Community and Communitarianism

Haig Khatchadourian

Community and Communitarianism

WIPF & STOCK · Eugene, Oregon

Wipf and Stock Publishers
199 W 8th Ave, Suite 3
Eugene, OR 97401

Community and Communitarianism
By Khatchadourian, Haig A.
Copyright©1999 by Khatchadourian, Haig A.
ISBN 13: 978-1-61097-056-3
Publication date 5/1/2011
Previously published by Peter Lang, 1999

in memory of
my aunt Astghig, whose love
and caring knew no bounds
in space, in time

Contents

Acknowledgments

The author wishes to thank Professor Bernard Williams for permission to include quotations from his *Ethics and the Limits of Philosophy*; Rowman & Littlefield Publishers, Inc. for permission to include quotations from Thomas E. Hill, Jr.'s "The Importance of Autonomy," in *Women and Moral Theory*, edited by Eva Feder Kittay and Diana T. Meyers; Oxford University Press, Oxford, for permission to quote from Brian Barry's *Justice as Impartiality;* and Cambridge University Press, North American Branch, for permission to quote from Michael J. Sandel's *Liberalism and the Limits of Justice.*

Introduction

Despite the growing interest in communitarian forms of social organization by American and British philosophers and social scientists during recent years, mainly in reaction to the theoretical flaws and practical excesses of post-Enlightenment liberalism in the West, not much has hitherto been done by communitarian philosophers themselves (as opposed to social scientists, see chapter 3) to develop systematic, articulated accounts of what a good and moral community, as a desirable form of social organization, looks like or would look like. To my knowledge, Loren L. Lomasky, in *Persons, Rights, and the Moral Community*, and Daniel Bell, in *Communitarianism And Its Critics,* are among the few philosophers who attempt to do so, each in his own way.

To a considerable extent, the present work is an attempt to help remedy that deficiency, by presenting, in two stages, in Parts I and III, a concrete account of a good and moral community. Chapters 1 and 2 provide an analysis of the ordinary nonevaluative uses of "community," together with some nonevaluative social-scientific uses of it, followed by a sketch of an ideal good and moral community. Chapter 3 develops the concepts of a community and a moral community by briefly looking at certain aspects of three conceptions of the "good society" through the work of a number of social scientists.

In Part III, that account is further developed and completed by the inclusion, in the concept of a fully moral community, of the protective norms of human rights, fairness, and justice. Because of the centrality of the concept of caring, the account of a moral community given in the book is significantly different from various other accounts of moral

Part II lays the theoretical ethical groundwork or foundations of the ideal of a moral community that was sketched in Part I, and developed further in Part III, with caring as the presiding moral concept. It lays down that groundwork by elaborating the fundamentals of a general "ethic of caring." In that way it aims to clarify and to provide the raison d'être or justification for the salient features of the ideal of a moral community. In formulating the essentials of the ethic of caring, it draws, both constructively and critically, on the contemporary feminist ethic of care, thus forging a moral theory with its own distinctive character. Specially noteworthy is the sustained attempt to bring together, in a harmonious union, the care approach, or "perspective," and certain fundamental elements of the "rights and justice" approach or "perspective": two perspectives (note the word) that many feminist moral philosophers deem hopelessly opposed and irreconcilable.

The attempt to harmonize the two approaches is done in two stages: first, by attempting to show that the protective norms of human rights, and fairness and justice, are indispensable for an adequate, full-fledged, care-centered ethic and second, by endeavoring to assign to these norms their rightful places or roles within that ethic. Consequently, several chapters are devoted to an account of the nature of human rights and of fairness and justice themselves, after which these concepts are applied to the ethical theory being developed.

With some qualifications, the model of human rights defended in Part II is the "constructive" model proposed by Ronald Dworkin in *Taking Rights Seriously*, a model he opposes to the traditional "natural" model. On the latter model, human rights are some sort of "natural" property possessed by us as human beings. In defense of the view that we must acknowledge (equal) human rights possessed by all humans, it is argued that they are strong moral entitlements and protections/defenses, necessary for our being able to satisfy our basic "survival" and "social" needs and interests, including the basic psychological needs that are posited by well-known contemporary American personality psychologists. It is contended that the satisfaction of our basic needs and interests is necessary for the attainment of our welfare and happiness, and for the actualization of our potentials.

Turning to justice, the analysis of that concept in general, in Part II, reveals that contrary to various familiar "essentialist" accounts that define it as impartiality, equality, or desert, justice is a "quasi-essentialist" concept: second-order impartiality (Brian Barry) is a general defining feature of the formal aspect of all forms of justice, including social or "distributive justice" in a broad sense, but that in the latter case, impartiality is only a secondary defining feature. The primary, hence lexically prior defining feature, is desert.

A central claim of both Michael Sandel and feminist moral philosophers is that, in contrast to the "unencumbered" or nonrelational account of the moral self that underlies Enlightenment and contemporary liberalism, the moral self is an "encumbered" self, partially constituted by its "values and ends" (Sandel), and, therefore, a self-in-relation (feminists). Because of the crucial role it plays in Sandel's account of community and the equally crucial role feminists believe it has in the ethic of care, the last chapter of Part II is devoted to a critical examination of Sandel's and the feminists' "encumbered"/relational account of the moral self.

Although Part II contends that the protective norms of human rights and justice must form an integral part of a full-fledged, adequate ethic of caring, the question remains whether these norms are indispensable in the special circumstances of community existence. Indeed, in his *Liberalism and the Limits of Justice* Sandel argues that they are relatively dispensable in the teleological (moral) community he envisages. In opposition to that view, it is argued, in Part III, that these norms are indeed indispensable in certain senses or ways specified there, and their place in a moral community is described in detail.

The discussion of moral community in Part III concludes with a series of responses to a variety of important challenges to the ideal of community by some "postmodern" and feminist thinkers.

As I have reiterated, what this book portrays is an ideal of moral community, hitherto only imperfectly approximated, and only capable of imperfect approximation in the future. But my own experiences as a past member of a close and remarkably moral community, the small fifteen-hundred-year-old Armenian community in the Old City of Jerusalem, right in the shadow of the Armenian monastery of St. James, has been both the inspiration and, to a considerable extent, the model for my vision of a moral community. In a recent letter to me, a relative and close friend of mine, John Peterson, now residing in Pennsylvania, described his formative years in that community in a way reminiscent of Philip Slater's description of a community, in which people "live in trust and fraternal cooperation with one's fellows in a moral and visible collective entity." John wrote: "I miss them [the past days] very much . . . . Life is never complete until one has successfully relived . . . [one's] childhood. In those days, life was different and joyful.

. . . We were somewhat saintly, we respected and honored our parents, elders, and our neighbors, we helped each other and [offered]
solace [to] those who were in need. We loved to be with our kind and
[to] exchange . . . thoughts, as we were indeed each other's reflection
and "mirror," and thus . . . able to look into each other's heart and
soul. Our neighbors were part of our own extended families. They
were precious in that respect, we were rich!"

In addition to the remarkable Armenian community in the Old City
of Jerusalem, I wish to thank Professor Charles Webel for suggesting
various improvements in the text, and for suggesting that I include a
section (the present chapter 3) on the views of Robert N. Bellah et al.,
Amitai Etzioni, and John Kenneth Galbraith concerning "The Good
Society." I also wish to thank my colleague, Professor Carl Hedman,
for directing me to some of the important writings of contemporary
British and American communitarian philosophers and for his stimu-
lating discussions of communitarianism and related subjects. These
writings and the exchanges brought home to me the fact that I have
always been, in an important sense, a communitarian at heart. The
quest for community exemplified in this book is, therefore, in essence,
an existential as well as an intellectual odyssey: a personal and a cultural *recherche du temps perdu*.

MORAL COMMUNITY

The musicians of the Vienna Philharmonic Orchestra are all paid the same. Whatever they take in from any source they divide equally among themselves. They are not there to make money. They are there because they are so proud of being part of this great tradition, so loving of what they do and of who they are. I operate the way they do. I operate in terms of love. And if it's not there, forget it.

—Leonard Bernstein

PART 1

MORAL COMMUNITY

—Leonard Bernstein

Chapter 1

Why Community?

I

I believe that a good and moral community provides optimal human conditions for the nurturing and developing of our needs and real interests as human beings and for the full realization of our human and individual potentials. Indeed, that it also enables us to realize our full personhood as moral beings, our moral personhood. In addition, a good and moral community respects its members' human right to be treated as moral persons, including their human right to equal opportunity, to enable them to satisfy their basic needs and real interests, and to realize their potential.[1] Note that the claim that a (good and moral) community is a desirable form of social organization goes considerably beyond the classical Greek view that "man" is naturally a social animal, that human *society* is a *natural outgrowth* of man's social nature, consequently social existence is essential for the individual's self-actualization as a human being; though, significantly, the model of society Plato and Aristotle had before them was the Greek city state—e.g., Athens, Corinth, or Sparta—which was a certain type of community (what I shall refer to as a "teleological community" or T-community).

Michael Sandel and other contemporary communitarians, as well as feminist moral philosophers, defend a metaphysical conception of a person as an "encumbered" or "embedded" self, as a self partially defined by its important attachments and relationships (and for Sandel, its ends and values) to others; of a self-in-relation. A form of that conception will be explored and defended in Part III. If that view of a person or self is correct, a community in which, in Philip Slater's words, people "live in trust and fraternal [and sisterly] cooperation with one's fellows in a moral and visible collective entity," would be a highly desirable form of social organization.

The intimate relation between the "encumbered" or "embedded" self and (a good and moral) community—in particular, a teleological community, a community in which the members are bound, among other things, by shared values and a communal end or "telos or a number of such ends or teloses"—underlies Michael Sandel's advocacy of what he calls the "constitutive conception" of community in *Liberalism and the Limits of Justice*.[2] It also underlies Alasdair MacIntyre's, and other communitarians' attack, in *Liberalism and Its Critics*,[3] on what they take to be the liberal, "unencumbered" conception of the self. At the same time the failure of some feminist moral and political thinkers to see the natural connection between the "embedded" self and community has led them to reject communitarianism. (The issues surrounding the Hegelian, "organic" conception of community, and its implications, considered by Sandel in *Liberalism and the Limits of Justice*, will be discussed in chapter 12; while the concerns of some anticommunitarian feminist thinkers regarding conformism and uniformity will be considered in chapter 13.)

In criticizing what he considers Rawls' individualistic conception of a person, Sandel speaks of that conception as, among other things, ruling out "the possibility that common purposes and ends could inspire more or less expansive self-understandings and so define a community in the constitutive sense, a community describing the subject and not just the objects of shared aspirations . . . . Unlike Rawls' conception, inter-subjective and intra-subjective conceptions do not assume that to speak of the self, from a moral point of view, is necessarily and unproblematically to speak of an antecedently individuated self."[4] Again, "intersubjective conceptions allow that in certain moral circumstances, the relevant description of the self may embrace more than a single individual human being, as when we attribute responsibility or affirm an obligation to a family or community or class or nation rather than to some particular human being."[5] Again, and stated most clearly:

> On this [Sandel's] strong view, to say
> that the members of a society are bound
> by a sense of community is not simply to
> say that a great many of them profess
> communitarian sentiments and pursue
> communitarian aims, but rather that *they
> conceive their identity*—the subject and not
> just the object of their feelings and

aspirations—*as defined to some extent by
the community of which they are a part.*
For them, community describes not just
what they *have* as fellow citizens but also
what they *are*.[6]

The relation between the "encumbered/embedded" conception of
the self and the concept of (a good and moral) community becomes
still stronger (a) if, as Slater maintains, there exists a human desire for
community, and that the frustration of that desire—a desire that he
believes is "deeply and uniquely frustrated by American culture"[7]—
leads to profound loneliness and other expressions of a *maladie
d'esprit* powerfully described in his book.

The proposition that an intimate relation exists between the "encumbered" conception of the self and (good and moral) community in
the constitutive sense receives further support from (b) the view[8] that
human beings have (or have, *inter alia*) certain basic psychological
needs, among which are a basic need for love, for belonging and acceptance, and for achievement or recognition. Similarly, if as the exis-
tentialist psychiatrist Viktor Frankl believes, human beings have a "will
to meaning," they are "meaning-seeking" beings.[9] In fact, if Maslow
and those other personality psychologists who hold similar views of
our basic psychological needs are correct, Slater's view of a human
desire for community can be readily seen as an expression of the basic
need for love, belonging, recognition, and so on. Moreover, it can also
be readily shown that the impulse or desire for the satisfaction of
these needs would also satisfy the putative quest for meaningfulness.

Some of the main challenges to communitarianism—those from some
feminist moral and political thinkers and others—which will be considered in the last chapter of this book, include several important criticisms of Richard Rorty's conception of community[10] by Barbara
Herrnstein Smith.[11] But one criticism of what she calls Rorty's "vague
but strongly demoting characterization of contemporary high culture"
is also directed at other communitarians as well, and so is pertinent
here. I mean about her speaking of the "more or less reactionary
nostalgia of various other current social critics, such as Charles Taylor
and Alasdair MacIntyre, who also invoke a (lost) sense of "community."[12] By its very meaning, "reactionary nostalgia" is bad; but the
word "reactionary" is ambiguously used in that phrase, implying without warrant that any backward-looking nostalgia, whatever its nature,
is undesirable. Whether or not the nostalgia that characterizes

MacIntyre's communitarianism in *After Virtue* (whether or not it also characterizes Taylor's view) is reactionary in Smith's intended sense does not concern us here. The important thing for us is that the conception of a constitutive community—or what I call "a good and moral community" in that strong sense—is quite independent of any nostalgia, *reactionary* or not.

I said that the word *reactionary* in "reactionary nostalgia" plays on an ambiguity in its meaning. For the nostalgia for a more harmonious and satisfying past is not necessarily reactionary in Smith's intended pejorative sense but can be quite salutary if it does not rest on the illusory glamorization and idealization of a past created by distance ("distance lends enchantment to the view"). That is, if the backward gaze perceives the past "steadily and as a whole." In particular, if one is not led to a delusory hankering to turn the clock back. In other words, if the past is used only as a guideline, if one learns from it in order to try to avoid its failures and to emulate its strengths; with full awareness of and consonant with the different historical, cultural, and other societal circumstances and forces that inform or animate the present. That would mean, say, envisaging of communities that can fit well into and form an integral part of the complex postindustrial modern Western world on the threshold of the third millennium A.D. The practical challenges and difficulties that attempts to revive, revitalize, create, or recreate good and moral constitutive communities in the United States or in Western Europe would face may be formidable but that does not argue against the desirability—if, as I believe, it is desirable to do—of such close-knit societal organizations.

More to the point is the fact that constitutive communities are alive and well, and have survived for centuries or millennia in many parts of the globe—in Africa and the Middle East, in Latin America and the Far East, and in ethnic communities in North America and Europe—even leaving alone the Native American tribes in North America and the so-called primitive tribes in such places as Polynesia and Micronesia. In some ways these communities provide better guidelines for us than those of the distant European past.

In my own case the writings of contemporary British and American communitarians have brought home to me the fact that I have always been a communitarian at heart; and though circumstances made me—to some extent, forced me to—leave behind the community in which I had, as a child and youth, moved and had my being, its vision and memory have been an inspiration in writing this book; while its virtues, indefinitely extended and magnified, have formed the basis for the ideal of the good and moral community sketched in chapter 2.

Before we turn to the question of what constitutes the ideal of a good and moral community as the present author envisages it, it is necessary to state what the term "community" in general means or provide an analysis of the concept(s) of *community* in general, as that term or that(these) concept(s) occur in everyday discourse and in the social sciences, to supplement the brief sketch of Sandel's conception of *constitutive* community that I have already given. To that task I now turn.

II

Community

When we speak of a particular community in some part of the world, we ordinarily have in mind either some ethnic, racial, religious, or other social group or an educational or scientific institution or organization. We speak of the East Indian community in London or Nairobi, the Greek Orthodox community in Chicago or Jerusalem, the Italian community in New York, and so on. We also speak of a university community, a scientific community, and the community of scholars. *The Random House Dictionary of the English Language*, College Edition (1968) defines "community" as "1. a social group of any size whose members reside in a specific locality, share government, and have a common cultural and historical heritage. 2. a social, religious, occupational, or other group sharing common characteristics or interests (usually prec. by the): the business community; the community of scholars. . . . 5. Similar character; agreement: community of interests. 6. the community, the public; society." In my discussion of community in this book I will be solely concerned with senses (1) and (2) of the word.

In *Community Structure and Change*[13] the authors—Lowry Nelson et al. define a community as "the structuring of elements and dimensions to solve problems which must be or can be solved within the local area."[14] By 'structure' they mean the "complex of relations among people within the local area. . . . Variations in area and people are conditions affecting community but are not the community per se."[15] "*Elements* and *dimensions . . .* make up the community *structure*."[16] The "elements" of a community are the relationships "among institutions, groups, formal organizations or other component units within the community, . . . and are described in terms of functions."[17] The influences of these elements are variable and extend "through the breadth and depth of a community. . . . A community may be oriented toward tradition, and this traditionalism will be seen as influencing decisions within a family, between the family and the school, and among all institutions. It will permeate the entire structure of the local area. . . .These all-pervasive patterns [of individual and group behavior] will be referred to as *dimensions*."[18] The needs and values of different communities may vary, and "there are orders of needs or values which vary with structure. These orders may be called the hierarchy of values."[19] The societal problems a community continually faces and attempts to resolve, which constitute an important part of its *raison d'être*, include its striving to satisfy its members' needs and to make possible or facilitate the realization of their individual and social ends and values. Nelson et al. write that "the structuring of elements and dimensions to solve problems" seems to imply that by definition a community is deliberately created to solve certain (human) problems. The same idea that a community necessarily has a common goal, purpose, or *telos* is assumed by MacIntyre, Sandel, and other contemporary communitarians. Finally, "the boundaries of the community are not precise, since they are different for each element of a sociocultural organization."[20]

The everyday senses of "a community" noted by the dictionary, and the more precise sociological concept, are purely descriptive, nonevaluative, and do not include the idea of goodness or desirability in their meaning. Whether a particular community in any of these senses is good or desirable, or bad or undesirable, is a matter of fact, not part of the meaning of "community" or the concept expressed by the term. By contrast, contemporary American and British communitarian philosophers tend to employ the term—without the indefinite article—as an honorific term; as shorthand for "good or desirable (perhaps also, moral) community." Such examples occur in the writings of Michael Sandel, Fred Berger, Alasdair MacIntyre, and other communitarian authors represented in *Liberalism and Its Critics*. In this book I shall use "community," with or without the indefinite article, in its ordinary dictionary meanings (senses previously mentioned, except for an important proviso to be noted later). But I shall also draw on the sociological usage insofar as it tightens and refines its everyday uses. I shall qualify the expression "a community" with either *good as*, *desirable*, or *bad as*, *undesirable*, and the like whenever the desirability or undesirability of certain sorts of communities is being considered.

Teleological and Nonteleological Communities

We saw earlier that Nelson et al. speak of a community as having a structure of interrelated parts. Further, their definition makes a community a necessarily goal-directed or teleological organization, with its structure providing the mechanism for its operations as a unit and its striving to realize its particular communal *telos* or *teloses*. But to include the idea of a shared, communal *telos* in the definition of "community" would unjustifiably exclude sense (1)—from which the idea of a *telos* is absent—and restrict its meaning to sense (2), which appears to involve that idea. There is a difference between (a) a group's having certain common interests and goals and (b) their working together to further these interests and goals. Moreover, (a) does not entail (b).

There are, of course, fairly obvious reasons why one may tend to suppose that all communities are necessarily, by definition, teleological. One is the fact that when scholars, educators, scientists, or other professional men and women form communities they do so to further the shared goals that bind them together as scholars, educators, or scientists. Again, it is not surprising that the communitarians I mentioned earlier actually assimilate what are in fact nonteleological (on N-) communities to teleological ones; since their paradigms of community are classical Greek and Roman, and medieval and Renaissance European communities, all of which were teleological (or T-) communities. Indeed, it may well be a historical fact that most or even all actual communities come into existence or are deliberately created to serve a particular group's special desires, aspirations, needs, and/or interests; whether or not these ends are subsequently realized.

All this may be true, especially as the members of a community, in the primary ordinary sense (1) have a "common historical or cultural heritage." Still, that does not disprove the conceptual fact that an N-community is logically possible in that sense. Further, it is certainly possible that some communities, which start off as teleological communities, eventually lose their teleological character and "lapse" into nonteleological communities, without thereby ceasing to be *bona fide* communities in sense (1). This process is illustrated by the community in which I grew up, the Armenian community in the Old City of Jerusalem described in the Introduction. That community almost certainly originated (around the fifth century A.D. or earlier) no doubt because of the Church's felt need for a community of worshipers. Consequently, Armenians converging on Jerusalem from different parts of the Near East as pilgrims decided, or were persuaded by the Church, to settle down in what became the Armenian Quarter of the Old City of Jerusalem. Gradually a sizable community came into existence. However, at some point in its very long history it lost its original telos, although it continued (and continues) to exist as a non-teleological community.

Those who maintain the opposite view may argue that the word "community," in all its everyday senses, is a "functional word," like other expressions that refer to or describe human artifacts or activities, such as "organization," "institution," and "practice." By that I mean expressions that include the idea of some function, use, aim, goal, or purpose in their meaning or uses, and so, in the concepts they express. But reflection on the ways in which "a community" is ordinarily employed shows that, like "a society," the opposite is true: precisely what sense (1), the primary dictionary sense of the word, reflects. A community in the sense of a teleological "social group of any size whose members reside in a specific locality" is only one species of a community in the preceding primary, generic sense.

We must be careful in this connection not to suppose that the fact that the members of a single community play a variety of societal roles, in many of which they find themselves as human beings or as members of the particular community, entails that all communities are necessarily teleological. For first, societal roles, in addition to certain natural, genetically determined roles, are an inseparable characteristic of all group living, of all types of societies, communal or other; though the specific nature of these roles varies. Second, though societal roles—e.g., the role of ruler, leader, slave or serf, warrior, hunter, worker or manager, subordinate or boss—are teleological, so that their proper fulfilment constitutes their characteristic or peculiar excellence or "virtue" (areté), they have reference to or form part of some collective telos or complex of teloses, only in teleological organizations. For then they, together with their corresponding excellences, are determined or defined by the particular collective telos(es) of the particular teleological institution, practice, or community.

The existence or nonexistence of a communal telos has important consequences for the overall nature of teleological and nonteleological communities and is the reason for my emphasis on the distinction. For one thing, if a community has a communal telos, some of the problems "*which* [in Nelson's words] *must be or can be solved within the local area*"[21] would be, or would include, problems that normally *all* the community's members would have in common and would endeavor to resolve. That is not true of nonteleological communities.

Frequently, but by no means necessarily, the members of a (T- or N-) community have, or would have, a common cultural and historical heritage. Whenever present, a common heritage forges strong and lasting bonds in a community, in addition to the bonds forged by common needs, interests, goals, and so on.

In traditional T-communities the telos(es) of the community are, or would be, bequeathed by the members' dead ancestors or are borrowed or adapted from some earlier or contemporaneous community. An N-community too may be traditional, though not in exactly the same way as a T-community, since it would lack communal teloses.

Earlier in this chapter I referred to Sandel's conception of a constitutive community. That conception is intimately tied with Sandel's equating "community" with "teleological community"—in fact, it is necessarily the fact that if the members of a community share common values and strive together to realize these values or ends (teloses), the community would necessarily be a constitutive community in his sense. As subjects or selves they would be partially defined by their membership in that community, by their shared attachments and relationships as members of that community.

If that is so, the question arises as to whether a nonteleological community, in the primary ordinary sense or in the sociologist's sense of "community," *can* be a constitutive community in Sandel's sense. The answer is yes; though clearly in a different way from a teleological community.

It can be so if, as I shall argue later, human beings, by their very nature as social animals, their existence in some type of society or other—whether communal or no—are partially defined by their personal and other close attachments and relationships to others, and by their collaborative pursuit with other human beings, in the public as well as the private domain, of certain common albeit limited aims and ends. A *fortiori*, "a social group . . . whose members reside in a specific locality, share government, and have a common cultural and historical heritage"—which describes nonteleological no less than teleological communities—would have certain common values and ends. The basic difference between these and teleological communities would be that the values and ends in question may or may not be common to *all* the membership. Further, even when the entire community shares certain values and ends, the pursuit of these values and ends would not be a community affair. It would remain a matter for individuals or limited groups within the community as a whole to pursue their shared social, economic, educational, athletic, or other interests.

III

We saw earlier what Sandel means in using the epithet "constitutive" in qualifying "community," but not how he employs the term "community" itself; what he understands by "community" in the phrase "constitutive community." That is, the kind of community he contrasts to and defends against what he calls the "instrumental" and "sentimental" conceptions of community: the latter as exemplified, according to him, by John Rawls' conception of community in *A Theory of Justice*.

In his comments and criticism of Rawls' individualist conception of the self or person, and so, his conception of a community, Sandel states at one point that "on Rawls' conception of the person, my ends are benevolent or communitarian when they take as their object the good of another, or of a group of others with whom I may be associated, and indeed there is nothing in his view to rule out communitarian ends in this sense."[22] Again, "these assumptions [those "contained in the original position"] do not admit all ends, but rule out in advance any end whose adoption or pursuit could engage or transform the identity of the self, and they reject in particular the possibilities that the good of community could consist in a constitutive dimension of this kind."[23] Again—

> For the community as a whole to deserve the natural assets in its province and the benefits that flow from them, it is necessary to assume that society has some pre-institutional status that individuals lack, for only in this way could the community be said to possess its assets in the strong, constitutive sense of possession necessary to a desert base. But such a view would run counter to Rawls's individualistic assumptions, and in particular to his view that society is not "an organic whole with a life of its own distinct from and superior to that of all its members in their relations with one another" (Rawls 264).[24]

The "instrumental" conception of community, Sandel says, is individualistic, though in a different way from Rawls' own individualistic conception. On the instrumental account, those who cooperate are assumed to be motivated by self-interest alone, and the community's good lies solely in the gain individuals derive from their cooperation in pursuing their egoistic goals.[25] The "sentimental" individualistic conception Sandel identifies with Rawls' conception of community. But neither account, "presupposing as they do the antecedent individuation of the subject, can offer a way in which the bounds of the subject might be redrawn; neither seems capable of relaxing the bounds between the self and the other without producing a radically situated subject."[26]

Despite his many references to community in his book, including his constant attempts to distinguish his "strong" conception of community from Rawls' and other conceptions, Sandel's use of community in "constitutive community" remains quite elusive and undefined. He simply fails to provide a definition of the term as distinct from explaining what he understands by the epithet "constitutive" as it qualifies "community" in "constitutive community."[27] The reasons are not far away. The failure results from the error of thinking that qualifying "community" by "constitutive"—which he does adequately define— enables him to distinguish a special type of community. For first, as will be argued in Part II, the individual is partially defined by his or her important attachments and relationships, as an "empirical" and a moral self, in any and every kind of human association, society, or organization, without exception. He or she is not partially defined only by his or her important attachments and relationships in a "constitutive community" in Sandel's sense, or in a community in the primary ordinary sense.[28]

Second, in examining his various statements about "community" and "constitutive community" in his book, it becomes clear (as already noted in section I) that Sandel mistakenly assumes the existence of a necessary, logical connection between a "constitutive community" and a "T-community": indeed, that a constitutive community is identical with a T-community. That too leads him to believe that he has succeeded in defining, or in sufficiently defining "community" by (a) speaking of a community as, essentially, a form of social organization which partially defines its participants as persons or selves. He is also mistakenly led to believe that by virtue of the fact that on his conception (b) a "constitutive community" is, necessarily, one that partially defines the participants by virtue of their sharing communal values and ends. But as we have seen earlier in this chapter, a T-community is but one possible sort of community in the generic dictionary meaning of the term. Therefore, on that ground also *no* necessary, logical connection exists between a community's being a T-community and its being a constitutive community. The participants in an N-community too are partially defined as persons by their close attachments and relationships and by the values and ends they may share with other members, or even—as may sometimes happen—with the majority or even all of the community members. But even when the latter occurs, the essential difference between an N-community and a T-community remains. In the former type of community the members pursue the shared values individually or cooperatively in limited groups, within particular institutions of the community, etc., rather than in concert with everyone else in, and for the sake of, the community as a whole.

Finally, it is clear from the passages I have quoted, as well as from his book as a whole, that Sandel employs "community" in an evaluative—an honorific—sense; as a desirable, nay, the most desirable form of social organization. That is, as equivalent to "moral community" in the ordinary and the social scientist's nonevaluative uses of community, which is how I employ the term throughout this book. My vision of what would constitute a good and moral community in that sense is the subject of the next chapter, to which I now turn.

To sum up. This chapter set the stage for the conception of a moral community that I envisage. In the first, introductory section, it was maintained that a good and moral community provides optimal conditions for the nurturing and developing of our basic, human needs and real interests, the full realization of our human and individual potentials, and our moral personhood. The relationship between Michael Sandel's conception of "constitutive" or "encumbered" self and his teleological conception of community, or his conception of constitutive community, was next explored.

In Section II, the everyday and the sociologist's nonevaluative, "descriptive" concepts of a community were distinguished from Sandel's and certain other communitarians' normative and honorific concept of community. Drawing on the former concepts, and in opposition to Sandel's equation of "community" both with "teleological community" and with "constitutive community," a second, nonteleological sort of community was distinguished and analyzed.

Finally, Sandel's failure to provide a positive account of community in speaking of constitutive community, as well as his equation of a "constitutive community" with teleological community, was criticized: in the latter case, inasmuch as a nonteleological community too is "constitutive," in Sandel's sense. In the present regard, the fundamental difference between the two sorts of community is that a non-teleological community lacks the special bond that exists between the members or participants of a teleological community, arising from their striving to realize the communal telos or teloses.

Notes

1   It should be noted that I spoke of a good and moral community as providing optimal human conditions for the above. I did not say that it would provide "*the* optimal conditions"—that it is "essential or necessary" for the realization of the values I mentioned. To make the stronger claim, to claim that a good and moral community constitutes the very best or most desirable form of human association possible would be to go considerably beyond what I claim in this book, or can properly claim; even if it is (or were) actually *possible* to argue convincingly in support of that extremely strong thesis.

       If that claim is shown to be true, the right to be treated as a moral person would entail a moral *right* to membership in a good and moral community or a number of good and moral communities.

2   Cambridge, 1982.

3   Michael Sandel, ed. *Liberalism And Its Critics* (Oxford, 1984).

4   Ibid., 62.

5   Ibid., 62—63.

6   Ibid., 150. My italics, except for the words "have" and "are," which are in the original. In *Communitarianism and Its Critics* (Oxford, 1993) Daniel Bell follows Sandel's constitutive conception but (mistakenly) goes beyond Sandel in speaking of constitutive communities not just as partially constituting but as (wholly) constituting the members' identity; and even speaks of the "good of the communities" as constituting their identity. (Op. cit., 93.)

7   Op. cit., 5.

8   Put forth by Abraham Maslow. A similar view is presented by Carl Rogers. The agreements and disagreements of various personality psychologists or schools of personality psychology regarding the existence and nature of the basic human psychological needs are discussed in Part II, chapter 6.

9   *Man's Search for Meaning: An Introduction to Logotherapy* (New York, 1977).

10   In "Solidarity or Objectivity?" *Post-Analytic Philosophy*, John Rajchman and Cornell West, eds. (New York, 1985), 3—19.

11   *Contingencies of Value* (Cambridge, MA, 1988).

12   Op. cit., 172.

13   New York, 1962.

14   Ibid., 24. Italics in original.

15 Ibid., 12.

16 Ibid., 21. Italics in original.

17 Ibid.

18 Ibid., 21. Italics in original.

19 Ibid., 21. Italics in original.

20 Ibid., 25.

21 Op. cit., 24. Italics in original.

22 *Liberalism and the Limits of Justice*, 60.

23 Ibid., 64—65.

24 Sandel, ibid., 101.

25 Ibid., 148.

26 Ibid., 149. It should become clear in chapter 2, when we describe a "good community" (*a fortiori*, a "moral community"), that a good community, including an N-community, in my conception, is neither an "instrumental" nor a "sentimental" conception. It is a "constitutive" conception in Sandel's sense, but, for one thing, without identifying "constitutive community" with "T-community," as Sandel does.

27 For instance, even as late as on page 150, Sandel observes that a theory of community which included the subject as well as the object of his motivations, would be "individualistic in neither the conventional sense [which he does not define] nor in Rawls'." The nature of the community would be manifested in the participants' values and goals: for example, as "fraternal sentiments and fellow-feeling . . . But . . . that community would describe not just a *feeling* but a mode of self-understanding partly constitutive of the agent's identity." The participants conceive of their identity as partially constituted by *the community* of which they are a part. And so on in the same vein. (My italics.)

28 I leave aside the fact that individuals may also be partially defined by their close relationship to pets or other animals, including those in the wild.

Chapter 2

Good and Moral Community

I

A. Good Community

In attempting to discover the qualities that characterize a good community we must distinguish between two common senses of "good" in relation to community: (1) a nonmoral sense (sense 1) and (2) a moral sense (sense 2). Proper functioning or efficiency is an important part of what "good community"designates in sense (1),[1] as in the case of "functional words"in general, such as the names of artifacts and of various human activities; where "good" means "efficient" For instance, a "good knife" or a "good chair" is an efficient knife or chair; performs its normal function(s) efficiently and so is a useful (or very useful) knife or chair.

To be efficient, particularly an efficient T-community, considerable teamwork is essential. In a T-community a high degree of cooperation and collaboration is required between its individual members and its institutions and practices for the realization—and the most efficient realization—of, *inter alia*, the community's communal telos(es).

On the other hand, people sometimes appear to use "good community" to mean a *morally* good, morally desirable community; just as when people speak of a "good person" they frequently have in mind moral goodness (sense 2 of "good"), perhaps in addition to other (nonmoral) kinds of desirable personal qualities, i.e., in a broader, more inclusive sense of "good community." In sense (1) but clearly not in sense (2) it is perfectly meaningful to speak of a "good community of thieves or murderers," though such a community would be clearly immoral.

By distinguishing a "nonmoral" and a "moral" sense of "good" in relation to community, I may have given the impression that I am assuming the existence of a clear or sharp demarcation between the two senses and that people have sense (1) or sense (2) exclusively in mind when speaking of a "good community." But that is not the case. As we shall presently see, the actual situation is quite different. In fact the demarcation line between the two senses is not only quite hazy and uncertain but also shifts with time and place: at least in "liberal," nontraditional societies, with changes in general attitudes and mentality and with scientific or technological changes and advances. In addition, as I said earlier, "good community" appears to be sometimes used in an inclusive sense, to designate both moral and nonmoral "good-making" qualities, combining senses (1) and (2) in a more inclusive (or g-) sense. In that sense the concept of a "moral community" is included in the concept of a good community in the broad sense.

Nonetheless, the distinction between senses (1) and (2) is a useful one because (a) some of the good-making qualities of a "g-good community" are normally thought of as paradigmatically nonmoral, while others are thought of as paradigmatically moral qualities. Cooperativeness and efficiency are examples of nonmoral qualities, while loyalty, solidarity, kindness, and caring are examples of moral qualities, in a community as well as in individuals. But (b)—and this is what connects senses (1) and (2) in the g-use of "good community"—the aforementioned and other "nonmoral" qualities can contextually cut across the distinction between the two senses of "good"; in the appropriate contexts or circumstances they *function* as—and in that way are *transformed into*—moral qualities. The same may be true, *mutatis mutandis*, of "moral qualities" in relation to communities. The distinction between a "moral" quality and a "morally neutral" quality *may* be contextually determined. This can be clearly seen from a consequentialist moral perspective. For example, communal cooperativeness and solidarity in the pursuit of a common goal (which abstractly considered would be normally classified as nonmoral qualities) become morally right or wrong, good or bad qualities in that context if the goal pursued is (or is considered to be) itself morally good or bad.

The haziness and uncertainty of the demarcation line between moral and desirable but morally neutral qualities (experiences, states of being, actions, and activities) infect theories of "the good," such as utilitarianism and other forms of consequentialism, particularly in relation to pleasure and/or happiness, which consequentialists, for example, consider to be *moral* goods (in some theories, "the moral good"). But are they moral or are they nonmoral "goods"? Note for instance how Plato and Aristotle, in trying to distinguish good qualities (dispositions) and actions on the one hand and desirable but morally neutral qualities and actions on the other, did not draw a distinction between moral and nonmoral excellence (or "virtue," *areté*).[2] Again, among the qualities and actions they regarded as morally virtuous, they included qualities and actions now no longer regarded as moral qualities or actions. For example, wisdom and physical courage (Plato), and liberality and magnificence (Aristotle). As with certain other concepts that have become restricted in Western culture in the course of time, the concept of virtue is now normally restricted to what are presently thought of as *bona fide* moral qualities.[3] On the other hand, Plato's "temperance" or "moderation" is, I believe, still widely regarded in the Western world (as well as in other societies) as a moral excellence.

B. Good Community Member

Among other things, a good community member, especially a good member of a T-community, is a "(good) team player." Although team-playing is not a moral quality, some of the qualities of a team player minimally presuppose the player's possession of certain moral qualities. These include helpfulness and the absence of vanity, egotism, or self-righteousness—together with the presence of friendliness if considered a moral quality. It also includes willingness to pursue a T-community's telos(es), and, whenever necessary, to subordinate one's own projects and goals to them. I say subordinate, not sacrifice because it is essential even for a team player not to give up her personal ambitions or be untrue to herself. In a T-community, part of team-playing lies in the members' identification or harmonization of their personal goals and ambitions, as much as possible, with the communal telos(es).

All adults have a private and a public "side" or life. Generally the "good community side" of a team player is mainly the social, public side. The private side includes kinships and friendships. One's being a good parent, son or daughter, spouse or friend requires one's possession of certain moral qualities that indirectly relate to team playing in the community at large. To be good in the former respects or relationships requires sensitivity to others: considerateness, gentleness, kindness and warmth, self-giving, and a sacrificing spirit. Given the right circumstances, these qualities tend to carry over into one's public, e.g., community, life. Consequently, an often complicated interplay exists between one's private *moral* and other private qualities on the one hand, and one's social, e.g., team, qualities on the other.

In talking about a good community in sense (1) we need to distinguish at least two things:

1 That which is "objectively" and universally good, i.e., qualities which it is desirable for any community to have, irrespective of its particular character. I refer to desirable political, socioeconomic, educational, or artistic qualities that characterize a good social, political, economic, or artistic community. A community that exhibits in a high degree an appreciable number of good-making qualities of any of these sorts would be a good community of its kind in sense (1).

2 A second sense of "what is good" is "what is desirable for a particular community C." Here goodness is relative to C's specific character and circumstances and depends upon its members' desires and goals, preferences and interests, and their way of life as a whole. What is good for a particular community can only be properly ascertained by periodic, uncoerced polling of its members.

Senses (1) and (2) of "what is good for a community" are contingently but closely connected; since the good-making qualities of all good communities (1) depend for their specific instantiations on the particular community's specific and even special, character and circumstances (2). Thus a community "Y" would be a good community in general if it satisfies two sorts of conditions. First, it must exhibit the relevant desirable qualities (1) and must ascertain by democratic means the appropriate ways in which, given its special character, it may attain or conserve, transmit, or disseminate its desirable qualities (2).

Cutting across and thus involving both types of good-making qualities, (1) and (2), is the further distinction between (a) qualities that it is desirable for any community to have in its relations with other communities, and (b) qualities that are desirable for its elements to have in their dealings with the community as a whole. Some of these qualities may be of both sorts, though they would naturally differ in their specific exemplifications. A community that possesses desirable qualities of type (b) in an appreciable degree would exhibit them in relation to its elements.

Let me illustrate. It will be generally agreed I think that a good community is characterized by its members' solidarity, loyalty to one another and to the community as a whole, cooperativeness, and general harmony. These are all type (1)(a) qualities, since they characterize relations between individuals, families, and organizations, however variously they may be exhibited or sought in particular communities. But loyalty also encompasses virtues of type (1)(b). One can be loyal to one's community as a whole as well as to its individual members and to its institutions and other elements. Of course, loyalty to a community differs from loyalty to an individual or to a family. It differs at least in its felt quality. If a sizable segment of a community's institutions and members is loyal to it, the entire community is likely to reciprocate. Further, some "regional" good-making qualities may expand into global good-making qualities. For instance, interinstitutional harmony may prove infectious and pervasive.

The basic psychological-existential needs and corresponding real interests shared by all human beings, together with their physiological needs and dispositions, dictate a formidable list of complex conditions and objectives that any community must realize to deserve the title of a "good" or "excellent" community. It must also be capable of sustaining that achievement as long as the ravages of time allow. An ideal community would satisfy all these needs and interests to the fullest, for all its present and future members. But that goal can only be indefinitely approximated by mere humans.

In *The Pursuit of Loneliness: American Culture at The Breaking Point*,[4] Philip E. Slater suggests "three human desires that are deeply and uniquely frustrated by American Culture":

1 The desire for *community*—the wish to live in trust and fraternal[5] cooperation with one's fellows in a total and visible collective entity.
2 The desire for *engagement*—the wish to come directly to grips with social and interpersonal problems and to confront on equal terms an environment which is not composed of ego-extensions.
3 The desire for *dependence*—the wish to share responsibility for the control of one's impulses and the direction of one's life.[6]

Later on, Slater attributes the suppression of these "three variables" in American society "to our commitment to individualism."[7]

In a good community as I envisage it, the desire for "dependence" in Slater's sense would be satisfied in a high degree. But the community would also *exemplify* considerably more than the satisfaction of the desire for community in Slater's sense, "the wish to live in trust and fraternal cooperation with one's fellows."[8] Yet community in that sense and the satisfaction of the desire for dependence are closely related. In fact, the latter is difficult to satisfy without the former. Positively speaking, a good community in my sense (and in Slater's sense of "community") is the optimum matrix for the satisfaction of the desire for dependence. Whenever people live in trust, as they do for example in loving and caring families, they depend on one another's advice and guidance, admonition and gentle warning. Likewise with close relatives and friends.[9]

As I shall argue later in this book, the jealous guarding of one's physical and emotional-mental privacy and the continual insistence that they be respected are inimical to intimacy, consequently to dependence in Slater's sense. They put people continually on their guard, tend to pit them against one another and turn them into potential adversaries. We see that most clearly in relation to physical privacy or personal "space" and its natural extension into the jealous guarding of one's material possessions; e.g., in exaggerated, even pathological sensitivity about "trespassing."[10]

The insistence on psychological privacy makes it difficult for trust to exist, and tends to stunt or kill it. It tends to erect walls between individuals, sometimes so towering and massive as to make even a glimpse of the other side—let alone the holding or even touching of hands across it—impossible. In short, it can and does lead to alienation. (I use "alienation" here in a general, not necessarily in Marx's special, sense or senses.)

Again, "private" persons tend to resist other people's attempts to identify with them and adopt their projects. They consider that as meddling, "psychological trespassing." As valuers of their privacy they *may* also value other people's privacy. But that is far from certain, considering that human beings frequently do unto others precisely what they don't want others to do unto them.

It must be conceded, however, that the total absence of physical privacy—endemic to poor tenements and slums—breeds resentment and conflict, even violence: not least from the contempt bred by the over familiarity of extreme proximity.

I said that dependence in Slater's sense flourishes in a good community: in fact it is part of its very nature. Living in trust leads to dependence in that positive, "symbiotic" sense. For that to transpire, one must not look on dependence as a weakness and must not be deluded into thinking that to be a "strong" person means being as independent of others, as self-reliant and self-sufficient, as emotionally and spiritually self-sustaining, as one possibly can. Nor must one think that love and friendship are frailties to be resisted. That attitude makes love, especially being in love, seem to be a surrender of one's identity and integrity, one's individuality; a turning of oneself into an "object" to be toyed with, to be "used"[11] or abused.[12] That is adolescent psychology. I call it that because it appears to be an adolescent syndrome, though it may be present at any age. But infirmity and old age make it difficult to sustain that attitude with regard to one's physical and emotional condition.

Great physical dependence, even in the young, can also be very painful for everyone concerned, including someone who prizes psychological and spiritual dependence—or better, *inter*dependence. Physical dependence in anyone but a child is a result of debility and tends to be profoundly humiliating, dehumanizing, and alienating; whereas psychological *inter*dependence can be a rich source of inner satisfaction. At least equally satisfying is the sense that another draws emotional and spiritual sustenance and strength from oneself, giving one a sense (or an added sense) of worth and meaning. In that way the ideally good community involves a high degree of interdependence, in Slater's sense of "dependence," between its members. It is an important dimension of "fraternal cooperation with one's fellows," especially in a T-community. Interdependence is of course also desirable in an N-community. Despite my strictures against the insistence on privacy, which is an obstacle to what Religious Existentialists call "I-Thou relationships," it is essential that the right to privacy be acknowledged in practice as well as in principle.[13] There are basic human needs, interests, and values that need to be protected by proper respect for privacy in the relevant sense or senses. The protection of privacy is a protection of one's autonomy as a person in a sense or senses distinguished in Part II. That protection includes freedom to pursue one's own projects and goals, particularly the most cherished and meaningful, and is closely connected with Bernard Williams' concept of a person's integrity.[14] Without the assurance of privacy in the present sense, the pursuit of one's projects, particularly of one's "commitments" in Williams' sense—viz, projects "with which one is more deeply and extensively involved and identified"[15]—which, as he emphasizes, are essential for one's integrity as a person—becomes very difficult. Williams maintains in effect that a man cannot "come to regard as one satisfaction among others, and a dispensable one, a project or attitude round which he has built his life,"[16] one with which he is identified "as flowing from projects and attitudes which in some cases he takes seriously at the deepest level, as what his life is about (or, in some cases, this section of his life)."[17] To demand of such a man . . . that he should step aside from projects and attitudes which in some cases he takes seriously at the deepest level, as what his life is about," "is to alienate him in a real sense from his actions and the source of his action in his own convictions. . . . It [i.e., that demand] is thus, in the most literal sense, an attack on his integrity."[18]

II

A. Moral Community

What are the specifically moral virtues that characterize an ideal moral community, as part of an ideal good community in the broad, g-sense? That is the question to which we must now turn. My answer is the following.

To begin with, a moral community is a fair community, treats fairly all its elements without exception. In the case of a political community, a moral community is also just and equitable. But as with equity vis-à-vis justice, a moral community also provides special opportunities to its most disadvantaged elements, to enable them to catch up with the more advantaged. Concerning justice in relation to community, Michael Sandel observes that what distinguishes a community in the constitutive sense, in addition to benevolence, the values shared by the community, and shared ends (teloses), is "a common vocabulary of discourse, and a background of implicit practices and understandings" within which the participants become partially, though never wholly, transparent to one another. Since justice depends for its preeminent status on the cognitive "separateness or boundedness of persons, . . . its *priority would diminish*" as the transparency increased and the community deepened.[19]

If this is true, it highlights an important difference between justice and fairness in relation to a (good) community. But as I shall argue in chapter 12, *contra* Sandel, the importance of justice would not diminish in a moral community, however close it may come to the ideal moral community.

Among other things, a moral community would be a fair community. But as I just said, it would also be a just community. It would treat all its elements both in a fair and just way. It would not legally or otherwise discriminate against or ignore any of its elements because

of their differences from other elements, but would give them their due. The community as a whole would also lend its material and moral support to the strengthening and nurturing of fairness and justice in all its elements.

The institutions and practices in a moral community too would be fair and just, internally and externally: in relation to their own membership and in relation to other institutions. These things can be seen more clearly in the case of T-communities. In a T-community questions concerning a community's fairness arise in relation to the pursuit of the communal telos(es), for example, with regard to the classification and ranking of benefits and tasks, and the apportionment or distribution of the tasks.

Again, a moral community is a caring community: a quality it shares with a good community. An ideal moral community would be universally caring. In actual communities all that one can realistically expect or hope for is for caring to spread as widely as is humanly possible, out of altruism, together with (at least) self-interested concern for the community's survival and success.

The concepts of caring *about* and caring *for* tie in with the right of all individuals to be treated as moral persons and will be discussed in Part II. I refer to the view that an essential part of that moral right is the right to become the subject of "consideration" in the sense of "concern and caring." The caring that is part of the treatment of human beings as moral persons, includes concern for the well-being of all others, involves helping them with opportunities to satisfy their basic needs and real interests, and to realize their human and individual potentials.

One problem here is the seeming conflict between the moral obligation to treat equally *all* other humans, as moral persons, and the differential concern and caring that people naturally have in relation to a limited number of special others—normally those existentially close to them. I shall leave a detailed resolution of the matter for another occasion; the following brief answer must suffice for the present. Suppose we adopt as a moral principle the injunction that we ought to care most about the most disadvantaged among our fellow humans, inasmuch as, by definition, some or all of their basic needs are greatest. The injunction to give them preferential treatment would conflict with the equal-treatment right *only* if the latter is treated as absolute. If it is not *absolute*—and in my view no moral rights, not excepting human rights, are absolute—the conflict would be sometimes resolved or attenuated, though perhaps not always to the satisfaction of all concerned. Moreover, need—for example, as embodied in Karl Marx's principle of distributive justice, the Socialist Principle of Justice, as Edward Nell and Onora O'Neill call the principle "to each according to his need"[20]—is one of the canons of distributive justice I accept and will defend in Part II. If the Socialist principle is accepted, it would sometimes appropriately qualify the right of all human beings to be treated as moral persons.[21]

Caring about and for others naturally springs from affection, benevolence, and, above all, love. As David Hume observes, "love and hate are not completed within themselves . . . but carry the mind to something farther—love is characterized by a desire for the happiness of the person loved, hate by the opposite tendency."[22] Were human beings angelic creatures rather than a perplexing and exasperating mixture of the angelic and the demonic, we could envisage an actual as against a merely possible moral community animated by pervasive love. Then solidarity, loyalty, caring, and all the other virtues that would grace a most excellent community would follow in its train. But apart from the obvious fact that such a social group would constitute a community of angels, not of beings of flesh and blood, certain practical problems would (alas) follow to which an angelic community would be immune. The constant willingness to set another's good above or before one's own is a wonderful quality. But particularly with great love there goes a willingness, nay an eagerness that knows almost no limits or bounds and sometimes borders on the irrational, to sacrifice one's interests and desires to those of the loved one. (That is one meaning of the saying that love is blind!) The result, especially if that tendency is widespread—as it would be in a loving community—would tend to make the chores and humdrum activities of daily life well-nigh impossible to perform! For instance, the community would pretty soon find itself in danger of starving to death with love! Unless the lover draws the line in her readiness to make sacrifices, endless impasses are likely to ensue. For instance, practically nothing of the everyday business of life can get done. Such things as business and other economic and financial enterprises and transactions would become well-nigh unthinkable.

As F.H. Bradley warns in a remarkable essay entitled "The Limits of Sacrifice,"[23] the (negative, second-order) virtue of sacrifice[24] must have limits if it is not to become counterproductive or destructive. A sacrificing spirit that knows no bounds—like boundless ambition "that falls on the other"—harms those who stand too ready to act on it for the sake of those they cherish. As often noted, the rational and moral opposite of selfishness or self-centeredness is not total selflessness but altruism, which involves concern for self as well as for others. That is true of Christian love, *caritas* or *agape*, as well as of friendship and spousal, parental, and filial love. The Golden Rule of Love enjoins loving others as oneself, not loving them above oneself—or not loving oneself at all! Again, love cries for reciprocation, and so is additionally heir to all the familiar heartaches and heartbreaks that human beings know only too well; particularly as loving or not loving, and falling in love or falling out of love are beyond the power of mere mortals to decide. Friendship too is prone to fruitless reaching-out, is vulnerable to rebuffs and indifference, to jealousy, resentment, even hatred. But the hurt of a rebuffed or failed friendship is sometimes measurably less acute, and sometimes not as lasting as the agonies of a failed (or even of reciprocated) love. "Jilted" friends rarely take their own lives, as jilted (or star-crossed) lovers are known to do.

In the last analysis the acid test of a good and moral community is its ability to provide optimal conditions for its members' pursuit of their happiness and well-being. As a consequence, the prospects for their realization are perhaps most uncertain in those circumstances in which the overriding and most pervasive attachments and relationships are those of love!

Yet when all this is said and done, one may still agree with Tennyson's memorable lines: "'Tis better to have loved and lost / Than not to have loved at all." In fact love's potential for heartache *may* be counterbalanced, though perhaps not outweighed, by the creativity that is often born of unhappiness or pain. For creativity is a further fundamental condition of a good community.

In sum, love is indispensable for a healthy community or society. In the absence of love, life would be deadly dull, bloodless, bleak, and dreary. It would lack much of what makes life worthwhile or meaningful. We would have to go down quite a distance on the biological ladder, below the "rungs" of mammals, to reach organisms that subsist in the absence of the most elementary forms of motherly or parental love. A community or society that takes the attitude of the teenage gangster leader Trevor in Graham Greene's short story, "The Destructors," that "all this hate and love, ... it's soft, it's hooey. There's only things,". . . would be ultimately doomed. That statement expresses the *non plus ultra* of human isolation and alienation; and in so far as Western society is fast approaching the position that "there's only things," it is in for increasingly profound depersonalization and dehumanization. These ills are essentially the implications of the common complaint that "the world is becoming increasingly materialistic." For materialism in this sense is the view that material possessions alone matter—at least that they matter more than beings that feel and hurt; hence that the latter may be exploited, even sacrificed, to the insatiable hunger for more, ever more material acquisitions.

To return to love. The English writer E.M. Forster is surely right in arguing, in a thought-provoking little essay entitled "Tolerance," that what democracy needs in order to exist is not love but toleration.[25] His thesis is that "unless you have a sound attitude of mind, a right psychology, you cannot construct or reconstruct anything that will endure."[26] And "surely the only sound foundation for a civilization is a sound state of mind."[27] He then argues that although "love is a great force in private life; it is indeed the greatest of all things; but love in public life does not work. It has been tried again and again: by the Christian civilizations of the Middle Ages, and also by the French Revolution, a secular movement which reasserted the brotherhood of Man. And it has always failed."[28]

Forster continues

> The fact is, we can only love what we know personally. And we cannot know much. In public affairs, in the rebuilding of civilization, something much less dramatic and emotional is needed, namely tolerance. . . . It merely means putting up with people, being able to stand things. . . . This is the only force which will enable different races and classes and interests to settle down together in the work of reconstruction.[29]

Forster's point concerning love in public life is similar to a point I made earlier, and, with qualification, is well taken, for instance, with respect to what Forster considers to be the absurdity, unreality, and dangerousness of expecting "that business concerns or marketing boards should love one another, or that a man in Portugal should love a man in Peru of whom he has never heard."[30] But one can take issue with his statement that love in public life has been tried in Medieval Europe and by the French Revolution. Indeed, one can seriously question the supposition that it has ever been tried.

More to the point, a moral community as I am envisaging it would have to be, like the ancient Greek city-states, relatively small and occupy a relatively small territory. If it is a good community at all, its members *would* tend to know one another personally. This is an important point, and I shall return to it later in this book.

Tolerance, which Forster rightly urges, is "the sound attitude of mind" necessary to public life, is also essential in private life. Lovers are quite vulnerable to possessiveness and exclusivity, which are death to tolerance, to acceptance of the other's right to freedom of choice and her unhindered pursuit of her interests and goals. Possessiveness stifles the loved one's individuality and creativity, stunts or twists one's life and personality. Resentment and rebelliousness, even hatred, are the usual rewards of the jealous, possessive lover, parent or spouse. Moreover, experience teaches that intolerance is endemic to small, close-knit, especially authoritarian groups, including communities. Aggressiveness and violence are two of its main banes. Thus in addition to the reasons mentioned earlier, a loving person's propensity to possessiveness is perhaps the most serious threat to the existence or survival of "a would-be love-informed" community.

I hasten to add that possessiveness and intolerance are not part of love itself. Rather, they spring from the imperfections of human nature: they vitiate and sully love. Aristotle's perceptive observation that to love is to desire the realization of the loved one's potentialities (echoed, as we saw, by Hume) is not impugned by our all too human propensity to egocentrism.

Benevolence triumphs where love fails in broad-mindedness and tolerance. Not surprisingly many philosophers extol it in their writings. Even in very small communities benevolence is free from the drawbacks of love in relation to public life, as pinpointed by the passages I quoted from Forster's essay. Benevolence can extend across oceans and continents, from people in Portugal to people in Peru; as we saw a few years ago in the outpouring of *sympathy*,[31] manifested in massive private and public aid that went from the four corners of the earth to the starving millions in Africa and the victims of the earthquakes in Armenia, Iran, and other countries. As with love, caring can come from benevolence but can embrace many more humans than love normally can. The danger of possessiveness and exclusiveness, hence of intolerance, also tends to be less evident in the case of benevolent persons. Again, benevolence is possible in the absence not only of love but of liking *and* dislike as well. It can be extended to total strangers. At the same time, one may dis*like* certain things about those one loves and that may engender painful inner conflicts in oneself. One may be caught between the desire to try to change those one loves or to see them change and the need to accept them as they are, with all their faults and frailties. In trying to change others one runs the risk of alienating them; and, in any event, such attempts are frequently a constant uphill fight.

The Random House Dictionary of the English Language, College Edition, defines "benevolence" as "1. desire to do good to others; good will or charitableness. 2. an act of kindness; charitable gift." It defines "beneficence" as "1. the doing of good; active goodness or kindness; charity." In the Treatise Hume classifies beneficence among the "natural virtues." A natural virtue is "a disposition which people both naturally have and naturally approve of."[32] Hume holds that "sympathy" is "a tendency to share what one takes to be the feeling of another, of whatever kinds they are,"[33] and supposes that it "is a very powerful principle of human nature."[34]

"Sympathy is not benevolence or altruism; but sympathy normally engenders benevolence. Insofar as I share another's feelings, his or her happiness and misery will matter to me; I desire his or her happiness in the same way that I desire my own, though usually in a lower degree. Thus Hume [Treatise, III, iii 1–5], unlike Hutcheson, Shaftesbury or Butler, does not consider benevolence as a basic given element in human nature but considers it as resulting from sympathy."[35] But in the Enquiry "Hume falls back on the mere fact of benevolence: 'It is needless to push our researches as far as to ask, why we have humanity or a fellow-feeling with others. It is sufficient, that this is experienced to be a principle of human nature.'"[36]

Mackie argues that "whereas Hume offers a sociological explanation of the artificial virtues but a psychological explanation of the natural virtues, it is . . . clear [in the light of his criticism of Hume in op. cit., p. 123] that at least a partly sociological explanation is needed for the natural virtues also."[37] But whether sympathy and benevolence are natural or artificial, or involve both nature and nurture, does not matter for us here.[38]

John Rawls thinks that love or benevolence needs justice for its completion. He writes

> Benevolence, even at its most expansive, depends on justice for its completion. "A love of mankind that wishes to preserve the distinction of persons, to recognize the separateness of life and experience, will use the two principles of justice to determine its aims when the many goods it cherishes are in opposition" 191). Even in the face of so noble a virtue as the love of mankind, the primacy of justice prevails, although the love that remains is of an oddly judicial spirit. This love is guided by what individuals themselves would consent to in a fair initial situation which gives them equal representation as moral persons (191).[39]

Sandel comments: "where for Hume, we need justice because we do not *love* each other well enough, for Rawls we need justice because we cannot *know* each other well enough for even love to serve alone."[40] He thinks that on Rawls' view justice is needed in relation to love as a result of the "opacity" of the good that the benevolent person or lover wishes another. For Rawls that opacity is the result of "the separateness of persons and the intractability of the bounds between them."[41] He continues: "on Rawls' view, love is blind, not for its intensity but rather for the opacity of the good that is the object of its concern. 'The reason why the situation remains obscure is that love and benevolence are second-order notions: they seek to further the good of beloved individuals that is already given'"[42] (191). Again, Sandel notes that according to Rawls, "only the person himself can 'know' what he really wants or 'decide' what he most prefers. 'Even when we take up another's point of view and attempt to estimate what would be to his advantage, we do so as an advisor, so to speak' (448), and given the limited cognitive access Rawls' conception allows, a rather unprivileged adviser at that."[43]

It is true that only the person herself can know what she wants or decides what she most prefers. The existential isolation or "solitariness" of the human being, even in the deepest, most intimate love or friendship, is an ineluctable part of the human condition and creates an unbridgeable cognitive chasm between the friend or the lover and the beloved. The other's deepest experiences, feelings, and emotions can only be barely glimpsed at or experientially shared. On the other hand, as H.L.A. Hart contends against J.S. Mill, grown-ups not infrequently do not know what is *good* or *best* for them, what they *should* want or prefer;[44] and that is precisely what Rawls is supposed to be talking about. A familiar example is the way in which people are gulled by seductive advertisements, especially on television, to acquire preferences that are patently not in their best interest. Here Rawls appears to confuse what people actually want or prefer with what is good for them, what is in their interest. His use of the phrase "one's own good" lends itself to the confusion.

To sum up the discussion of love, benevolence, and sympathy: realistically speaking, a moral community is a close-knit social organization that contains a mix of the following things: (a) love, mainly between family members and between the nuclear and extended families, together with affection binding together at least some of these families: those related by blood or by ethnicity or culture; (b) affection between friends and, perhaps, less close relatives; and (c) sympathy in Hume's sense and benevolence toward strangers and mere acquaintances, if any, as well as good will toward and concern for the success of the community's institutions and practices. These would flow both from a developed sense of duty and from self-interest and moral or religious sentiments. But as Mackie observes, "we sympathize more with people who are in one way or another nearer to us than with strangers, foreigners, and those remote in time or place, but we set the same moral evaluation on similar characters and actions wherever they are found."[45] In fact, "since the desire to do good to others," and the like, is part of affection and love, a community that satisfies conditions (a) through (c) above would be an eminently sympathetic and benevolent community in Hume's sense of "sympathy," and so, a moral community. In short, it would be a good community in the expression's inclusive sense.

Notes

1 But as we shall see, far from being the whole of what "good community" means in that sense.

2 Aristotle, of course, distinguished "theoretical" and "practical" virtue, but that is another matter.

3 The older, broader use is occasionally encountered in such sentences as "she is a woman of many virtues—a quick wit and a sense of humor, courteousness and sensitivity."

4 (Boston, 1970).

5 We should add the word "sisterly" to "fraternal."

6 Ibid., 5.

7 Ibid., 25.

8 Ibid., 5. I have excluded Slater's "*in a total and visible collective entity*"— which is part of the first "human desire" he claims is frustrated by American culture—since it is clearly inapplicable to an N-community. Indeed, the term "total entity" seems to imply an "organic," a Hegelian sort of T-community, which I consider unacceptable.

9 We should distinguish "depending on someone" and "being dependent on someone." The danger is that dependence on another may turn into overdependence, into one's becoming dependent on the other to such an extent that one becomes a psychological cripple. However, that would be unlikely if the dependence in Slater's sense is mutual, is interdependence. (This should be distinguished from what is now labeled "co-dependence," i.e., mutual or two-way overdependence.) Attachments too, though, like dependence, laudable in themselves, are vulnerable. Overdependence can result from overattachment. Almost inevitably the price of overdependence is often mutual resentment and the souring or the demise of the love or friendship.

10 I am, therefore, suggesting a very close connection between the concept of privacy and the concept of private property. It is significant that John Locke conceived of property as an extension of the self.

11 Note the American colloquial use of the word "use" and "being used"—words which are synonymous with "exploit" and "being exploited" respectively. Also note the profound fear of "being used": the widespread, almost pathological mistrust or distrust of others that the common employment of these words reflects.

12 One cannot help thinking of Jean-Paul Sartre's view that all human relationships tend to rob the other of her freedom, reducing her to an "object"—in sharp contrast to Albert Camus' humanism in *The Plague*.

13 See chapter 7.

14 *A Critique of Utilitarianism,* in *Utilitarianism For and Against,* J.J.C. Smart and Bernard Williams (Cambridge, 1973), 113ff.

15 Ibid., 116.

16 Ibid.

17 Ibid.

18 Ibid 116–117.

19 *Liberalism and the Limits of Justice* (Cambridge, 1982), 172–173. Italics in original.

20 "Justice Under Socialism," in *Justice: Alternative Political Perspectives,* ed. James Sterba (Belmont, CA, [1980]), 200. The other half of the Socialist Principle: "From each according to his ability," does not concern us here.

21 This, in a way, would fit in well with Nicholas Rescher's Canon of Claims in *Distributive Justice* (Indianapolis/New York, [1966]), which states that "[d]istributive justice consists in the treatment of people *according to their legitimate claims,* positive and negative. This canon shifts the burden to— and thus its implementation hinges crucially upon—the question of the nature of legitimate claims, and the machinery for their mutual accommodation in cases of plurality, and *their reconciliation in cases of conflict*". (Op. cit., 82) In the type of case under consideration, the competing claims and the possible conflict would arise, *vis-à-vis* need, not in relation to equality as a possible basis of distributive justice (the Canon of Equality, ibid., 74–75) but as the egalitarianism embodied in the human right of all individuals to be treated as moral persons. (See Part II, chapter 8.)

22 P. L. Gardiner, "Hume's Theory of the Passions," in David Pears, *David Hume, A Symposium* (London, 1963), 39.

23 "The Limits of Individual and National Self-Sacrifice," *Collected Essays* (Westport, CT., 1970), 165–176.

24 It is a negative or second-order virtue because it would not exist in a world in which suffering did not exist.

25 In *Two Cheers for Democracy* (London, 1972).

26 Ibid., 43.

27 Ibid.

28 Ibid., 44.

29 Ibid.

30 Ibid.

31 Both in its ordinary meaning and in Hume's use of the word.

32   J. L. Mackie, *Hume's Moral Philosophy* (London, 1980), 76.

33   Ibid., 120.

34   Ibid., 120–121.

35   Ibid.

36   Ibid., 12.

37   Ibid., 123.

38   It might be worth noting that my earlier discussion of the virtues that charac-
      terize a good community is compatible with psychological egoism; though like
      Hume I reject that view as an inadequate account of human motivation in
      general.

39   Quoted from Michael Sandel, *Liberalism and the Limits of Justice*, 171–
      172.

40   Ibid., 172.

41   Ibid., 170–171.

42   Ibid., 171.

43   Ibid.

44   *Law, Liberty, and Morality* (New York, 1963), 32–33.

45   Op. cit., 121.

Chapter 3

"The Good Society": A Comparative Sketch

Each of the authors I shall discuss in this chapter—Robert N. Bellah, Amitai Etzioni, and John Kenneth Galbraith—has his own distinctive vision of the Good Society. The former two are communitarians in a sense yet to be explained, while Galbraith is a liberal (where liberalism is contrasted with conservatism). Since this chapter continues the sketch of a good and moral community begun in chapter 2, it will focus, in the first two cases, on what is distinctive about the conceptions of a good/moral community as their authors understand it, and on what they add to our understanding of it. I shall begin with Bellah, Richard Madsen, Willaim M. Sullivan, Ann Swidler, Steven M. Tipton, and their *Habits of the Heart*, subtitled "Individualism and Commitment in American Life,"[1] but will also briefly refer to their *The Good Society*.[2] Next I shall consider Etzioni's views, mainly in *The New Golden Rule*,[3] and will conclude with some of the fundamentals of Galbraith's "broad specifications" of the good society.

I. Bellah et al.

Two main themes in *Habits of the Heart* will concern us: first, the relation of communities in general to their history, their tradition, and the increasing loss of that tradition in contemporary America in its modernist "culture of individualism," and "the . . . individualistic achievement and self-fulfillment that often makes it difficult for people to sustain their commitments to others, either in intimate relationships or in the public sphere."[4] Their solution in *Habits of the Heart,* as summarized in *The Good Society*, is to hold up "older traditions, biblical and civic republican, that had a better grasp on the truth that the individual is realized only and through community . . . but showed that contemporary Americans have difficulty understanding those traditions today or seeing how they apply to their lives."[5] And, "recently one way of posing the argument about how to deal with the problems emerging in this new form of society ["a radically new and rapidly changing kind of society was coming into existence"] has been to pit philosophical liberals against communitarians; *Habits of the Heart* was often termed communitarian."[6]

Relations of Communities to their Past: In defining "community" in the glossary of *Habits of the Heart*, the authors note that they are using the term in a strong sense, different from the very loose way it is used by Americans today. They contrast "real" or "genuine" community, community in the strong sense, with a "lifestyle enclave," which is "formed by people who share some feature of private life. . . . They are not interdependent, do not act together politically, and do not share a history."[7] A community, on the other hand, is "a group of people who are socially interdependent, who participate together in discussion and decision making, and who share certain *practices* . . . that both define the community and are nurtured by it.[8] Such a community is not quickly formed. It almost always has a history and so is also a community of memory, defined in part by its past and its memory of its past."[9] Ethnic and racial communities, "each with its own story and its own heroes and heroines" are examples.[10]

Communities are almost always "communities of memory,"in that "they have a history—in an important sense they are constituted by their past—. . . one that does not forget its past."[11] "In order not to forget that past, a community is involved in retelling its story, its constitutive narrative, and in so doing, it offers examples of the men and women who have embodied and exemplified the meaning of the community. These stories and collective history and exemplary individuals are an important part of the tradition that is so central to a community of memory."[12]

If we look at actual communities, we find that the gradual fading of their collective memory, in the course of time (not an uncommon occurrence) may, but also may not, result in the communities' demise as communities. The Armenian community in the Old City of Jerusalem, to which I have alluded elsewhere in this book, illustrates the point that, as long as other forces that bind people together into a community continue to operate, the fading of collective memories would not destroy, or even weaken, a community. The community in question consists of two groups, one very old, going back to, at least, the fifth century A.D., the other much more recent, and each with its own different history. Many of the members of the latter group are descendants of survivors of the 1915 Turkish genocide who found shelter within the confines of the Monastery of St. James. Both groups survive, greatly diminished in number; but one cannot find, at present, "examples of the men and women who have embodied and exemplified the meaning of the community,"[13] assuming that, at some time in the past, it did have such exemplary men and women. In contrast to it, the men and women who reside within the monastery continue to have a strong collective memory of suffering and loss—but also memories of the martyrs, and the heroes and heroines, of the tragic period in their families or their own lives. And like their compatriots everywhere, they annually commemorate the death of some million-and-a-half men, women, and children in the genocide.

Bellah et al. emphasize the importance of a community's keeping memories of suffering alive; but as in the case of the survivors of the Nazi Holocaust, the memory of *personal* suffering and loss is often suppressed by the survivors, exemplifying Freud's insight that if such memories are suppressed, they continue to "dominate a person in unhealthy ways." For as our authors comment, "only by remembering can one be free to act without being dominated by unconscious memory."[14] Whether the painful memories are verbally shared or no, they may make the sufferers kindred souls, partially constituted by their mutual suffering as moral selves, especially if it impels them to pursue some common goal or goals, such as to seek justice or redress for the wrongs. In that way a community may come into existence, united by a deep special bond or burden. But it must be added that a community must be careful not to be bogged down in the past by constantly harping on it—perhaps, especially, if it is a painful past. Thus the "communities of memory that tie us to the past" may, instead be turning us "toward the future as communities of hope,"[15] as Bellah et al. say.

If "community" is used to mean a "T-community," as Bellah et al. do, a community's teloses may become repositories of communal memories, including memories of the community's creators, the history of these goals, the stories of the pioneers who worked hard to realize them, and their success or failure. If a community's telos is a rallying cry for political, economic, or religious liberation from domestic or foreign oppression, the narratives would normally include, as Bellah et al. say, stories of the heroes and heroines who fought—perhaps died—for the cause.

The preceding process may also occur if an existing N-community becomes politicized, and is consequently transformed into a T-community. One example is the Palestinian communities on the West Bank and Gaza, who became politicized with the rise of Arab nationalism in the early part of this century, and more so, as a result of the Israeli occupation of the whole of Palestine in 1967. Other examples are the various Middle Eastern and North African Arab countries and, indeed, other former Western colonies, during their struggle for independence from their colonial masters.

"Transforming American Culture"

Like other critics of the contemporary American science, Bellah et al. believe that, despite "our enormous achievements," "we seem to be hovering on the very brink of disaster, not only from international conflict but from the internal incoherence of our own society. What has gone wrong? How can we reverse the slide toward the abyss?"[16] Their answer is that what has failed is "integration" or "coherence" at every level, "from the society of nations to the national society to the local community to the family,"[17] or "the extreme fragmentation of the modern world."[18] The reason for the failure is that we have "put our own good, as individuals, as a nation, ahead of the common good."[19] What we need, therefore, is "a more genuinely integrated societal community," a "new integration,"[20] by "reappropriating tradition," which means bringing the "moral concerns of the American biblical and republican traditions," republican civic virtue, actively and creatively into our social, political, economic, and other structures. In *The Good Society*, for instance, the authors state that "[in *Habits of the Heart*] we held up older traditions, biblical and civic republican, that had a better grasp on the truth that the individual is realized only in and through community."[21]

That any desirable economic, political, or social systems or structures are "dependent on the existence of virtue among the people" is, I think, important and true. Certainly caring and related virtues described in Chapter 2 and later sections of this book are the sort of "civic virtues" that I believe make for a better society and world.

In addition to the biblical and republican tradition, Bellah et al. believe that we also "need to learn again from the cultural riches of the human species and to reappropriate and revitalize those riches so that they can speak to our condition today."[22] That is also important. Much can be learned from the ongoing experience of the European Union's attempts gradually to integrate financially, economically, politically, and, through NATO, militarily. We can also learn from the longer experience of the United Nations. Learning from them, as well as from the tragedy of Yugoslavia and other countries in the throes of civil war or war, should help considerably the cause of domestic and international tranquility and peace.

The problem, of course, is learning to learn, and to learn to apply (both difficult matters) the wisdom and experience of those countries or societies that are most similar, as well as from those most dissimilar to America—or whatever particular country or society one is concerned with. That involves difficult choices, and there is no sure way of knowing whether what has been learned would help when applied under the different historical and current conditions. But, and in this I fully agree with Bellah et al., the effort must be constantly made. It means overcoming national pride, hubris, chauvinism, and an insular or superior attitude.[23]

Despite the authors' belief that the loss of the traditional biblical and civic virtues, not, perhaps, the "diversity and pluralism of American life," is what divides Americans, one may wonder if the reappropriation of these values would be sufficient to reintegrate American life and restore community to it, especially in light of the great, ever-increasing ethnic, racial, religious, and cultural diversity of contemporary American society. The recovery of the biblical values taught by such later Old Testament prophets as Isaiah, and by the New Testament, means widespread caring. But appeal to the Judeo-Christian moral tradition *as part of Judaism and Christianity* would be limited to Christians and Jews, and possibly Muslims, not also to the non-white, non-Western cultural/religious groups and communities.[24] In fact, attempts to restore the biblical tradition are more likely to create tensions and conflicts between the latter and mainstream America since they are likely to resent and resist a push in that direction as oppression and unwanted assimilation.

In short, the solution offered by our authors to America's ills applies best, if not only to, the white, middle-class majority of present-day Americans, leaving out the rich, and the poor, the millions who have a non-White cultural or religious heritage. (It is not an accident that all the interviewees for *Habits of the Heart* were white, middle-class men and women.)

The situation is significantly different with the pursuit, in practice, of the ideals of democracy, human rights, equality, liberty, and justice that is embodied in the U.S. Constitution and Bill of Rights (as opposed to the reappropriation of the actual political history of America). That, indeed, should go a long way toward restoring the coherence and integration that Bellah et al. hope for. The restoration of democratic values, of participatory democracy, should strengthen the existing bonds between the members of real communities. It should also help create a more nearly harmonious relation between the different ethnic, racial, and religious communities.

In the Third World, whether the transformation of existing institutions and practices by democracy or democratization may also bring about peace between warring countries in the Middle East, Asia, Africa, and Latin America is another question.

II Amitai Etzioni

Like Bellah et al. in *Habits of the Heart,* Etzioni applies the term 'community' very broadly in *The New Golden Rule,* i.e., not only to small-scale communities, such as constitutive neighborhoods, villages, or small towns, but also to nations and to groups of nations. In fact, he is primarily concerned with community in the term's broad applications and advances a communitarian paradigm "of what makes any social entity, from a village to a group of nations, into more of a community. Community is a set of attributes, not a concrete place."[25]

A. The New Golden Rule and the Good Society (Community)
The paradigm of the good society/community that Etzioni advances and applies in his book is "the notion of the golden rule at the social level," "one which nourishes both social virtues and individual rights."[26] Such a society requires "a carefully maintained equilibrium of social virtues and individual rights,"[27] i.e., equilibrium between "individual rights [and preferences] and social responsibilities [or commitments], individually and communally, and autonomy and social order."[28] The new golden rule requires that the tension between one's preferences and one's social commitments be reduced "by increasing the realm of duties one affirms as moral responsibilities," not forcibly imposing them by law. Rather, "the realm of responsibilities one believes one should discharge and that one believes one is fairly called upon to assume."[29] What that means becomes clear from his statement that "the order of a good communitarian society relies heavily on normative means (education, leadership, consensus, peer pressure, pointing

out role models, exhortation, and, above all, the moral voice of communities)."[30] "In that sense, the social order of good societies is a moral order."[31] The "civic order" is part of the good order, but it is not enough. The "more" required is autonomy. Like social order, it is a primary virtue. That is the "rights" part of the paradigm's equilibrium. In short, autonomy too is "basic to the communitarian paradigm,"[32] and is a "primary virtue." But autonomy is socially bounded in the sense that human beings are social by nature, are "encumbered" in Sandel's sense, and that "their sociability enhances their human and moral potential. . . . The social fabric sustains, nourishes, and enables individuality rather than diminishes it."[33] "In good measure, communal attachments and individuality go hand-in-hand, enrich one another, and are not antagonistic. The self is enriched and, . . . ennobled by being social; it is the social self that is held back by the lack of positive multiple attachments."[34] It follows that nourishing social attachments is "part of the effort to maintain social order while ensuring that such attachments will not suppress all autonomous expressions."[35]

B. Autonomy and Order; Social Order; Etzioni's Communitarian Paradigm

At least three basic questions immediately arise in relation to the desired equilibrium between the "two dual virtues" of autonomy and social/moral order, between social good and individual choice: (1) How the equilibrium is to be achieved, not just in principle but also, and particularly, in practice. For it may seem obvious that, contrary to Etzioni's claim, the individual's social embeddedness would militate against his or her autonomy and choice. And (2) how we would know when equilibrium has been reached, or what are the criteria for it in a given community or society. Since a community with "too much" autonomy at the expense of social/moral order, or vice versa, would be a morally and socially bad community, it becomes also important to ask (3)(a) how much disequilibrium between the two virtues must exist in a given community, *conceptually speaking,* for that community to change from a "good community" into a bad one, and (b) at what further "point" in that conceptual process would a community cease to be a community at all. Or what is the conceptual dividing line between community and its absence. I shall later argue that Etzioni offers no answer to question (3)(b) (if not also to question (3)(a)), since (like Sandel, for example) he uses "community" in the sense of good/

moral community, and fails to provide a value-neutral definition of "community."

Etzioni's general answer to question (1) is that it requires (a) "a reliance mainly on education, leadership, persuasion, faith, and moral dialogues, rather than the law [36] for sustaining virtues," (b) defining a "substantive core of values" that need to be promoted, a core "richer than those that make procedures meritorious, but not a pervasive ideology or the kinds of religion that leave little room for autonomy."[37] In a good society the order "has to be of a special kind: voluntary and limited to core values rather than imposed or pervasive. And autonomy has to be contextual within a social fabric of bonds and values rather than unbounded."[38]

Etzioni's general answer to question (2) is essentially the following. First, as a communitarian, Etzioni correctly views autonomy, freedom, or liberty as contextual: "It is futile to argue that people in general require more liberty or more order, more individual rights or more moral duties."[39] Rather, for him, the equilibrium or lack of equilibrium between the dual virtues in a given community is determined by its consequences for the community. Second, in a communitarian society the rare relationship [of equilibrium] between autonomy and order is one of "inverting symbiosis": "*a blending of the two basic formations that—up to a point—enhance one another (so that in a society that has more of one, the other grows stronger as a direct result), a symbiotic relationship; but if either element intensifies beyond a given level, it begins to diminish the other: the same two formations become antagonistic.*"[40] For example, if a community "continuously increases its expectations of its members, a point will be reached at which . . . the members' autonomy . . . [will] decline" . . . "the communal bonds will fray . . . and opposition to the community will grow, which in turn will undermine the social order."[41] Similarly if, in a community, "autonomizing formations grow stronger and stronger."[42]

We may grant Etzioni's rather obvious and commonsensical view (which is also supported by history) that, beyond "a certain" contextually determined point, autonomy and order in a given community become antagonistic. It is much less obvious that, contextually speaking, *before* such a point is reached, autonomy and order *would* (always, or even generally) *be* mutually enhancing, would strengthen each other—if Etzioni means that freedom to *exercise* one's rights would be enhanced. In trying to support his contention, he imagines a "low level community in a recently-completed high-rise building," where the strengthening of the residents' social bonds will make the residents have a "stronger sense of self" and "feel less isolated" (presumably meaning that the freedom to exercise their rights would, thereby, be enhanced). As a result, he thinks, the residents will voluntarily perform their responsibilities well. That may be true; but by his own admission, the increasing closeness of the residents' relationships would make their freedom more and more "bounded," which can be plausibly interpreted to mean that the residents would voluntarily limit the exercise of their rights against the other residents. That is, they would voluntarily avoid standing on or asserting their rights vis-à-vis the others. The rights themselves would not be restricted or otherwise affected, in principle, in any way. They would not be actually restricted—or enhanced.

I shall not pursue this question further, but in a later chapter I shall advance the more modest thesis that the acknowledgment of human rights in practice, not just in principle, is not only compatible with community existence but, in certain ways to be explained, is essential to a community's being, or becoming, a moral community.

C. Order and Autonomy Among Communities

As we recall, Etzioni, like Bellah et al., applies the term "community" very broadly, and in the chapter entitled "Pluralism Within Unity" turns to the relation between communities within a given nation or society and between a group of nations. But before we look at his views on the subject, it is necessary to examine the concept of "community" as he broadly applies it. Now it may be remembered that on the two ordinary meanings or senses of community, particularly the first, as e.g., defined by *The Random House Dictionary of the English Language*, it is possible for a nation or country to be a community. They are: 1. "a social group of any size whose members reside in a specific locality, share government, and have a common cultural and historical heritage," and 2. "a social, religious, . . . or other group sharing common characteristics or interests." Even in sense (1) the concept of community does not presently apply to any existing group of countries or nations, but it may perhaps apply to the European Union if, at some future date, its members become politically united and acquire a common cultural and historical heritage. (For the latter to transpire, hundreds of years or a millennium may perhaps be necessary.)

According to Etzioni, a group of communities would form a community as a whole, a "community of communities," if "systematic attention is paid to ensuring that communities will relate to one another in a manner that is respectful of both order and autonomy."[43] Otherwise, they will only be "communitarian islands" in a "noncommunitarian sea,"[44] with the likelihood of hostilities and strife erupting between them. If the islands are autonomous and share a moral social order, the "sea" would be orderly and peaceful. The question is whether respect for order and autonomy would be sufficient to make the sea a community of communities—just as an island in the sea is supposed to be a community if it satisfies that condition? Or does Etzioni here commit the fallacy of composition? It would seem that unless the islands are related or united by some *additional* important value or values, by certain special relationships, the country or society in question would not be community as a whole, a community of communities. A fortiori, with a group of nations.[45] It is true that, according to Etzioni, the substantial core of values a community needs to exist includes democratic structures, which are presupposed by a group's respect for order and autonomy. But once again, would these three core values or complexes of values be sufficient?[46] The crucial point is that there appears to be no possible answer to this persistent question in Etzioni's book, precisely because, as I shall now argue, Etzioni offers no definition, or a criterion or criteria, for "(single) community." Without either, one cannot define "community *of* communities" or provide criteria for its application.

In discussing his views regarding community so far, I have assumed without examination that Etzioni employs "community" as a purely descriptive, value-neutral term, as, for example, in ordinary usage (though, obviously, not defined the way ordinary language does). A little reflection shows that that is not, at least, not generally, the case;[47] that like Sandel and Bellah et al., he generally uses the term with an honorific (hence normative) meaning, as equivalent to "(good and?) moral community" as they are used in the present book. That is, a social entity that *achieves equilibrium or near equilibrium* between autonomy and order would be an ideal or near-ideal society-*siv*-community.

Whether the last proposition is true it is difficult to say without detailed examination, but it is unquestionable, I think, that respect for individual human and other rights, a social order of mutual commitments, responsibilities, and obligations, and democratic social, economic, and political institutions and practices, are eminently good-making qualities in any social entity of any kind, including a community in the value-neutral sense. And although Etzioni does not think of these admirable qualities in terms of the notion of caring about others, they do very much involve, or amount to that!

The fact that Etzioni generally uses "community" in an honorific sense—that the extent of a social entity's goodness/badness varies with the extent of autonomy vis-à-vis moral social order in it—fits in with his conception of the (variable) relation between (the extent of) autonomy and (extent of) social order, since moral and other kinds of values clearly vary in extent or degree. A social entity would be good to the degree that autonomy and order approach equilibrium and bad to the degree of their disequilibrium: provided it does not cross the conceptual "line" that would make it cease to be a community at all. As I have argued, that conceptual line is never defined or demarcated and is only an imaginary line we must assume exists somewhere. But we know that, wherever it is, it must be a fixed, not a variable, line since community in the value-neutral sense is a non-scalar term, or the concept it expresses does not admit of degrees. (For instance, a "lifestyle enclave" in the sense in which Bellah et al. use it is not "a community in some degree but not so in some other degree!")

III. John Kenneth Galbraith

I shall not tarry long on Galbraith's "broad specifications" of the good society.[48] Unlike Bellah et al. and Etzioni, Galbraith is a philosophical liberal: his "good society" is not envisaged as a community (or a community of communities) either in the ordinary senses or in Bellah et al.'s strong sense of the term. But like Bellah et al. and Etzioni, his concern is with what he calls the "good and achievable society," not with the perfect or ideal society, thereby distinguishing his aims and their aims from our consideration in chapter 2, and in this book as a whole, which is to sketch an ideal of a good and moral community.

A further similarity between Galbraith and the other two authors is that the good society he describes is essentially what he conceives to be *the* morally good and desirable society. He writes that his aim is "to explore and define what, very specifically, would be right."[49] Again, he too devotes considerable attention to the economic, social, political, educational and other changes and improvements that he believes need to be made to realize the good society, cognizant that "some barriers to achievement are immobile, decisive,"[50] namely, "the institutional structure and the human characteristics."[51] But there are other constraints that must not be accepted. He writes: "as there are shaping forces, some deep in human nature, that must be accepted, so there are constraints that the good society cannot, must not accept. Socially desirable change is regularly denied out of well-recognized self-interest."[52] He claims that neither classical capitalism nor socialism is the "controlling framework of the good or even plausible society."[53] The controlling, immutable framework of the good society consists in market economy and social and political democracy. But he stresses that decision and action must be based on the specific case, on "the ruling facts of the specific case," on "practical judgment." Thus "nothing can be decided by a recourse to free market,"[54] capitalist, liberal, or socialist principles. In the good society, policy decision and action are not ideological but made on the "social and economic merits of the particular case."[55] "This is not the age of doctrine; it is the age of practical judgment,"[56] he says. Only in the way described are "social decency and compassion, perhaps even democracy itself, . . . preserved." Personal liberty for all, "basic well being," "racial and ethnic equality," and the "opportunity for a rewarding life" are essential components of the good society.

Not surprisingly, Galbraith accords economics pride of place in the good society. In it the economic system would "work well and for everyone. Only then will opportunity match aspiration, either great or small."[57] The economy would be strong and stable, and the opportunity it provides would not leave anyone without a decent income. Basic support would be given to "the retired, single mothers with young children, the medically or mentally infirm and physically and mentally incapable."[58] Although adequate employment must be ensured, "there must still be a safety net for all."[59] Consequently, the state must have a large role in the economy, especially, on behalf of "the less fortunate of the community."[60] But equality in income is not either realizable or socially desirable. It is not desirable because some seek income and wealth and others do not, but seek satisfaction elsewhere. "It is the essence of liberty that these differences in motivation and reward be accepted."[61] Still, "the economy must accord everyone a chance both to participate and to advance according to ability and ambition."[62]

To achieve these goals, the economy must be stable, not "recurrently deny employment and aspiration because of recession and depression. And it must not frustrate the efforts of those who plan diligently and intelligently for old age and retirement or for illness or unanticipated need."[63] It must therefore grow substantially and reliably in productivity and employment, "from year to year," reflecting "the needs and desires of a people who seek to enjoy greater economic well-being."[64]

Internationally, the good society must live in "peaceful and mutually rewarding association with its trading partners on the planet. It must be a force for world peace," cooperating with other nation-states to realize that end. "War is the most unforgiving of human tragedies, and is comprehensively so in an age of nuclear weaponry. There must also be recognition of, and effective support for the needs and hopes of the less fortunate members of the world community."[65] In short, the good society would have "a cooperative and compassionate foreign dimension."[66]

(A) Ends and (B) Means

(A.) There is little or nothing in my brief and highly selective outline of Galbraith's admirable broad specifications of the nature and purpose of the good society I disagree with. But leaving aside his rather surprising silence about the place and role of art, culture, science, and technology in the good society, a fundamental question arises about the envisaged good society's realizability in practice. *Theoretically speaking*, the broad specifications of Galbraith's good society are all realizable, I believe. But it is very doubtful that many of them are *actually* achievable, perhaps even in the unforeseeable future, and even if we confine ourselves to America and the other Western nations and leave aside the bulk of humanity. In other words, one may wonder how the fully democratic, egalitarian, caring and compassionate domestic social-economic and political goals of the good society—for example, "employment and an upward chance for all," "reliable economic growth to sustain employment," "education and, to the greatest extent possible," "the family support and discipline that serve future participation and reward," "freedom from social disorder at home and abroad," and so forth—can be realized in the modern world, given that they go, first, against people's human, all-too-human tendencies and propensities toward self-interest and self-centeredness, greed and acquisitiveness, aggressiveness, territoriality, laziness, and almost insatiable lust for power. Similarly with regard to transnational and international cooperation and peace, the deteriorating world ecology, the world's poor; and so on. Galbraith does not tell us how people, and governments, would be persuaded or can be given the needed motivation or incentives, say through education to do what is right.

What I am saying it that, to achieve the good society, a profound, even revolutionary change in men's hearts and minds (especially hearts), if not in human nature itself, is absolutely necessary, when no fundamental moral improvement has been discernible in Homo sapiens since he emerged, or thought he emerged, from the jungle. Yet it is essential for Galbraith's own non-utopian conception that, as he says, "the good society must accept men and women as they are."[67]

But even if we assume that, in many quarters, the will and desire to create a better society does exist, there would remain further obstacles to translating them into action. Among the most obvious are the world's runaway population explosion coupled with the depletion or diminishing of its natural and other material resources; the ever-increasing poverty and squalor, disease, malnutrition, famine, and starvation in the Third World; the continuing polluting and poisoning of our water, food, and air; global warming and the greenhouse effect; and—to cut a long list short—the destruction of the ecology, resulting in the extinction of numerous plant and animal species. All these, leaving aside man's inhumanity to man that culminated, in our sad century, in the bloodiest wars and most horrifying genocides in human history.

(B) further kind of problem Galbraith's conception faces concerns the *means* he proposes for the achievement of the good society. The two fundamental means he proposes are, (a) the role of *government*, and (b) the "decisive role" of *education*. For example, with regard to (a), he states that "Economic success depends on the support and supervision of a stable, efficient, effective governmental structure. Without it, the most essential of the requirements for economic development is unrealized. . . . In the last century, . . . a question as to what economic progress demanded would have brought a prompt reply in the United States, as also in Europe: good government, good education and possibly good transportation. This is still a controlling role in our own time."[68] This is perfectly true, especially with regard to good, democratic government, and good public education. But even a modicum of democracy is only a dream in many parts of the world, and the so-called Western democracies have a long way to go before they truly become governments of all the people, for all the people, by the people.

(b) Concerning education, Galbraith starts with the important economic contribution of education to society, but quickly adds that education has a "larger political and social role."[69] It "has a vital bearing on social peace and tranquillity; it is education that provides the hope and the reality of escape from the lower, less-favored social and economic strata to those above."[70] But its "deepest justification in itself" is allowing people to "enjoy life itself to the fullest."[71] That the latter is sometimes true is undeniable, but only part of its "deepest justification." Good education also enables us to understand who or what we are as humans and as individuals, and our place in the universe. Consequently, it gives, or adds meaning to our lives. The surprising thing is that despite his emphasis on education, Galbraith says nothing at all about the importance of moral (and religious) education for the achievement and maintenance of the good society. For example, the role of good role models and the right kinds of heroes, or the importance of our inculcating the sorts of moral virtues described in Chapter 2 in the younger generations, for the raising of decent individuals who would work, individually and collectively, to bring about the kinds of difficult changes and improvements Galbraith advocates.

But when all is said and done, and despite the odds against the real possibility of achieving a "good society" anytime in the foreseeable future, it is absolutely necessary that we hope and believe (as Galbraith obviously does) that we are redeemable as a species. Never yielding to despair, we must never stop trying to redeem ourselves. We have no choice: otherwise we perish.

To sum up. As will be recalled, Chapter 2 presented an ideal of good and moral community. To compare that ideal with a few other "communitarian" and non-communitarian visions of "the good society," the present chapter outlined three such conceptions. The first two—those of Robert N. Bellah et al. and Amitai Etzioni—identify the good society with some conception of community, while John Kenneth Galbraith provides a non-communitarian, liberal account of the good society.

The brief, highly selective expositions and critiques of the three conceptions focused on the distinctive aspects of each view, especially in relation to the account of the good and moral community I gave in Chapter 2. In that way the discussion aimed to increase and deepen our understanding of, or provide added insight about, the good society in general and good and moral community in particular. Likewise the critical remarks about each view were designed to provide a better understanding of some of the main difficulties that attempts to create a good society and/or a good and moral community (particularly a "community of communities" in Etzioni's sense) would encounter, and need to be resolved or overcome.

Notes

1 Robert N. Bellah, Richard Madsen, William M. Sullivan, Ann Swidler, Steven M. Tipton, *Habits of the Heart* (Berkeley and Los Angeles, CA.)

2 Berkeley and Los Angeles, CA, 1985. The book is co-authored by Bellah, Richard Madsen, William M. Sullivan, Ann Swidler, and Steven M. Tipton.

3 New York, 1996.

4 *The Good Society*, 5.

5 Ibid.

6 Ibid., 6. In distinguishing their communitarianism from philosophical liberalism, they note that they maintain that "more substantive ethical identities [than 'autonomous individuals'] and a more active participation in a democratic policy [than a "market economy, and a procedural state"] are necessary for the functioning of any decent society" (ibid.). But they think that the term communitarian may be misunderstood if one supposes that "only face-to-face groups . . . are communities" and that "communitarians are opposed to the state, the economy, and all the large structures that so largely dominate our life today," and consequently, avoid the term "communitarian" in *The Good Society*. In fact, their view is that "only greater citizen participation in the large structures of the economy and the state will enable us to surmount the deepening problems of contemporary social life" (ibid.).

7 *Habits of the Heart*, p. 335.

8 Thus, like Michael Sandel, they identify "community" with "T-community."

9 Ibid., 333. Italics in original.

10 Ibid., 153.

11 Ibid.

12 Ibid. Cf. Alasdair MacIntyre's *After Virtue*.

13 Ibid., 153.

14 Ibid., 321, Note 17.

15 Ibid.

16 Ibid., 284.

17 Ibid., 285.

18 Ibid., 286.

19 Ibid.

20 Ibid.

21 Op. cit., 5. My italics.

22 *Habits of the Heart*, 282–83.

23 More of this when we turn to Galbraith's internationalism.

24 The great diversity of religions and moral-religious beliefs in the world is a main reason why caring and related virtues championed in this book are based (in Part II) on a secular "ethic of caring," enabling them to have universal appeal, in principle.

25 Etzioni, op. cit., 6.

26 Ibid., 4.

27 Ibid., 5.

28 Ibid.

29 Ibid., 12–13.

30 Ibid., 13.

31 Ibid.

32 Ibid., 16.

33 Ibid., 26.

34 Ibid., 26–27.

35 Ibid., 27.

36 One of the things conservative American legislators keep forgetting or not being aware of, for example, in their futile efforts to legislate not only public but also private morality, is the limits of the law's efficacy, apart from the basic moral question of whether such activities as abortion, euthanasia, assisted suicide, homosexuality, prostitution, and drug use are morally wrong.

37 Ibid.

38 Ibid., 28.

39 Ibid., 39.

40 Ibid., 36. Italics in original.

41 Ibid.

42 Ibid.

43 Ibid., 189. In other words, the same conditions are supposed to apply in both single communities and a "complex" of such communities: a country or society as a whole.

44 Ibid.

45 Our question does not imply that a "community of communities" must be an "organic whole" either in the Hegelian sense or in G. E. Moore's sense in *Principia Ethica*.

46 Similar problems arise in relation to Bellah et al. It is not clear, for instance, what is the precise logical relation in *Habits of the Heart* between a "communal country" as a whole and the individual communities in it. Perhaps these authors would say that if a country is bound and integrated by reinvigorated biblical and republican virtues, and so is a community in their strong sense, any and all communities would, as a result, become reinvigorated and integrated, and all lifestyle enclaves would be transformed into real communities.

47 I say this because Etzioni inconsistently oscillates between a normative/honorific and some undefined and unclear, watered-down sense or use of "community," as when he speaks of the United States and Canada as communities. For these countries are not communities themselves in either of the two ordinary senses of "community" or in Etzioni's normative use of the term.

48 *The Good Society* (Boston. New York, 1996).

49 Ibid., 1.

50 Ibid., 4.

51 Ibid., 3.

52 Ibid., 4. In this respect too, although to a considerably lesser extent, his specific practical (or more practical) prescriptions about how the good society can and needs to be realized, distinguish his book from the present one, which, as we shall see in Parts II and III, does not attempt to provide detailed, specific, prescriptions about how progressively to approach or approximate the ideal of good and moral community.

53 Ibid., 18.

54 Ibid., 29.

55 Ibid., 20.

56 Ibid., 24.

57 Ibid., 26.

58 Ibid., 28.

59 Ibid., 30.

60 Ibid., 28.

61 Ibid., 30.

62   Ibid., 30–31.

63   Ibid., 24.

64   Ibid., 31.

65   Ibid., 32.

66   Ibid., 60.

67   Ibid., 130.

68   Ibid., 69.

69   Ibid.

70   Ibid., 70.

71   I say "sometimes true" since education, to the extent that it may heighten consciousness, may also, and not infrequently, result in greater sensitivity to suffering and pain, in ourselves and others. Schopenhauer and Dostoevsky are, of course, the masters in describing this phenomenon.

PART 2

AN ETHIC OF CARING

Chapter 4

An Ethic of Caring–I

Introductory

We saw in Part 1 the centrality of the concept of caring in the conception of a moral community presented there. It is, therefore, necessary to try to gain a better, clearer, analytical understanding of that concept and what an ethic of caring can and would consist in and entail, at least for the special purposes of this book. The development of a full-fledged ethic of caring must await a future occasion.

I spoke of the need for gaining a "better, clearer understanding" of the concept of caring rather than of "an understanding" of it. The reason is obviously that the everyday, pre-analytical idea of caring, and caring itself, are quite familiar to people everywhere, and have been so throughout human history. But caring is also widely present among sentient nonhuman animals, not just *Homo sapiens*. Indeed, with regard to human beings, caring can be called the "natural piety" of humankind: a natural piety prior in time to the idea of a *duty*, including a moral duty to care about others—spontaneous, unreasoning, unquestioning caring—flowing from love or affection for those close to oneself and, even sometimes, not close to oneself. Correspondingly, an ethic of caring provides what we might call the "commonsense morality" of humankind. In traditional, close-knit, unalienated societies the idea of a *duty* to care about others becomes important in practice, mainly in relation to acquaintances and total strangers. But in highly industrialized alienated modern societies, where caring even about members of one's own family has become increasingly rare, the moral imperative to care about others has become increasingly important. It is not surprising, therefore, to see the recent emergence of an ethic of caring in contemporary American feminist moral thought, in reaction to what many of its advocates consider to

be the traditional "male ethic of justice and rights."[1] But it is equally
understandable that many of these feminist thinkers shrink from the
idea of a moral duty to care about others, fully cognizant of the moral
superiority of that natural piety, that natural milk of human caring
(which is much more than mere kindness), to caring from a mere moral
sense of duty.

It should be added in a nonpolemical spirit, and without minimizing
the centrality of caring in relation to women, that in calling caring
"the natural piety of humankind" I am not thinking that women practice an ethic of caring more (or much more) than men.[2] Suffice it to
say here that if the answer turns out to be "yes," it is partly explicable
by the fact that in the vast majority of human societies, women's important roles have hitherto been mainly confined to the private domain, particularly the household, that is, where nurturing and caring
are of paramount human and moral importance[3]; while the male's life
has largely centered on the public domain of business, politics, and
the like; where, as I shall later contend, the principles of fairness,
justice, and rights are especially important. In fact, in opposition to
Sandel's and the general feminist view, I shall further contend that
these principles are also important in the private domain, though the
roles they play there are different from and perhaps are less central
than the roles of caring itself.

The Random House Dictionary of the English Language gives
no less than eleven meanings and senses of "caring about"—which is
this chapter's and the present book's primary concern—and of "caring for" ("taking care of," "care-taking"). The relevant ones for an
ethic of caring are the following.

> Care, caring . . . n. 2. a cause or object of concern, worry, anxiety, distress,
> etc.: *Her child is her major care.* 3. serious attention; solicitude; . . . *He
> devotes great care to his work.* 4. protection; charge or temporary keeping:
> *He's under the care of a doctor.* . . . 7. take care of, to watch over; be
> responsible for: *to take care of an invalid,* . . . v.i. 8. to be concerned or
> solicitous. 9. to make provision or look out (usually fol. by *for*): *Will you care
> for the children while* I *am away?* 10. to have an inclination, liking, fond-
> ness, or affection (usually fol. by *for*): *She doesn't care for desserts.* Syn. 1.
> Solicitude, trouble.

The relevant meanings or senses of "concern" (note sense 8 above)
are: 5. n. A matter that engages a person's attention, interest, or
care, or that affects his welfare or happiness. 6. worry, solicitude, or
anxiety: *to show concern for someone in trouble.* Briefly, therefore,
to *care about* someone is to be concerned about her welfare and hap-

piness—with all that that entails; while to *care for* someone is to make provision or look out for, or to look after her if and when she needs help in one way or another.

A little reflection reveals the following main characteristics of caring about another:

(1) Caring normally consists in a set of complex mental, emotional, attitudinal, and behavioral dispositions, hence a settled tendency to act in certain ways in relation to those cared about. Experience shows that it may be spontaneous, unlearned, or acquired or instilled, especially in the young.

(2) Caring behavior includes a gamut of kinds of actions and activities designed to serve the other's interests. Among them are measures designed to protect her from harm and to come to her aid if threatened with harm.

(3) When caring is spontaneous rather than acquired by dint of habituation or effort, it is like love and perhaps affection,[4] which are the main springs of caring, in having no *reasons* but only (psychological) causes. For instance, if a mother's caring about and for her children is part of her loving them, her response to "Why do you care about them?" with "Because they are my own flesh and blood!" provides no reason but only a causal explanation for her loving/caring about them. Of course we frequently expect or at least hope that people we care about would reciprocate our caring; and we may be lovingly, affectionately, or benevolently disposed toward others partly in the hope or expectation that our feelings toward them will be returned. But if it is spontaneous, the caring—as it always is with love and affection—would be without a reason.

The expectation or hope of reciprocation is perfectly natural and morally in order. For in my view, our caring about (and for) ourselves and our desire for our happiness and well-being, are perfectly moral. But that desire must not be confused with psychological or ethical egoism. Feminist moral philosophers, such as those represented in *WMT*, are perfectly correct in emphasizing caring about oneself in addition to caring about others. The Golden Rule of Love is noteworthy in this connection.

(4) The fact that we can and normally do care about ourselves as well as (certain) others marks an interesting difference between caring and benevolence, since one cannot be meaningfully said to be benevolent toward oneself. Indeed, as feminist moral philosophers also emphasize, it is *morally* necessary to care about oneself as well as others; quite apart from whether, as a matter of psychological fact,

one's caring about oneself is a causal (psychological) condition for one's caring about others. (Another question for psychologists is whether it is possible to love others and not love oneself.) Unfortunately the opposite—caring only about oneself—is far from uncommon.

(5) In combining, *inter alia,* a beneficent teleological disposition and a matching attitude (assuming that not all dispositions are necessarily goal-directed), an ethic of caring is like utilitarianism in being a form of consequentialist ethic. We now turn to the first part of our sketch of an ethic of caring in this and the following two chapters.

Outline of an Ethic of Caring–I

Caring about others (unless stated otherwise, hereafter referred to as "caring") is a cardinal moral virtue and the central virtue of an "ethic of caring." Indeed, it is not a single virtue but an "omnibus" virtue as one might call it, embracing or subsuming, in a sense, a variety of important traditional moral virtues, including concern and responsibleness, kindness and compassion, sensitivity and considerateness, helpfulness and supportiveness, cooperativeness and solidarity. Great caring also includes selflessness and great eagerness to further the other's welfare and happiness, even if at the expense of one's welfare or happiness.

Alternatively, instead of thinking of caring as an omnibus virtue as described, we can consider the moral virtues it "embraces" as flowing from it, and so conceive of it as just one virtue among these others. Whichever way we look at the matter, caring remains of central importance as a moral virtue and as the central virtue of an "ethic of caring."

The same dual analysis is applicable to the vice of being uncaring, both (1) in the sense of being cold-hearted, insensitive, and indifferent to the weal or woe of others; especially (and more culpably) (2) in the sense of being positively cruel, disposed to hurt others. Sadism is the absence of caring in the present sense, carried to the extreme. Whether in sense (1) or (2), being uncaring includes cold-heartedness and self-centeredness, selfishness; while especially in sense (2) it involves the trampling of other people's rights and flagrant violation of their freedoms. Again, both (1) and (2) involve an indifference, sometimes extreme, as to whether one's behavior toward others is fair or unfair, just or unjust.

Although caring is a cardinal moral virtue in my view, it is like other virtues, if thought of as a single rather than as an omnibus virtue, in not providing, by itself, a full-fledged ethic. (This view goes counter to the position of some feminist moral philosophers.) One reason is that an adequate, comprehensive ethic would reserve a proper place for other major virtues: e.g., justice as "the chief artificial virtue," as well as, at least, the "natural moral virtues"[5] (other than "parental love and solicitude," and "family cooperativeness and inventive self-interested reason," and so on, which may be included in caring itself). For Hume these "natural" virtues include gentleness, self-esteem, generosity, gratitude, integrity, temperance, clemency, equity, honesty, truthfulness, fidelity, and good temper.[6]

There are additional reasons why, besides other major virtues, a comprehensive caring-centered ethic needs to reserve (*contra* some feminist moral thinkers[7]) an important place for human rights and the principles of fairness and justice, i.e., for certain elements of the conventional Western "male" morality of "justice and rights." That view will be defended in Part II.

But if caring is a necessary feature of a moral community as I envisaged it in chapter 2—indeed, I believe of all forms of social organization without exception—the inculcation and nurturing of caring in the young by example and by training and habituation becomes of paramount importance as a fundamental moral duty of parents, guardians, teachers, communities, and society as a whole. Since, as the philosopher Brand Blanshard and others have observed, morally wrong action is frequently the result of lack of imagination, of people's inability (or unwillingness) to place themselves in other people's shoes, it is incumbent that adults take pains to develop their sensitivity and empathic imagination in relation to others. Such efforts are aided by the fact that, as noted in chapter 2, caring can exist in the absence of love or affection, which (particularly love) are difficult or impossible to bring about by sheer conscious effort. Liking, by contrast, can be cultivated or developed by sincere, sustained efforts to find likeable qualities in another and can become a source of caring.

Caring and Knowledge of Means and Ends

The discovery of the environmental and possible genetic factors that make for caring persons, and those that make for uncaring persons, is of great psychological, pedagogical, and moral importance, and re-

quires concerted efforts by geneticists,[8] psychologists, and other social scientists, as well as the insights of moral philosophers. It is crucial for the success of efforts to make the alienated, generally uncaring
post-industrial contemporary societies in the West and elsewhere more
humane and caring—whether or not with the intention of making them
good and moral communities in our sense.

Like all goal-directed dispositions, actions, and activities, and affections, such as love and benevolence, caring requires proper knowledge not only of the best *means* for the realization of the other's real
interests, and so forth, as, for example, Bertrand Russell emphasizes
in relation to love, but also proper knowledge or understanding of
these interests, and so forth, themselves. But as we all know, knowing
or understanding what, in the particular circumstances, another's "interests" or "best interests" are, is often a tricky and risky business:
more so when her welfare or happiness at the particular juncture in
her life, or in her life as a whole, is concerned. (Cf. the familiar difficulties regarding utilitarian conceptions of "the general welfare," as well
as the famous Greek saying: "Call no man happy until he is dead.")
For instance, how often do well-meaning, caring parents, relatives, or
friends go wrong when they think they know or understand what is in
their children's, relatives', or friends'—or a particular child's, relative's,
or friend's—"best interests"? Indeed, how difficult it is for us sometimes to know or understand what our own best interests are! Yet
even if we suppose that a caring person knows or understands another's
best interests in the particular circumstances, caring can often lead to
great harm instead of good in the absence of proper knowledge of the
best means for bringing about the desired good. St. Augustine's famous "Love and do as thou wilt," is unfortunately far from enough
with respect to caring as it is with respect to love or benevolence:
ignoring such complicating factors as, e.g., a parent's, relative's, or
friend's projecting or foisting his or her own needs, desires, dreams,
and aspirations, or fears, frustrations, and anxieties, on to or upon
the other. Nor am I considering here moral and legal problems about
privacy, or individual freedom and autonomy; hence difficult issues
surrounding "due intervention" and "undue interference" in the other's
life or affairs, in relation to caring. These thorny issues will be dealt
with in the next chapter.

The question of knowing how best to serve the other's real interests is especially difficult inasmuch as caring acts are often highly
contextual, and aim to further the interests, or a particular interest, of

others in specific situations.[9] Helpful precepts or rules are difficult to come by that are designed to guide caring persons; since, in addition to knowing the relevant physical, social, and other relevant circumstances, they must also have intuitive, empathic understanding of the others' general psychological makeup and immediate mental and emotional state or condition. What rough guidelines that are available are based on the collective experience and wisdom (or lack thereof) of humankind: prudential precepts derived from very imperfect experiential generalizations.

Like other teleological moral concepts, the concept of caring determines general ends but no specific, or relatively specific, means for the realization of the ends of caring. What would be caring actions in a particular context or circumstance, and what a caring individual in it is morally obligated to do or refrain from doing, depends upon and varies with that context or the circumstances. It is true that, in general terms, caring includes such things as kindness, consideration, compassion, and solidarity. But what solidarity, kindness, consideration, compassion, and so forth, consist in or specifically involve varies in different circumstances and in relation to different others. It is crucially dependent on the particular relationship between the caregiver and the other: for example, does caring sometimes involve being "cruel only to be kind"? In this respect the aforementioned virtues, and caring itself, are unlike "telling the truth" or "not lying," "not stealing," "not killing," and so forth, which provide the content of various moral concepts and rules.

Because of the foregoing features of caring, feminist moral philosophers correctly stress the necessity for a caregiver's empathetic understanding of the other as a "concrete other,"[10] as a unique person in a specific context or circumstance, at a particular time. They also correctly stress that that understanding includes an awareness of the other's important attachments and relationships. The latter is particularly important since as they also correctly claim, as I mentioned in chapter 1, our important attachments and relationships (as I shall also argue later) partially define us as individual selves or persons.

I spoke of empathic knowledge or *understanding* of the other and her concrete circumstances, and so forth, not of mere knowledge about her. Although empathic understanding, or "existential knowledge" as we might also call it, requires varying sorts and amounts of knowledge about the other, it is considerably more than, and in some ways significantly different from, simply being in possession of the abstract intellectual information about her that is called "knowledge about."

But if the preceding is true, would it not seriously limit the possible reach or scope of caring? This apparent problem vanishes once we distinguish between (a) the conditions for the existence or acquisition of a caring disposition and (b) the conditions for successful caring acts. Empathic understanding of particular others is only necessary for (b), and has nothing to do with (a). That logically explains how, once in a while, some remarkably selfless persons can dedicate their entire lives to caring about suffering humanity as a whole, or future generations, with minimal general, abstract knowledge about them as individuals. It remains that existential knowledge or empathetic understanding is essential for a would-be caregiver to effectively serve another's best interests in a particular situation (b).

That knowledge is especially critical in people's relation to nonhuman animals, plants, and the physical environment. Although, and partly because people have become increasingly aware of the need to protect Nature, the paucity of our scientific knowledge about many animal and plant species and the habitats they need for their flourishing and survival, and our complete ignorance of the very existence of many unknown species in remote parts of the world and in the depths of seas and oceans, many attempts by caring scientists and ecologists, and by various nations and international organizations to protect Nature, have resulted in more harm than good. No wonder the eminent ecologist Aldo Leopold was leery of well-intentioned but misguided conservationist interventions designed to protect Nature.[11]

As with many current calls for the protection of the environment, people's self-interest and caring for their physical well-being and the well-being and survival of their descendants, are becoming, but still far from universally, a potent force toward conservation of the ecology if not also of the world's nonrenewable resources.

Cultivation of the Virtue of Caring

If caring is an essential feature of a moral community as I envisage it, and, indeed, of any form of social organization, the inculcation and nourishing of that virtue in the young, by example and by training and habituation, becomes of paramount importance as an integral part of their moral education and gives the adults entrusted with their care a special moral responsibility. As I mentioned, morally wrong acts are too often the result of lack of imagination, of people's inability or unwillingness to imagine themselves in other people's shoes; thus, from a failure to empathize with them. Fortunately, efforts to develop and increase the sensitivity and empathic imagination of all—young and old—are aided by the fact, noted in the previous chapter, that love and affection, which are difficult or impossible to acquire by dint of effort, are inessential for caring. In that respect caring is more similar to liking, which can be acquired by sustained efforts to find likeable qualities in those one does not care about. Liking itself can also lead to caring.

Scientific research to understand the social-cultural and possibly genetic factors and mechanisms that give rise to a caring disposition in individuals, and those that give rise to the opposite disposition, is of great pedagogical and social importance. Such understanding is, for instance, crucial for the success of any efforts in the deeply alienated and increasingly callous and cold-hearted present postindustrial capitalist Western countries, to make them more sensitive to the plight of the ever-increasing poor and destitute in their midst, and in the rest of the world and, above all, of the one million or more children in the world—the ultimately "insulted and injured"—who are sexually and in other ways exploited and abused every year.

I shall end this chapter by outlining some actions that I believe can help bring about, in the absence of emotional attachments in the form of love or affection, concern and caring for others. These are:

(1) bonding with like-minded persons, with those who share serious ideas or interests, aspirations and goals, and/or projects and commitments. As mentioned in chapter 2, these things are among the important forces that lead people to form T-communities;

(2) liking another for whatever reason or reasons;

(3) being habituated or trained to care for others;

(4) holding strong altruistic moral or religious beliefs and being habituated to practice them;

(5) being compassionate, in so far as all human beings are heir to pain and suffering, loss and tragedy, and, in Martin Heidegger's famous phrase, are "beings-unto-death."

These possible sources of caring about (and in the case of (2), sometimes of caring for as well) color and inform the caregiving. For instance, the caring is frequently lifelong in (1), while in (5) it tends to end if or when the misfortunes, and such, that occasioned the compassion are over.

The satisfaction that the caregiver may experience can be a spur to continued and even greater caring; but it cannot be its primary *moral* source in truly caring persons. Otherwise the other is treated, in Kant's sense, as an "object," not as a "person"; though not in the sense that the caregiver violates the other's autonomy in the relevant sense or senses but in the sense of lacking respect for her personhood. (See chapter 5.)

To sum up. Part 2 endeavors to develop a fairly systematic outline of the fundamentals of a caring-centered ethic that can serve to ground the conception of a good and moral community as put forward in Parts 1 and 3 This, introductory chapter attempted to provide a clear, analytical understanding of the central concept of *caring about*, and of some of its important implications. After a brief analysis of the relevant ordinary meanings and senses of, and the concepts expressed by, "caring about" (and, to a much lesser extent, of "caring for," "taking care of," and "care-taking"), the main characteristics of the cardinal moral virtue of "caring about another" were discussed. It was maintained (*contra* some feminist moral philosophers) that a comprehensive caring-centered ethic must reserve an important place for human rights and the principles of fairness and justice, i.e., for certain elements of the Enlightenment and post-Enlightenment "male" morality of "justice and rights."

The relation between caring, and means and ends, was next explored. The importance of the caring person's knowledge of the other's real needs, interests, goals, and so on,—as well as of the means for their satisfaction or realization—was stressed, as well as the difficulty that is frequently encountered in the caring person's attempts to know what the other's real needs, interests, and so on, are, particularly in light of their often highly contextual nature. Helpful precepts or rules to guide the caring person are difficult to come by; since, in addition to knowing the relevant physical, social, and other relevant circumstances, he or she must also have intuitive, empathic understanding of the other's general psychological makeup and immediate mental and emotional state or condition. In other words, the other must be empathically understood as a "concrete," not as an "abstract" other. The available guidelines are based on the collective experience and wisdom (or lack thereof) of humankind: prudential precepts derived from very imperfect experiential generalizations. The problem of how best to care for Nature, it was noted, is especially critical and difficult.

The preceding considerations seem to seriously limit the possible reach or scope of caring; but it was observed that they only pertained to the success of caring acts, not to (or not also to) the conditions for the existence or acquisition of a caring disposition.

The chapter ended with a list of the ways in which, in the absence of love or affection, a caring disposition may be cultivated. The list consisted of (1) bonding with like-minded persons, (2) liking another, for whatever reasons, (3) being habituated or trained to care for others, (4) holding strong altruistic moral or religious beliefs and being habituated to practice them, and (5) being compassionate, insofar as all human beings are heir to pain and suffering, loss and tragedy, and are, in Heidegger's words, "beings-unto-death."

Notes

1   To mention a recent anthology of feminist moral philosophy, see for instance the excellent collection, *Women and Moral Theory,* edited by Eva Feder Kittay and Diana T. Meyers (Lanham, MD, 1987), hereafter referred to as *WMT.*

2   But see, e.g., Sandra Harding, "The Curious Coincidence of Feminine and African Moralities," in *WMT,* pp. 296–315, in which Harding "argues that feminists must face the challenges posed by the comparison of worldviews and the highlighting of the problems endemic to each." She suggests a "unified field theory" that can account for the embeddedness of gender differences within a larger context of difference, as structured by oppression and exploitation" (Summary, ibid., p. 296).

3   For research by American developmental psychologists about the putative differences between the moral concepts that certain samples of young American females, as opposed to American males, appealed to in wrestling with various ethical dilemmas, see e.g., Carol Gilligan, *In a Different Voice: Psychological Theory and Women's Development* (1982), *WMT,* passim, and Lawrence Kohlberg, *The Psychology of Moral Development* (1984).

4   I say "perhaps affection" because I feel that affection (like liking) may be sometimes based on the other's personal qualities and so may have a reason.

5   I say "natural *moral* virtues" since quite a number of the "natural virtues" David Hume lists are no longer regarded as moral virtues but only virtues in the broader Greek sense of "special excellence" or *areté.* They include "agreeability, indulgence . . . due pride, or self-esteem, and the proper ambition and courage that may involve, as well as generosity, liberality, zeal, . . . industry, perseverance, activity, vigilance, application, . . . economy, resolution, . . . discretion, caution, presence of mind." Quoted from Annette C. Baier, "Hume, The Women's Moral Theorist?" *WMT,* p. 42.

6   Baier, ibid.

7   But, notably, not Carol Gilligan. For though she thinks of a feminist ethic of care and the conventional male ethic of justice and rights as alternative ethical viewpoints, she does hope for reconciliation between women's and men's moral insights, as e.g., Annette Baier points out in "Hume, the Women's Moral Theorist?", in *WMT,* p. 39. Annette Baier herself thinks that for various reasons, the comparison of Hume's and Kant's moral theories holds out "the same hope of reconciliation that Gilligan wants, or in her book, wanted to get, between men's and women's moral insights" (Ibid). Other examples will be mentioned in the appropriate contexts.

8   To ascertain, for example, the role of possible genetic factors that may help bring about a caring disposition in children.

9   Cf. the additional, even more difficult problems utilitarianism faces with respect to the realization of the putative "*general* good or welfare."

10   Borrowing the term from Seyla Benhabib's "The Generalized and the Concrete Other . . . ," in *WMT*, pp. 154–177.

11   See, for instance, Edward Johnson, "Treating the Dirt: Environmental Ethics and Moral Theory" on Leopold's "respect for land" or "land ethic," in *Earthbound*, ed. Tom Regan (Philadelphia, 1984), pp. 352ff., as well as Leopold's *A Sand County Almanac*.

Chapter 5

An Ethic of Caring–II

I

In chapter 4, I claimed that, as human beings, we are morally obligated to care about others, that caring should not be confined to ourselves, and I then attempted to provide some evidence that caring about others is a moral virtue, not just a virtue in the classical Greek sense of *areté*. One principal aim of the first part of this chapter is to attempt to justify the claims (a) that we have a special moral obligation to care about those with whom we have a special relationship; and (b) that we have a general moral duty to care about (some or all) others, including (some or all of) those with whom we have no relationship at all, such as total strangers.

I. The Obligation/Duty to Care

The duty to care is either (A) a special moral obligation[1] or (B) a general moral duty.

A. The Special Obligation to Care. The special moral obligation to care arises in both the private and the public spheres. Special moral obligations are created in the private sphere by the various personal bonds and other close relationships and attachments that exist between two or more individuals: members of a household, relatives, and friends. In the public sphere they are created by the social, political, economic, or other kinds of transactions and relationships between different parties. I shall begin with the special obligation to care in the private sphere: with the obligations of parents, children, relatives, and friends, in that order.

(a). The moral obligation of natural parents to care about—indeed, to lavish care on—their offspring results from the obvious but fundamental fact that parents are responsible for their children's existence, as well as, directly and indirectly, for their genetic characteristics, and so are partly responsible for what they become as individuals. In addition to the obligation to care about and nurture them and their natural capacities and abilities, parents have the special moral obligation to care for their minor children to the fullest extent of their means and ability. If a child is handicapped or disabled in her adult life the parents are obligated to continue to care for her (or to see to it that she is professionally and properly cared for) within the limits imposed by their financial condition and physical and mental health.[2]

(b). Adoptive parents, though lacking the biological link to their adopted children, nonetheless have similar special moral obligations toward their adopted children by virtue of their having freely and voluntarily adopted the children as their own.

(c). As with the societal as opposed to "natural" special legal-moral relationships between adoptive parents and their adopted children, the two-way special societal, legal-moral obligations spouses or live-ins have toward each other arise from the marital bond between them.

(d). The basis of a child's special obligation to care about his or her natural or adoptive parents is, once again, different from either (a), (b), or (c), because of the different nature of the child-parent relationship. Similarly with (e) the special relationship between siblings.

It is more difficult to show that children have a special obligation to care about their parents or their siblings. For one thing children "do not ask" to be brought into the world—and have no say in who their natural parents, or who their siblings will be. (Older children may, however, have some say about whether their parents should or should not have other children.) Similarly, in the case of adopted children.

At this point, reciprocity seems to be the only basis for the putative obligation of children to care about their natural or adoptive parents, namely that children ought to give their parents as much (or as little) love as their parents give them. On that view, if their parents care little or nothing about them and give them little or no care, they too would have little or no special obligation to care about their parents, or to help care for them in later life, financially or otherwise, if they need such help. Any caring or love that children may have toward derelict parents would be supererogatory, would flow from the sheer kindness of their hearts.

In the same vein, it may be wondered if siblings have any special obligation at all to care about one another. "Natural" siblings are, of course, biologically related; but that relation is quite different from their natural relationship to their parents, or their parents' natural relationship to them. Even more complicated is the societal relationship of adoptive siblings to one another, and their relationship to their natural siblings, if any.

Should we then, again, suppose that the only moral relationship that can exist between siblings is one of reciprocity? That—like the view that reciprocity is the basis for whatever moral obligations exist between children and their natural or adoptive parents, or between siblings—seems somehow artificial, unsatisfactory. I think we have a sense that it is morally wrong for natural or adoptive siblings not to care about one another or about their parents. In the case of natural siblings the biological bond is, I think, generally thought of[3] as providing a sufficient basis for the putative obligation. It seems repugnant, even preposterous to me[4] to suppose that I am absolved from any obligation to care about my brother or sister if he or she does not care about me or at any time stops caring about me.

But why does it not seem equally repugnant or preposterous to me (perhaps also to others), as regards children vis-à-vis cold and indifferent, uncaring (let alone abusive) parents? Is it that parents have a greater moral responsibility, consequently a greater moral obligation toward their children than children normally have toward one another?[5] That can only be part of the reason.

The preceding difficulties, I think, dramatize the fundamental fact that reciprocity can hardly provide a basis for caring: a point variously stressed by feminist philosophers. For example, by Carol Gilligan's criticism of Lawrence Kohlberg's hierarchy of stages in the individual's (or community's or other social organization's) moral development, which includes reciprocity as one stage in the process; although, on his account, reciprocity is far from the highest stage of moral development. In fact, it may be questioned whether reciprocal acts can count as moral, rather than prudential, acts.[6]

For a systematic holistic, more adequate understanding of the nature and grounds of the special moral obligations—and the corresponding and correlative special rights—of the various members of a nuclear or extended family and close relatives, we need to turn to the concept of the family[7] as a basic societal institution and practice.

A family of any sort, whether traditional or no, extended or nuclear, is defined by certain constitutive conventions that define it as a particular type of institution and practice. These conventions are part of the conventions/rules of the particular community or society that a particular sort of family forms part of. I mean the body of conventions/rules that define the various types of societal institutions/practices constituting that community or society.[8] The traditional family's constitutive conventions define (1) its basic structure and intended *modus operandi*, hence also (2) its members' special roles together with (3) their special duties and responsibilities, correlative powers, prerogatives, and rights. That is, in the same way as, *mutatis mutandis*, the appropriate conventions/rules define the members' or participants' obligations, responsibilities, rights, and so on, in any other sort of societal institution/practice.

As determined by the particular defining conventions/rules, the duties and responsibilities, correlative powers and prerogatives that the different family members have are *non-moral as such*. But they acquire a moral dimension, become transformed into special moral obligations and rights, or are given a moral dimension, as a result of being evaluated as moral duties and responsibilities, and so on, by the appropriate *moral regulative principles/rules* applied to them. Likewise, the family as a whole, as an institution and a practice, is seen as a morally good or bad institution and practice, in terms of the moral roles it is traditionally intended to play, or the moral purposes it is traditionally intended to serve. A particular family is judged morally good or bad depending on (the degree of) its conduciveness, or the opposite, to these societal moral purposes or ends.

The regulative principles that regulate and evaluate the traditional family and its members as morally good or bad, are, in turn, defined by the overall *societal ends* the traditional family is designed to serve; viz, to create an optimum matrix or conditions for the healthy physical, mental, emotional, and moral/spiritual development of human beings, particularly children from birth to majority. These goals—but here only contingently—also determine the family's constitutive conventions.[9]

The participants in an institution or practice logically acquire their various (moral, legal, and so forth) rights by virtue of the correlative obligations defined by their particular office or position in the institution or practice. That is, insofar as these rights are deemed necessary for the participants being able to fulfill their special obligations, and to fulfill them as well as possible. The obligations are the *raîson d'etre* of the correlative rights. This is true of the special rights and obligations of the members of a family, including their special obligation to care about (and in the appropriate circumstances, for) one another. For instance, the obligation of parents to fulfill their parental responsibilities requires that their young children obey them and that requires that their children trust and respect them and their judgment and guidance, secure in the belief that their parents love and cherish and care about them. Lack of respect (and of trust) makes it very difficult for the parents to take care of their children as they should.

The institutional conception of the family provides, I think, a satisfactory answer to the questions raised earlier concerning the obligation of children toward their parents and toward their siblings: in the latter case, whenever the relationship is involuntary.[10] For it is a fundamental moral principle that, like involuntary actions, no involuntary relationship can give rise to moral obligations.

Parents have special prerogatives and rights in relation to their children, and special prerogatives and rights in relation to each other, necessitated, and defined, by their special obligations toward the children. Further, the parents' special rights in relation to the children define correlative special obligations in the latter toward their siblings. The parents' obligation to take care of and nurture their children gives rise to the children's special obligation to trust and respect them, and, if minors, to obey them.

The special obligation of siblings to care about one another can also be explained in terms of the parents' responsibilities and obligations toward their children. Unless siblings act cooperatively and in harmony, as a family, to realize their common aspirations and goals, a family cannot fulfill its intended function as a loving, caring, nurturing family. Or it cannot fulfill its function in the particular society in terms of the latter's conventions, traditions, and moral rules. A family's very survival depends on its members working hand-in-hand to make it work. This is particularly true of the relationship of the spouses to each other.

Like the traditional family, friendship is a basic societal institution and practice, set up by certain constitutive conventions that define the personal bond of friendship, the mutual special obligations and responsibilities, and the special prerogatives and rights of friends. The bond of friendship is ideally understood as one of mutual affection and caring, and of unqualified loyalty, truthfulness, honesty, and implicit mutual trust.

These virtues, which qualify ("true") friendship, also clearly qualify a morally good family: indeed, such a family, besides being blessed with mutual love and caring, trust and unqualified loyalty, would be one in which genuine friendship exists between parents and children, and between the siblings. These friendships may flourish, even get stronger, after the children grow up and leave the family home.

Friendship is always voluntary, created by avowals of affection, caring, trust, and loyalty, or by actions signifying these dispositions and sentiments, thus constituting an explicit or implicit promise or quasi-promise. (Compare and contrast the marriage vow "to love and cherish," and so forth, and the conditions under which friendship, or a family, ceases to exist.)

Friendship, though voluntary like modern marriages, differs from marriage in lacking its fundamental legal dimension, such as the spousal legal obligations and rights.

With the necessary changes, the logical analysis I have sketched in relation to the family is applicable to the public sphere, to the obligations and special rights involved in economic, political, legal, and other types and forms of public institutional arrangements. But with regard to caring, an important difference between the public and private spheres needs to be noted. That is, that with the exception of the educational domain,[11] the parties to a "public" contract or agreement have no *special* moral obligation as opposed to a possible *general* moral duty to care about one another as persons. They have an obligation to help make the common enterprise work, and for that to be possible they must care about, if not love, the enterprise. Any caring about the other party to the relationship may be due to self-interested, prudential, or other practical reasons; i.e., for the sake of the institution or practice.

From society's standpoint, public institutions have a genuinely moral purpose in addition to their utilitarian functions. In fact, public institutions have been historically designed to promote the general good in addition to, for example, helping to ensure society's survival and stability.

The same goals—society's survival and well-being—are the traditional *raison d'être of* society's creation of the private institutions and practices of kinship, marriage, and the family/household, and the institution and practice of friendship.

Finally, whatever the kind of special transaction or relationship between two or more parties may be, caring has (a) the same general nature in all cases. Similarly, with caring, when only the abstract bond of a common humanity is present. Further, (b) caring has special features that vary with the kind of personal or public relationship involved. In fact, caring also has (c) an individual quality determined by the parties' own personalities.

In sum, all institutions and practices, private and public, are essentially goal-directed. But in *good* and *moral* families, and in good friendships, the operative forces are not prudential, or even utilitarian in the philosophical sense: rather, they are caring, and love or affection.

II

B. The general duty to care about others. A major claim of this chapter and this book is that human beings, as human beings, have a general moral duty to care about others, perhaps about all other human beings, apart from whatever special moral obligations they have to care about particular individuals, groups, institutions or practices, nation-states, and so on. Consequently, I shall presently consider various possible attempts to substantiate that claim.

But first, some obvious but important preliminary remarks. If all human beings were caring, and if their caring were always spontaneous, and sprang from universal affection or love, the concept of a (moral) duty to care would not arise at all; in the same way that it does not arise in relation to the angelic hosts, who, we may imagine, spontaneously care about all of God's creations out of overflowing love. That ideal state of affairs, above all, is believed to characterize the Supreme Being, whose caring about His entire creation is thought to flow from infinite love. Unfortunately, experience teaches that human beings are notoriously uncaring. In particular, spontaneous caring is often limited in degree and quite circumscribed. That makes it necessary to put forth the idea of a general moral duty to care about others, however averse some feminist moral philosophers and others may be to the idea of such a moral imperative. Such familiar statements as "You ought to care about others—including strangers in need," make perfect sense. But they leave open the fundamental question of whether the "ought" in question is or is not a moral one.

Accordingly, I shall critically examine a number of arguments that may be thought to establish the proposition that we have a general moral duty to care about others. I shall begin with an argument that takes as a major premise Plato's view of justice in the *Republic*, namely that justice is giving each person what he or she is owed, is his or her due. In bare outline, it would proceed thus.

Argument I

1. An essential part of being treated as a person is being treated fairly and justly. That is, all human beings, as moral persons, are entitled to or owed fair and just treatment; inasmuch as all human beings have a (an equal) basic right to fair and just treatment.

2. To be fairly and justly treated includes, other things being equal, being treated with equal consideration. That, *inter alia*, means being entitled to be cared about.

3. Therefore, all human beings are morally entitled to be cared about, which means that all human beings have the corresponding general moral duty to care about everyone else.

4. It also seems to follow that society must recognize the achievements of the meritorious, giving them the encouragement and praise they deserve. That is an essential way of caring about others. Similarly with other forms of desert. For instance, the just distribution of caring would importantly include aiding the disadvantaged to satisfy their basic physical and social needs, in proportion to their need. That is, respectively, "those [needs] which must be satisfied in order not to endanger . . . [one's] health or sanity,"[12] and those "for companionship, self-esteem and self-development in the society in which . . . [one] lives."[13]

Argument I has some attractions but suffers from fairly obvious difficulties. Thus,

(a) basing caring on justice is an attractive idea, since I believe that no adequate moral theory can dispense with some theory of justice, including some principles of formal and social justice. This belief is by no means shared by all contemporary feminist moral philosophers, for example, Seyla Benhabib, to mention just one notable example. As we shall see in our later discussion of justice and the ethic of caring later in Part II, she argues that what an ethic of caring—moral philosophy in general—requires, is equity not abstract, impartial justice. But as I shall try to show there, the relevant concept of equity logically presupposes the concept of justice, since equity involves the modification of an impartial second-order rule or principle as it is applied to special cases. If so, the present objection to justice can be met and does not affect the merits of Argument I, if it has *any*.

(b) A more serious problem with the argument is that equality, in Aristotle's sense, viz, the equality of equals and the inequality of unequals, is of the essence of justice; hence, in Argument I, equality is of the essence of the duty to be just. But it is humanly impossible, if not also contrary to Aristotle's principle, for everyone (if not also for anyone) to care *equally* about everybody toward whom he or she has a duty to care. To reiterate, the strength of caring, like the strength of affection and love, cannot but vary with the degree of closeness of those one cares about. It is natural for us to care more about the members of our immediate family than for our other close relatives, and we are often unlikely to succeed if we try to care equally about all of them.[14]

But what does it mean for two persons, "A" and "B," to be cared about equally (hence, also for them to be treated unequally)? Does it mean for "A" and "B" to be treated (i) strictly or literally in exactly the same way, (ii) in a manner befitting their individual, including special needs, interests, and circumstances in light of the essential contextuality of caring? If the answer is (ii), as I think it is, the idea of "equal caring" in sense (i)—the counterpart of the impartial, objective, and, in that sense, abstract equality, an equality that is "no respecter of persons"— is inappropriate and inapplicable to caring and to the duty to care.

Argument II

Let us see whether the following argument, which appeals to both justice *and* human rights, is more satisfactory than Argument I.

1. All human beings have an equal human right to equal treatment, as part of their equal human right to being treated as moral persons.[15]

2. The equal human right to equal treatment includes the equal moral right to legal and social justice: justice before the law (procedural and judicial) and substantive or social justice, including distributive, rectificatory, and retributive justice.

3. Justice, as Plato correctly defines it, is giving everyone his or her due.

4. But for everyone to be justly treated means or includes being (equally) caringly treated in sense (ii) above.

5. Therefore, all human beings have a moral duty to care about others.

6. Indeed, aiding the needy and rewarding the meritorious (the deserving in general), and other possible forms of *distributive* justice, are forms of caring, forms of just distribution of caring in accordance with need, merit, or other canons of desert.

In addition to the difficulties involved in premises (3) and (4) regarding abstract equality arising from the appeal to the idea of justice, a crucial question is whether premise (4) follows from premise (3); or if it does not, whether it can be made to follow from it by the addition of any justifiable premises. That is, the question is how the desired conclusion that "everyone is owed care" can be derived from the putative *right* to being justly treated.[16]

A further question is whether a right to be cared about can be directly derived—if such a putative right can be shown to exist at all—from the general right to equal treatment, rather than indirectly from the putative right to justice or just treatment as part of everyone's human right to be treated as a person.

Again, and as pointed out in relation to Argument I, being treated equally as a "subject" of caring,[17] means giving the interests of everyone cared about equal consideration, in the sense of caring about them in ways that fundamentally depend upon their individual needs, interests, and so forth.

Further, if the *equality* of everyone's human rights is based on justice, can caring be based, without circularity, on the human right to be treated as a person? The answer is, I think, yes; since it is only the idea of the *equality* of the human right to be treated as a person, not the human right itself, that is based on the idea of justice.

Argument III

It might be thought that a more satisfactory argument than Argument II can be constructed by appeal to John Rawls' decision procedure in *A Theory of Justice*; that is, to the original position, the veil of ignorance, and so on, Unfortunately, that approach too would not work in this case; just as Thomas Hobbes' method in laying the foundations of his ethics and social-political philosophy would not work here. As with Hobbes' *Leviathan*, the persons in Rawls' original position are imagined to be rational and wholly self-interested, and choose, in Rawls' case, principles of justice they reason would be to their greatest advantage in society once the veil of ignorance is lifted. They do not choose the particular principles of justice they do because of sympathy or benevolence, let alone out of concern for or caring about the needs or interests of anyone else in the original position. In Hobbes's view, as well as the view of other ethical egoists with the notable exception of Ayn Rand, serving the interests of others is prudent, is a useful policy, but of course is not a moral duty or obligation. The individual has no moral duty or obligation to seek the welfare of others for their own sake. Seeking the welfare of others can only be a means for one's own welfare.[18]

Returning to Rawls, it may seem that his decision procedure would enable the parties in the original position to acknowledge a universal moral duty, say in addition to the Two Principles of Justice. For if their being rational and self-interested persons would not impede their choice of the Two Principles, it would seem that their rational self-interest—not sympathy, benevolence, or any altruistic sentiments—would likewise lead them to acknowledge a universal moral duty to care about others. That is, that acknowledging such a duty would, in the last analysis, serve their self-interest since they may need being cared about (and even for) by others at some point or other in their life. (Cf. the earlier references to Hobbes.)

Whether that supposition would in fact be true will be considered later in this chapter. Here we need to note certain putative difficulties in Rawls' decision procedure which, if correct, would prevent it from satisfactorily serving our purposes. Two of these putative difficulties are urged by Ronald Dworkin in *Taking Rights Seriously*. The first is that "a hypothetical contract is not simply a pale form of an actual contract: it is not a contract at all."[19] That means that the persons in the hypothetical original position would not be bound by the principles they choose once the veil of ignorance is lifted: in our own case, they would not be bound by the principle (Principle C) that they have a moral duty to care about others.

Dworkin further maintains that "it is not in the best interests of everyone to choose the two principles, because when the veil of ignorance is lifted some will discover that they would have been better off if some other principle, like the principle of average utility, had been chosen."[20] The crucial question for us, which will be considered later in this chapter, is whether that would also be true in relation to Principle C.

The second basic difficulty Dworkin correctly urges is that Rawls' original position does not provide a rational basis for Rawls' Two Principles of Justice.[21] This criticism also applies to the attempt to employ Rawls' procedure to provide an argument for the adoption of Principle C.

In *Justice as Impartiality*,[22] Brian Barry defends Rawls against a charge similar to a part of Dworkin's first criticism, leveled by Henry Phelps Brown in *Egalitarianism and the Generation of Inequality*.[23] Brown writes:

> It is hard to see why an engagement that appears rational, and binding, to a person of one kind, allowed very limited information should continue to be acceptable or to be binding upon that person when he and all others like him have been greatly changed and are altogether better informed.[24]

Barry notes that Brown "concedes that 'at one point Rawls does speak as if the principles adopted by the hypothetical persons would commend themselves to the actual persons in ordinary life,'[25] but he does not appear to understand why Rawls thinks that they should. . . . Phelps Brown is apparently incapable of recognizing that Rawls invites people to put themselves in others' shoes in order to concentrate their minds on what they should think is fair while wearing their own shoes."[26]

According to Rawls, people are willing and able to put themselves in others' shoes, i.e., to be objective and impartial, because, Barry says, Rawls believes that people can (and may) have "an effective sense of justice." For as Barry points out (correcting Phelps Brown's patent misconception), it is false that 'the view of human nature that informs Rawls' "approach" is "that people are actuated solely by self-interest."[27] Barry adds

> Naturally, if people are self-interested in real life the conclusions reached in the original position will cease to attract them once they know their real situation. But Rawls' conclusions are intended to appeal to his readers' sense of justice, not their self-interest. What they would think when pursuing their self-interest (or more precisely their conception of the good) within the constraints of the original position is supposed to guide their thinking when they consult their sense of justice in real life.[28]

But "putting oneself in others' shoes," or "inviting people to put themselves in others' shoes," in Barry's statement, is ambiguous. There are two ways in which one can "put oneself imaginatively (and empathetically) in another's shoes": in (a) a more inclusive or (b) less inclusive way. In (b)'s case, one would properly understand the nature of the other's good, or what particular needs, desires, goals, and the like she has at the time. Consequently, one would appreciate the other's pursuit of that good, and its value for her. In (a)'s case, in addition to being objective or impartial, one judges that the other's good, etc. is worth pursuing by anyone, including oneself. But unless that judgment is accompanied or informed by (c) sympathy, benevolence,[29] or caring—in general, unless one is capable of altruistic sentiments—toward the other, the objectivity and impartiality, and even the empathy one achieves in (a) above, would not be enough to make one acknowledge a general *moral duty* to serve the other's good, etc., "for its own sake" rather than for whatever benefit one expects to receive from it. The same applies to the sense of justice Rawls posits. Therefore (*pace*

Barry), Brown's criticism of Rawls concerning the persons in the hypothetical original position, remains.[30]

Barry's dismissal of what he considers to be misdirected criticism leads him to his own criticism of Rawls' original position. He writes:

> The crucial problem lies in the lack of fit between the specification of Rawls' original position and his objectives in constructing it. The people in the original position are to pursue their conception of the good. But if we were to leave things there, we would have justice as reciprocity: the motive for compliance with the principles would be fairness but the principles themselves would arise from mutual advantage and thus reflect the bargaining power of the parties.[31]

And so on.[32]

Argument IV

In "The Welfare Rights of Peoples and Future Generations,"[33] James Sterba presents a modified Rawlsian decision procedure that escapes some of the difficulties in Rawls decision procedure in *A Theory of Justice*. But on examination, as we shall see, it too turns out to be inadequate for our present purposes (just as, as I argued elsewhere,[34] it is inadequate for justifying need as a canon of distributive justice).

Sterba attempts to discover the requirements of fair treatment by employing a decision procedure that stipulates, instead of a veil of ignorance, a state of affairs such that "we . . . discount the knowledge of which particular interests happen to be our own . . . [and] so we would just not be taking that knowledge into account when selecting the requirements for fair treatment. Rather, in selecting these requirements, we would be reasoning from our knowledge of all the particular interests of everyone who would be affected by our decision."[35] And "assuming that we are well-informed of the particular interests that would be affected by our decision and are fully capable of rationally deliberating with respect to that information, then our deliberations would culminate in a unanimous decision."[36]

The utilization of Rawls' decision procedure in Argument III was motivated by the idea that since the parties in the original position would be ignorant of the extent to which their survival and social interests would be satisfied by, among other things, their being cared about by those on whom they may depend, these parties would choose Principle C. They would do so on the supposition—the worst case scenario—that unless the principle is adopted by all, they would find themselves uncared for by, or would not care about, anyone. In the case of Sterba's decision procedure, we similarly need to ask: "But what requirements would we select by using this decision procedure?" If we adapt to our present concerns Sterba's answer to that question, we would not exclusively favor either the interests of those who presently receive, or in the future are likely to receive, the most care (e.g., members of a highly caring community), or the interests of those who presently receive, or in the future are likely to receive, the least care (e.g., the homeless and others who are completely alone in the world). "Rather we would compromise by endorsing . . . [a principle] to fair treatment [in the form of Principle C]."

But this immediately leads to the special difficulty that, to be acceptable, Principle C must stipulate a general moral duty to the *greatest* degree and widest scope of caring that individuals and groups, institutions, and society as a whole are capable of lavishing on others; limited only by, for example, the capacity of individuals, groups, etc. to have a caring disposition and to act caringly. But the right to fair treatment that Sterba's decision procedure supposedly selects can only be a *minimal* right. In the case of distributive justice, to which Sterba applies his procedure, the right to fair treatment would consist of "a right to accumulate goods and resources that was limited by the guarantee of a minimum sufficient to provide each person with the goods and resources necessary to satisfy his or her basic needs."[37]

It will be correctly replied that, supposing it to be adequate, Sterba's procedure would provide a rational ground for a general moral duty to care about others *in their own right*—precisely what we set out to justify—while a further argument or decision procedure would be capable of justifying the imperative to *maximize* the caring. An argument of that nature, it might be thought, can be readily devised along consequentialist lines; since as noted in chapter 3, an ethic of caring is, *inter alia*, a special form of consequentialism.

The following argument is an attempt to establish the existence of a moral duty, not just to care *simpliciter* but to care maximally.

1. Human welfare and happiness are (great) goods;

2. But goods ought to be realized (conserved, promoted, etc.) as much as circumstances permit;

3. By definition, caring about others is designed to promote their happiness and welfare, and when combined with empathic understanding of the proper means for the achievement of those ends, caring would tend to achieve these desirable ends.

4. Therefore, we have a moral duty to care, and so, to seek to promote the happiness and welfare of others;

5. But the maximization of everyone's happiness and welfare is a greater good than their realization in a lesser degree;

6. Therefore, it is our moral duty to seek to promote the maximum happiness and welfare of others, by means of a caring disposition and caring actions, guided by empathic understanding of the appropriate means for promoting them (Principle C').[38]

There are obvious logical gaps in this argument, for example, between premises (1)–(3) on the one hand and premise (4) on the other. Premises (1)–(3) only entail that it is *desirable* to seek to promote other people's happiness and welfare. They do not entail that we have a *moral duty* to do so. In addition, the argument as a whole is far from sufficiently tight.

To return to the attempt to adapt to our ends Sterba's decision procedure. Although that procedure avoids some of the difficulties due to Rawls's positing a veil of ignorance in the original position, it too suffers from various difficulties.[39] It escapes Dworkin's first but not second criticism of Rawls' decision procedure. It avoids the first difficulty since the persons in the original position would be fully cognizant of their best interests, etc. Although Sterba's contract, like Rawls' contract, does not describe an *actual* contract, it does describe a *bona fide* contract in the crucial sense in which Rawls cannot do so. That means that the requirements of fair treatment, once selected, would be binding on the society for which the adopted principles are designed. Unlike Rawls' procedure, there would be no unwarranted passage from an artificial state of ignorance to the more realistic situation of real people in regard to their interests and position in society.

Dworkin's second criticism of Rawls' procedure also applies, *mutatis mutandis*, to Sterba's decision procedure, as adapted for our present purposes. As noted earlier, a crucial element in Sterba's imagined original position is that the parties in that position "would not be using [their] knowledge of which particular interests happen to be [their] own"[40]; that is, their knowledge of where they belong in society: in relation to our present concerns, whether they happen to be among those who receive a great deal of care, or the opposite. But why would they not use that knowledge, and so, why would they compromise, as Sterba thinks? Essentially, Sterba's answer is that "like judges who discount prejudicial information in order to reach fair decisions,"[41] they "would be able to give a fair hearing to everyone's particular interests."[42] But since they are imagined to be wholly self-interested, the crucial question remains whether they would be willing—not whether they would be able—to discount their prejudicial knowledge. In terms of my adaptation of the procedure, would not those who are deprived of caring choose an *unlimited* (certainly more than a bare minimum) right to be cared about, while those on whom care is lavished would choose to limit that right for fear that if they opted for an unlimited right to caring, or to any amount of it above the *minimum* that Sterba's procedure would envisage, it would be at their own expense. They would opt to limit the right on the perfectly valid ground that people's capacity to care is limited. In both types of cases, more than a minimum degree of caring would be opted for. Only if the parties (a) are imagined to be "other regarding" in some degree, or (b) recognize a moral obligation to be fair to all other members of society, would the kind of conclusion that Sterba draws naturally follow.

Can we ourselves assume (b), or would doing so beg the question in favor of Principle C? Yet even if we do not assume it, or if assuming it does not beg the issue, (a) remains a problem for our adaptation of Sterba's procedure. When we turn next to Benhabib's proposed approach to conflict resolution in the hope that it would finally provide our long-sought support for Principle C, we shall see that Sterba's problem in relation to (a) disappears; since in her model the participants are conceived of as "other regarding." Unfortunately, it will turn out that Benhabib's method of conflict resolution is not without its difficulties.

In "The Generalized and the Concrete Other . . . ,"[43] Benhabib proposes a decision procedure which, like Sterba's modified Rawlsian procedure, does away with the veil of ignorance but also avoids the difficulties of the modified procedure, and is, therefore, superior to both procedures.

Benhabib describes her procedure as "the communicative model of need interpretations," distinguishing it from "the justice model of the original position."[44] She writes

> Questions of the most desirable and just political organization, as well as the distinction between justice and the good life, the public and the domestic, can be analyzed, renegotiated, and redefined in such a process. Since, however, all those affected are participants in this process, the presumption is that these distinctions cannot be drawn in such a way as to privatize, hide, and repress the experiences of those who have suffered under them, for only what all could consensually agree to be in the best interest of each could be accepted as the outcome of this dialogic process.[45]

Whether that procedure would achieve the above goals does not concern us here. For us the question is whether Principle C would be among the matters the participants could consensually agree are in their best interest. The question boils down to whether the "actual dialogue situation in which moral agents communicate with one another," and do so without any "epistemic constraints upon such an actual process of moral reasoning and disputation,"[46] would further rather than hinder the agents' acceptance of the principle. Benhabib believes that "the more knowledge is available to moral agents about each other, their history, the particulars of their society, its structure and future, the more rational will be the outcome of their deliberations. Practical rationality entails epistemic rationality as well, and more knowledge rather than less contributes to a more rational and informed judgment."[47]

Whether it is adequate for the purposes for which Benhabib intends it, her model, once again, cannot provide a rationale for Principle C, if we suppose that (a) the participants are wholly "self regarding" or "self interested." Indeed, it appears that the attempt to establish Principle C by means of any decision procedure on which the participants are wholly self-interested, is bound to fail. This can be seen generally as follows.

The adoption of Principle C presupposes the acceptance of a weaker principle, Principle B: viz. "Always care about others, not only about yourself." But I think the participants in Benhabib's model would not adopt that weaker principle, if they are supposed to be wholly self-interested. Rather, they would adopt a still weaker principle, Principle A. They would not adopt Principle B because they would believe that caring about (certain) others may not always be in their, the participants', interest. Principle A, which they would adopt, would enjoin: "Care about (and only about) those who care about you; or those who are likely to return any caring you may have toward them." Being completely self-interested, knowing the relevant facts about human nature, and being rational, they would adopt Principle A.

Finally, and contrary to what one might expect, Benhabib's model would not fare better even if (b) the participants are supposed to be other-regarding, caring rational persons (which I believe she assumes). Though they may reach agreement that everyone has a moral duty to care about others, such agreement would only be a result of their belief that (i) caring about others is a good thing and that (ii) it is desirable to increase the amount of altruism in the world, by lending it the considerable weight of moral authority. In short, Benhabib's open,

essentially democratic procedure of "advice and consent" is not designed to establish ethical altruism or, in particular, to establish a moral
duty to care. Rather, *starting* from the *assumption* that being a rational moral agent includes being altruistic and caring, the procedure
may make it possible[48] for rational agents to arrive at a fair decision, a
consensus as to who, besides those toward whom they have a special
moral duty to care, they have a general moral duty to care about. In
particular, whether caring ought to be accorded to total strangers.

The justification of the claim that we have a general moral duty to
care about others, even on the supposition that human beings are
capable of unselfishness and altruism—a basic assumption of this
book[49]—therefore remains so far an open question.

III

In the sketch of an ethic of caring that I drew in chapter 4, and earlier
in this chapter, I naturally focused on the concept of caring itself, the
central normative concept of such an ethic. But the fact that an ethic
of caring, as a virtue ethic, is, among other things, a special form of
consequentialist ethics in a broad sense, may seem to render it open
to some or all of the abuses to which pure consequentialism in its
modern varieties, particularly (pure) classical utilitarianism and contemporary preference utilitarianism, is vulnerable: for example, to
scapegoating, and other forms of inequity or injustice. In this, the
second part of the chapter, I shall take pains to show that it is not
open to these abuses. In that respect, it is like Platonic/Aristotelian
consequentialist virtue ethic.

I shall begin by attempting to show (I) that a caring-centered ethic
avoids certain serious but familiar difficulties that plague classical utilitarianism, hence that in these, if not also in other respects, it is more
adequate than the latter. However, and (II) that as a (special) form of
consequentialism, a care-centered ethic, like all forms of "pure"
consequentialism, would suffer from certain *other* difficulties unless
reinforced and enriched by the protective norms or side-constraints of
human rights.

A. Superiority of a Care-Centered Ethic
to Classical Utilitarianism
Philippa Foot opens her essay, "Utilitarianism and the Virtues,"[50] with
the following words:

It is remarkable how utilitarianism tends to haunt even those of us who will not believe in it. It is as if we forever feel that it must be right, although we insist that it is wrong. T.M. Scanlon hits the nail on the head when he observes, in his article "Contractualism and Utilitarianism," that the theory occupies a central place in the moral philosophy of our time in spite of the fact that, as he puts it, "the implications of act utilitarianism are wildly at variance with firmly held moral convictions, while rule utilitarianism . . . strikes most people as an unstable compromise."[51] He suggests that what we need to break this spell is to find a better alternative to utilitarian theories, and I am sure that that is right.[52]

Foot wishes to argue that "what is most radically wrong with utilitarianism is its consequentialism,"[53] which "in its most general form simply says that it is by "total outcome," that is, by the whole formed by an action and its consequences, that what is done is judged right or wrong."[54] This definition is unsatisfactory as it stands and excludes what on a more adequate definition would include the virtue ethic of caring as well as Greco-Roman and Medieval Christian virtue/consequentialist ethics. Foot's definition would also leave out her own brand of virtue ethic.[55] Foot's definition is also defective in its inclusion of the unclear idea of a "total outcome," consisting of a supposed "whole formed by an action and its consequences." No such idea is included in either classical, Benthamite or Millsian, or contemporary consequentialist theories. These theories hold that the criterion of the rightness or wrongness of individual actions, or of kinds of actions, consists in the overall goodness or badness of their consequences. Further, the idea of "total outcome," even if applied to the consequences of actions alone, is too restrictive or at least too vague to be of any use, in relation to, for example, the Platonic/Aristotelian form of consequentialism.[56]

A care-centered ethic is superior to a utilitarian ethic in two sorts of ways: (A) in the superiority of the concept of caring itself to the concept of benevolence, the central concept of utilitarianism; and (B) in its avoidance of certain crucial difficulties that plague pure utilitarianism: utilitarianism unconstrained by the norms of human rights and/or independent principles of fairness and justice. John Rawls gives a good definition of the *classical* utilitarian doctrine/principle (as having received perhaps "its clearest and most accessible formulation in Sidgwick"), as follows: "A society is properly arranged when its institutions maximize the net balance of satisfactions."[57] Bernard Williams speaks of benevolence in relation to utilitarianism. He notes, for instance, the inclusion of (some) animals in the "primary constituency" of "most versions" of utilitarianism, as a conception which "appeals to one moral motivation, benevolence."[58] Again, "for utilitarianism the characteristic moral motive is benevolence."[59]

B. Benevolence and Caring

(1) We can begin to see in what ways caring is superior to benevolence, by noting first Williams' description of the inadequacy of the term "benevolence" as it occurs in utilitarian ethics. He writes

> The term ["benevolence"] is vague, and it can also be misleading, particularly if it suggests warm feelings of personal attachment or, again, any kind of sentiment one naturally feels in greater degree for some people than others. Utilitarian benevolence involves no particular attachments, and it is immune to the inverse square law. The term stands for a positive relation to other people's desires and satisfactions, which the benevolent person has only because they are the desires and satisfactions of others. [60]

This passage also captures the basic differences between caring and utilitarian benevolence; since caring is "a kind of sentiment one naturally feels in greater degree for some people than others," and often but not always includes "warm feelings of personal attachment." The "strength" or "nobility" of utilitarian benevolence—its universality, the "noble" element in its welfarism, which is its "positive relation to other people's desires and satisfactions" in general—is bought, among other things, at the price of abstractness and pallidness, lack of warmth. One reason is precisely that it does not involve any "particular attachments" to any particular person or persons. As we shall see later in this chapter, that is no less true of R.M. Hare's treatment of "the agent's relation to others' desires . . . in terms of imaginative identification."[61]

In the preceding chapters, references to "benevolence" were to the *ordinary, everyday* uses and concepts of benevolence, not to any philosophical, such as the utilitarian, use(s) or concept(s) of it. It is necessary, therefore, to distinguish more clearly the former uses from the utilitarian use(s) of it.

According to *The Random House Dictionary of the English Language* the (ordinary) term "benevolence" means: "1. desire to do good to others; good will or charitableness. 2. an act of kindness; charitable gift." It is obvious that an act of kindness or a desire to do good *may* spring from "warm feelings," and, of course, is normally part of caring, especially in relation to those close to us. But as pointed out earlier, caring always includes more than such feelings. Similarly, the idea of a desire to do good to others, which utilitarian benevolence shares with benevolence in the word's ordinary employment, is also included in caring, but without excluding other important things. Other things being equal, the greater richness of the concept of caring helps make an ethic of caring superior to an ethic of benevolence, whether in the ordinary or the utilitarian employment of "benevolence." In addition, as we shall see later in this chapter, its greater richness also makes it superior in a certain respect to a utilitarian ethic as a welfare ethic.

The classical utilitarian (and, *mutatis mutandis*, the contemporary preference utilitarian) will reply that the universalism of utilitarian benevolence and welfarism—the principle of the greatest happiness of the greatest number—is ethically nobler than, and consequently, superior to an ethic of caring. Indeed, that utilitarian benevolence can embrace all sentient nonhuman animals in addition to all human beings, whereas caring, precisely because it involves more than a sentiment of sympathy or fellow-feeling, is normally more limited in scope. Caring loses in scope what it gains in warmth, attachment, and, generally, in specificity and concreteness. Moreover, utilitarianism is superior to an ethic of caring in morally enjoining us to seek to *maximize* the general welfare.

To the preceding, the following retort can be made. First, that in *practice* as opposed to theory, both utilitarianism and an ethic of caring are essentially in the same boat. In the majority of real-life cases, utilitarian benevolence as well as caring acts affect limited numbers of individuals, groups, institutions, and so on.[62]

Second, although the duty/obligation to care may be considered (just like the utilitarian's maximalist duty) a duty/obligation to seek another's *greatest* good possible in the circumstances, the duty/obligation to care is not a duty/obligation to seek to maximize the *general welfare*, in the utilitarian's sense of the phrase. Although that may seem to make utilitarianism more high-minded than an ethic of caring—to borrow the term from Williams—its actual result is the very opposite. As I shall presently argue, the utilitarian's duty to seek to maximize the "general good" saddles her with what Williams calls the "strong doctrine of negative responsibility." And that, as Williams argues, is one of utilitarianism's main difficulties.[63]

Williams holds that that difficulty faces consequentialism in general. If that is true, any ethic of caring would suffer from the same difficulty. Williams writes:

It is because consequentialism attaches [intrinsic] value ultimately to states of affairs, and its concern is with what states of affairs the world contains, that it essentially involves the notion of *negative responsibility*: that if I am ever responsible for anything, then I must be just as much responsible for things that I allow or fail to prevent, as I am for things that I myself, in the more everyday restricted sense, bring about. Those things also must enter my deliberations, as a responsible moral agent, on the same footing.[64]

The strong doctrine of negative responsibility[65] flows directly from consequentialism's assignment of ultimate value to states of affairs.[66] In *Ethics and the Limits of Philosophy* he states the matter thus: There are states of affairs I can affect with respect to welfare which, because I can do so, turn out to be my concern when, on nonutilitarian assumptions, they would be someone else's concern.[67]

In *Utilitarianism For and Against*, Williams gives two examples to show what is wrong with the strong doctrine of negative responsibility. The first example involves George, a chemist with heavy family responsibilities who is facing a moral dilemma: viz, whether to accept, against his moral principles, a job "in a certain laboratory which pursues research into chemical and biological warfare."[68] If he refuses the position his family will be in financial difficulty, and the position "will certainly go to a [chemist] who is . . . likely . . . to push along the research with greater zeal than George would."[69] George's wife, "to whom he is deeply attached," appears to think that, at least, "there is nothing particularly wrong with research into CBW."[70]

The second example finds Jim, an American traveler on a botanical expedition, "in the central square of a small South American town," where the captain in charge has rounded up a random group of Indians who, "after recent acts of protest against the government, are just about to be killed to remind other possible protestors of the advantages of not protesting."[71] The captain tells Jim that if he kills one of the Indians he will let the other Indians go free.

The utilitarian's resolution of the two dilemmas, Williams thinks, would be as follows: "In the first case, that George should accept the job, and in the second, that Jim should kill the Indian";[72] whereas he himself thinks that "many of us [including himself as a nonconsequentialist] would certainly wonder whether, in (1) [the George case], that could possibly be the right answer at all; and in (2) [the Jim case], that even one who came to think that perhaps that was the answer, might well wonder whether it was obviously the answer."[73] In its strong doctrine of negative responsibility, utilitarianism "cuts out" the fact "that each of us is specially responsible for what *he* does, rather than for what other people do."[74] For Williams "this is an idea connected with the value of integrity," a value he thinks utilitarianism makes "more or less unintelligible."[75]

Integrity as Williams understands it involves "the relations between a man's projects and his actions."[76] The idea of integrity essentially arises in relation to a person's projects, which Williams calls "commitments, those with which one is more deeply and extensively involved and identified."[77]

Williams clearly thinks that in ascribing "ultimate" (intrinsic) value only to states of affairs, a consequentialist ethic denies that dispositions, motives, actions, "commitments" and so, personal "integrity" in his special sense, have or can have "intrinsic" value. For utilitarianism, these things can only have instrumental value or "dis-value."

Williams' strictures are true of "pure" consequentialism, such as utilitarianism, but not necessarily true of "enriched" consequentialism. Williams errs in thinking that the preceding criticism of pure consequentialism means that consequentialism in general must be abandoned.

Among "enriched" consequentialist theories one can envisage theories that ascribe considerable value—including "intrinsic" value—to commitments and integrity in Williams' use of these terms—[78] not just to states of affairs. But there are other ways in which a consequentialist-cum-deontological theory can avoid the strong doctrine of negative responsibility, and preserve the value of the individual's integrity. I mean, by the addition of the protective norms of human rights and of fairness and justice, as side constraints independent of any consequentialist goods, to the care-centered ethic being outlined in this book. Whenever these side constraints come into play, they impose additional duties/obligations, or other moral constraints, on the caring-agent.

In the Jim example, these constraints would enjoin that Jim categorically refuse to kill any Indian, out of respect for the Indians' human right to life, and would place the responsibility for the consequent death of the twenty Indians, squarely on the captain's shoulders.

For this to be possible, the consequentialist-cum-deontological theory described must reject maximalist universalism, thereby eliminating that important source of the strong negative doctrine of responsibility.[79] In that way it would also limit Jim's moral responsibility to act in such a way that he would not be morally responsible for refusing to kill a single Indian.[80]

Human rights can provide even more fundamental grounds for the rejection of the strong doctrine of negative responsibility than the elimination of a maximalist imperative from any form of consequentialism. Jim would be morally enjoined to respect the human right to life of the captive Indians by not killing any of them, even if we suppose that he also has a duty to maximize the good or minimize the evil possible in the circumstance, if that duty is regarded as constrained by respect for people's human rights.

Suppose now, that the pure consequentialist were to abandon the duty to maximizing the general good, and is enjoined instead only to increase the general good or to decrease the general evil possible in the circumstances. Would that be enough to avoid the strong doctrine of negative responsibility? The answer is "no." For the answer to be "yes," both the universalism and the maximizing element must be eliminated. If only the maximizing element is eliminated, and if, at any time, my project "X" would produce less good than, say, pursuing my neighbor's project "Y," I would still be obligated to pursue "Y" even if I am committed to doing "X" and not "Y."

Williams is certainly correct that utilitarianism's denial of "ultimate" value to anything but states of affairs—which, in the context of Williams' line of reasoning, I take to mean the utilitarian's denial of "intrinsic" value to a person's "integrity"—has the result, among other things, that,

> For utilitarianism, agency comes in only secondarily: our basic ethical relation to the world, as agents, is that of being the cause of desirable or undesirable states of affairs. Our basic ethical concern is to bring about, so far as we can, that there is more welfare or utility in the world rather than less, [81] and, in the simplest version of utilitarianism, we should simply act in the most efficient way to bring that about. It is a question of what causal levers are at that moment within reach. Sometimes the causal connections through which I can affect outcomes run through other people's actions, but this makes no special difference. It is simply a matter of what changes produce most welfare. [82]

That is true because a person's "commitments" are a fundamental aspect of one's agency, and because, as Williams maintains, one's identity is crucially connected with (indeed, partially defined by) one's "commitments." But Williams is mistaken in apparently thinking that the *ascription* of "ultimate" ("intrinsic") value to integrity enables a pure consequentialist theory to avoid the strong doctrine of negative responsibility. Even if such a theory ascribes "intrinsic" value to integrity (or, even, to still other things besides states of affairs), it would still suffer from the strong doctrine of negative responsibility if (a) it ascribes greater "intrinsic" value to desirable states of affairs than to integrity, and (b) these desirable states of affairs are thought to consist in the maximization of the general welfare. From (a) and (b) together, it would follow that, whenever the pursuit of the general welfare conflicts with the agent's integrity, the latter ought to be set aside. It would be morally incumbent on one to pursue another's projects and set aside one's projects and commitments whenever the other's projects are likely to produce greater good, or less evil. Indeed, in these circumstances "one's integrity" would lie precisely in one's commitment to the other's projects! For example, if George turns down the job offer, he would be unable to minimize the evil that would result from research into chemical and biological weapons. Similarly, if Jim refuses to kill one Indian he would be unable to minimize the evil of the death of twenty innocent Indians. Here I assume, what I think is true, that Jim's saving the lives of nineteen innocent human beings would be a greater good than his continuing his botanical expedition without delay.

Returning to utilitarianism, Williams is clearly correct in maintaining that (1) for the utilitarian, George's accepting the offer would be the right course of action. Similarly, with Jim's killing one Indian to save the rest of the group. Therefore, Williams is also correct in holding that in enjoining these courses of action, (2) the utilitarian would violate George's and Jim's integrity. In short, Williams is correct that the right course of action for both George and Jim is to preserve their integrity by sticking to their commitments. That is what the more adequate, "weaker" or "modest" doctrine of negative responsibility entails.

Unfortunately, Williams provides no reasons for the adequacy of the foregoing "weaker, modest" doctrine; nor does he provide reasons for his view about the value of integrity. Athough the question of individual, and, especially, collective, moral responsibility involves complex and thorny issues that do not concern us here, the following might be briefly noted in preliminary defense of the weaker, more modest doctrine. The basic idea is that one is responsible for, and only for, what one intends, plans, envisages, desires, and pursues as a goal or end; things for which one is causally responsible as an agent, in a broad sense of causally responsible that includes mental as well as physical causation. This means that one is responsible for what one freely or voluntarily undertakes, and not responsible for what one is physically or psychologically forced to undertake. One makes another's project one's own and becomes partly or wholly responsible for it, if and when one freely and voluntarily accepts to undertake it on the other's or on one's own behalf. The fate of the Indians can become Jim's responsibility only if he freely accepts that responsibility, but there is no valid moral reason why he should do so, and every moral reason why he should not do so. Indeed, the captain is morally wrong in trying to manipulate Jim's conscience or compassion, forcing him psychologically to adopt his, the captain's, proposal.[83] Similarly, *mutatis mutandis*, with George. But clearly, the moral dilemma Jim faces is much more difficult than George's dilemma. Whatever he does, or does not do, will be inevitably tragic.

In sum, we normally think that unless we freely adopt or consent to another's project, or participate in a joint enterprise or project (whether by explicit or formal agreement or no), we are not, in any degree or way, responsible for his or her actions and their consequences. Not so with utilitarianism, by virtue of its ultimate maximizing universalist imperative. Stupidity, irrationality. selfishness, and insensitivity are among the many reasons for people's forcing their projects on others, or placing them willy-nilly in situations in which they are unable to avoid shouldering some of the projects and responsibilities of others. Perhaps the most horrendous example is that of war, when a government or the head of a state decides to fight a war without the people's advice or consent. Such highhanded behavior is by no means limited to dictatorial governments or heads of states. Sometimes, of course, people freely and voluntarily, out of caring (not benevolence!) flowing from affection or love, may give up or postpone a project, even a commitment, for the sake of projects or commitments of others. By becoming identified with the projects and commitments of others they become partially defined by them as persons or selves.

In addition to one's responsibility for what one does or does not do, one sometimes also bears some responsibility for the actions of individuals, groups, institutions, etc., with whom or with which one has a special relationship. The responsibility extends, *inter alia*, to the foreseeable impact on other people's projects and commitments of what one does or does not do.

The acknowledgment of a human right to individual autonomy, including the free pursuit of one's projects and commitments,[84] can provide a logical basis for the weaker doctrine of negative responsibility and for the value of integrity. For instance, the captain's attempt to force Jim into his project violates Jim's integrity by assaulting his autonomy. Similarly, George has a moral right to act in accordance with his moral principles, and so, is only responsible for whatever he contributes to nonmilitary research.

In some instances, integrity can be viewed as "being true to oneself" (and as Shakespeare wrote, if one is true to oneself, one cannot be "untrue to any man"). But the George and Jim examples demonstrate in significantly *different* ways what the betrayal of integrity may involve or mean. In George's case integrity means "truth to oneself," to one's moral principles. Likewise in Jim's case, if we imagine Jim to be, say, a universal pacifist, who flatly refuses to betray his pacifism by accepting the captain's "invitation." As Socrates clearly saw, only through betrayal of one's principles can one become untrue to oneself.

The implications of this for individual autonomy, in a sense closely related to integrity in Williams' sense, are quite important. Although one's autonomy can be assaulted and, in that sense, violated, one can, in principle, always resist the attack, even if, in the most extreme cases, it costs not less than everything, including one's very life.[85]

To sum up the discussion of negative responsibility, an ethic of caring avoids the strong doctrine and respects the individual's integrity. It does not abstractly prescribe a general duty to produce the greatest good for the greatest number, but is concerned with the happiness and welfare of particular, concrete persons that one has a general moral duty to care about. Of course, exceptionally caring persons may embrace the entire human race or even the whole of Nature in their concern and caring, and, in an obvious sense that all-embracing caring cannot but be abstract. For no human being can possibly know, or know about and personally empathize with, every human being and every plant and animal on earth. Since caring is directed toward people as individuals, it can only be abstractly directed toward each member of the human race, and only collectively in relation to the rest of Nature. The general duty to care itself cannot be justifiably considered a duty to care individually about each and every living person on earth.

IV

Contemporary "Preference Utilitarianism" and Benevolence

I shall now turn to Hare's theory of "imaginative identification" and relate it to the classical utililitarian concept of benevolence. In his examination of Hare's preference utilitarianism, Bernard Williams writes that Hare "treats the agent's relation to others' desires [what I vaguely call "benevolence"] in terms of imaginative identification,"[86] "of thinking oneself into someone else's position."[87] Briefly, Hare's imaginative identification, as Williams understands it, consists in "the use of a role-reversal test":

> In considering what I ought to do, . . . I must consider what it would be like to be the other people affected, in doing this. I apply a "role-reversal test" and think that what I would want or prefer if I were in their positions. I should, if thinking ideally, conduct this thought experiment with regard to every person, or indeed every sentient creature, involved in similar situations.[88]

This form of imaginative identification is clearly different from benevolence either in the ordinary or in the traditional utilitarian's sense explained earlier; though it *can result* from a benevolent attitude (in Hare's theory, it is a logical requirement of his universalizability principle). But it has an obvious similarity to empathy,[89] which is crucial for caring as well as for Hare's preference utilitarianism. For our present purposes, the important difference between the two, as we have seen, is that a caring person's empathy is anything but the purely detached and impartial cerebral attitude of the "omniscient, impartial, and benevolent" Ideal Observer—and far far from omniscience.[90] Moreover, unlike Hare's own version of it—of preference utilitarianism in general—sympathetic understanding and empathy are not expected to imaginatively take on everyone's preferences.

The differences are even greater between the empathy involved in caring and in another version of the Ideal Observer theory. In that version, as Roderick Firth states it, "the observer is 'omniscient, disinterested, dispassionate, but otherwise normal,'"[91] since that version "leaves out the condition of benevolence and does not imagine the observer actually to take on everyone's preferences."[92]

Notwithstanding its superiority to classical utilitarianism in some respects, preference utilitarianism does not fare better in relation to the Jim and George dilemmas. In the Jim example, as with classical utilitarianism, it would judge Jim's killing one Indian as morally right. Since the Indians would naturally want nothing better than to remain alive and to be given their freedom, they would prefer that Jim make that happen by shooting one Indian—provided it is some other Indian in the group. Only the captain would presumably prefer to have all the Indians shot by his men; although he would, perhaps, not mind too much, for the sake of public relations, if only one Indian is shot. For his purposes, that would be enough to teach a lesson to the Indians in the area and, at the same time, demonstrate his magnanimity!

Because all twenty Indians would prefer to live, their aggregate preference would far outweigh the captain's preference(s), in amount and strength. By shooting one Indian, Jim would therefore maximize the good, the aggregate preference.

A familiar difficulty facing preference utilitarianism is the assessment of an interest's or preference's amount and strength, and weighing it against the amount and strength of other interests or preferences. Note, for instance, Hare's following statements: "Where the conflicting interests of individuals are affected, the question of what morally ought to be done cannot be answered without comparing the strength of the interests, and this involves some kind of cost-benefit analysis.

Antiutilitarians may not like this; but it is hard to see how else we can be fair to the different parties. Not only utilitarians, but anyone who needs to assess the amount of harm or good done to those affected . . . has to have a method for assessing it; and this will be cost-benefit analysis under another name."[93]

In judging that killing one Indian would be the right course of action—indeed, a moral duty—*for Jim*, preference utilitarianism, like classical utilitarianism, would violate Jim's integrity and autonomy.

In George's case the same problem of making an adequate assessment of the weights of the conflicting interests involved in cost-benefit terms would also arise. Williams imagines George and his wife to have opposite preferences with respect to the position he has been offered. If the strength of their opposite interests is imagined to be equal, the preference utilitarian would find himself in an impasse. To avoid it the interest of their friends in seeing George accept the offer would then have to be added to the interest of George's wife, resulting in the judgment that George ought to take the job.

An ethic of caring avoids the George and Jim dilemmas and unqualifiedly acknowledges the value of integrity. For if one really cares about someone, one would not impose—certainly one would try hard to avoid imposing—one's projects on her, forcing her to betray her commitments, and consequently her integrity.

A Christ-like resolution of the Jim dilemma not contemplated by Williams would be to imagine Jim making the Indians' interests his own, saving them all by offering himself as a "sacrificial lamb," and making sure that the Indians are released and safely disperse before either killing himself or letting the soldiers shoot him. To be sure that the captain will not recapture and kill the Indians, he would secure the assurance of the captain's superiors that that will not happen. Since his choice would be free and voluntary, his autonomy and integrity would remain intact.

George's dilemma would be likewise resolved if we imagine George freely adopting his wife's and friends' urgings (here I again imagine that she would agree with their friends) and, making their preference his own, deciding to accept the position, with a view to working within the system to slow down the manufacture of the dangerous chemicals.

Because of the essential contextualism of caring, an ethic of caring avoids still other difficulties that plague Hare's preference utilitarianism, such as those that stem from its aggregative character, since caring is nonaggregative in a fundamental sense. One does not care about others in the abstract, as "abstract others," simply as part of the human race or even as a sentient being, or simply as part of the majority affected by a particular action, but as a "concrete other," in his or her own right.[94] It follows that an ethic of caring is immune to the evils of telishment ("punishing" the innocent) and scapegoating, which are among the chief difficulties from which pure utilitarianism suffers.[95] The caring person, or a community of caring persons, does not sacrifice anyone's happiness or welfare for the majority's happiness or welfare.

In sum, an ethic of caring does not suffer from the fundamental defect of utilitarianism that Rawls notes, viz, that "utilitarianism does not take seriously the distinction between persons."[96]

Further, the classical utilitarian general principle of utility makes unfairness and injustice, even toward the majority, always an open possibility. A fortunate minority, rather than the majority, may sometimes be its beneficiary. The principle of average utility eliminates that possibility, but not the problems connected with the aggregative aspect of that principle.[97]

Finally, the utilitarian would, I think, agree that caring about others is a desirable, indeed, admirable quality, given that caring includes sympathy (and benevolence in the word's everyday meaning), and that a society whose members are caring people would contribute to the "general welfare," as a group. In that sense, caring can be the utilitarian's ally. That view would be especially congenial to such utilitarians as Henry Sidgwick and G. E. Moore. To quote Williams:

It is important that, for utilitarian theories, systematizing everyday attitudes and dispositions does not necessarily mean replacing them. Theory may sometimes justify those attitudes; moreover, it may sometimes do this even if the attitudes are not themselves utilitarian in spirit. Sidgwick saw that it must be an empirical question what motivations lead to the greatest good; . . . Sidgwick came to the conclusion that in many departments of life it [utilitarian consciousness] should not be too much encouraged. He hoped to save utilitarianism from the old charge that it led to a denial of all natural affections and the stifling of impulse and spontaneity in the interests of a calculative spirit directed toward universal good.[98]

Nonetheless, the utilitarian would, I think, insist that acts of caring, if they are more than just acts of benevolence in his sense, are supererogatory. Our moral duty, he would add, is always to (strive to) maximize the general good.

To sum up. This chapter continued the sketch of the ethic of caring begun in chapter 4 by offering support for the following claims: (1) that we have a special moral obligation to care about those with whom we have a special relationship and (2) that we have a general moral duty to care about (some or all) others, including those with whom we have no relationship at all, such as total strangers: a claim for which some support was provided in chapter 4.

Starting with (1), it was argued in some detail that in the case of the private sphere, that special obligations arise between (a) natural and adoptive parents on the one hand and their children on the other. Likewise, (b) special obligations arise between spouses, and, on different grounds, between (c) children and their parents, and (d) siblings.

To establish the more difficult claims (c) and (d), a systematic, holistic account of the family's institutional nature was provided, applying to that fundamental institution-practice a conceptual framework developed elsewhere in the author's writings. That framework was next applied to friendship, both in relation to the family and independently of it.

Turning to claim (2) above, the second part of the chapter was devoted to a critical examination of four possible arguments that attempt to establish the existence of a general moral duty to care about others.

Both Argument I and Argument II endeavored to base the putative moral duty to care on the individual's moral right to be treated fairly and justly; but Argument II appealed to human rights as well. Although both arguments had certain attractions, both were found to have serious flaws. Arguments III and IV approached the matter from the standpoint of social contract theory, appealing, respectively, to John Rawls' decision procedure in relation to his hypothetical original position in *A Theory of Justice*, and to a modified Rawlsian decision procedure utilized by James Sterba. Despite their promise to provide strong evidence in support of claim (2), they too were found wanting.

For the evaluation of Argument III, Rawls' decision procedure in *A Theory of Justice* was examined in light of three basic criticisms. The first two, put forth by Ronald Dworkin in *Taking Rights Seriously*, were (a) that a hypothetical contract, such as Rawls', is not a contract at all, and (2) that Rawls' original position does not (and cannot) provide the needed rational grounds for his two principles of justice. The third argument, partly similar to Dworkin's first criticism, was urged by Henry Phelps Brown. Although that argument was shown by Brian Barry to rest (in part) on a misconception of Rawls' original position, the defense was marred by some ambiguities and left Dworkin's, as well as the essentials of Brown's criticisms, unanswered. What Barry made clear was that, on Rawls' theory, the parties in the original position are imagined to be endowed with a sense of justice, and in that sense, can be "other-regarding." Since the success of Argument III depended on the adequacy of Rawls' decision procedure, it too had to be ultimately rejected.

Unlike Argument III, Argument IV avoided Dworkin's criticism (a) above and came closer to successfully establishing claim (2) than any of the three other arguments. Following Sterba's decision procedure, it stipulated (i) reasoning "from our knowledge of all the particular interests of everyone who would be affected by our decision" after having discounted our particular interests.

Since the Argument, like the decision procedure on which it is based, failed to meet Dworkin's second criticism, it too is ultimately unsuccessful. To succeed, the persons in the original position must be supposed to recognize a moral obligation to be fair to all other members of society, and not only be "other-regarding" in some degree.

Finally, it was noted that a method of conflict resolution proposed by Seyla Benhabib, which will be considered in a later chapter, avoids Sterba's problem with Dworkin's first criticism, though it too is not completely free of difficulties.

Notes

1   Following H.L.A. Hart's usage in "Are There Any Natural Rights?", in *Rights*, ed. David Lyons (Belmont, CA, 1979), 14–25, I shall distinguish "duty" and "obligation," reserving the latter term for those duties that arise from special transactions or relationships between particular individuals, groups, institutions, nations, etc.

2   Indeed, I firmly believe that parents are morally responsible not only to continue to give their *adult* children moral support and the benefit of their experience, but also to provide whatever financial assistance they can give, whenever such assistance is needed. The fact that in the U.S. for instance, an individual becomes legally independent at 18 does not end the parents' special moral responsibilities toward him or her. (Nor does it end the child's moral responsibilities toward his or her parents.)

3   At least in traditional societies, where family bonds are strong and are prized as the most precious kinds of human relationships. The situation may be significantly different in Western countries where family bonds have tended to become weaker and have lost a good deal of their traditional value and importance.

4   Perhaps because of my traditional Middle-Eastern background and upbringing!

5   I say "normally have" since there are instances in which, e.g., older siblings voluntarily or involuntarily replace their parents in relation to their younger siblings. For instance, as a result of their parents' early death or incapacitation.

6   Acts based on reciprocity must be distinguished from the reciprocal moral rights and *duties/obligations* of individuals, groups, institutions, and practices, etc. For example, general and special moral rights and correlative obligations. They must also be distinguished from *just acts*, which too are not based on reciprocity. See chapter 8.

7   For simplicity's sake I limit myself to the traditional family. But what I say will apply, with the necessary changes or modifications, to nonconventional kinds of families.

8   Nontraditional families (or "families") are logically "parasitic" on, and are also made possible, with some modification or extension, by the societal conventions that define the traditional family.

9   For a fuller account of the general nature of an institution/practice see my "Institutions, Practices, and Moral Rules," *Mind*, LXXXVI, no. 344 (October 1977): 479–496, and "Language and Speech as Institution and Practice," *Teorema*, IX-1 (1979): 5–38, reprinted in my *Philosophy of Language and*

Logical Theory: Collected Papers (Lanham, MD, 1995). See also Part II of this book.

10   I leave aside the case of children who have a say in their parents' having, or adopting, another child.

11   It is of the essence of a good teacher that she care not only about her charges' academic success but also about them as persons. Her caring would take the form of genuine interest in and concern not only for the students' formal education but also for their general intellectual, emotional, and, yes, moral growth and self-actualization as human beings and as individuals.

12   James P. Sterba, "The Welfare Rights of Distant Peoples and Future Generations," *Morality in Practice*, James Sterba, ed., 3rd ed (Belmont, CA, 1991), 108.

13   Ibid., 114.

14   Christian as against profane love demands equality between self-love and love for one's "neighbor," even if we are only enjoined to love our enemy, not love him as ourselves. But it is secular love we are concerned with in this chapter and book.

15   "The Human Right to Be Treated as a Person," *Journal of Value Inquiry*, 19 (1985), 183–195.

16   I shall leave it to the interested reader to determine whether an analogous problem arises in relation to Argument I.

17   By "subject" here I do not refer to the agent, the caring person herself. I use the expression "subject of caring" to avoid any idea that the "cared about" person is an "object" in any sense, is treated differently from a "Thou" in Søren Kierkegaard's sense of "I" and "Thou," in an "I-Thou relationship."

18   By the same reasoning, Hobbes maintains that "when a covenant is made, then to break it is *unjust*," provided that there already exists a civil power or commonwealth, "sufficient to compel men to keep them [their covenants]." (*Selections from Leviathan*, in *Great Traditions in Ethics*, 5th ed, Ethel M. Albert et al., eds. (Belmont, CA, 1984), 140. Italics in original.

19   Ronald Dworkin, *Taking Rights Seriously* (Cambridge, MA, 1977), 151.

20   Ibid., 153.

21   For Dworkin's reasons, see op. cit., 150ff. It can be readily seen that Dworkin's second criticism follows from his first. For if a hypothetical contract is not a contract at all, and so, is not binding, it follows that the appeal to such a contract fails to provide a rational basis for any principles of justice—indeed, for any principles at all.

   I shall return to Dworkin's second criticism in chapter 8, in relation to justice vis-à-vis a care-centered ethic.

22 Oxford, Clarendon Press, 1995.

23 Oxford, 1988.

24 Ibid., 444. Quoted from Barry, op. cit., 56.

25 Brown, ibid.

26 Barry, ibid.

27 Barry, ibid., 57; Phelps Brown, op. cit., 500.

28 Ibid., 57.

29 In either the ordinary or the utilitarian sense.

30 One may ask how the parties in the original position can have a sense of justice, which by definition is general, applies to other persons in the original position and in society as a whole, and at the same time be distinterested in the sense of being "concerned to advance their interests" (*A Theory of Justice*, 19. Cf. Also how Rawls describes "mutually disinterested rationality" on p. 144).

According to Rawls, the parties' being capable of a sense of duty means "that . . . [they] can rely on each other to understand and to act in accordance with whatever principles are finally agreed to. *Once principles are acknowledged the parties can depend on one another to conform to them*" (ibid., p. 145. My italics). Thus, by defining "a sense of justice" in the foregoing way, Rawls tries to guarantee compliance with the contract when the veil of ignorance is lifted. Apart from whether the question begs the issue, and granting for the sake of argument that the parties' being capable of a sense of justice is part of their supposed rationality, the question remains whether they would "realize" that capacity, would in fact act in accordance with the principles they choose once the veil of ignorance is lifted.

31 Ibid., 57. See also 58ff. This criticism is strikingly similar to my critical remarks in relation to the idea of "putting oneself in another's shoes." Although I raised the objection apropos of the attempt to use Rawls' original position to justify a general moral duty to care about others, it can be generalized to include Barry's criticism of Rawls' attempt to justify his two principles of justice by means of a contractarian decision procedure. The connection between Barry's and my criticism can also be seen if we connect Barry's criticism to Hobbes' psychological (and ethical) egoism in the *Leviathan*; since for a psychological (and ethical) egoist, such as Hobbes, justice can be no other than reciprocity (see also chapter 8).

32 Other important criticisms of Rawls' decision procedure, even more central to an ethic of caring, are urged by Seyla Benhabib. See chapter 8.

33 "The Welfare Rights of Distant Peoples and Future Generations," *Morality In Practice*, James Sterba, 3rd ed, ed. (Belmont, CA, 1991), 109.

34 In "Need and Distributive Justice: A Defence," *Practical Reason and Theories of Justice*, Werner Maihofer and Gerhard Sprenger, eds. (Stuttgart, 1992), 119ff.

35 Sterba, op. cit., 109.

36 Ibid.

37 Ibid.

38 Principle C' is more stringent than Principle C, which only imposes a moral duty to seek to promote—not to seek to promote the maximization of—the welfare and happiness of others.

39 What follows is drawn from my "Need and Distributive Justice: A Defence," 119ff.

40 Sterba, op. cit., 109.

41 Ibid.

42 Ibid.

43 *WMT*, 154–177.

44 Ibid., 169.

45 Ibid.

46 Ibid.

47 Ibid., 169–170.

48 For my reasons for saying "may make it possible . . ." rather than "would make it possible . . . ," see chapter 9.

49 Although I believe that strong empirical and philosophical evidence can be readily given in support of that contention, I shall not attempt to do so in the present inquiry. Here I shall merely appeal to the reader's recollection or awareness of actions he or she has performed or witnessed others perform, that, as honestly as one can say, have been partly or wholly motivated by unselfish impulses or desires.

50 In *Consequentialism and Its Critics*, Samuel Scheffler, ed. (Oxford, 1991), 224–242.

51 T.M. Scanlon, "Contractualism and Utilitarianism," *Utilitarianism and Beyond*, A.K. Sen and B. Williams, eds. (New York, 1982), 103–128.

52 Foot, ibid., 254.

53 Ibid.

54 Ibid.

55   For her brand of virtue ethic see, for example, "Virtues and Vices," *Virtues and Vices* (Berkeley and Los Angeles, CA, 1978), 1–18, as well as other essays in that collection.

56   Bernard Williams offers a more adequate characterization of consequentialism. He says: "A distinctive mark of consequentialism might . . . be . . . that it regards the value of actions as always consequential (or, as we may more generally say, derivative), and not intrinsic. The value of actions would then lie in their causal properties, of producing valuable states of affairs; or if they did not derive their value in this simple way, they would derive it in some more roundabout way, as for instance by being expressive of some motive, or in accordance with some rule, whose operation in society conduced to desirable states of affairs" ("Consequentialism and Integrity," *Consequentialism And Its Critics*, 21).

57   "Classical Utilitarianism," op. cit., 14.

58   *Ethics and the Limits of Philosophy* (Cambridge, MA, 1985), 76. Another important feature of utilitarianism is its welfarist consequentialism (ibid., 76ff.). The importance of benevolence in relation to utilitarianism is clearly seen in Hume's ethics, which includes a significant "utilitarian" element in its emphasis on sympathy and benevolence. See, e.g., Annette C. Baier, "Hume, The Women's Moral Theorist?" *WMT*, 37–55.

59   Ibid., 81.

60   Ibid., 81–82.

61   Ibid.

62   Theoretically, utilitarian benevolence extends to all human beings.

63   "A Critique of Utilitarianism," in *Utilitarianism For* and *Against*, with J.J.C. Smart (Cambridge, 1973). Also in *Ethics and the Limits of Philosophy* (Cambridge, MA, 1985).

64   Op. cit., 95. Italics in original.

65   The "weak doctrine of negative responsibility" as we might call it, which Williams accepts, is described by him as "a fairly modest sense of "responsibility," introduced merely by one's ability to reflect on, and decide on, what one ought to do" (ibid., 95, footnote 1).

66   Ibid.

67   Ibid., 77. He adds: "Moreover, because the class of beneficiaries is larger than that of agents, there are situations that turn out to be someone's concern when on nonutilitarian assumptions they would have been no one's concern" (ibid). For our purposes this aspect of the utilitarian strong doctrine of responsibility can be ignored.

68   Ibid., 98.

69   Ibid.

70   Ibid.

71   Ibid.

72   Ibid., 99.

73   Ibid.

74   Ibid. Italics in original.

75   Ibid.

76   Ibid., 100.

77   Ibid., 116.

78   I use "intrinsic"in "intrinsic value" in shudder quotes since even if we suppose
     that "intrinsic value" is adequately defined by "value that something has 'in
     itself,' apart from (the value of) its consequences," the troubling question of
     the lack of a viable criterion or criteria of "intrinsic value" remains. (See, for
     example, my "'Intrinsic' and 'Instrumental'" Value: An Untenable Dichotomy,
     Journal of Value Inquiry, IV, no. 3 (Fall 1970): 172–190. Thus, even if
     Aristotle is correct that (a) it is meaningless to ask, in the case of happiness:
     "Why be happy?" and that (b) shows that happiness is an (indeed, is the
     ultimate) good, that criterion does not seem to be applicable with any clarity
     or degree of assurance to things other than happiness; e.g., pleasure, integ-
     rity—even caring.

     Again, from the fact or supposition that something "X" or that seeking to
     bring about something "Y" is a moral duty does not entail that "X" or "Y" has
     "intrinsic" value. Thus, from my view that we have a moral duty to care about
     others, it does not follow that caring has "intrinsic" value. And to say: "we
     have a moral duty to X 'as such,' 'for its own sake,'" raises the perplexities I
     had in mind above in asking what that exactly means or can mean.

79   There is another way in which it can do so while preserving maximalist uni-
     versalism, namely by maintaining an absolutist conception of human rights
     (and/or of justice). In that case it becomes one's duty to maximize the general
     good, but only when doing so would not violate anyone's human rights, or
     any principles of justice. But maximalist universalist moral principles are out
     of tune with the nature of caring and a caring-centered ethic.

80   Cf. Elizabeth Anscombe's definition of "murder" in "War and Murder," *War
     and Morality*, Richard A. Wasserstrom, ed. (Belmont, CA, 1970), 42–62,
     passim.

81   Actually, for classical utilitarianism, in order to bring about the *greatest* amount
     of good, or the least amount of evil possible, in the circumstances.

82   Ibid., 77. See also *Utilitarianism For and Against*, 108ff.

83 The attempt to force Jim to do the captain's bidding would become overt coercion if we imagine the captain threatening to kill Jim unless he kills one Indian.

84 My claim that such a human right should be acknowledged will be defended in the next chapter. That right is part of the basic human right to be treated as a person.

85 Socrates is, of course, the most famous historical example of a person who fully maintained his integrity, at the cost of his imprisonment and death. But note that we do not *ordinarily* consider dying or being killed as an option, and classify dying for one's principles, or to save others, as a supererogatory rather than a morally obligatory act. (But there are extreme cases in which committing suicide is a *legal*, e.g., military, duty.)

86 Ibid., 82. Compare that with Barry's interpretation of Rawls' decision procedure in *A Theory of Justice*, discussed later in this book.

87 Ibid., 83.

88 Ibid. It is clear that the role-reversal test would work in relation to Sterba's and Benhabib's decision procedures, but not Rawls' decision procedure in *A Theory of Justice*.

89 *The Random House Dictionary* defines "empathy" as follows: *Psychol.* 1. Intellectual identification with or *vicarious experiencing of the feelings, thoughts, or attitudes of another person.* 2. The imaginative ascribing to an object, as a natural object or work of art, feelings or attitudes present in oneself." Clearly the sense of "empathy" relevant to caring is only part of sense (1) that I have italicized.

90 Williams, op. cit., 83.

91 Ibid., 83–84.

92 Ibid., 83. For Williams' telling criticism of Hare's version of the Ideal Observer theory and his form of utilitarianism as a whole, see ibid., 84ff. Let me merely note one point that Williams considers as "a compact illustration of a truth about all utilitarian politics, that benevolence gets credentials from sympathy and passes them on to paternalism" (ibid., 89). Caring involves sympathy as well as empathy: in personal relationships, out of affection or love, and in their absence, out of empathy. And, in contrast to utilitarianism, the sympathy that is part of caring, does not "pass on to paternalism."

93 R.M. Hare, "Moral Reasoning About the Environment," *Applied Philosophy: Contemporary Debates in Morals and Metaphysics*, Brenda Almond and Donald Hill, eds. (London, 1991), 15–16.

94 Note also that, as a consequence of the contextual character of caring, the general moral duty to care is not, and cannot be, abstractly universal.

95 Indeed, the (pure) utilitarian's rejection of human rights, and his subordination of fairness and justice to the principle of utility, are another major source of these difficulties. According these protective norms their proper place, in a care-centered ethic, would result in greater harmony between caring on the one hand and rights and fairness/justice (and equity) on the other hand than from strengthening utilitarianism with these protective norms, conceived, for example, as side constraints.

96 "Classical Utilitarianism," from *A Theory of Justice*, 22–27. Reprinted from *Consequentialism and Its Critics* (Oxford, 1991), 19.

97 In *Utilitarianism For and Against*, J.J.C. Smart favors the general principle of utility against average utility. He writes: "In most cases the most effective way to increase the total happiness is to increase the average happiness, and vice versa" (ibid., 28). The first part but not the second part of the statement is true. It is far from obvious that even in most cases increasing the total happiness would increase the average happiness (utility). In fact, both history and the present situation in the world provide ample evidence against Smart's optimistic view.

98 Op. cit., 106–107. My italics.

Chapter 6

Human Rights and the
Ethic of Caring–I

Since the pioneering work of Carol Gilligan in *In a Different Voice* and other writings, feminist moral philosophers who advocate an ethic of care have, with some notable exceptions,[1] stressed what they believe is the sharp opposition between the care perspective and what they call "the ethic of rights and justice." Consequently, with some notable exceptions, they reject or tend to reject appeals to abstract justice and/or human rights in moral decisions. They have thus tended to force moral solutions, in my opinion, into untenable "either/ors": a situation directly traceable to the polemical *contretemps* between Gilligan and her feminist followers and supporters on the one hand and her Harvard psychologist colleague Lawrence Kohlberg and his followers on the other.[2] In this and the next chapter, as in my outline of an ethic of caring in the preceding two chapters, I intentionally steered away from the psychological debates about the ways certain American and other adult men and women attempt to resolve certain favorite moral dilemmas of the writers.

Human Rights

In chapter 4 I claimed that an ethic of caring would be incomplete if not complemented and constrained by the inclusion of the protective norms of human rights, fairness, and justice. In this chapter I shall try to support this central claim by considering some of the main problems that would arise in the absence of a proper place for human rights, in a care-centered ethic. I shall also try to show how the protective norms of human rights, if properly applied, would eliminate or help avoid these difficulties. I say "eliminate or help avoid" the difficulties because the elimination of some of the difficulties may require, or require in addition, an appeal to fairness and/or justice.

But first, a brief outline of my conception of human rights, starting with a look at a distinction Ronald Dworkin draws between what he calls a "stronger" and a "weaker" sense of "a right." Next I shall consider Dworkin's criticism of what he calls the "naturalist" model (N-model) and his defense of the "constructive" model (C-model) of human rights. Following that I shall outline my own views about some of the basic human rights I believe all human beings have, as I have sketched them to some extent elsewhere.[3]

In *Taking Rights Seriously* [4] Ronald Dworkin describes the stronger sense as follows: "in most cases when we say that someone has a 'right' to do something, we imply that it would be wrong to interfere with his doing it, or at least that some special grounds are needed for justifying any interference."[5] Dworkin distinguishes that stronger sense from the weaker sense in which we say of someone that he or she has a "right to perform a certain action," meaning that it "is the 'right' thing for him to do, or that he does no 'wrong' in doing it."[6] In the stronger sense, according to Dworkin, someone may have the right to do *something "that is the wrong thing for him to do*, as might be the case with gambling. Conversely, something may be the right thing for him to do and yet he may have no right to do it, in the sense that it would not be wrong for someone to interfere with his trying."[7]

The reason why it is wrong to interfere with someone who has a moral right to do something in the stronger sense is precisely that, other things being equal, what the right-holder has a right to do is *morally right*.[8] A right X in the stronger sense *makes* it right to exercise X in the appropriate situations or circumstances. "A has a right to (do, etc.) Y in the stronger sense" entails that doing Y (in the appropriate circumstances) is morally right. Or the concept of moral rightness is included in, is part of the concept of a human right—of any kind of moral right (which, by being a moral right, is necessarily a right in the stronger sense). Consequently, when Dworkin says that "it would be wrong for anyone to interfere with you" when "you propose to use your money in a way that I think is wrong," Dworkin is mistaken if he is thinking of a person (anyone) as having a *moral* right, a right in the stronger sense, to gamble with his money. But what he says is perfectly correct if he is thinking of a *legal* right to gambling; for then it would be legally (though not necessarily morally) wrong to interfere with him.[9]

Since human rights are very strong moral rights, the foregoing, *mutatis mutandis*, applies to them as well as to special moral rights. But we must distinguish between having a right and exercising it. Although my having a human right R (i.e., a strong moral right) to do X, makes it wrong for anyone to interfere with my exercising R at time t, *provided that my exercise of it at that time* is not overridden by another's stronger moral claim to exercise his moral right Y, whose exercise is incompatible with my exercise of X at that time.

Our concept of a right is applicable to all kinds of rights, including all kinds of rights in the stronger sense as well as to rights in the weaker sense, since to do that which is right in the latter sense is to do nothing wrong. It is to do what is right or what is legally, morally, and so forth, indifferent or neutral. Consequently, Dworkin's account of the stronger sense of right is inadequate insofar as he incorrectly thinks that we can meaningfully speak of one's having a strong (moral or legal) right to do wrong! By the very meaning of 'a right' in general, the proper exercise of a right is in principle necessarily right: that is, provided that no overriding circumstances exist at the time that would make it *improper* or wrong for the right-holder or right-holders to exercise it at that time.[10]

The preceding remarks have important implications. For instance, with regard to the question of whether something is a moral right, a right in the stronger sense. For if the concept of moral rightness is part of the concept of a moral right, or something's being morally right is a necessary—though not sufficient—condition for its being a moral right, to argue that there exists a moral right to X, one must first show that doing X is morally right. For example, in order that, say, a human right to life (in the negative sense of "a right to life") may be justifiably posited, it is necessary first to show the moral rightness of self-defense against attempts on one's life; e.g., by showing that human life as such is an "intrinsic" value, or on the ground that human life is a condition for the very possibility of an individual's being able to experience, enjoy, create, or disseminate any kind of value whatever. In the case of gambling this would mean (a) that gambling is morally wrong and so one has no moral right to gamble, or (b) that gambling is right and so, in addition to a right in the weaker sense, a moral right to gamble *may* exist.

Our concept of a right, and so, of a right in the stronger sense, applies without difficulty to special moral and other rights, to rights created by special transactions or relationships, which are also rights in the stronger sense. Special rights imply, in the sense of "determine or entail," certain courses of action (and kinds of reactions or responses) as rights: morally, legally, etc., as the case may be. It *becomes* right for the right-holder to perform a certain kind of action, A, or B, or C, etc., to exercise her special right, in the appropriate circumstances. Consequently it would be (morally or legally, etc.) wrong to interfere with the exercise of that right, if (a) it is exercised in the appropriate circumstances, and (b) is not, in these circumstances, overridden by someone else's stronger (moral, legal, etc.) right.

The stronger sense of "a right," in my understanding of it, corresponds to Shelly Kegan's notion of a "full right" in *The Limits of Morality*[11]; since someone's having a full right to X entails her option to do X or not to do X, as she chooses, an injunction protecting her decision, and an enforcement privilege (though that may or may not include the use of force). Kegan's "thin right" does not correspond to Dworkin's weak sense of "a right"; since, for one thing, to ascribe a thin right to someone is to ascribe to her the relevant *injunction*: an element absent from a weak right as Dworkin defines it. Kegan thinks that it is the thin right that is "the heart of most rights-talk."[12] This is not true at least when people complain, say, about the violation of their human rights, or of their special moral rights. In addition, the "thin sense" is not what I understand by "a right" in speaking of human rights or of special rights.

Dworkin[13] equates "a right in the stronger sense" with "an absolute right,"[14] and describes it as a "trump." He maintains that "if someone has a right to something [in the stronger sense], then it is wrong [for example] for the government to deny it to him even though it would be in the general interest to do so. This sense of a right . . . might be called the anti-utilitarian concept of a right."[15] Although I agree that all rights, particularly in the stronger sense, must be taken very seriously, I do not share his view that rights in the stronger sense, not excepting human rights, are absolute. On my understanding, a right in the stronger sense is less strong than Dworkin's.

I now turn to Dworkin's cogent criticism of the traditional "Natural" (or N-) model of human rights, according to which human rights are inborn and inalienable attributes of human beings and are apprehended by our alleged intuitive powers. Dworkin explains that he avoids the phrase "natural rights" "because it has, for many people, disquieting metaphysical associations. They [the defenders of the N-model] think that natural rights are special attributes worn by primitive men like amulets to ward off tyranny."[16] That, he correctly says, is a "preposterous notion." I might add that to think of human rights as some sort of attribute human beings have is to commit essentially the kind of mistake G.E. Moore committed in maintaining that "good" names some sort of "nonnatural" property of "intrinsically good things." Unless the N-model's advocates are ethical naturalists or descriptivists rather than, like Moore, ethical nonnaturalists or prescriptivists, they must consider a "natural or human right" as a "nonnatural" attribute of human beings, different from the "natural" properties or attributes human beings have *qua* human. For "a right," like "good," is a normative expression. But if a human right is regarded as a nonnatural attribute, the N-model would be plagued with all the familiar difficulties of Moore's notion of a "nonnatural property"; including what J.L. Mackie calls "the problem of queer (metaphysical) entities,"[17] and the utter obscurity of the supposed *supervenience* of "nonnatural properties" on certain "natural" properties; e.g., how that mysterious relation between certain natural properties can "give rise" to an alleged supervenient "nonnatural" property, bridging (to my mind, the unbridgeable) gap between the "is" and the "ought."[18] In sum, supervenience is but a name for its advocates' ignorance.[19]

Dworkin notes that the N-model presupposes, among other things, that theories of morality, hence theories of natural rights, "describe an objective moral reality."[20] Moral principles, including the principles of natural rights as well as the principles of justice, are not "created by men or societies but are rather discovered by them, as they discover laws of physics."[21] "The main instrument of this discovery is a moral faculty possessed by at least some men, which produces concrete intuitions of . . . morality [here, intuitions of natural rights] in particular situations."[22] In the case of natural rights these intuitions would presumably be "clues" to the existence and nature of the objective attribute, "a natural right."[23] Consequently the N-model is tied to some form of ethical intuitionism—in fact, is essentially an intuitionist model—with its own well-known special difficulties.

The C-model too, as Dworkin describes it, (a) appeals in a fundamental way to moral "intuitions" or "immediate convictions"; but (b) it treats these "not as clues to the existence of independent principles [here the alleged attributes of "natural rights"], but as stipulated features of a general theory to be constructed, as if a sculptor set himself to carve the animal that best fits a pile of bones he happened to find together. This 'constructive' model does not assume . . . that principles of . . . [morality] have some fixed objective existence, so that descriptions of these principles must be true or false in some standard way."[24] On that point it is noncommittal. For (c) it "does not deny, any more than it affirms, the objective standing of any of these convictions; it is therefore consistent with, though as a model of reasoning it does not require, the moral ontology that the natural model presupposes."[25]

Dworkin maintains that John Rawls' theory in *A Theory of Justice* utilizes the C-model. He also maintains that unlike the N-model, the C-model "makes sense of John Rawls' technique of 'reflective equilibrium,'" described by Rawls as "the technique of seeking a "reflective equilibrium" between our ordinary, unreflective moral beliefs and some theoretical structure that might unify and justify these beliefs."[26]

Although the C-model is more adequate than the N-model, it is not without its own difficulties. Some of them can be exhibited by drawing some of its important implications:

(1) I said that according to Dworkin the C-model does not either affirm or deny that "human right" refers to any objective attribute, relation, etc., possessed by human beings *qua* human; so that to say that "human right" refers (or does not refer) to some objective attribute, etc., of human beings . . . is not to say something that must be true or false "in some standard way." But what can that mean? Dworkin does not say. A *prima facie* plausible interpretation, but one that must be ruled out on the basis of what Dworkin says about the C-model, is that since moral principles are normative, they cannot be true or false in the way (nonvague) statements of putative fact are either true or false, but are true or false in the way normative judgements are true or false. The reason this interpretation will not do is that the C-model "does not assume that principles of morality have some fixed objective existence"; though Dworkin says that the C-model is consistent with the moral ontology of the N-model. That makes it possible for moral principles to have reference to some objective reality, in his view. As a result, "human right," say, may refer to an attribute possessed by all human beings!

Dworkin's view that the C-model makes sense of Rawls' technique of reflective equilibrium strongly suggests that in saying that moral principles are not true or false in the standard way, he is thinking of their truth or falsity in terms not of correspondence but of the putative coherence, the best "fit" or "match" between considered moral judgments (beliefs or opinions, or intuitions as Dworkin also calls them) and a set of moral principles.

(2) Dworkin speaks of the C-model's subordinating "troublesome intuitions"—intuitions that apparently fail to fit our moral principles, or *vice versa*—to the "responsibility that requires men to integrate their intuitions and subordinate some of these, when necessary, to that responsibility."[27] But how then does the model escape circularity; or what independent moral or nonmoral facts can support a moral theory? For as we saw, the C-model does not appeal to any putative objective moral reality. Dworkin's answer is that the moral principles "must have independent appeal to our moral sense."[28] These moral principles, which are to support our moral intuitions, convictions, or judgments, must explain them "by showing the underlying assumptions they reflect."[29] and provide guidance in those cases about which we have either no convictions or weak or contradictory convictions.[30] What that putative "moral sense" is and how it differs from the "intuitions" of traditional intuitionism we are not told; and no evidence is provided for its existence and its uniformity or universality. Dworkin's use of "belief" or "opinion" interchangeably with "intuition" suggests that the C-model's "intuitions" simply consist in people's (settled) beliefs or convictions about moral matters. Not coincidentally, it is this that R.M. Hare understands Rawls' "intuitions" to consist in, in his interpretation of Rawls' thesis that "[t]here is a definite if limited class of facts against which conjectural principles can be checked, namely our considered judgments of reflective equilibrium."[31] Hare identifies these "facts" with moral opinions or beliefs and argues *contra* Dworkin that Rawls' technique of equilibrium commits him to what is essentially Dworkin's N-model.[32]

The model of human rights in the present book and in the present author's articles referred to earlier, differs significantly from both N- and C-models; though in rejecting the N-model it shares some negative features with the C-model. It agrees with it in rejecting the view that human rights are some kind of natural or nonnatural attribute of human beings. A protective moral norm cannot be an attribute of any kind. It makes no sense to think of a human right as an object of, and discoverable by, some kind of ethical intuition. To perceive that everyone has a human right or has certain human rights is to realize that everyone is entitled, in certain circumstances, to do certain kinds of things or be treated in certain kinds of ways. It is, if you like, to discover an "objective fact" about all human beings, though not in the N-model's sense. To understand this more clearly we must understand more precisely what someone's "acknowledging the existence of a human right" involves.

Human rights are not *prima facie* entitlements, hence open to forfeiture, as William Blackstone cogently argues in "Human Rights and Human Dignity."[33] Only the entitlement to their exercise is a *prima facie* entitlement. One attraction of the view that human rights are *prima facie* entitlements is that it provides an attractive moral justification for legal punishment by incarceration or execution, and for the political assassination of dictators and others who commit heinous crimes. But Blackstone correctly argues that human rights are "inalienable" and, consequently, not *prima facie* rights. As he says:

> What could it mean to renounce, transfer, or waive one's right to be treated as a person, for example? Such renouncement seems to make no sense as long as one *exists* as a *person* [i.e., as a human being, I should add]. [And with respect to renouncement or transfer of one's human rights, he adds:] If being respected as a person means that one's preferences, needs, choices, and actions are to be respected, surely it is nonsensical to speak of *someone else* having or being given *my* right to have *my* preferences, needs, choices and actions respected. [34]

Similarly, it makes no sense to speak of the forfeiture of one's right to be treated as a person "as long as one exists as a person." Blackstone's argument against the claim that human rights are *prima rights* rests on his rejection of the view that persons are "open to forfeiture of all rights. This . . . amounts to allowing the conceptual possibility of viewing persons as *things*,"[35] as not worthy of respect. Blackstone's argument is cogent if by "all rights" we understand "all human rights," not necessarily also civil or (some?[36]) legal rights.

Basic Rights

In the two articles on human rights referred to in footnote 4, I argued that all human beings have an equal human right to be free to pursue their well-being and welfare as human beings and as individuals, to find meaning in their lives, and to actualize their potentialities. Further, that the effective pursuit of one's welfare and self-actualization, etc., requires our acknowledging an equal human right to equal opportunity and equal treatment. Again, that the equal right to be free is an essential part of the basic human right of all human beings to treatment as moral persons and that the right to equal treatment and opportunity is either part of that foundational right or is entailed by it.

Briefly,[37] to treat someone as a moral person in my sense is to treat her (1) with "respect," and (2) with "consideration." To treat her with "respect" (1) in my special sense is, among other things, to respect her freedom of choice and action, by virtue of her capacity to make reasoned choices and decisions on her own and seek her and others' welfare and well-being or happiness. In other words, it is to respect her autonomy in that sense (see chapter 7). To treat her with "consideration" (2) is to have a certain positive attitude and corresponding ways of thinking and feeling about her and of acting in relation to her: a positive attitude that is the very antithesis of the attitude exemplified in insulting and humiliating, and even depersonalizing and dehumanizing her. That is, treating her ideas, feelings, actions, and relationships, even her life as a whole, and in the most extreme cases, her culture, religion, and ethnic or racial heritage or identity, as "dirt" or "trash." Treating her with "consideration," on the other hand, means being sensitive to her needs, aspirations, interests, concerns, projects, and goals. It means concern about her welfare and happiness. It also means making her feel that she matters, and her life matters. In sum, in Bernard Williams' words, it means identifying with her in the fullest sense.[38]

As fundamental moral protections and entitlements, or "protective norms" in Stephen Lukes' apt phrase,[39] human rights need to be acknowledged in their constitutions and laws by all countries and guaranteed in practice to everyone: young and old, rich and poor, healthy and ill, nonhandicapped and handicapped. Everywhere, but above all in the developing world, they are sorely needed to help and protect people in their lifelong striving to satisfy their basic survival and social needs and to realize their full human and individual potentials. "Social needs," as I understand the phrase, include what various personality psychologists consider to be the universal psychological needs of human beings. Following the work of Abraham Maslow (and, to some extent, Carl Rogers) in the articles alluded to earlier (*TFHR, HRTP*), the psychological needs I took to be basic are the need to be loved, to belong or be accepted, and to achieve and be recognized. The first two of these and, normally, the third, involve interpersonal relations and so can be called "social needs" in a broad sense.[40] At any rate, I shall use "social needs" as an umbrella term to include these putative basic psychological needs in addition to James Sterba's "social needs."[41] I also continue to be strongly inclined to accept Viktor Frankl's thesis that human beings have a "will to meaning," are meaning-seeking beings; which seems to me essentially to involve the need of human beings for achievement and recognition. In addition, the need for love and for belonging often arise from or are, likewise, expressions of the need for meaning. (I include the need for meaning among our "social needs.") Stated in terms of the preceding basic psychological and existential needs, my thesis boils down to the claim that any object, activity, situation, or state of affairs that is directly or indirectly conducive to the satisfaction of one or more of these (or these together with one's survival) needs would be desirable to have or to promote. Consequently, the opportunity to seek to satisfy these needs, and to satisfy them as fully as possible, is a basic human right.

"Meaning in one's life" and "the meaning(s) of one's life as a whole" can be defined in terms of the preceding four basic social needs. For example, I think we tend to feel that our life is meaningful so long as we are able to strive for success in our chosen endeavors; insofar as we achieve recognition for our attempts to create things of value and for the realization of these goals. Similarly we value our life, or value it more, if we are loved; or if we ourselves love and strive to make those we love happy or increase their happiness.

It is worth noting, particularly in relation to the ethic of caring and the ideal of a moral community discussed in earlier chapters, that Frankl maintains that meaning in life is achievable in three sorts of ways: "(1) by doing a deed; (2) by experiencing a value; and (3) by suffering."[42] Concerning (2) he says: "The second way of finding meaning is by experiencing something, such as a work of nature or culture; and also by experiencing someone, i.e., by love."[43] True. But we need to add that satisfying our survival needs is also necessary for a meaningful life.

As one might expect, psychologists differ to a greater or lesser extent in their classification of our basic psychological needs. I shall, therefore, present the classifications of some personality psychologists other than Maslow. Conceptual differences of this sort are not unexpected in any empirical science, especially in a relatively new social science; and though the empirical facts on which the theory of human rights I am presenting partially rests may change with increased understanding of human psychology, we need to remember two essential points. First, that many personality psychologists *do* posit a set of basic psychological needs. Second, that despite noteworthy differences in emphasis or classification, they have a good deal of ground in common. For instance, psychologists in general appear to agree about the fundamental role the need for love or affection (hence for acceptance and belonging) plays in the individual's mental health: above all, in the child's ego development.[44]

The following lines from F. Helm Sierlin illustrate the importance of love and belonging:

> There are . . . those numerous . . . families where the expelling mode [as opposed to those that are more or less homeostatically deadlocked] prevails, i.e., where children, rather than being excessively bound and/or delegated, are neglected, abandoned, and pushed into premature autonomy. And these children, as well as their parents, appear no less in need of help than those subjected primarily to the binding or delegating modes.[45]

Again:

> How should we treat these wayward children and their parents? Clearly, before we can unbind them, we must bind them, i.e., must instill in them that sense of belonging and of being loved which should be every child's birthright. Yet such primary binding—the implanting of love and concern where none existed before—seems more difficult a therapeutic task than the unbinding.[46]

B. Sullivan stresses the importance of the infant's experience of security in addition to its "relief of bodily tension" by the satisfaction of its physical needs, including "physical closeness." These two factors, according to him, are the two components on which the fulfillment of the infant's needs has rested from birth. The experience of a sense of security has to do with "the need to feel accepted and approved by the person providing this relief. The absence of this sense of security is a highly unpleasant sensation, namely anxiety, which is disruptive, interferes with other pursuits, and may stand in direct opposition to the satisfaction of other concurrent needs."[47] And: "The pursuit of security is the more important factor in shaping the personality and it modifies in many ways the needs for satisfaction. It has to do with the development of the human potential in a social, cultural setting, with the development of self-esteem, the feeling that one enjoys the respect of others, and the assurance of competence in pursuing one's goals."[48]

As a therapist, Carl Rogers stresses wholeness, integration, and self-actualization, hence autonomy; and caring and empathy by the therapist; while Seeman stresses mutual liking and respect in the therapeutic process.[49]

Like Rogers's theory, G. Albert Ellis' Rational-Emotive Theory (RET) tries to give the client what Rogers (1961) calls "unconditional positive regard"—or, more concretely, the knowledge and feeling that the therapist fully accepts him or her, as a human being, even though the therapist may clearly indicate that his or her behavior [the patient's "transference" reactions] is objectionable, immoral and self-defeating."[50]

It is clear that the feelings and assurances described are connected with the possibility of self-actualization (also emphasized by Maslow and Rogers among others).[51]

The Right to Be Free

In his classic essay, "Persons and Punishment," Herbert Morris, like Rogers, envisages individual freedom as negative freedom, as freedom from interference by others. He also views the "capacity to make rational choices" as a necessary condition for one's having the human right to make free choices. But I think he is wrong if he means the individual's actual ability, at a given stage of her physical and mental development as a human being, consciously to seek to satisfy her welfare and happiness. I do not think that such a capacity is at all essential for a human being's actually *having* the human right to make free choices, as opposed to being able properly to *exercise* that right. I therefore also disagree with H.L.A. Hart in maintaining that children lack the human right to be free.[52]

The capacity to make rational choices, although part of what I mean by a human being's being moral, hence of being morally entitled to treatment as a moral person, is a sufficient but not necessary condition for moral personhood. Treating a human being—normally an adult—as a moral person frequently involves treating her as capable of rational choices in the sense that is relevant here. But as I shall argue later, that is not always true.

Autonomy in the sense of being able to make rational choices, and so being able to act rationally, is only one of that term's several (often imprecise) philosophical uses. To respect an individual's autonomy in that sense (1) is to respect her right to make her own decisions and choices and to take responsibility for them and for the actions and foreseeable consequences that flow from them. It includes autonomy in Gerald Dworkin's understanding of it as "the capacity of individuals to critically reflect on and take responsibility for the kind of persons they want to be."[53] A fuller discussion of this and other uses or senses of "autonomy" is found in chapter 7.

If I am right in claiming that we have an equal human right to autonomy, respect for that right is part of what treating an individual as a moral person consists in.

In his definition of the "notion of the respect owed to all men," freed from the Kantian transcendental-based concept of a "moral agent," Bernard Williams maintains that in addition to the universal human characteristics of feeling pain and desiring affection, "there seems to be a characteristic which he calls 'a desire for self-respect'; . . . a certain human desire to be identified with what one is doing, to be able to realize purposes of one's own, and not to be the instrument of another's will unless one has willingly accepted such a role."[54]

If such a universal desire/need does exist, treating an individual as a moral person would include one's respecting her desire/need for self-respect. But an individual is self-respecting if and when she believes she has self-worth, which rests on the belief that she has achieved or is achieving something she values; consequently, that her life is meaningful.

Since we saw that the need/desire for meaningfulness is a combination of the basic needs for achievement and recognition, and sometimes also of the need for love and for belonging, the desire/need for self-respect involves these basic psychological-existential human needs.

Williams explains that "being regarded from the human point of view" means in part that "each man is owed an effort at identification: that he should not be regarded as the surface to which a certain label can be applied, but one should try to see the world (including the label) from his point of view."[55] This is a sound and significant notion and carries us beyond sheer respect for an individual's autonomy or integrity (1) (above) to (2) above, to what I call "consideration." Let us, therefore, turn to it.

The Right to Be Treated with Consideration

As I stated in chapter 5, treating someone with consideration in the present sense involves a wide variety of interrelated things: a certain cluster of attitudes toward, and corresponding ways of acting, thinking, and feeling, in relation to her. Perhaps I can explain what it is by describing what *not* treating someone with consideration involves; since that, unfortunately, is much more common than the opposite. An important part of not treating one with consideration is treating her as though she has no feelings at all—in fact, as incapable of feeling anything, particularly mental pain. Or as though her feelings, if she has any, are utterly worthless and matter not a whit. In fact, it involves treating her as though she has little or no worth; that she is "trash" or "dirt": meaning by that that her life as a whole—the sum total of what she has felt and experienced and done, strove for or aspired to, including her human relationships, attachments, and memories—add up to nothing. An even more extreme and more invidious form of not treating her as a moral person is denigrating and dismissing her culture or ethnic heritage.

This leads me to two final questions about consideration. First, whether we actually have a human right to be treated with consideration, as I have claimed; and second, what relation exists between being treated with consideration and the human right to equal opportunity.

That the answer to the first question is "yes" can be briefly seen as follows: the right to consideration, in our sense, is a moral protection of the "human" side of our nature, of our very humanity; and any threat to it is a threat to our very being as humans. Moral personhood, including the dimension of our personhood that consideration harks to, is an important value, requiring the protective norm of a human right. But that right must be an equal right since it is designed to protect a universal dimension of our being. The capacity to feel, the need or desire for self-respect, for a sense of self-worth, for a meaningful life, appears to characterize human beings in general.

In Part I of his *Man's Search for Meaning* Frankl sketches a graphic and poignant portrait of the brutalization, depersonalization, and dehumanization that millions of innocent Jews and other Nazi victims suffered during World War II. Slavery, including white slavery, pornography, and the sexual exploitation of children, are other paradigms of the most egregious type of depersonalization of human beings. Modern warfare, particularly saturation bombing, the massacre of civilians, ethnic cleansing, genocide, and nuclear war are other horrible examples.

Williams adds a dimension to "respect" that goes beyond the effort at identification. He writes

> There are forms of exploiting or degrading them [people] which . . . cannot be excluded merely by considering how the exploited or degraded men see the situation. For it is precisely a mark of extreme exploitation or degradation that those who suffer it do not see themselves differently from the way they are seen by the exploiters; either they do not see themselves as anything at all, or they acquiesce passively in the role for which they have been cast. Here we evidently need something more than the precept that one should respect and try to understand another man's consciousness of his activities; it is also that one may not suppress or destroy that consciousness.[56]

The importance of what Williams says in this passage can hardly be exaggerated. It has been endlessly illustrated and chronicled throughout history whenever men have conquered, colonized, or dominated other peoples, and whenever a dominant group has lorded it over, oppressed, or disenfranchised the majority or a minority.[57]

A great deal of morally right conduct consists precisely in treating people as moral persons; and a great deal of wrong conduct consists in treating them as less than moral persons, as nonpersons.

Consideration in our sense provides a rational basis for treating as moral persons the mentally handicapped, the insane, the comatose; those who either temporarily or permanently lack the capacity to make rational choices (the first part of the concept of a moral person, which physically and mentally normal individuals have) and so would not, on that condition, qualify, either temporarily or permanently, as moral persons. In other words, their lacking that capacity does not make them any less worthy of consideration in our sense than anyone else, hence, for being treated as moral persons. In fact, precisely because of their special needs and because of their special conditions, they are morally entitled, on grounds of distributive justice, to special consideration and greater solicitude than normal persons. But their entitlement to treatment as moral persons is no more, no less, than the entitlement of everyone else. Except perhaps in the case of those in a deep coma, they feel physical and mental pain and have qualitatively the same basic survival and social needs, and basically the same kinds of aspirations, interests, and desires as other human beings.[58] They also have, though often in a lesser degree, the human potential of normal people. The moral obligation to treat them as moral persons is of particular importance in their case because of the crucial role it can play in their recovery or rehabilitation: in the case of the insane and the comatose, in helping them regain, if possible, the capacity for rational choice they had lost; hence to being restored to moral personhood in the fuller sense. The essential fact that their inability to function as moral persons is not due to any loss of humanity (which only death can bring about) but to a severe medical condition, argues for continual vigilance on our part, to avoid wronging them by treating them as less than moral persons.

The Right to Equal Opportunity

I now turn to the final question of this chapter, which conerns the putative equal human right to equal opportunity. The justification for positing such a right is, I think, essentially this: treating someone with consideration either essentially (a) includes or (b) implies providing her with equal opportunities to realize her good. It also implies that these opportunities must be equal opportunities, insofar as the "human" dimension of the concept of treating someone as a moral person is found equally in all human beings. If I am right in claiming that we have a (an equal) human right to be treated with consideration, it follows that that right (a') includes, or (b') implies, the equal human right to equal opportunity. Stated from the standpoint of the correlative obligation, the obligation to treat people with consideration either includes or implies the obligation to give them opportunities equal to everyone else in order to satisfy their basic survival and social needs, and to realize their potential. I say "includes or implies" because both the concept of a moral person and the concept of an individual's being treated as a moral person must be firmed up before one of the two alternatives can be settled on. Which of the two alternatives it would be desirable to stipulate would depend on their logical implications. For example, Occam's razor would suggest that we define broadly the concept of a moral person; or to understand the human right to be treated as a moral person broadly enough to include the human right to equal opportunity. A consequence of the latter would be to acknowledge only one complex basic human right, consisting of two relatively specific human rights: the right to autonomy and the right to equal opportunity. On the other hand, the same desire for simplicity may perhaps lead to the overbroadening of the concept of a moral person. For the present, I shall stay with the weaker claim that the relation in question is one of logical implication. That claim rests on the fact that denying someone the opportunities to satisfy her basic needs and realize her potential would be the very opposite of consideration. But the consideration and concern owed her must be equal to the consideration and concern owed everyone else; and the opportunities owed to all as human beings must be equal opportunities.

In describing consideration in sense (2) above as a fundamental part of treating people as moral persons, I mentioned caring as importantly connected with consideration in that sense. Caring is also connected with consideration in sense (1), in its relation to individual autonomy. These connections, among others, bring together the key concepts of caring and human rights, which I shall now briefly discuss as a prelude to arguing that respect for everyone's equal human right to be treated as a moral person (together with all other general moral rights derivable from it together with the requisite additional premises) must be included in any adequate ethic of caring.

It is clear, I think, that consideration for another in sense (2) would naturally follow from caring: it would be odd for a mother, say, to claim that she cares for her children when she does not treat them with consideration in that sense; or for a friend not to treat her friend with consideration. If a "friend" and she does not treat her friend with consideration in that sense, we would describe her as a "bad friend" or as "not a good friend." In the latter cases, we attribute the lack of consideration to the "impurity" of the caring, due to our human tendency to possessiveness and self-centeredness and apart from our common psychological hangups. The same—and the same proviso—is, I think, true in relation to caring vis-à-vis the other's autonomy in the sense(s) described earlier. Because of the impurity of people's caring, we see much less actual consideration for the autonomy (and privacy) of those they may sincerely care about. Indeed, as we all know, love and caring themselves make it quite difficult for caring persons—e.g. parents and close relatives—not to interfere in the lives of their children and friends. At least in traditional cultures, parents and close relatives tend to think that they would be quite remiss, and feel downright guilty, if they did not "intervene" (unasked) in the personal affairs of their children or close relatives.

To sum up. Continuing the sketch of the ethic of caring begun in the previous chapter, this chapter focused on human rights in relation to that ethic, devoting the first part of the author's conception of these rights. It was claimed that we must acknowledge the existence of human rights as fundamental moral norms designed to defend and protect the individual's quest for the full satisfaction of her basic physical, psychological-existential, and social needs and interests, in pursuit of her welfare and happiness. The views of various contemporary personality psychologists were adduced to show the existence of certain basic, universal psychological needs, such as the need for love, for belonging, and for achievement—and perhaps, as Viktor Frankl maintains, a need as well to find meaning in our life. The individual's equal human right to be treated as a moral person was taken as fundamental, as including an equal right to be free and an equal right to treatment with consideration, and as either including or entailing a right to equal opportunity. Two opposed models of human rights, the "natural" model and Ronald Dworkin's "constructive" model, were next examined. The former was rejected as inadequate, and the latter was adopted with certain modifications.

Notes

1 Virginia Held is a notable exception. She holds that the ethics of the "public" and the "private" spheres, of "justice" and of "caring," can be harmonized, and employs the concept of rights to "unite" the two approaches. Similarly, Michael Stocker, Christina Hoff Sommers, and Thomas E. Hill, Jr. think that the two approaches are compatible and use various moral concepts to link the two approaches. See later.

2 The fact that the controversy started between psychologists, not moral philosophers, has tended to muddy the ethical waters and has caused a good deal of confusion in regard to the strictly normative ethical issues and the empirical psychological and pedagogical debates; sometimes steering the discussion away from the strictly philosophical-ethical issues. This is clearly seen in many of the articles in *WMT*.

3 In "Toward a Foundation for Human Rights," *Man and World*, 18 (1985), 219–240, and "The Human Right to Be Treated as a Person," *Journal of Value Inquiry*, 19 (1985), 183–195.

4 (Cambridge, MA, 1977).

5 Ibid., 188.

6 Ibid. Dworkin's whole sentence is "*is the 'right' thing for him to do*, or that he does no 'wrong' in doing it." If I am correct about the logical relation between having a right to do something in the stronger sense, in the case of *human rights,* and the rightness or wrongness of that (kind of) act, then the part of Dworkin's above phrase I have italicized obliterates the distinction between the weaker and the stronger sense. But the distinction does hold, as Dworkin defines it, in the case of special moral rights (see the text above).

   Dworkin's distinction between a stronger and a weaker sense of "a right" is similar to Robert Nozick's distinction in *Anarchy, State, and Utopia*, between a stronger and a weaker interpretation of "a right." There Nozick equates the latter with "a liberty." For instance, he claims that talk about "a right to punish" makes sense only in the sense of "a liberty to do it, which liberty others also may have" (New York, 1974).

7 Ibid., 188–189.

8 Note that the same is true of a moral right in the weaker sense, since it would also be right to interfere with someone's, e.g., doing something that it is not morally wrong for him to do. In other words, this does not mark a difference between the two senses of "a right." One *difference* between the two senses of "a right" is that, if someone has a right to do *X* in the weaker sense, *X* is either (morally, legally, etc.) right *or* neutral, neither right nor wrong. By contrast, if *Y* is what someone has a strong right to do, it is (morally, legally, etc.)

right, period. A more fundamental difference is that, stronger countervailing considerations would be needed to justifiably override the exercise of right Y, than to override the exercise of right X.

9   Dworkin's statement that someone may have the right to do something "that is the wrong thing for him to do," is ambiguous. It is correct only if by "right" is meant "legal right," not "moral right." If someone has a legal right to something, it would be clearly unlawful, legally wrong, to interfere with the right's proper exercise. But if that legal right is a morally unjust (e.g., discriminatory) right, it would be *morally right*, not wrong, to interfere with its exercise.

10 I think that to say that A has a right to Y in the weaker sense simply means, among other things, that A is free to do (have, etc.) Y. If, as it appears, Dworkin believes in negative freedom or liberty. his distinction between the stronger and the weaker sense of "a right" would follow. For in both types of cases a right would constitute a negative liberty. Since I reject a moral right to negative freedom except as necessitated by the effective (proper) exercise of a human right to positive freedom, my view conflicts with Dworkin's on rights.

11 (Oxford, 1989).

12 Ibid., 222–223.

13 Op. cit., 269.

14 Ibid., 92. See later.

15 Op. cit., 269.

16 (Cambridge, MA, 1977), 15.

17 *Ethics, Inventing Right and Wrong* (London, 1977), 36ff.

18 For a discussion of how not to derive "ought" from "is," in the case of institutions and practices, see my "Institutions, Practices, and Moral Rules," *Mind*, LXXXVI, no. 344 (October 1977): 479–496.

19 For some of the basic difficulties of ethical intuitionism, see, e.g., P. F. Strawson, "Ethical Intuitionism," *Readings in Ethical Theory*, Wilfrid Sellars and John Hospers, eds. (New York, 1952), 250–259.

20 Dworkin, op. cit., 160.

21 Ibid.

22 Ibid.

23 Ibid.

24 Ibid.

25 Ibid., 162.

26 Ibid., 155.

27   Ibid., 162.

28   Ibid.

29   Ibid., 155.

30   Ibid.

31   "Critical Study of *A Theory of Justice*," *Philosophical Quarterly*, 23, no. 9 (April 1973): 144–145.

32   Ibid., 146, and *passim*. In his review of *A Theory of Justice* Hare interprets Rawls as "advocating a kind of subjectivism, in the narrowest and most old-fashioned sense," (Hare, op. cit., 145; see also 146) and dismisses ethical intuitionism as "nearly always a form of disguised subjectivism" (ibid., 146). For instance, he argues that appeal to "intuition" boils down to the appeal to one's subjective beliefs or convictions: with the consequence that the "intuitions" are relativized. This is essentially correct, even if the relativity is societal or cultural and not individual, hence not subjective in the usual sense. With it the N-model's claim to the certainty of intuitions goes by the board. But Dworkin does not consider ethical intuitions on the C-model to be certain, in contrast to the claim of the advocate of the N-model. (Dworkin, op. cit., 162f.) Although Hare criticized ethical intuitionism in 1973 as "nearly always a form of disguised subjectivism," he later did appeal to ethical *intuitions* in his *Moral Thinking* (1981), in relation to his two-level theory. Ethical intuitions were appealed to in what he called the first, intuitive level of moral thinking. In that book the "relatively simple principles [which are used at the intuitive level]" (ibid., 39) are seen as nothing more than empirical generalizations from past experience. Where the principles conflict, critical thinking (the theory's second level) adjudicates between them in an "act-utilitarian" way (ibid., 43).

33   *Philosophical Forum* (DEKALB), 9 (March 1971): 3–38.

34   *Ibid.*, 6. Italics in original.

35   Ibid., 7. Italics in original.

36   I say *some*? because it can be plausibly argued that a society's stripping a criminal of *all* of his or her legal rights amounts to treating him or her as a thing: an argument that may have some force against capital punishment.

37   For a detailed description of what, I believe, constitutes treating an individual as a moral person, the reader is referred to my "The Human Right to Be Treated as a Person," *passim*.

38   See his "The Idea of Equality," *Justice and Equality*, Hugo A. Bedau, ed. (Englewood Cliffs, NJ, [1971]), 123–124.

39   As rights, human rights are, first, moral immunities or "a basis for justifying . . . [the right-holder] against, at least certain sorts of criticism for the things . . . [one] does, even when these are things which he would be properly criticized for doing in other circumstances or others would be properly criti-

cized for doing even in these circumstances. . . . Moreover, these others would often be criticizable for interfering or even for not helping with what he did, where such interference or help is appropriate" (Alan White, in Maurice Cranston, *What Are Human Rights?* [London, 1973], 14–15). This characterization is applicable to both negative and positive, or passive and active rights. "Protective norm,"used as an umbrella term for "protective norms and entitlements," covers both negative and positive rights: the latter being entitlements to do certain things and/or to expect (or demand) certain kinds of help from others, "where such interference or help is appropriate" (Ibid., 5). Some complex rights, for example, the human right to privacy and the right to autonomy in certain senses of the word, combine both passive and active, negative and positive rights-elements.

In "Moral Rights and Animals" (*Inquiry*, 22 [1970]): 23–24) White correctly argues against the view that only passive rights are rights and that "the so-called "active"rights are really only liberties" (e.g., G. L. Williams, "The Concept of Legal Liberty," *Columbia Law Review*, 56 (1956), 1129–1150). He also correctly argues against what he considers to be H. J. McCloskey's and others' one-sided concentration on "active rights."

Finally, a right is not a (valid) claim: claims and entitlements are distinct, and neither is identical with or entails a *title* to something. But one's having a justified or valid claim to something means one's being entitled to it, and vice versa. Thus, to have a valid claim to something is to be entitled to it.

40   In addition to the abovementioned, Maslow posits two other basic psychological needs: the need for self-actualization and the need for self-esteem. Both of these are largely social needs and depend on other people, e.g., their peers, valuing what one is and realizes. The need for self-actualization and the need for self-esteem—or for self-respect—are also posited by other personality psychologists.

41   The concept of need, which is "generally accepted by personality psychologists" (Bernard Weiner, *Theories of Motivation*, 23), is described by Weiner in relation to C.L. Hull's Drive Theory as follows: "Since a need, either actual or potential, usually precedes and accompanies the action of an organism, the need is often said to motivate or drive the associated activity. Because this motivation is characteristic of needs, they are regarded as producing primary animal *drives*. . . ." (Ibid.)

For the "generally accepted" definition of "need,"and regarding the entire discussion in this section, see my *TFHR* as well as *HRTP, passim.*

42   Op. cit., 176.

43   Ibid.

44   For example, David P. Ausubel writes in *Theory and Problems of Child Development* (New York, 1958), 341: "In discussing the ego development during early childhood we have . . . considered the importance of parental *affection* as part of a larger pattern of *acceptance* and *intrinsic valuation* necessary for satellization and the development of intrinsic feelings of *security* and *adequacy* [hence self-esteem or self-respect]" (italics in original).

45   *Operational Theories of Personality*, Arthur Burton, ed. (New York, 1974), 295.

46   Ibid.

47   Ibid., 153.

48   Ibid. See also 156 and 157 top, where Sullivan again speaks about self-respect and confidence, as well as a sense of belonging.

49   See, e.g., ibid., 230–231. For example, Rogers writes: "A tentative conclusion, which I have reached after years of experience with troubled individuals in psychotherapy is that man has an inherent tendency to develop all his capabilities in ways which serve to maintain or enhance his organism--the total person, mind and body. This is the single basic postulate of client-centered therapy." (Ibid., 214.)

50   Ibid., 314.

51   See also the rest of 156, and 157 top, for Sullivan's further remarks about the importance of a sense of belonging and of self-respect and confidence in one's capacities.

      In *A Theory of Justice* (pp. 440–446) John Rawls assigns an important place to the value of self-esteem or self-respect, "defined as [the] most important primary good" (index). On p. 440 he defines self-respect or self-esteem "as having two aspects. First of all, . . . it includes a person's sense of his own value, his secure conviction that his conception of his good, his plan of life, is worth carrying out. And second, self-respect implies a confidence in one's ability, so far as it is within one's power, to fulfill one's intentions."

52   "Are There Any Natural Rights?" op. cit., 14–25. If Hart is (or were) right, the insane, the mentally retarded, and the comatose would also lack the human right to be free.

53   "Paternalism: Some Second Thoughts," *Philosophy of Law*, Joel Feinberg and Hyman Gross, eds. (Belmont, CA, [1991]), 243. Dworkin correctly maintains that "There is nothing in the idea of autonomy which precludes a person from saying: I want to be the kind of person who acts at the command of others. I define myself as a slave and endorse those attitudes and preferences. My autonomy consists in being a slave."

      If this is coherent, and I think it is, one cannot argue against slavery on grounds of autonomy. The argument will have to appeal to the idea of what is "a fitting life for a person, and, thus, be a direct attempt to impose a conception of what is 'good' on another person." (Ibid., 244.)

      A partial answer to "What is a fitting life for a person?" I am proposing in this book, is: "Life as a good member of a good and moral community."

54   "The Idea of Equality," *Justice and Equality*, Hugo A. Bedau, ed. (Englewood Cliffs, NJ, [1971], 123. Italics in original. As we saw, this is what Williams calls integrity.

55   Ibid., 123–124.

56   Op. cit., 124.

57   The experience and writings of Franz Fanon and Kwame Nkrumah about this in relation to European colonialism in Africa, are telling examples. See, for example, Fanon's "Colonialism," and Nkrumah's "Philosophy and Ideology for Decolonization," *Philosophy for a New Generation*, 3rd printing, A.K. Bierman and James A. Gould, eds. (New York, 1970), 286–290, and 291–304, respectively.

58   The relation of these things to need as a canon of distributive justice is discussed in chapter 8.

Chapter 7

Human Rights and the
Ethic of Caring–II

In chapter 5, I maintained that the protective norms of human rights, together with adequate principles of fairness and justice, are essential for an adequate and comprehensive ethic of caring; that they add side constraints to and complement the central concept of caring. In this chapter I shall argue in support of that claim, in relation to human rights. In chapter 8 I shall argue in support of a similar claim about fairness and justice.

Some feminists reject outright the concept of human rights in relation to an ethic of caring; and one can think of reasons why the "protective norms" of human rights would be considered to be superfluous in relation to, if not in conflict with, a caring-based ethic. (1) One such reason might be that a caregiver would invariably treat the other as a moral person, respecting her freedom to shape her own life and destiny in her own way, as she desires. Indeed, that caring itself consists in, or includes, treating the other as a moral person. (2) A second possible reason is that caring may be thought to be incompatible with a putative human right to privacy in some sense or senses of that word; at least in the sense that the exercise of that putative right would always be a barrier to that closeness—e.g., to the solidarity and interdependence, and the empathy, between the self and the other—which is of the essence of a caring relationship. For instance, that acting independently of another, without regard to her needs, interests, etc., is sometimes tantamount to one's acting in opposition to her best interests. (3) A third and conceptually more fundamental and historically based reason is the view shared by many feminists that the norms of human rights are part and parcel of the so-called "ethic of rights and justice" or "male ethic": an ethic that some feminists view as the diametrical opposite of the feminist ethic of caring.[1] A basic assumption that they believe underlies the ethic of caring is (a) that the moral self or agent is partially defined by her attachments and important relationships to others, that it is an essentially relational self. Correlatively, (b) that the liberal Enlightenment and post-Enlightenment "ethic of rights and justice" presupposes an untenable nonrelational, "unembedded" conception of the moral self. Because of the importance of claim (b)—as well as Michael Sandel's analogous claim that the relational or "encumbered" conception of the moral self is a fundamental logical presupposition of the idea of a "constitutive community"—chapter 10 will be devoted to a detailed consideration of that subject. But as I noted in chapter 5, not all feminist moral philosophers think that the ethic of caring is incompatible with an ethic of rights and of justice.

I shall now present some reasons why I think that the protective norms of human rights are not only compatible with but necessary for an adequate ethic of caring.

I agree that, ideally speaking, caring would invariably include respect for the other's personhood, including her autonomy in sense 1. But as I stressed in earlier chapters, caring, like love and affection, is in reality almost always mixed with and sullied by, for example, one or more of the vices of self-centeredness, selfishness, possessiveness, aggressiveness, lust for power, and domination,[2] in addition to the fact that caring is naturally unequal and so needs to be "corrected" by universal egalitarian moral principles. Further, as reiterated in this book, caring is often limited in scope; although I believe that it ought to be a determining factor in individual, group, and institutional activities and relationships in the public spheres. I shall now spell out these and related reasons for these claims.

(1) First and perhaps most obviously, human rights are needed as moral protections against unfair discrimination and exploitation—in general, egregious unequal treatment—of targeted individuals and groups in the economic, social, political, educational, and other public areas because of color, race, ethnic background, gender, sexual orientation, or age. That is, in those areas where social, political, economic, or other kinds of gain or advantage, prestige and power, or self-aggrandizement—in short, not caring but naked self-interest—is often the primary, sometimes the consuming concern. For even in countries that can boast a modicum of democracy, those individuals, groups, or classes that hold the reins of power are frequently more

interested in furthering their own or their circle's or class's interests than in caring about the people and the country as a whole.

In fact, like their basic constitutional and other civil and legal rights in countries with a modicum of democracy, human rights are first and foremost rights against the state's overwhelming powers over the citizens. Worth noting in this connection is Ronald Dworkin's statement that "the concept of [moral, human] rights, and particularly the concept of [moral, human] rights against the Government, has its most natural use when a political society is divided, and appeals to co-operation or a common goal are pointless.[3] A little later Dworkin adds: "The debate [and I should add: increasingly all over the world] does not include the issue of whether citizens have *some* moral rights against their Government. It seems accepted on all sides that they do."[4]

Although they are perhaps more commonly used as defenses against a government's overweening power in the public domain, human rights are no less important as defenses against the government's intervention (or interference) in the private domain, in relation to various fundamental ethical issues of life and death that may face a family or household: issues that I strongly believe ought to be left to the decision of the individuals concerned. For example, whether the life of a terminally ill or deeply comatose family member should be painlessly ended, and, if so, whether assisted suicide or passive or active euthanasia would be best in the circumstances. Or whether to authorize a physician to terminate an encephalic newborn's life. It is clear that the Law would need to enact the necessary legal safeguards to prevent abuses. A good example is the recent legislation in the Netherlands concerning active euthanasia.

(2) Second, for women and minorities in general—and even for the majority in dictatorships and other authoritarian countries—to become economically, socially, and politically empowered and to gain equality or at least reduce inequality in these and other vital areas, it is absolutely essential that they gain the requisite *legal* and civil rights. A good example is a woman's legal right to abortion in the United States (subject to certain restrictions imposed by the United States Supreme Court in Roe v. Wade), which is usually grounded on a human right to privacy.

Like all other such rights, these legal rights serve as entitlements and defenses against the government as well as against individuals and public institutions. But, and this is the important point here, to make a valid case for the need for such rights, the historically discriminated against and disadvantaged need to present generally accepted or rationally defensible moral principles in their support. These principles would importantly include human rights. (Cf. the founding fathers' grounding of the United States Constitution on certain putative "natural" rights.)

(3) In addition to their use as defenses against government intervention in the private sphere, human rights have an important positive role in relation to the nuclear and extended family, relatives, colleagues and friends. I mean as counterbalances against the unequal nature of caring about, and consequent unequal treatment of, others who are biologically or otherwise at equal "distances" from the caregivers. Such unjustified "discrimination" may produce deep emotional scars or other ills in those discriminated against, unless their "discriminatory" treatment is offset, or the potential hurt is prevented, by equal respect for their legal and moral, including human, rights. For instance, in counterbalancing or offsetting the not uncommon partiality of parents toward some of their children, or the not uncommon partiality of children toward one parent, or some sibling or siblings. As we know, that kind of partiality tends to embitter the less-favored child or sibling, filling him or her with envy, jealousy, and resentment, unhealthy competitiveness, and even aggressiveness toward the unfair parent and the favored sibling or siblings.

In saying that the inequality of caring and concern *may* be morally unfair and unjustified, and that it may sometimes harm the less favored individuals, I am making provision for circumstances in which the inequality is not either psychologically harmful or morally unjustified. I am thinking, for example, of a bright child whose parents give her a good college education but at the cost of depriving her sibling of a college education, or of a good college education, provided that the "favoritism" is (say) due to (a) the former's academic superiority over her sibling and (b) the parents' inability to send both children to college, to the same good college, or to equally good colleges.

In these types of cases too, the protective norms of equal human rights, along with other rights, need to be acknowledged and appealed to in practice by families in relation to all their members, to avoid unfairness. These rights, and the legal and civil rights created in their light, are also needed for other reasons, some of which are also connected with love and caring themselves. They include:

(4) the familiar dangers of "*too much love and caring*," hence the temptation of the loving-caring person continually to interfere—albeit

from the noblest motives—in the other's life, threatening or undermining her ability to think, choose, and act as she wishes, to pursue, or to pursue in her own way, her well-being and happiness.

(5) The tendency to possessiveness on the part of those who love but not too wisely, is another, closely related phenomenon, although possessiveness is, of course, plentiful in the absence of love or caring. Part of what may cause an "excessively" loving person to meddle in the life of those she loves is precisely her viewing the other as "belonging"—and belonging exclusively—to her; as if the latter were her property. That is why we speak of such people as having a "propriety interest" in the other. Relatives or members of a family who have to take care of their old, bedridden, or handicapped relatives sometimes have the same propensity for meddling and possessiveness: with similar or worse consequences for the indigent person or the patient.

The human right to be free to seek our good entails that the tendencies described under (4) and (5) above, and the behavior they give rise to, violate the right to be free of those who are subjected to them. It is essential, therefore, that everyone acknowledge and do her utmost to respect that right in all others, always vigilant against any tendency to shackle and smother those she loves.

The awareness that all human beings, irrespective of gender, age, ethnic background, race, sexual orientation, color, or creed are entitled to equal consideration in the two senses distinguished in chapter 6 has fortunately increased among ordinary people the world over, not least in the third world. But the unfortunate fact remains that too many nations, including the advanced Western states, often only pay lip service to their citizens' human rights and to their pledge to abide by the principles of the UN's Universal Declaration of Human Rights. In their international dealings also, economic, political, strategic, or other so-called "national interest" considerations too often prevail over human rights and other moral considerations. A glaring example is the United States essentially brushing aside China's human rights abuses for commercial and political gain,[5] producing and selling to other nations weapons of torture,[6] and, at least until recently, instructing the military of various Latin American dictatorships in the use of weapons of torture.[7]

Although human rights, if properly guaranteed by law and safeguarded by the citizenry's continual vigilance and habitual conformity to them, can be a powerful moral shield and deterrent against the abuses noted above, they always remain at the mercy of the state's power structure. What then is the solution? Can we expect government, as well as the big companies and corporations, to care about people, or is that a contradiction in terms or a "counsel of perfection"? If it is not a contradiction in terms or a counsel of perfection, the countries of the world need to create an almost-ideal moral order, a fully democratic social, political, and economic system for such an enviable state of affairs to become a reality. What such a fully participatory democracy would be like—for example, whether it could be exemplified by a so-called representative democracy (assuming that that is not a contradiction in terms)—is obviously a very large and complex but vital theoretical and practical issue. Similarly, the question of how real concern for human rights may be extended to the entire world, both through and outside the United Nations, continues to be a burning issue, especially in the face of the recent ethnic cleansing and genocide in the former Yugoslavia, and in Rwanda and Burundi.[8]

Against these ideals must be placed the cold facts about the practical limits of people's caring about remote strangers, due to the barriers created by cultural differences and people's perceived social, political, economic, and/or national self-interest.

(8) Finally, the appeal to human rights is necessary whenever one's desire to act in what one perceives to be one's self-interest conflicts with one's duty, obligation, or desire to care about others in general, or about certain others. Circumstances sometimes make such conflicts inescapable, whether between spouses, parents and children, siblings, relatives, friends, partners, colleagues, superiors and subordinates, or employers and employees. When such conflicts arise the tendency of self-love to prevail over the other's best interests may be avoided or minimized if one is able to place one's duty/obligation to respect the other's human rights before one's self-interest. Though perhaps uncommon, such transcendence of self-interest is not impossible.

Autonomy and Privacy

Earlier in this chapter I used the word *autonomy* in relation to the individual's basic positive human right to be free (together with the limited but variable negative freedom its exercise requires). In that sense the human right to be free is a right to individual autonomy in sense 1. But moral philosophers employ "autonomy" in a variety of meanings or senses, or give the concept different interpretations. I shall now consider these meanings or interpretations in relation to human rights *vis-a-vis* caring, to ascertain whether any of them is incompatible with caring, as some feminist moral philosophers maintain. Finally, I shall consider the relation of "privacy" to autonomy in the relevant meanings, senses, and so on, of the latter term, to find out whether the human right to autonomy in any of them entails a human right to privacy in some sense.

A. Autonomy

In "On the Limits of Terrorism,"[9] Igor Primoratz distinguishes what he calls three interpretations of "autonomy" in describing the "principle of respect for persons." The three interpretations are:

(1) "the principle [of respect for persons] enjoins respect for the core of individuality of each and every person, a concern for seeing things from the point of view of the other person, in terms of his or her character or 'ground-project.'"[10]

(2) "On another interpretation, the principle demands that we recognize certain basic, 'human' rights of every human being, which safeguard a certain area of personal freedom: persons are to be respected as sources of rights."[11]

(3) "On still another interpretation, the principle prohibits using another person as a means only. The Kantian statement of the principle is not as clear as one would wish; but at a minimum, it requires that the other person be able to "share in the end" of my action, that is, to consent to it."[12]

In "The Importance of Autonomy,"[13] Thomas E. Hill isolates three putative ways in which "autonomy" is important. Since "'autonomy' means different things to different people," he wants "to focus upon three *senses*, or ideas, of autonomy and explain why, despite recent [feminist] critics, I still believe each of these ideas has an important place in an ideal conception of morality."[14] He adds: "Extravagant reactions to extravagant praise of autonomy, I fear, have put us in danger of overlooking some elementary points embedded in the autonomy-glorifying reaction [by liberal philosophers]. These points should be rather obvious and nonthreatening once they are disentangled from certain unnecessary accompaniments; and they are fully compatible with recognition of the moral importance of compassion."[15]

The senses Hill isolates are these:

(1) Autonomy as "impartiality in the review and justification of moral principles and values":

For present purposes, two points in this conception [which comes from Kant] are crucial. First, having autonomy means considering principles from a point of view that requires temporary detachment from the particular desires and aversions, loves and hates, that one happens to have; second, autonomy is an ideal feature of a person conceived in the role of a moral legislator, (i.e., a person reviewing various suggested moral principles and values, reflecting on how they may conflict and how they might be reconciled, and finally, deciding which principles are most acceptable, and whether and how they should be qualified.[16]

(2) "Autonomy as a right to make certain personal decisions":

The autonomy here is . . . a right that every responsible person has, a right to make certain decisions for himself or herself without undue interference from others. To respect someone as an autonomous person in this sense is to acknowledge that certain decisions are up to him or her and thus to refrain from efforts to control these decisions. It is a right to make otherwise morally permissible decisions about matters deeply affecting one's own life without interference by controlling threats and bribes, manipulations, and willful distortions of relevant information. Like other moral rights, this right of autonomy may be defeasible—or overridden in special circumstances; but it is nonetheless important.[17]

(3) "Autonomy as a goal for personal development": Taking his clue from the word "autonomy," which suggests "self-governance," Hill appears to suggest—since he does not make it explicit—that "autonomy" in this third sense means "self-governance," and involves "having a unified personality in general" as "a morally worthy goal." For instance, he says: "ideally autonomous, or self-governing, moral agents would respond to the real facts of the situation they face, not to a perception distorted by morally irrelevant needs and prejudices. The principles and values they try to express in their decisions would be genuine guiding considerations and not mere epiphenomena unrelated to their real moral motivation."[18]

Starting with Hill's putative first sense of "autonomy," it is certainly true that in responsible human beings, impartial, objective deliberation is a desirable trait in the moral sphere. It is, in fact, one sense of "rationality" as philosophers use that expression. But it is puzzling why Hill considers it a sense of "autonomy"; especially since it is only within the context of "the more extreme Kantian baggage that usually travels with these . . . [three senses of autonomy he wishes to explain] that it would be thought of as a way of someone's being autonomous."

In explaining the third putative sense of "autonomy" as "self-governance," as the goal of a unified personality, Hill states that "people are not self-governing, in a sense, when their responses to problems are blind, dictated by neurotic impulses of which they are unaware, shaped by prejudices at odds with the noble sentiments they think are moving them. When we make decisions like this we are divided against ourselves."[19] Thus, the goal of a unified personality is to try "to face important moral decisions with as few as possible of these self-fracturing obstacles."[20] This characterization, like Hill's characterization of the putative first sense of "autonomy," is a good description of a common sense of "rationality" we find in psychology and philosophy. Rationality in this, second, sense (sense 2) is psychologically necessary for rationality in the first sense (sense 1). A person divided upon herself in the sense Hill describes would be incapable of impartial or objective deliberation about moral principles. One who is *not* a slave to passion, prejudice, and the like can be said to be, psychologically, "internally" autonomous, the "captain" of her soul. In fact, this sense of "autonomy" is the internal counterpart of Hill's second sense, which is nothing other than the responsible person's freedom from interference from others in the form of physical pressure or coercion; i.e., so-called negative freedom. This sense of "autonomy" corresponds to or is included in Primoratz's second interpretation of "autonomy."

The next question is whether autonomy in Primoratz's three interpretations of "autonomy" and Hill's third sense of autonomy are compatible with caring.

B. Autonomy and Caring

Earlier I attempted to show that caring needs to be constrained by the other's human right to positive freedom or autonomy in sense 1, and so, assumed without evidence that the putative human right to autonomy in that sense is compatible with regard to both sense 1 of "autonomy" and Primoratz's three interpretations of the term.

(a) On Primoratz's first interpretation, autonomy is "concern for seeing things from the point of view of the other person." Concern, on this interpretation, is an important part of "consideration" as respect for others as moral persons. (For instance, respect for Bernard Williams' "ground-projects" or "commitments," essential to one's "sense of moral identity," to one's "integrity.") Here respect for the other's autonomy means (Primoratz says "enjoins") respect for her as a moral person.

(b) Primoratz's second interpretation, insofar as it includes safeguarding "a certain area of personal freedom" (our sense 1 of autonomy) as well as the recognition of everyone's human rights, is, once again, clearly compatible with caring.

(c) Primoratz's third interpretation of "autonomy,"shorn of the questionable Kantian idea that a person has (inestimable) "intrinsic" value, provides an additional sense (sense 2) of "autonomy." In that sense it includes being free to weigh and consider other people's actions without being constrained in her deliberations by others and being free to decide for herself whether or not to assent to the actions. Autonomy in this sense (and the moral responsibility it entails) is thus part of negative freedom. Compare the Kantian sense of autonomy that Sandel distinguishes in relation to Rawls in speaking of "the imperative to respect above all the autonomy of the individual, to regard the human person as the bearer of a dignity beyond the roles that he inhabits and the ends he may pursue."[21]

As noted earlier, positive freedom presupposes a non-sharply-demarcated area of negative freedom, varying in scope with the particular conditions for the exercise of positive freedom in concrete situations or circumstances, including the conditions for "voluntary exchanges" (Nozick) that are probably always necessary for the pursuit of one's self-actualization, welfare, and happiness. But the negative freedom involved in Primoratz's present sense of autonomy seems to be more extensive than the negative freedom to which I believe we have a conditioned human right. Similarly, with Hill's view that we have a (presumably human) right to negative freedom.

Primoratz's interpretation (2) of autonomy fails to distinguish positive and negative freedom, if, on that interpretation, autonomy consists in a more extensive negative freedom than the limited negative freedom necessitated by the individual's equal human right to positive freedom. In particular, if on that interpretation, autonomy is envisaged as "freedom to do as you please,"[22] in which case the need to acknowledge such a human right must be defended on other grounds than those I have adduced in the two articles on human rights summarized in chapter 5. In considering whether the human right of autonomy is compatible with caring, I shall consequently limit myself to positive freedom together with the negative freedom required for the exercise of positive freedom in different circumstances.

The negative freedom I am talking about cannot properly include or be identical with free choice, independent of the influence of the individual's wants, needs, passions, and desires, a radically free choice. Such a choice would be completely arbitrary, the kind of freedom Jean Paul Sartre envisages in *Being and Nothingness* and other philosophical writings of the period. But even he subsequently rejected the extreme conception of a person as "nothingness," and, with it, the absolute freedom that went with that view.[23]

C. Autonomy and Privacy

At the end of his article, Hill asks whether the third idea of autonomy he distinguishes is "compatible with compassion"—compassion being what some feminist moral philosophers appear to identify with "care." He then correctly answers his question thus:

> Of course, it is. Holding autonomy of this sort as an ideal is neutral in disputes about which is more important, compassion or respect for rights. What it tells us is merely that we should try to face moral decisions with integrity and self-awareness. Or, perhaps better, if it favors either side, the ideal of autonomy for particular moral decisions urges us to face such problems with [sic.] compassion: [really "with due care or concern"] for I suspect that without compassion one can never really become aware of the morally relevant facts in the situation one faces. The inner needs and feelings of others are virtually always relevant, and without compassion [substitute "empathy" for "compassion"] one can perhaps never fully know what these are—or give them their appropriate weights.[24]

Except for his rather idiosyncratic use of "compassion," Hill's remarks are well taken; as well as (but substituting "two" for "three") his general conclusion that:

> There are at least three modest but important ways that autonomy is needed in a complete conception of morality. None is incompatible with recognition of the importance of compassion; and, though one ideal of autonomy puts some constraints on the reliance on compassion alone, another ideal of autonomy itself seems to require compassion. If, as Carol Gilligan's work suggests, autonomy represents a male value and compassion a female value, then my conclusion is that we must get the sexes together.[25]

Even cursory, everyday observation of people in different cultures tends to show that Gilligan's male/female dichotomy is a distortion and oversimplification of the facts and is ultimately untenable. At best, ours and Hill's second sense of autonomy is a largely modern Western philosophical and cultural phenomenon, associated with the Enlightenment and the post-Enlightenment period, not predominantly (let alone wholly) a "male value" in world history or even Western history as a whole. Similarly, it is doubtful whether women have ever had a monopoly or near-monopoly on compassion—on caring in general—in the West or the world as a whole.

Given the right to autonomy in our sense and in Hill's second sense, a caring act must generally be consensual in order to be morally justifiable. Advising, persuading, cajoling, or working to convince someone—or extracting personal information from her—without her tacit or explicit consent, normally violates her human right to privacy and may also violate her right to autonomy in our sense. (Hill's third sense of "autonomy" would not be involved here.) The issue is complex and has many ramifications. One example is the issue of confidentiality in the private and public spheres. In the discussion of privacy in chapter 2 we saw that the confidentiality of personal or other private information is an essential part of privacy. Since we are concerned with privacy and autonomy in relation to caring, I will limit myself to the private sphere.[26]

In the private sphere the "consent rule" obviously needs to be qualified or modified in relation to caring; taking into consideration the nature of the personal relationship involved and the age and emotional and mental state of the subject of caring. As far as the family is concerned, I believe that at least certain forms of parental caring and concerned nonconsensual intervention on behalf of a teenage child (the issue of consent does not arise in relation to younger children) do not violate her autonomy or privacy. Giving advice is one example. In fact, the parent's moral and other responsibilities and obligations toward the minor child's nurture and care arguably give the parent the correlative moral right to intervene whenever, in light of the available facts, a parent rationally deems it in the child's best interests to do so. For example, if the parent discovers that the teenager is using drugs. But physical or mental pressure in the form of bribes, threats, and, above all, physical or mental punishment, violate the teenager's entitlement to exercise his or her right to autonomy, within the limits imposed on it by the parent's correlative rights/obligations toward him or her.

In the absence of consent, a parent's reading her adult child's private mail or diaries, or attempting to extract information about her private life, would violate her privacy and may also violate her autonomy in our sense.

In the preceding, I coupled the right to autonomy and the putative right to privacy. But going back to the characterization of privacy in Part 1, chapter 2, what is the precise relation between (1) privacy and autonomy and (2) the reasons for believing that we need to acknowledge a human right to privacy in addition to a human right to autonomy? For instance, is privacy a special part or form of autonomy? Or if the two are distinct, does the human right to autonomy entail a human right to privacy? Finally, (3) how are autonomy and privacy compatible with caring?

The relation between privacy and autonomy is quite complex, like the relation between the putative human right to privacy and the human right to autonomy in our sense. As I claimed in chapter 2, privacy consists of both mental and physical privacy. Ideal or total as opposed to actual, partial autonomy would consist, first, in one's having the freedom to do whatever one wishes with one's body, limited only by respect for one's other human and special moral rights and consequentialist moral principles.[27] Physical privacy in this sense is an important form of autonomy in our sense. Positively, it consists in freedom to use one's body—always with the proviso I noted—in pursuit of self-actualization, wellbeing, and happiness. Negatively, physical privacy means the absence of interference by others in matters pertaining to one's use or treatment of one's body. The ability to provide or to withhold private information about one's physical state or condition and about one's inner life, as one chooses, is sometimes desirable, even necessary, for the proper exercise of one's positive freedom.

D. The Right to Autonomy and the Right to Privacy

Caring and the right to privacy. It should be remembered at the outset that all rights must be sparingly and judiciously exercised. Parsimony in the exercise of rights is especially important in close personal relationships. The wise caring person would especially avoid standing on her right to autonomy or privacy. Fortunately, the need or temptation to insist on these or other rights would rarely arise in truly loving, caring relationships. On the contrary, the free sharing of one's inner life with those one loves is an expression and measure of closeness, even in cultures that set great store by privacy; since we are basically social animals and have a natural need to express our deepest and most important feelings, thoughts, fears, and concerns, and to communicate them to a kindred spirit—even to a pet or plant. More than any other, the relationships of spouses and lovers can scarcely be sustained for long in the absence of openness, trust, and sharing.

It would be clearly unwise to bare all if it is likely to jeopardize a relationship. That does not mean lying to keep certain facts about oneself private. It only means not disclosing information that may stunt, damage, or end the relationship. But every loving, caring person must always carefully weigh the likely consequences of revealing particular facts about himself or herself against the likely consequences of not revealing them. The Golden Mean depends crucially on the particular relationship and the personality and life history of the parties as they know them. In general, prudence guided by knowledge of human nature, and the strength of the love and caring, should carefully dictate the degree of openness, and continually readjust it to the varying strength of the dynamic relationship.

Like different cultures, different individuals and families show different degrees of tolerance for the curious eyes of others; and some individuals and families tend to be secretive about matters that others would not at all hold close to their chests.

To highlight the central thesis of this chapter and a central thesis of this book about the indispensability of human rights for an adequate ethic of caring, I shall conclude with some observations about certain aspects of the moral problems relating to abortion and pregnancy. Some feminist moral philosophers dismiss the traditional rights approach out of hand, while other feminist philosophers contend that that approach is insufficient to resolve the moral dilemmas connected with abortion. I, on the other hand, will argue that these moral issues, rather than showing the uselessness of the human rights approach, demonstrate the need for an adequate theory of human rights as an integral part of a comprehensive care-centered ethical theory.

The feminist view that the human rights approach is insufficient to resolve the moral dilemmas of abortion is well summarized by the editors of *Women and Moral Theory*, in these words: "The view that a morality of rights is insufficient to moral issues that concern women, particularly those of pregnancy and abortion, has been anticipated [in a number of collections of feminist philosophy] by a number of feminist philosophers who presage morality of care."[28] Again, in "Moral Passages," Kathryn Pyne Adelson writes: "The 'classical' philosophical analysis of the moral problem of abortion is to treat it as a conflict of rights: the fetal right to life in conflict with the woman's right to decide what happens in and to her own body. . . . If one decides that fetuses are not persons, morally speaking, then abortion becomes a practical decision, not a moral one."[29]

Significantly,[30] in describing what she calls the "classical philosophical" "conflict of rights" approach, Addelson ignores the utilitarian and other consequentialist approaches to the dilemmas; but by ignoring fundamental aspects of them, even her and the other feminists' discussion of the rights approach, grossly oversimplifies if not caricatures it and the "conflicts" involved.

It is obvious that the rights approach alone does face an impasse whenever pregnancy threatens the mother's life and the fetus is at the stage at which it becomes a moral person and acquires a human right to life equal to the mother's human right to free choice and to life (i.e., at conception, viability, birth, etc., as the case may be). At that stage that approach fails to resolve the moral and human dilemma of whether the mother's or the fetus' life ought to be saved. Only if personhood is assumed to begin at (say) (a) viability, or (b) birth, would the rights approach be importantly relevant to the morality of abortion *prior* to (a) or (b). For then the mother's human rights to life and to free choice would outweigh whatever (nonhuman) moral rights the fertilized ovum or the nonviable/unborn fetus would have. It remains, however, that a pregnant women is morally responsible for being pregnant if she had voluntarily indulged in intercourse, even if she and her partner had taken all available precautions to prevent pregnancy; given that it is common knowledge that no birth control methods are foolproof. Consequently, her reasons for deciding to abort must be morally very strong to override her responsibility to carry the pregnancy to term (see note 32). For example, if the pregnancy threatens her life or if the fetus is very severely handicapped, physically or mentally; above all, if it has no chance of surviving after birth (e.g., if it is encephalic). In these instances, in addition to human rights considerations, the nature of the woman's motives (hence the degree of her caring about the fetus, about herself, and about the members of her immediate family, her spouse or lover, and her children, if any) and the fetus' own fate and future if the pregnancy is carried to term, all become morally important.

I shall return to these matters later. But first, some main feminist criticisms of the putative "conflict of rights" approach.

(1) Reporting on Beverly Harrison's view, Addelson writes that

> She says that the conflict of rights analysis does not take women seriously as moral agents. (Harrison 1984) One major reason is that the "classic" philosophical approach takes abortion as a "discrete deed" to be decided on in abstraction from the circumstances in which women make their procreative

choices. . . . She is saying that procreation must be considered as part of the good life of women, children, and the community as a whole. . . . Women do not simply decide to abort or not to abort. Harrison is saying that we should see women's moral choice as making, at every moment, the choice to go on with the pregnancy, and after it, at every moment to rear the child. That is what procreative choice is about.[31]

(a) Seeing women's moral choice as Harrison describes it is undoubtedly necessary; and it is true that (b) nonfeminist philosophical writings tend to take abortion as a "discrete deed."[32] But I do not see how the conflict of rights analysis fails to take women seriously as moral agents; how a serious consideration of (a) above would materially affect the validity or invalidity of approaching the problem in terms of the relevant human rights: if, to begin with, one subscribes to the idea that moral persons have a human right to life and that women—and human beings in general—have a human right to make free choices and decisions as part of their human right to be free. According to Addelson, Harrison does accept a rights analysis, "but modified, and put in its proper place."[33] But Addelson does not tell us *how* a rights analysis is to be modified "and put in its proper place" in order to succeed in resolving, or helping to resolve, the abortion dilemma.

(2) Caroline Whitlock argues that "neglect of matters that cannot be adequately expressed in terms of 'rights' and the employment of an atomistic model of people (a model that represents moral relationships as incidental to being a person) confuses many moral issues, but especially those concerning pregnancy, childbirth, and infant care."[34] The alternative ethics of responsibility she offers is "one in which women take responsibility for the circumstances within which they make procreative choices."[35] Such responsibility is certainly of the utmost moral and practical importance; for instance, in terms of the implications and consequences of the pregnant woman's decision whether or not to have an abortion, and, in the latter case, whether to keep the child or put him or her up for adoption, as well as whether or not to have other children. And so on. However, since Whitbeck, like Harrison, accepts a (partial) rights analysis, the question becomes once again (a) how the relational conception of a moral person (which I accept[36]), and (b) how consideration of the "larger context" in which the moral situation alone can be adequately understood,[37] would in fact help deal with the issues. The moral relationship between mother and fetus is certainly of great moment for her decision-making process; since aborting the fetus would mean severing a profound bond

between the fetus and her, and a profound moral and existential change in her very being as a person—indeed, a decided loss to her as a person-woman, if not a considerable impoverishment of it as well. These considerations are morally and existentially important for a pregnant woman's decision process, and part of the "larger context" that should be taken into serious account. Still, as far as I can see, they do not materially affect the *rights* that come into play, or their putative conflict: either the fetus' right to life (at the stage or stages in which it has a human right to life) outweighs the mother's right to free choice and to life, or the opposite.[38]

A woman's love for, and care about, the fetus she is carrying, if she does love and care about it, is unquestionably a very important part of the larger moral and human context involved (which includes her caring for her spouse or lover, and for her children, if any), and can play a decisive role in her decision to abort or to keep the fetus, if it is found to be severely handicapped. For instance, that very love and caring can lead her to abort the fetus precisely to save it, herself, and her family from a life of suffering and pain. Or it may make her decide to carry the fetus to term and to dedicate her life to taking care of him or her. But here the future child's *positive* right to life, his or her right to a modicum of well-being, becomes important. For if the child is doomed to a life of grave physical or mental disability, and so would be deprived of any chance for happiness and self-actualization, it would be selfish and wrong in my view to bring him or her into the world, however much love and caring the mother may be able to lavish on him or her.

Consider again the situation in which, prior to the fetus' becoming viable, a pregnancy seriously threatens the mother's physical or mental health, or even life; or when the pregnancy is the result of rape or incest. In the former case, it can be plausibly argued that the value of the mother's life outweighs the evil of the fetus' death, that it would be, therefore, morally permissible to abort the fetus.[39] In the former case, the morally right course of action would most likely be, in my view, for the woman to carry the pregnancy to term but put up the child for adoption, to spare it a life devoid of a loving and nurturing parent-child relationship. In the case of incest, the termination of the pregnancy may be the most compassionate course of action, if the evidence (e.g., through amniosynthesis) shows that the child's genetic makeup would prevent it from leading anything like a normal life, physically or mentally.

Finally, anticipating the discussion of the place of human rights in a moral community in chapter 10, it might be thought that my claim that what is dispensable in caring relationships is not the rights to autonomy and privacy themselves but undue insistence on them, is untenable; that in a good and moral community imbued with caring, the protective norms of human rights in general—or, at least, the rights to autonomy and privacy—would be superfluous. To that criticism, I shall respond in chapter 10.

To sum up. This chapter continued the elaboration of the fundamentals of a comprehensive ethic of caring begun in the previous chapter, by attempting to ascertain the proper place of human rights in that ethic. Since some feminist moral philosophers reject outright the concept of human rights in relation to an ethic of care, the first part of the chapter provided a number of important reasons why the protective norms of human rights are not only compatible with but necessary for an adequate ethic of caring.

Since two putative rights were singled our for special consideration, viz, the putative rights to autonomy and privacy, the discussion opened with an analysis of various proposed senses or interpretations of autonomy. Three interpretations distinguished by Igor Primoratz, and three putative senses of the term (or three ways in which autonomy, he thinks, occupies an important place in an "ideal conception of morality"), isolated by Thomas E. Hill, Jr., were analyzed. Examination revealed that in its putative first sense, viz, "impartiality in the review and justification of moral principles and values," "autonomy," which Hill defines as "impartiality in the review and justification of moral principles and values," is nothing but "rationality," in one of the term's philosophical uses. As for his second sense, namely, "autonomy as a right to make certain personal decisions," examination showed that it essentially corresponds to, or is included in, Primoratz's second interpretation of "autonomy," namely, the demand that "we recognize certain basic, 'human' rights of every human being . . . persons are to be respected as sources of rights." Finally, that Hill's third sense—"autonomy as 'self-governance,' as the goal of a unified personality"—is identical with a second philosophical/psychological sense of "rationality," and is the internal counterpart of his second sense.

Based on the analysis of autonomy, it was then argued that, contrary to the view of some feminist moral philosophers, Primoratz's three interpretations and Hill's third sense of "autonomy" are perfectly compatible with caring.

The chapter next explored the relation between (1) autonomy and privacy, and (2) the right to autonomy and the right to privacy. With regard to (1), it was maintained that, given the right to autonomy in the present author's and in Hill's second sense, a caring act, to be morally justifiable, must be, generally speaking, consensual. In the private sphere, the "consent rule" needs to be qualified or modified in relation to caring, taking into consideration the nature of the personal relationships involved (e.g., in the case of the family), and the age and emotional and mental state of the subjects of caring. In general, the precise relation between autonomy and mental and physical privacy was found to be quite complex. With regard to (2), it was noted that, as with all other rights, parsimony in the exercise of one's right to autonomy or to privacy is especially important in close personal relationships, but that the need or temptation to insist on them would rarely arise in truly loving, caring relationships. Still, like different cultures, different individuals and families show different degrees of tolerance for the curious eyes of others.

To highlight the central thesis of the chapter and a central thesis of the book about the indispensability of human rights for an adequate, comprehensive ethic of caring, the chapter concluded with some observations about certain aspects of the moral problems relating to abortion and pregnancy. It was argued that these moral issues, rather than showing the uselessness of the human rights approach, demonstrate the need for an adequate theory of human rights as an integral part of a care-centered theory.

Notes

1   Carol Gilligan herself speaks of them as different "perspectives" and hopes that they may be somehow reconciled.

2   Note that aggressiveness and lust for domination are widely attributed by feminists to the male of the species. See, for example, Nancy C.M. Hartsock, "Gender and Sexuality: Masculinity, Violence, and Domination," and Roger S. Gottlieb, "Masculine Identity and the Desire for War: A Study in the Sickness of Power," *Rethinking Power*, Thomas E. Wartenberg, ed. (Albany, NY, [1992]), 249–276, and 277–288, respectively. But the proposition that the male is "from Mars," is (naturally?) prone to aggression, violence, and lust for "power *over*" others as opposed to the female's desire for "power *to*," is a tremendously sweeping generalization. It ignores such things as the fact that throughout history vast numbers of males have been peaceful and peace-loving, as well as loving and caring; as parents, husbands, friends, and/or as humanitarians or saints.

3   *Taking Rights Seriously*, 184. The view expressed here is reminiscent of Sandel's view in *Liberalism and the Limits of Justice* in relation to justice, critically considered in chapter 12 of this book.

4   Ibid.

5   See, for example, the article "Farewell My Trade Status," *Time* (March 21, 1994): 47–48, regarding the collision course between the U.S. and China concerning the latter's human rights' abuses.

6   Amnesty International Report, summer 1996.

7   *The Milwaukee Journal-Sentinel* (September 22, 1996).

8   The United Nations' attempt at peace-making in Somalia temporarily broadened its de facto scope of activities beyond its traditional peace-keeping mandate, and may continue in the future whenever gross violations of the human rights of entire peoples or, perhaps, even large minorities, occur in a "sovereign" country. Although the United Nations' attempt at peace-making in Somalia failed, the *de jure* broadening of its activities may turn out to be salutary. Indeed, I hope that sooner rather than later the member states would vote to broaden the UN Charter by giving it the de jure mandate to continue to do so, albeit cautiously and judiciously.

9   Shaping Revolution, ed., Espeth Attwooll (Aberdeen, Scotland, 1991).

10 Ibid., 202–203.

11 Ibid., 203.

12 Ibid., 204. In a footnote, Primoratz refers to H. J. Paton, *The Moral Law: Kant's Groundwork of the Metaphysics of Morals* (London, 1972), 92.

13 *WMT*, 129-138.

14 Ibid., 130.

15 Ibid. Like many feminist moral philosophers, Hill employs "compassion" more broadly than in everyday usage. I myself would prefer to use "caring" instead, which in ordinary discourse is broader than compassion. Compassion is an important expression of caring whenever misfortune, tragedy, or other problems human flesh is heir to, afflict someone one cares about.

16 Ibid., 131.

17 Ibid., 134.

18 Ibid., 137.

19 Ibid., 136.

20 Ibid., 136-137.

21 Michael Sandel, *Liberalism and the Limits of Justice* (Cambridge, 1982), 20. Cf. also the "ideal of autonomy" that, according to Rawls, his social contract in *A Theory of Justice* realizes. For an extended discussion of Kant's conception of autonomy, see Sandel, op. cit., 6ff.

22 Note that, by definition, the putative exercise of the right to [positive or negative] freedom must not violate any relevant ethical principles or imperatives if it is to be a proper exercise of the right. This is no less true of so-called "freedom of indifference" or "doing as (or what) one pleases."

23 See, for example, Jonathan Grover, *The Philosophy and Psychology of Personal Identity* (London, 1988), 135, and William Alston and George Nakhnikian, eds., *Readings in Twentieth Century Philosophy* (New York, 1963), 176. Nakhnikian writes: "According to a recent report, Sartre would probably no longer propose his thesis of radical freedom." And so on to the end of the paragraph.

24 Op. cit., 137.

25 Ibid.

26 The confidentiality of patients' medical records is one among a number of important issues in medical ethics. For a discussion of that issue, see, for example, Sandra E. Marshall, "Public Bodies, Private Selves," in *Applied Philosophy, Morals and Metaphysics in Contemporary Debate*, Brenda Almond and Donald Hill, eds. (London, 1991), 260-271. The concepts of "permission" and "informed consent" are also crucial in both medical ethics and in law: for instance, in relation to passive and active euthanasia, assisted suicide, etc.

27   For example, I would draw the line at self-mutilation (in some cases, until death occurred), which some would-be artists in the United States practiced some time ago as an alleged form of art.

       Some champions of a right to privacy, e.g., in defending a woman's right to choose to have an abortion, speak of a person's owning her body. An example is Judith Thomson's classic "A Defense of Abortion," *Morality in Practice*, James Sterba, ed. (Belmont, CA, 1984), 126–134. But that is an error. It is a misuse of the concept of ownership—or a bad metaphor. One's body is not something one owns, like one's clothes, furniture, or house. One's body is part of the whole of oneself, of what one is as a person.

28   Introduction, 9.

29   Ibid., 89.

30   Since feminist moral philosophers reject utilitarianism, along with a rights and justice approach.

31   Addelson, ibid., 89–90. In summarizing her view at the end of her article, Addelson writes: "They [Harrison and Whitlock] are right in saying that the conflict of rights analysis tears abortion out of the context of women's lives. In fact, the moral passages approach [to which she devotes her article] shows how the conflict of rights analysis tears abortion out of the context of women's, children's, and men's lives." (ibid., 107.)

32   Judith Thomson's famous article is I think a good example.

33   Addelson, ibid., 90.

34   Ibid. For the relational conception of persons, see chapter 9.

35   Ibid.

36   See chapter 9.

37   Addelson, ibid.

38   For the sake of simplicity, I am ignoring questions about the *precise* nature and scope of that right, or the circumstances under which its exercise, e.g., in the case of a pregnancy, is morally permissible. For instance, I personally reject the extreme view that a woman has the moral right to abort a fetus for just about *any* reason, e.g., to give the stock example—because she wants to be able to wear a bikini at the beach.

39   Compare the position of the Catholic Church on this issue, as it involves appeal to the principle of double effect. But see my "Is the Principle of Double Effect Morally Acceptable?" (*International Philosophical Quarterly*, XXVIII, no. 1, 109 (1988): 21–30), and *The Morality of Terrorism* (New York, 1998), for a detailed criticism of that principle.

Chapter 8

Justice and the Ethic of Caring

As will be recalled, chapters 6 and 7 attempted to show the place of the protective norms of human rights in a comprehensive caring-centered ethic. In this chapter I shall attempt to do the same with respect to fairness and justice. Section I will prepare the ground for it by an overview of the nature of fairness and justice and will attempt to show that justice, conceived in a certain way, is compatible with individual discretion in a broad sense of this phrase. It will also describe some important ways in which "individual discretion" plays important roles in moral/legal cases or situations. In Section I, I shall argue for the need for the protective norms of fairness and of justice in a care-centered ethic and will provide an account of the role(s) of these norms in that ethic.

I
What Is Justice?

Tom Campbell and others on Justice as Desert

Under the continuing influence of Plato's famous conception of justice as giving each person her due, the various theories of justice in Western philosophy appear to take for granted that justice is an "essentialist" concept. To give a few examples, John Rawls sees social or distributive justice as defining "the appropriate distribution of the benefits and burdens of social co-operation." Commenting on that view, Tom Campbell writes: "In this context, the concept of justice means 'a proper balance between competing claims,' while a conception of justice is a 'set of related principles for identifying the relevant considerations which determine this balance.'" Following Plato, D. Miller states that "'the just state of affairs is that in which each individual has exactly those benefits and burdens which are due to him.'"[1] But Miller "goes on to say that 'the important questions about justice emerge when we try to settle what a person's "due" actually means.'"[2] Other examples are Kai Nielsen's view of justice as equality[3] and James Sterba's view that justice consists in desert.[4]

Although Michael Walzer too (in Campbell's words) holds that "justice has to do with the distribution of goods," he goes on to say that

> Different considerations apply according to the type of goods in question, so that it is wrong to look for one criterion (or set of criteria) which covers the distribution of such disparate goals as social security, money, offices, work, leisure, education, love, religion and political power.[5]

The existence of different criteria for justice in relation to different goals, *may* mean that Walzer thinks of justice as a nonessentialist, "family resemblance" concept—or perhaps better, a "family of concepts," particularly as he holds that "there are different spheres of justice which ought to be kept distinct."[6]

Campbell finds Walzer's thesis regarding spheres of justice persuasive, as also his view that

> The tendency to erect a comprehensive and unitary set of principles of justice reinforces the politically and morally unfortunate practice of cumulating the inequalities which may arise legitimately in the distribution of particular spheres of good. Through the encouragement of the assumption that the good reasons for having inequalities in one sphere are also good reasons for inequalities in all spheres, the resultant distribution of wealth, political power and educational opportunity, for example, tend to coalesce around the same individuals and groups.[7]

And so on in the same vein. But under the clear pull of essentialism or quasi-essentialism, Campbell significantly responds.

> Notwithstanding the attractions of this thesis it is a part of the second (critical) level of presentation adopted here that a theory of justice should be able to identify common features which explain how we are able to speak of justice and injustice in such diverse spheres as taxation, liability in tort and equality of opportunity in education.[8]

Campbell finds the thesis that a "cardinal feature" of justice is desert plausible[9]; but in his detailed evaluation of "an impressive recent work by Wojciech Sadurski . . . [who "develops a largely desert-based analysis of justice which covers both legal and social justice"]," he finds important problems with, as well as certain strengths, in the desert theory.[10] Ultimately, on his second, critical level, in which he views

justice as "a specific rather than an all-encompassing social and political value,"[11] he does adopt what he calls "the meritorian analysis."
According to it,

> There is an essential connection between justice and desert, first in the broad
> sense that justice in all its aspects has to do with treating persons equally as
> responsible agents, normally entails dealing with people in accordance with
> their deserts . . . .The meritorian analysis is that the concept of justice is
> treatment in accordance with desert, while differing conceptions of justice
> have to do with what counts as desert. This develops into the general conten-
> tion that a just state of affairs is one which accurately reflects the equal worth
> and unequal worthiness of responsible agents.[12]

But, *pace* Campbell and other advocates of the meritorian analysis
of justice in general, *desert* is a narrower concept than *justice in
general*, and is specifically applied whenever (1) honors, awards, rewards, punishment, and other penalties are *merited* by individuals or
groups, institutions, and so on, *by virtue of what they do or refrain
from doing*, and of their intentions or motives; and whenever (2) some
individuals or groups (e.g., children, the poor, ill, and elderly) have
special needs which render them deserving of society's economic,
educational, and other forms of special treatment or support. Thus,
need, in my view, is a main canon or criterion of substantive—distributive—justice.[13]

In distinguishing desert from justice in general, I am, more precisely, distinguishing it from *formal justice*, that is, from justice in
general, in its purely formal general aspect. For later in this chapter I
shall argue, first, that desert is the primary defining feature of social
justice—or "distributive justice" in the broad sense, in which it includes
retributive and compensatory justice as well as distributive justice in
this term's usual meaning; and, second, that (second order) *impartiality* constitutes the other—secondary—aspect or feature of social
justice in the broad sense.

Merit is closely related to desert, being a species of it. The relation
between the two, as well as the relation between desert and justice in
general, can be seen by noting the close connection between merit
and what is said to be "one's due."

Like "merit" and "desert," which, as species and genus differ in
certain of their employments, the closely related concepts of "desert"
and "entitlement" also differ in some of their employments. For instance, one may be entitled to something "X," in the sense of having
a right to "X," but not in the sense of deserving "X." As a human

being, an individual is entitled/has the human right, to treatment with respect.

An important difference between justice in general and desert is that it would be ordinarily odd to speak of a human being as *deserving* such-and-such treatment simply because she is a human being. In contrast to that, justice in general applies to people *simply as human beings or persons* (Campbell says "as responsible agents").[14] Campbell's linking of desert to the putative "equal worth . . . of responsible agents," is the Kantian metaphysical-axiological underpinning of his second-level, desert-justice reconstruction, enabling him to make "desert" a cardinal feature of "justice": a Kantian view that, as I observed in earlier parts of this book, I found difficult to make sense of or accept. I mean the claim that (human) persons have "worth" simply as rational beings—for Kant himself, as moral legislators, as "members of the kingdom of ends." My inability to make sense of or accept Kant's claim that human beings have worth simply as rational beings was a main reason for my attempt to ground human rights not on any metaphysical-axiological grounds, but on human nature as we, at present, empirically but admittedly very imperfectly, know it.

All human beings, as such, are morally entitled to justice in general,[15] and one's acting justly toward other human beings is a very important way of acting rightly in relation to them. This follows from my belief that all human beings have a moral right to justice, to just treatment: a right entailed by their basic human right to be treated as persons in our special sense. More precisely, what human beings have as persons is (an equal) moral right to just social, economic, political, and legal systems with just institutions and practices. Correlatively, all human beings who possess the capacity for acting justly have a moral obligation to do so toward all others (see chapter 12).

The moral right of all human beings to justice in general includes their right to certain special societal burdens and/or benefits whenever they satisfy certain conditions that render them deserving. The general right to just treatment provides one important link between desert and justice in general, but justice in general must not therefore be identified with desert or with merit. It would be odd to speak of our entitlement to justice in general, as our "deserving" or "meriting" justice simply as human beings or persons, inasmuch as we deserve something or other not simply as human beings but by virtue of what we do or refrain from doing, and by virtue of our intentions and motives.

If I am right that, *pace* Campbell, the concept of justice is not to be identified with treatment in accordance with desert, in the everyday meanings of "justice" and "desert"—i.e., on what can be considered, at least by extension, as one example of Campbell's first-level of analysis,[16] viz, "ordinary language analysis"—Campbell's second-level thesis about the relation between desert and justice in general is a stipulated essentialist or quasi-essentialist philosophical redefinition of the ordinary concept of desert, and so, a redefinition of the concept of justice itself.

Campbell correctly sees a continuity between formal and substantive, social, justice, as well as that "the justice with which law is concerned [formal, legal justice] is continuous in kind with the justice of distributions which are not primarily the concern of courts of law, for both 'legal' and 'social' justice have to do with the treatment of persons as responsible persons."[17] But this is not an additional defining feature of justice in general; rather, it is a precondition for the applicability of principles of justice to human beings—indeed, to persons in general, human, divine, etc.

The following may be said in support of the claim that, as human beings, we have a moral right to justice, to just treatment. In a well-known article entitled "Persons and Punishment,"[18] Herbert Morris argues that humans, as free and rational, hence morally responsible, beings have a moral right to the system of punishment (as opposed to a system of therapy). Although it can be shown that he errs in completely ignoring a system of restitution, even as ancillary to punishment,[19] he is, I think, perfectly correct insofar as a (just) system of punishment is an integral part of an overall system of justice, to which human beings are entitled—not only if they are rational or act freely as rational beings, as he thinks, but even when they act irrationally or are morally and legally irrational because of mental illness or defect. That is, being a *responsible agent* is not a necessary condition for a human being's being entitled to (a general system of) justice.

A child, a patient suffering from schizophrenia or some other form of psychosis, or a mentally retarded person, as well as a person in a vegetative state, is as entitled to just treatment as a fully responsible, "normal" adult. As I have reiterated, he or she has a moral right to it—insofar as he or she has a (an equal) human right to be treated as a person, to be treated with consideration, in my two senses of "consideration." Thus, I am claiming here, in addition to what I claimed about the right to be treated as a person in chapter 5, that the right to be treated with consideration in the two senses, entails, perhaps even includes, a moral right to just treatment, and consequently, to a just system of justice. It is not that we have some kind of (equal) "worth" as persons and so ought to be treated (equally) with consideration but that justice is necessary so that the members of a society may be able to satisfy their basic needs and interests, to realize their potentials, and hence actualize themselves and attain a modicum of happiness. Without a modicum of justice, a society is unlikely to stand for very long, except by brute force. A main function of a system of justice is conflict resolution. In the absence of a just system of justice, or just institutions and practices, conflicts inevitably tend to lead to rampant crime and violence. In particular, the absence of an appreciable degree of penal justice would undermine the legitimacy of the state and the citizens' respect for the law, and the state could only maintain its power by the constant use of coercion and force. In other words, a democratic political system is impossible without a high degree of society-wide institutional justice, while the full development of human potentials and creativity, self-actualization and happiness, are very difficult to attain in the absence of an appreciable degree of political democracy.

In sum, a just society is absolutely essential for the full self-actualization of all its members. In an unjust society, only some—nearly always a (or the) dominant minority, at best, can have the means to satisfy their basic needs and interests.

But if a just system is indispensable in the way described, would it not also be true that human beings have a moral right to such a system, as a necessary condition for their being able to exercise, effectively and fully, their other human rights, as moral protections in their lifelong pursuit of their welfare, self-actualization, and happiness? Compare this with the human right to life, which is obviously necessary for one's experiencing and realizing any and all values, such as the various freedoms and liberties, etc.

Unlike the right to life and the other human rights, the right to just treatment[20]—consequently the correlative moral obligation to treat others justly—cannot be overridden, either by other, putatively more compelling human rights, or on the basis of consequentialist considerations. In that way at least, justice is the primary moral virtue, as, for example, John Rawls, for different reasons, maintains in *A Theory of Justice*. For example, if in any conceivable situation a conflict arises between an individual's desire or need to *exercise* a particular human right—the right to autonomy, privacy, speech, or expression, as part of the right to positive freedom—justice ought to prevail.[21] As with human rights, the principles of justice (and fairness), as I envisage an ethic of caring, are independent of putatively more fundamental or ultimate moral principles, such as the "principle" of caring itself, or some straightforward consequentialist or deontological principle(s).

Needless to say, justice must be tempered by compassion and mercy and must be "corrected" by the demands of discretion and equity, especially with regard to statutory, as opposed to case law. (See Section III.) But that does not mean that, consequently, it is not absolute.

In *Justice as Impartiality*, Brian Barry defends a different essentialist analysis or view of justice "in all its aspects" or forms; viz, the view that justice in general consists in universal second-order impartiality. Although I agree that second-order impartiality is a defining feature, being the purely formal element or dimension of justice in general, justice as including both formal and substantive or social justice,[22] I also maintain, as noted earlier, that the different aspects or forms of social justice—distributive, retributive, and compensatory—have a further defining feature of their own, viz, desert. Further, that desert is the logically primary or prior defining feature of the latter forms of justice, with impartiality (equality, or consistency) as a lexically secondary, or "subordinate," defining feature. In other words, once desert is assessed, all like cases, all instances of equal desert, are treated impartially or equally.

If these claims are true, the concept of justice in general is not an essentialist but a "quasi-essentialist" concept, in which (second-order) impartiality is the one feature shared—albeit differently—by both formal and substantive/social justice. The element of desert is confined to social justice alone.

II

Brian Barry on Justice as Impartiality

The following are Brian Barry's fundamental claims regarding justice "in all its aspects": (1) Justice is second-order impartiality, (2) (a) universal second-order impartiality does not entail universal first-order impartiality but allows for first-order partiality, i.e., individual discretion; indeed, (b) second-order impartiality is incompatible with universal first-order impartiality; (3) The "contention of the friends and foes of impartiality are equally valid"; hence (4) "there can be no contradiction between . . . the friends and foes of impartiality"; (5) The discussion in chapters 8 and 9 of *Justice as Impartiality*, taken together, provides evidence in support of proposition (2)(a), i.e., it "show[s] that none of the well-established forms of impartial morality [Kantian, utilitarian, Rawlsian, and Scanlonian moralities] entails universal first order impartiality," adding that "these forms of impartial morality are actually incompatible with universal first-order impartiality."[23]

I. Justice as Impartiality

In chapter 8, Barry sets the stage for a defense of proposition (1) against the "supporters of partiality," including feminist moral philosophers and social psychologists. He observes that the feminist critics of impartialism either maintain that "an ethic of caring" is equally valid as "the impartialist concern with rights and duties," or, "according to some, should drive impartialist ethics from the field altogether."[24]

The contemporary "self-styled antiimpartialists' central convention," as Barry states it, is that,

> There must, they maintain, be something fundamentally at fault with any moral system which has the implication that for example, children should not be regarded as having special claims against their parents, or that a fully conscientious man would toss a coin to determine whether he should rescue from a burning building his wife or a total stranger.[25]

In *Anatomy of Values*,[26] Charles Fried presents a similar dilemma. An understanding of that dilemma, and of a well-known dilemma presented by the psychologist Lawrence Kohlberg called the "Heinz dilemma," which also poses the issue between the two camps, will help us understand Barry's impartialism.

A. Fried's Case
In Fried's example,

> "A man could, at no risk or cost to himself, save one of two persons in equal peril," one of whom is "say, his wife." So long as this man "occupies no office such as that of captain of a ship, public health official, or the like," it would, Fried says, be "absurd to insist" that "he must treat both equally, perhaps by flipping a coin."[27]

In relation to this dilemma, as well as the earlier dilemma he imagines, Barry (1) agrees that it would be absurd for the man not to rescue his wife rather than tossing a coin. But he also (2) rightly rejects Fried's explanation, "that the requirements of equal treatment (assumed to mean random selection) are still met, albeit in a rather esoteric way: 'the occurrence of the accident may itself stand as a sufficient randomizing event to meet the dictates of fairness, so he may prefer his friend or loved one.'"[28] He also rejects Fried's view ". . . that 'where the rescuer does occupy an official position, the argument that he must overlook personalities is not unacceptable.'"[29]

With respect to (1) above, Barry agrees with Bernard Williams' view that "The consideration that it was his wife is certainly . . . an explanation which should silence comment."[30] Barry adds: "But beyond that, it *is*, on the basis of two-level impartialism, sufficient for him to have the thought that it was his wife."[31] And, with respect to (2) above, he notes that "the relevant conception of equal treatment here operates at the level of second-order impartiality. . . . I cannot say [as I would have to say if "the relevant conception of equal treatment operates at the level of first order impartiality"] 'I should rescue my wife and anybody else in a position to rescue one of two people should rescue my wife if she is one of the two.'"[32]

Note that, on Kant's, and, following it, on Barry's view, the maxim operating on the first-order level cannot be universalized without inconsistency; one cannot rationally will it to be a universal law. Further, first-order partiality cannot entail second-order impartiality. By contraposition, it follows that second-order partiality does not entail first-order partiality. The question remains whether second-order impartiality entails universal first-order impartiality.

The reason why it is morally right for one to rescue his own wife (or son) rather than the stranger in the kind of situation imagined, is that one's wife has special moral (and legal) rights against him, while one has the correlative special moral (and legal) responsibilities and obligations toward her—responsibilities and obligations he does not have toward strangers. On the other hand, as Barry says, if the choice is between rescuing a stranger or (in Barry's example) rescuing his horse or manuscript, his moral duty would be to rescue the former.

The stranger has a positive-cum-negative human right to life,[33] apart from the moral reprehensibility of not letting a human being die if one is in a position to rescue him or her, particularly without greatly endangering one's own life. In fact, in these circumstances, one would have the duty to care about the stranger as a human being, by rescuing her from death. In sharp contrast to that, one has neither a general moral duty nor a special moral obligation to rescue one's horse or manuscript. As we shall see in Section III, universal impartial first-order rules apply whenever no overriding conditions, such as special rights and obligations, are present.

In discussing Fried's example, Barry makes the important—and valid—point that the husband's duty to rescue his wife does not rule out one's saying that everybody should rescue one's own wife in the situation imagined by Fried. As Barry rightly says, that does not put one's wife in a privileged position at the second-order level, since one would be prepared to prescribe that anybody else, in a similar situation, do for his wife what one is prepared to do for one's own wife: "even if the consequence is that the person who is not rescued is . . . [one's] wife when the choice is between her and the wife of another rescuer."[34]

And: "it would be possible for anyone to satisfy all the requirements of impartiality, as they are understood in commonsense morality, and still be left with a lot of discretion."[35] This follows from the proposition that second-order impartiality does not entail universal first-order impartiality.[36] In support of that claim, Barry cogently argues, in chapters 8 and 9, that neither Kant's nor Rawls,' nor Scanlon's, nor the utilitarian form of justice as impartiality, "entails universal first-order impartiality."[37] For instance, in the utilitarian calculus, in which "everybody counts for one in that all want-satisfaction is given the same weight regardless of the identity of its bearer. Everybody is treated equally in a certain sense."[38]

In sum, Barry believes that "the core contention of the friends and foes of impartiality (as they conventionally represent themselves) are equally valid. If this is so, there can be no contradiction between them."[39] What the impartialists are defending is second-order impartiality, which Barry sees as "a test to be applied to the moral and legal rules of a society," while the "critics are talking about [rejecting] first-order impartiality—impartiality as a maxim of behaviour in everyday life. . . .They wish to insist on the common-sense view of the scope of impartiality . . ."[40] and resist the extension of the demands of impartiality to the whole of life."[41]

B. The Heinz Dilemma

I now turn to Barry's discussion of Kohlberg's "most famous example," the Heinz dilemma. A certain drug might save Heinz's dying wife, but Heinz can afford no more than half the price the druggist, who has discovered the medicine and wants to make a profit by it, asks for it. Heinz is unable to persuade him to sell him the drug for less than the asking price. Desperately, Heinz breaks into the drugstore [42] and tries to steal the drug. Barry asks: "The question is: should Heinz have

tried to steal the drug? Kohlberg's answer, is yes," as putatively following from both the utilitarian (stage five) and the Kantian/Rawlsian
(stage six) varieties of 'postconventional' morality. . . .The utilitarian
calculation is that the gain to the wife (a chance of surviving) outweighs the loss to the druggist (money), while the sixth stage tells us
that the right to life trumps the right to property."[43]

Earlier, Barry observes that Kohlberg's conception of a moral principle ["principled morality"] is "a mode of choosing which is universal,
a rule of choosing which we want all people to adopt always in all
situations."[44] This, Barry counters, makes morality "inconsistent with
any notion that there can be special duties attaching to certain roles
or positions": "precisely the same as the 'morality' repudiated by [Ber-
nard] Williams."[45]

Contra Kohlberg, Barry argues that "the maxim of Heinz's act in
stealing the drug would not withstand universalization."[46] Conceding
that life is more important than property, it is nonetheless plausible
that in the long run, if everyone in a similar situation did what Heinz
did, the consequences would be bad on the whole: more lives would
be lost than saved. The reason is that the repeated break-ins would
lead the druggist to stop manufacturing the drug: with the result that
nobody who needs the drug would be able to get it.[47]

Note that Heinz's action would be judged morally right on act-utilitarian grounds but wrong on rule-utilitarian grounds for the reasons
Barry gives in the preceding quoted passage in relation to Kant's Categorical Imperative.

As in Fried's example, the resolution of the Heinz dilemma lies in
the fact that Heinz has (*pace* Kohlberg) a special moral obligation to
(try to) further his wife's life and welfare; so his offer to buy the drug
must be seen as evidence of his taking his special obligation seriously—perhaps also as evidence of genuine caring and love for his
wife.

But the question remains whether Heinz's special moral obligation
and his imagined love and caring would justify violating the druggist's
right to his property.

Barry appeals to the Rawlsian 'principle of fair play,' which is essentially one important way of understanding Kant's Categorical Imperative, to show that Heinz's stealing the drug constitutes unfair behavior, a "'free rider' on the efforts or forbearance of the rest . . . [i.e.,
their not stealing the drug in similar circumstances]."[48] What the principle of fair play rules out is to say "'I shall do x, where it is possible to

do *x* (or possible to benefit from doing *x*), only because many other people similarly placed to me are refraining from doing *x* on the basis of moral constraints."[49]

The force of the Rawlsian-Kantian argument is patent. But I am more strongly pulled in the opposite direction by two other moral considerations: the positive-cum-negative right of Heinz's wife to her life, and Heinz's special moral obligation toward her. Despite the dilemma's patent artificiality and abstractness, I tend to consider it to be Heinz's moral obligation to steal the drug to save his wife's life.

More importantly, however, I agree with Barry's "major proposition" that "in a just society nobody would find himself in Heinz's situation. Drugs would be available as needed under some national system of health care provision, and the prices charged by drug companies would be regulated so as to leave them with enough incentive for innovation but rule out profiteering. (Alternatively, the right of patent might be restricted)."[50] Given an ideal of moral community informed by just institutions and practices and imbued with caring like the one sketched in this book, one can plausibly imagine the druggist to be caring and compassionate, leading him to accept, say, payment in small installments, with only modest interest added. Or one can imagine the caring druggist's generously selling Heinz the drug at a reduced price. Like Barry's view of a just society, these imagined alternatives would involve crucial changes in the Heinz example. But they would illustrate how caring people, even in an imperfect actual community, would tend to act.

In our discussion of the Fried and Heinz examples, as well as in other parts of the book, I took it for granted that special transactions or relationships, given the appropriate conditions, give rise to moral special rights and correlative moral special obligations. The question now is what rational justification can be given to that supposition or assumption.

It might be thought that it can be justified on consequentialist, utilitarian grounds, a course Bernard Williams suggests in relation to the Fried dilemma, although, as an anti-utilitarian, he himself would not accept it. I mean "that within a utilitarian framework one might allow for a division of labour, so that there can be special obligations which are justified on the ground that things go better overall with them."[51]

The general utilitarian answer would be that society's very existence and proper functioning, hence the general welfare, require that people be able to plan and act in the expectation that certain things would come about; in this case, that when someone makes a promise, the promiser can confidently expect that, whatever is promised would come to pass. This consequentialist line of thinking is, *a fortiori*, operative within the context of the law—for example, with regard to contract law; where in the Anglo-Saxon legal system "consideration," and sometimes even "detriment" on the part of one or all of the would-be contracting parties, is, among other conditions, necessary for a valid contract's coming into existence.

In *The Concept of Law*, H.L.A. Hart claims that "we can explain the self-binding quality of legislative enactment" as "the operation of a promise."[52] But in defining a promise, he assumes without argument that promising is saying "something which creates an obligation for the promiser; . . . [and that] in order that words should have this kind of effect, rules must exist providing that if words are used by appropriate persons on appropriate occasions (i.e. by sane persons understanding their position and free from various sorts of pressure) those who use these words shall be bound to do the things designated by them. . . . In lawyers' parlance we exercise 'a power' conferred by rules to do this."[53] The notion of a power conferred by rules is of great importance, as Hart amply shows. Such ("secondary") rules, which confer certain powers on members of a society to bring about various kinds of states of affairs, are absolutely essential for any form of societal existence, including the simplest or most primitive. That is, those that lack formal legislative or other legal institutions and practices.

Although, I too maintain that special rights/obligations arise from successful promises—that is, from promises that, *inter alia*, are made freely and voluntarily, and with understanding—I have elsewhere attempted to show in what way successful promises give rise to these obligations and rights,[54] and I shall, therefore, leave it to the interested reader to judge the success or failure of that attempt.

III

Justice and the Feminist Ethic of Caring

In this section I shall concentrate on the relation between justice and the feminist ethic of caring, in relation to Barry's claims concerning that relationship.[55] His relevant claims are: (1') "A characteristic line of argument against impartiality from a feminist viewpoint rests on a now familiar failure to distinguish between second-order and first-order impartiality."[56] (2') Since the feminist attack on Kohlberg "takes its origins in a critique of Kohlberg,"[57] the former's confusion between first-order and second-order impartiality rests on Kohlberg's conflation of first-order and second-order impartiality. (3') The "conflation of first-order and second-order impartiality among feminist writers" is "their taking seriously Kohlberg's theory of the stages of moral development, which (among other deficiencies) fails to distinguish between levels of impartiality."[58] (4') (a) "Much of the feminist criticism of impartiality is addressed to universal first-order impartiality and leaves second-order impartiality, properly understood, unscathed"[59] though (b) there are certain feminists (e.g., Nel Noddings) who reject second-order impartiality. Consequently, (5') once the objection to universal first-order impartiality is eliminated, it is seen that both justice and caring are valid, indeed, complementary, and both need to be incorporated "into any satisfactory account of morality."[60] From (5') it is also seen that (6') impartial second-order rules allow for "prior commitments, institutionally derived obligations, or perhaps relations";[61] consequently, it is difficult to see why feminists should be "skeptical of the value of abstract rules in dealing with particular moral problems,"[62] particularly as no society can dispense with some general moral and legal guidelines. For (6') ". . . what is surely true is that every society needs in addition [to legal rules] a . . . common system of guidance operating on the members of the society by internalization . . . ,"[63] etc. (7') Finally, with regard to proposition (4')(b), Barry maintains that the rejection of impartiality all the way down is incoherent.

The following comments about Barry's preceding propositions are in order.

1. Although the rejection of justice as (first-order) impartiality is by no means the only important reason for the feminists' general rejection of the (of any) "ethic of justice," it is true that the rejection of Kohlberg's theory would make feasible (or rather, more feasible) the reconciliation of the two. As Barry says, Kohlberg's "equation of justice with the kind of equal treatment that . . . [he] thought was mandated by his sixth stage of moral development . . . fills up the whole moral space and thus leaves no room for any other basis of moral judgement to be combined with it. We can therefore easily understand how the pervasive idea of an unavoidable conflict between an 'ethic of justice' and an 'ethic of caring' comes about."[64]

2. It should also be remembered, as Virginia Held states, that "nearly all who have tried to develop an 'ethic of care' think that at the very

least the dominant ethic of justice will need to be supplemented by an ethic of care. Some speak of a harmony between and integration of the two emphases. Others suggest that the incompatibilities between the interpretive frameworks each provides makes problematic any "marriage" between them."[65]

3. In agreeing with Barry and in opposition to the latter group, I believe that if justice is interpreted as a matter of having principles and rules compatible with second-order impartiality, there would be no conflict between justice and caring. Barry thinks that the cases that are supposed to demonstrate a conflict are of one of two sorts: (1) those where "plausible rules of justice do not determine the choice," so that a "caring" approach would be perfectly legitimate to deal with them; and (2) those where certain rules of justice determine the choice. In the latter cases, therefore, it would be a mistake to suppose that one must choose between caring and justice for a moral decision regarding them.[66]

We saw earlier that the Fried and Heinz cases fall into the first group, while first degree murders, that is, murders lacking any extenuating or mitigating circumstances, fall into the second group; since justice sans judicial discretion applies in their case. A third group Barry neglects to mention involve the cooperative application of both justice and care, where, in various ways, justice (including the system of legal justice) is rendered responsive to and informed by the caring consideration of special circumstances, i.e., discretion or equity. A good example is Gilligan's fictional example of the long-neglected wife who, after a "pattern of detachment and abandonment" by her husband, ended in his strangling her canary and, in turn, led to her killing him. Other examples are long-suffering battered women who, in desperation, end up killing the abusive husband or lover. In these cases understanding and compassion for the woman's ordeal, like the understanding and compassion Gilligan imagines to have been felt for the long-neglected woman by a neighbor woman and the sheriff's wife, who discover the strangled canary "buried under pieces of quilting,"[67] are essential. No less essential is the need to broaden the moral and legal concepts of self-defense to include acts of killing of the kind described, and so, as morally and legally justified acts. That would entail a corresponding narrowing of the present concepts of moral and legal murder respectively, and the appropriate modification of the laws pertaining to murder, in, for example, the United States. In these cases, caring fits into "the structure of rights and duties," to borrow Barry's words in connection with another imagined dilemma, faced by "a woman trying to decide whether to go out for the evening with her husband to some long-planned event or stay at home with her child, who is ill but not seriously or dangerously ill."[68]

4. As we saw in relation to the Fried and Heinz cases, as well as in other cases he discusses in his book, Barry envisages circumstances in which special moral/legal obligations can be overridden by actions mandated by caring. But he thinks that the circumstances "must be such as to activate a duty of greater salience than that entailed by the contractual obligation to look after the child."[69] For example, where a professional nanny, looking after a child while his or her parents are away, has to decide between her obligation to stay and look after the child, and an emergency where "the next door neighbor has to be rushed to the hospital and nobody else is immediately available to do it."[70]

In sum, Barry correctly believes that "it is not possible to find a plausible case in which there is a legitimate conflict between an 'ethic of justice'—construed in terms of justice as impartiality—and an 'ethic of caring.'"[71] The same can be said of the desert aspect of justice, insofar as (a) the concept of desert as such is not, as far as I can see, an issue between feminist and other moral philosophers. Similarly with (b) the element of second-order impartiality that forms part of the concept of desert. As we have seen, impartiality in that sense is compatible with first-order partiality.

5. I shall now turn to Barry's criticism of those champions of an "ethic of caring" who reject (formal) justice as second-order impartiality:[72] specifically, to Ned Noddings' view in *Caring*, described by Barry as "nothing less than a call for a moral revolution of a far-reaching and potentially catastrophic nature."[73]

Noddings claims that on the ethic of caring, "our obligation is limited and delimited by relation. We are never free, in the human domain, to abandon our preparedness to care; but, practically, if we are meeting those in our inner circles adequately as ones caring and receiving those linked to our inner circles by formal chains of relation, we shall limit the calls upon our obligation quite naturally. We are not obliged to summon the "I must" if there is no possibility of completion in the other. . . . [W]e limit our obligation by examining the possibility of completion."[74] Thus for Noddings, as Barry says, "There is no room for the idea that there can be obligations imposed by the requirement that the interests of other human beings are entitled to respect simply qua interests of other human beings."[75]

Despite her laudable view that we should be always prepared to care, Noddings' view is narrow in the extreme from the standpoint of the present book. I mean her implicit, and morally and humanly disastrous rejection, *tout court,* of human rights and justice (the latter, as second-order impartiality-*cum*-desert). In fact, she implicitly rejects the very distinction between *right* and *wrong* action, not only in relation to plants and nonhuman animals with whom we have or can have no special relationship, but also in relation to human strangers and possible intelligent beings in other parts of the universe. Again, her view renders the distinction between right and wrong, and the idea of moral duties, inapplicable in relation to God—except perhaps when a human being enters into a personal relationship with Him, in some kind of religious experience.[76]

Second, Noddings' view that we do have a moral obligation toward those with whom we have a relationship[77] implicitly commits her to second-order impartiality and to embracing second-order impartial moral rule R: that one has a moral obligation toward, and so, ought to care about those with whom one has a relationship, although the degree of that obligation normally varies with the closeness of the relationship, or the opposite. Rule R would state that all those who are equally close to oneself (presumably, for example, some or all members of one's family) ought to be treated equally. Similarly, those who are equally less close to oneself ought to be given equal, albeit less, consideration than the former, closer group. And so on. Only a "rule" S of the form: "Always treat differently everyone with whom you have some relationship; never treat any two of them with the same degree of sensitivity, concern, consideration, or respect," would eschew second-order impartiality.

"Rule" S—if the word "rule" may be meaningfully used in relation to it—would be the only kind of rule compatible with the idea that every moral situation is utterly unique and the only kind of rule Noddings may be willing to accept. But it is quite doubtful that such a "rule" can be applied even to individual cases, since it would provide no positive guidance as to how each case ought to be treated. (Later in this chapter, I shall argue against what I call the "strong uniqueness thesis," a thesis on which "rule" S rests.)

Barry offers several arguments against the kind of (Cereal) "ethic of caring" Noddings advocates. These are (1) that "if all the members of a society acted exclusively" on it, that ethic of caring would be "characterized by a variant of 'amoral familism.'. . . [That is] . . . 'the inability of the . . . [members] to act together for the common good or, indeed, for any end transcending the immediate, material interest of the nuclear family.'"[78] (2) "People would not even pay lip-service to impartially defensible principles. Perhaps 'relation' à la Noddings would create a sense of obligation extending beyond the immediate family. But nobody would feel that these obligations must be subordinated to the demands of justice as impartiality."[79] (3) "A Cereal society would suffer essentially the same inconveniences as a Hobbesian state of nature . . . . We might speculate...that people are prepared in general to act more ruthlessly in the pursuit of the interests of their nearest and dearest than in the pursuit of their own personal interests. In the absence of a sense of justice to set limits, . . .'confin'd generosity' poses an even greater threat to social order than pure egoism."[80] (4) "People with nothing but the 'ethic of care' to guide their actions would inevitably find that, because of the lack of any authoritative coordinating rules [since Noddings repudiates universalizability], their pursuit of their ends was constantly being frustrated by others' pursuit of their (different) ends."[81] But (5) "purely in order to pursue their ends more effectively, . . . people with divergent ends would find it in their interests to agree on some rules of justice. They would thus be led to discover the idea of justice as mutual advantage . . . . [Then] they would be led by the defects of justice as mutual advantage to embrace justice as reciprocity. But the lack of fit between the motive for behaving justly and the criteria of justice that is inherent in justice as reciprocity would propel them into the acceptance of justice as impartiality."[82]

It is clear, I think, that if these criticisms are valid, such a radical ethic of caring as Noddings advocates would be in deep trouble in any society, but especially in a community in our sense—above all, in a T-community—that aspires to be good and moral. They would also strengthen considerably the claim, made in Parts II and III of the present book, that an adequate and comprehensive "ethic of caring" must appropriately include justice (together with fairness and human rights).

Criticism (1) is rather extreme: there is no inherent reason why a caring relationship à la Noddings should not extend beyond the immediate family to the extended family, to other relatives, to friends, and to some associates—as Barry admits in his second argument. But, as I observed a little earlier àpropos Noddings, an extension of the scope of caring to include the ecology or the biosphere, even human-kind in general, is (to invert Spinoza's famous phrase) as rare as it is noble. Still, the usual restriction of most people's special moral duties and obligations to those with whom they have a special relationship does not, or would not, entail any inability on their part to act in concert, or to pursue a common good. They would be able to do so at least to advance their interests and the interests of those they care about. What they would not be able to do would be to work together for the common good out of a sense of morality; and the coordination of their endeavors would always be an uphill fight, frequently frustrated by their more limited overriding ends. Their obligations to those they care about would always override the demands of justice as impartiality—criticism (3). By definition they would "not even pay lip-service to impartially defensible principles." The human rights, at least of those who lie outside the circle of their caring relationships, would also be overridden.

As Barry says, his criticism (4) is speculative. I do not see how it would *tend* to follow even if one supposes that people's special moral obligations are restricted to those they care about, even granting Hume's belief that people's affection for their nearest and dearest makes them almost unfit for large societies, since it necessarily produces "an opposition of passions, and a consequent opposition of actions."[83] What is more likely than what Barry imagines—and that is perhaps what Hume meant—is that the relentless pursuit of their own interests and the interests of those they care about, and their *lack* of caring about mere acquaintances and total strangers, would render them ruthless toward the latter and "a threat to social order." That would be especially true as acquaintances and strangers, who would constitute the majority in any society other than a community, would not be protected by the norms of human rights or justice.

Barry's most fundamental criticism is clearly (5), in relation to his book's central theses. But that criticism goes far beyond our own purposes in this chapter and book, and will, therefore, be left to the interested reader to evaluate.

IV

The Place of Justice in the Ethic of Caring
As we saw in Section III, Barry maintains that caring, and justice considered as second-order impartiality, are complementary. But he does not show how the two would be actually related in an enlarged "ethic of justice-*cum*-caring," or the precise place of justice in an ethic

of caring. Since I have myself maintained that while formal justice consists in impartiality, substantive justice consists in desert-*cum*-impartiality, I shall next consider some of the ways in which formal justice and substantive justice relate to caring and to the comprehensive care-centered ethic I have been sketching in this book.

A. Formal Justice and Caring

In answering the question of the relation between formal justice and caring, I shall concentrate on some of the ways in which justice allows for individual discretion and for equity. Since judicial discretion plays an important role in common law legal systems such as the American system, I shall focus on certain ways in which judicial discretion is involved in the judge's interpretation and application of statutory and case law—especially, in the latter case, past precedents.

1. Justice and Individual Discretion

Laws consist of rules,[84] which imply the existence of legally relevant common or similar features in otherwise different situations or cases. The same is true of moral rules. Only if each moral/legal case or situation is *unique in all morally/legally relevant respects*—call this the strong sense of "moral uniqueness"—would the concepts of impartiality and impartial moral/legal rules be ruled out in principle. (Cf. the claims of aestheticians who defend the idea of "aesthetic uniqueness," in a corresponding strong sense, in relation to art.) The idea of "rules internal" to a unique case or situation in the present sense of "unique case or situation"makes no sense. By definition, a principle or rule is general, applies to a class of cases. Those feminist philosophers who reject either first-order or second-order impartiality in relation to morality and/or the law, presuppose the strong uniqueness thesis, rejecting all moral/legal rules.

In "The Generalized and the Concrete Other,"[85] the feminist philosopher Seyla Benhabib opposes equity to justice, and argues that equity rather than justice is what an ethic of caring requires. That is, an ethic whose concern is with the "concrete other," not the abstract, "generalized other" of the ethic of justice and rights. "Our relation to the [concrete] other is governed by the norms of equity and complementary reciprocity; . . . each is entitled to expect and to assume from the other forms of behavior through which the other feels recognized and confirmed as a concrete, individual being with specific needs, talents, and capacities. Our differences in this case complement rather than exclude one another."[86]

The following may be said in response. Benhabib's emphasis on the need to view "each and every rational being as a concrete, individual being with specific needs, talents and capacities" is perfectly valid. But her position is based on a false opposition between justice and equity. In fact, as we shall presently see, equity is not only not incompatible with justice: it presupposes it. In Benhabib's case the untenable contrast between equity and justice is a result of her unfortunate contrast between an inadequate concept of the "concrete other" and an untenable (Kolbergian) concept of the "generalized other."

The basic source of Benhabib's inadequate concept of the "concrete other" is her belief that to seek to comprehend the other's needs, "motivations, what he or she searches for and desires," is to abstract "from what constitutes our commonality," and so, to focus on what is supposed to be totally unique about our individuality. She therefore assumes the untenable strong uniqueness view. In fact, we cannot leave out *all* that is common to the needs, desires, motivations, experiences, and so on, of some or all human beings, without ending up with bloodless abstractions that correspond to no actual or possible human being, instead of what allegedly is a totally unique "individuality." To be able to empathize with, and so, to treat another as a "concrete other," one certainly needs to understand his or her special experiences, needs, aspirations, goals, and the like. But that is possible only if there are at least some similarities or commonalities, not just differences between one's experiences, needs, etc., and those of the other. In the absence of such similarities, if not commonalities, it would be impossible for us to fulfill the entitlement of each "to expect from the other forms of behavior through which the other feels recognized and confirmed as a concrete, individual being with specific needs, talents, and capacities. The norms of our interaction are . . . norms of friendship, love, and care."[87] In treating one with these norms, "I confirm not only your humanity but your human individuality."[88]

The champions of an ethic of "justice and rights" would be acting inequitably, and unfairly if, as Benhabib alleges, they focus exclusively on what is common to, and ignore any potentially or actually relevant individual differences between, the needs, desires, motivations, etc., of different persons. But by the same token, Benhabib's suggestion is likewise extreme and unjustified. For as I stressed a little earlier, there are always enough similarities between the needs, desires, motivations, and so on, of different individuals that warrant or, at least, may be relevant to, fair, equal (not the same), treatment. (I say "equal," not "the same" treatment precisely because of the possible existence of relevant differences.) In fact, both the attempt to abstract "just" what is purported to be common to two or more cases or situations, and the attempt to extract "just" what purports to be completely different and individual in them, are misguided. They rest on a common misconception of the relation between what is "common" to, and what is "different," between two or more individuals, with respect to a particular kind of need, desire, motivation, etc., they have. I mean the erroneous supposition that each individual case or situation involves two distinct and separable, hence conceptually abstractible, elements: common characteristics *simpliciter* and different, indeed, unique characteristics *simpliciter;* whereas individual differences are differences-in-shared characteristic—or shared characteristics are "imbued" with differences. Individual differences are well-nigh endless variations on that which is shared or "common." There are no shared characteristics without differences, nor differences without some similarities, something shared, between otherwise different actions, experiences, occurrences, motives, or states of affairs. And it is through that which is common or shared that we recognize and understand the actions, needs, desires, etc., of others. But our ability to do so does not entail that what is shared is some common "essence": the existence of certain specific or relatively specific crisscrossing "family resemblances" between them is sufficient. Of course, to ascertain what actions, experiences, etc., would constitute "sufficient" or even "relevant similarities" in a particular case calls for judicious interpretation and discretion, and is always open to challenge and revision, and is something on which rational "judges" (and judges and juries in the courtroom) may disagree.

So far I have spoken, as Benhabib appears to do, of equity in its everyday, extra-legal usage. Turning to equity as a technical legal concept, we find that, at present,[89] the concept of equity presupposes and makes sense only in relation to the concept of justice. As defined by *The Law Dictionary*,[90] "equitable defense" is

> A defense which is recognized by *courts of equity* acting solely upon inherent rules and principles of *equity*. . . . Examples of such defenses include *fraud, duress,* illegality [these are all exculpatory circumstances, consisting in "evidence and/or statements which tend to clear, justify, or excuse a *defendant* from alleged fault or *guilt*."[91] Such defenses can now be asserted in *courts of law* as well. . . . The term also refers to equitable doctrines such as *unclean hands* that may operate to *bar* a plaintiff from pursuing an equity action and thus constitute equitable defenses to such an action.[92]

Equity modifies or "corrects" an impartial rule in accordance with the special circumstances of the particular case before the court, thus presupposing that rule to begin with. To be equitable, i.e., fair to individual cases, the court has to appeal to some common measure or rule of equity itself as the above passage states. Such a rule of equity is increasingly needed in relation to a type of case we touched on earlier, namely, those battered women who, in desperation, kill their lovers or husbands. They are entitled to being treated with compassion and understanding, and either completely exonerated by a court of law on grounds of "self-defense," or given a light or relatively light sentence on the judge's discretion, depending, among other things, on whether viable psychological and practical alternatives to killing were available to them.

Ideally, the principles of formal justice (and the protections of procedural justice as well) are not put aside even when a court takes into full account a defendant's or a plaintiff's relevant special circumstances. Justice is not impugned by such attention to "detail,"[93] although the judge cannot possibly treat every case as a "special case," as unique in the putative strong sense, if any statutes or any common law rules are to exist and be applicable to anything.[94] In the case of formal justice as second-order impartiality, the element of truth in Benhabib's strictures essentially boils down to an admonition or warning to juries and judges to be as sensitive as possible to relevant differences between otherwise like cases that come before them; a reminder that they should pay special attention to the seemingly irrelevant details of each case.

A further legal meaning of "equity" noted by Harold J. Berman and William R. Greiner is equity *in the sense* of "the exceptional exercise of discretion based on mercy or fairness. . . ."[95] The marked sympathy American juries and judges in recent years have had toward the plight of long-abused women who end by killing their husband, reflected in relatively light jail sentences, or even no jail sentence at all, are I think good cases of judicial equity. But they are not examples of judicial discretion considered under (3) below.[96]

It is worth noting in this connection that some feminists, e.g., Christina Sommers and Paulia Camilli, distinguish "equity feminism" from "gender feminism," and describe the former as championing women's equal opportunity and equal treatment with men. In that sense of "equity," women's demand for equity requires the assigning of an important place for fairness and for formal justice in the ways described in Section I of this chapter.

(2) A further way in which impartial justice is essential—this time in relation to everyday life, and before the law—is with respect to *procedural justice*. Equal moral, civil, and legal immunities and rights are essential for the protection of individuals and certain groups, such as certain minorities, from bigotry and prejudice and the "tyranny of the majority."

(3) In addition to equity in the special circumstances in which fairness calls for it, there is need for discretion in the interpretation of the "general classifying terms" that are employed in rules of conduct of any kind. Thus, in *The Concept of Law*, H.L.A. Hart observes that "uncertainty at the borderline is the price to be paid for the use of general classifying terms in any form of communication concerning matters of fact."[97] When some general rule of conduct is framed, "the language used in this context fixes necessary conditions which anything must satisfy if it is to be within its scope, and certain clear examples of what is certainly within its scope [paradigm cases] may be sent to our minds."[98] But "blindly prejudging what is to be done in a range of future cases, about whose composition we are ignorant, . . . [enables us to] succeed in settling in advance, but also in the dark, issues which can only reasonably be settled when they arise and are identified."[99] Summing up, Hart writes that

> All systems, in different ways, compromise between two social needs; the need for certain rules which can, over great areas of conduct, be safely applied by private individuals to themselves without fresh official guidance or weighing up of social issues, and the need to leave open, for later settlement by an informed, official choice [by the judge], issues which can only be properly appreciated and settled when they arise in a concrete case. [100]

Since moral concepts too "suffer" from borderline indeterminacy or open texture, much of what Hart says applies to moral rules and calls for discretion in the interpretation and application of moral rules to particular cases or classes of cases.

(4) In addition to the borderline indeterminacy of general moral and legal concepts, key general concepts, in statutes and common law precedents, and other past rulings, tend to undergo changes in meaning over time, which reflect changes in the particular society's attitudes, beliefs, values, and circumstances. A good example is the significant change in the meaning of the term "family" during the past several decades, necessitating a broadening, and corresponding modification of the concept of the family in the Western world, to include not only the "house-mate" and common-law husband or wife, but also

same-sex"live-ins" and "families." The legal issues raised by recent "palimony" cases in the United States illustrate the related semantic-conceptual changes. Sensitivity to changing social beliefs, attitudes, values, and circumstances—what legal realists, who advocated "judicial activism,"[101] correctly called for—makes it desirable for legislators to modify or redefine the relevant laws, and for judges to use their discretion in interpreting them and the case law, in a manner consonant with these changes. Realism requires nothing less.[102] The relation between (2)[b] above and changes in the meaning of legal rules due to historical changes and changing in societal norms and attitudes, etc., is obvious: legislative and judicial (and jury) responsiveness to these societal changes is simply good social policy. In its absence, the law becomes rigid, in danger of becoming ossified, sacrificing fairness and justice for constancy, and so, increasingly irrelevant to new cases and situations.

(5) In assessing the merits of legal realism in American jurisprudence in relation to what Donald Dworkin calls "hard cases," which "seem non-determined or un-determined by rules," Jeffrie Murphy points out that a judge can appeal to [a] perceived intentions of founding fathers, [b] a conception of good social policy, [c] general moral principles built into the common law, or [d] do nothing at all; all of these (even the last) is a kind of activism because all represent ways of doing something other than simply applying rules.[103]

The above have possible analogues in relation to moral rules. For instance, in the interpretation and application of particular religious moral rules (e.g., the Ten Commandments, or the Beatitudes in the Christian Gospels), the analogue to [a] would be the interpreter's appeal to what she takes to be or to have been the intention of the rule's author in framing the rule (God in the first example? Jesus in the second example). The analogue to [b] would be the interpreter's appealing to the overall societal good or bad consequences of (i) applying a particular rule as it stands, or (ii) adapting or appropriately modifying it to apply to special cases more fairly. In light of our earlier discussion, both [a] and [b] would be well illustrated by the judge's interpretation and application (or nonapplication) of the law against murder to battered women who, in desperation, kill their husbands or lovers.

(6) In those instances in which a battered woman kills her husband or lover, the judge may consider the abuse she has suffered as a *mitigating circumstance*, ruling her act as manslaughter, and sentencing her to a relatively light prison term. A judge's appeal to mitigating or

extenuating circumstances constitutes a further way in which judicial discretion may be exercised. It is a way in which two cases of homicide or robbery, say, would be seen—legally speaking—as significantly dissimilar, with the result that the relevant laws regarding homicide or robbery are applied relatively differently. Note that such discretion—indeed, judicial discretion in any form described in this section—is quite different from *misapplications* of an impartial rule, which are unjustified partiality, a miscarriage of justice. (Cf. the miscarriage of justice in Socrates' case.)

(7) So-called "partial defenses" in criminal law are further states of affairs "where justice requires the mitigation of the applicable sentence." In such cases the jury's discretion plays an important role in the penalty phase, while the judge's discretion is important in the sentencing phase. Similarly with "complete defenses," which completely exculpate the defendant. Let me illustrate. In American criminal law, diminished mental capacity or "partial responsibility" constitutes a partial excuse or defense, while duress, irresistible impulse, drug induced insanity, legal insanity, and epilepsy constitute complete defenses. Partial responsibility lessens responsibility and guilt, while a complete defense renders the generally applicable law, for example, the law pertaining to murder or other felonies, inapplicable to the particular cases.[104]

B. Substantive/Social Justice and the Ethic of Caring

In the discussion of judicial discretion in relation to formal justice, we considered, in effect, a main form of social justice, namely, criminal, retributive justice, but only with respect to its formal aspect, *qua* (second-order) impartiality. In order to avoid over-lengthening a long chapter, I shall focus on distributive justice alone, and then only on the need criterion or canon of that form of justice.

In light of our discussion in the earlier parts of this chapter, it is readily seen that the feminist and other moral partialists' criticism of justice conceived of as impartiality is solely directed at formal justice, not at distributive or compensatory justice. But distributive justice is, clearly, an essential component not only of any adequate theory of justice but also of any moral theory, not least a care-centered theory. The struggle of women, certainly in the Western world, to force society and the law to acknowledge women's fundamental physiological and psychological differences from men, and their special needs as women and nurturers,[105] well illustrates the significant moral and legal role distributive justice can play in the lives of contemporary women and men.

In "Feminist Morality and the Role of Law,"[106] Virginia Held envisages a state of affairs where, "with a more adequate view of the wide range of moral considerations and context for which morality and ethical theory are needed, the place of law in the wider framework or more comprehensive [moral] view might be significantly more modest than previously thought. . . . The realm of law might be seen as a much more subsidiary sphere designed for those progressively fewer and fewer problems where enforcement is unavoidable."[107]

I cannot agree more with the preceding passage, even leaving aside the overabundance of laws in a country such as the United States, and even if we exclude ambiguous, inconsistent, or patently contradictory laws that confuse and unnecessarily restrict the citizen's freedom of action. I also fully agree that "when an actively working morality would break down would legal machinery need to be invoked."[108] But as long as the United States and the rest of the world fall far short of Held's ideal, the law will undoubtedly continue to play a much more fundamental role than Held envisages, and the struggle of women and minorities for legal equality would need to continue apace. Similarly with the need for affirmative action, until women and minorities attain at least approximate economic equality with men.[109]

It is also worth noting that in the United States at least, one can now discern the beginning of a significant reversal of the historical relation between law and morality, with respect to some of the most troubling ethical and legal issues on the cutting edge of medical technology. For example, in relation to the ethical and legal problems of genetic testing, surrogate motherhood, testtube babies, and genetic engineering. In these and similar types of cases, where traditional moral intuitions offer no help or give inconsistent directives, the law (howsoever hesitantly, stumblingly) has tended to take the lead and has begun to shape public morality. If this trend continues, the law's place vis-à-vis morality in the United States would be significantly enlarged, rather than the opposite.[110]

Another way in which the law appears to be influencing morality in the United States is in the area of punishment. I mean, with respect to people's tendency to consider legal punishment, commonly referred to as the criminal's "payment of his or her dues to society," as also automatic "payment" for the ethical wrong he or she has committed.

Elsewhere,[111] I argued that all human beings have a positive as well as a negative human right to life, and that the former is the fundamental moral basis of the "need principle"[112] as a canon of distributive justice. That directly ties in with, and provides a good example of, my earlier claim that all human beings, as possessors of the basic human right to treatment as moral persons, have a (an equal) moral right to a (just) system of justice: here, distributive justice. In terms of the need principle, that means that people who live below the poverty line[113] through no fault of theirs, morally deserve, and are entitled to society's help, proportionally to the degree of their need. The second half of Karl Marx's famous Socialist Principle of Justice (as Edward Nell and Onora O'Neill call it[114]) viz, "To each according to his need," stipulates society's obligation to aid the needy proportionally to their need. The principle as a whole states: "From each according to his ability, to each according to his need."

In addition to the moral basis of the genuinely needy person's entitlement to society's aid, and to what I think is the gut feeling that human beings are entitled to a decent living, perhaps support for the need canon sometimes also comes from people's self-interested awareness that "but for the grace of God I could be in that destitute or homeless person's shoes!"

To show some of the ways in which caring and distributive justice are based on need and are complementary, I shall assume the general validity of the Socialist Principle. I shall leave for the future a qualified defense of that principle against such libertarian critics as Robert Nozick, who advances a different kind of theory of distributive justice he calls "The Entitlement Theory";[115] a theory which, if correct, would undercut not only the Socialist Principle but also what he calls "patterned principles."[116] Nozick's theory is an excellent expression of the conservative, libertarian attitude toward the involuntary (re)distribution of wealth. To quote just one telling statement of Nozick's: "From the point of view of an entitlement theory, redistribution is a serious matter indeed, involving, as it does, the violation of people's rights . . . . From other points of view, also, it is serious."[117]

A few preliminary remarks about the Socialist Principle may be appropriate here.

First, the first half of the principle is crucial to its adequacy as a whole, as a principle of distributive justice. Without it, its "need" part, the principle would stipulate what is both patently unfair and unjust. The obligation to aid the needy can only fall on those who (a) are capable of contributing materially to them, and can only (b) fall on them to the degree in which they have the means of doing so. It follows that those who are capable of contributing materially (or otherwise) to society but willfully fail to do so, cannot consistently, i.e., justly, claim that *they* deserve society's help if they themselves fall on hard times.

The second half of the Socialist Principle differs significantly from the Socialist Incentive Principle, which essentially stipulates that those who do not work will not eat.[118] As Nell and O'Neill describe it, "The Incentive Socialist Principle rewards workers according to their contribution: it is a principle of distribution in which an incentive system—reliance on material rewards—is explicit."[119] "According to Marx, this is a form of bourgeois right that 'tacitly' recognizes unequal individual endowments, and thus natural privileges in respect of productive capacity."[120]

A commonly heard criticism of social welfare by conservatives is that the system is frequently abused, and that many who receive welfare do not deserve it. They are lazy and idle and exploit the system by preferring to be on the dole rather than working to earn an honest living. It is certainly true that the lazy or idle cannot claim a moral right to society's support, and follows from the nature of fairness itself; namely, that it is unfair to the hard-working, who earn a decent living by the sweat of their brow, to have to support the drones. Any contribution they make to help support the needy can only be an act of charity or compassion—in general, an act of caring. It cannot be the fulfillment of an obligation, whether of justice or of fairness.

All this is true. Nevertheless, it should also be clear that a welfare system, as embodying a Need Principle of Justice, cannot be validly judged—and dismissed—on the purely factual grounds that it is sometimes, or even often, exploited by parasites. What that criticism means is that the private and public sectors of society should always be alert to abuses of the system and always strive to make it more effective and more fair. Recent legislation designed to reform the current welfare system—notwithstanding its weaknesses—illustrates the United States government's attempt to improve on a palpably flawed system.

Since we are concerned with the need canon of distributive justice alone—on which the two Socialist Principles agree—the differences between them, which pertain to the first half of each principle, are immaterial for our present purposes. However, because of the importance of the concept of incentives in relation to need, some observations are in order about one aspect of a problem facing a canon of need with regard to, say, the Socialist Principle.

The special aspect of the problem in question concerns the any-thing-but-need-fulfilling drudgery of which human life is so full. In the face of such drudgery, normal incentives clearly fail. Should society then not provide special incentives in the form of, for example, higher pay or special privileges to motivate people to perform essential but deadening chores? But would that not mean abandoning, in their case, "To each according to his need," and embracing instead, "To each according to his work (or contribution, in the special sense of 'contri-bution' involved here)? The alternative Nell and O'Neill do not hesi-tate to advocate would be to compel some to train to perform these chores, thereby violating their human right to freedom of choice and action!

The real choice in these cases lies between the Incentive Principle, which provides the needed incentive, and the Socialist Principle. Nell and O'Neill think it unnecessary "to supplement the Socialist Prin-ciple of Justice with an incentive scheme, whether material or moral. The principle already contains the Kantian maxim: develop your tal-ents to the utmost, for only in this way can a person contribute to the limits of his ability."[121]

Unfortunately, that reasoning will not do, for the following rea-sons. First, the Kantian maxim imposes a duty, which, as we all know, may or may not be actually obeyed. Like any other, that duty does not, as such, give rise to a desire, motive, or incentive in people to develop their talents to the utmost—the fundamental question here. In order that a society or community may benefit maximally from the implementation of the Socialist Principle, it needs to provide both (a) the needed economic, educational, social, cultural, political, and legal institutional mechanisms and opportunities, and (b) special incentives to spur its members to serious and continued efforts to develop their abilities to the fullest.

Second, a "Kantian" Socialist Principle, whose relevant part, ex-panded, would mean: "It is each person's duty (dictated by distributive justice) to contribute according to the limits of his ability," would be significantly different from the Socialist Principle. For "According to his ability" is not the same as "According to the limit of his ability, one's ability developed to its fullest." The former means "According to one's ability at the particular times at which and the circumstances in which one is called upon to contribute of one's abilities, holdings, etc." That is to be expected, since a duty, such as the Kantian duty Nell and O'Neill refer to, cannot be strictly, or properly, part of a principle of (here, a principle of distributive) justice.

Nevertheless, I feel it would be right to allow everyone who contributes in any degree, not just those who take care of the meaningless drudgery of everyday life, and not just those who contribute a good, or a great, deal, to receive according to their contribution. But I also believe that it would be an egregious failing not to help those who are unable to contribute much or anything at all, not because of laziness or idleness, but because of limited abilities, age, illness, or physical or mental disabilities. Similarly, those who are unable to contribute much, or anything at all, because of discrimination that denies them opportunities to education, employment, and so on.

The importance of the problem of incentives in relation to the present discussion is clearly seen if we consider that in order for a country or community to have enough material and other resources to distribute or to redistribute to the really needy, those who are able and have to contribute, must have the incentive to contribute as much as, or close to, what they are capable of contributing. But the incentive to contribute tends to vary inversely with the size of the expected contribution, in the form of, for example, the taxes they have to pay.

II. The Complementarity of Caring and Distributive Justice Based on Need

Caring and the need principle of distributive justice are often complementary, or work in tandem, in that, in certain kinds of situations I shall briefly describe, the two converge—albeit for different moral reasons—in their concern for the amelioration of the condition of those genuinely in need, by material and other kinds of aid. Caring about others is not caring unless it importantly includes caring about the needy, just as concern for their welfare, as possessors of a positive moral right to life, therefore, to a decent life, is an imperative of distributive justice, on those who have the means or ability to help.

The types of societal situations in which the need principle and caring may be involved, are situations of (a) extreme scarcity, (b) moderate scarcity, (c) relative abundance or abundance, and (d) superabundance. By considering them, even briefly, we will see more precisely how caring and the need principle are, or may be, related in different kinds of actual or possible situations.

(a) In situations of extreme scarcity, distributive justice based on need, hence the Socialist Principle, is inapplicable. I said "distributive justice based on need," since other principles than the Socialist Principle and other canons than need, such as moral merit, may conceivably still apply. That is precisely what Marx and Engels maintain. According to them, the Incentive Socialist Principle would apply, although they reject it as the putative ultimate principle of distributive justice. The reason is that on that Principle, "Each worker receives back the value of the amount of work he contributes to society in one form or another . . . . This principle holds for a still deficient society where the needs of particular workers, which depend on many things other than their productive capacity, may not be met."[122] But "although it may be less desirable than the Socialist Principle of Justice, the Incentive Socialist Principle . . . provides a principle of allocation that can be applied equally well to the various situations of scarcity, sufficiency, and abundance."[123]

Although the Socialist Principle of Justice and, in general, the need canon, become inapplicable in situations of extreme scarcity, caring about the needy has its finest moment. In such dire circumstances as famine, war, or other calamities, caring's self-denying, sacrificing spirit may be very much in evidence. Even in the absence of such disasters, concerned needy parents may allocate the little they have for their children's basic needs, denying themselves some basic necessities.

(b) In the case of situations of moderate scarcity, at least two sorts of circumstances need to be distinguished: (i) where much of the resources, etc., are monopolized by one powerful individual or a small group of powerful individuals, and (ii) where monopoly is absent, but for certain reasons the resources are not uniformly or equally distributed.

In the case of both (i) and (ii), need does provide a canon of distributive justice: first for everyone's survival needs, then for their basic educational and social welfare needs. But in both types of cases, for two main reasons, the distribution or redistribution of benefits would unavoidably be less than perfectly fair or just. First, because forced distribution would be unavoidable. Second, because, as in situations of extreme scarcity, not enough would be available to satisfy the basic needs of all those in need and because even a minimal amount of redistribution of benefits would considerably diminish the ability of those who contribute, to satisfy their own needs. Here, to a greater extent than would be possible in situations of extreme scarcity, voluntary contributions out of caring or of a sense of justice would reduce the forced contributions of those who do not care, or have no sense of distributive justice.

(c) In situations of relative abundance or abundance, we must distinguish at least two sorts of circumstances; (i) where much of the resources are monopolized by one powerful individual or a small group of powerful individuals, and (ii) where much, or most, of the holdings and other resources are widely distributed among the members of the society or community. Under (i) part or the whole of the redistribution, if it occurs at all—i.e., if the state has the will and authority to take from the individual or group in question—would inescapably be forced. Unless, that is, those who have the greatest wealth happen to be great philanthropists. But outside the realm of idealized fiction, that is not very easy to imagine!

Under (ii), where the needs of many, or most, people are fortuitously satisfied, the need canon, including the "need" part of the Incentive Socialist Principle, would have little place. Still, the desire of the financially well-endowed to lavish material things on particular others, whether out of caring or ostentation, may play a considerable role. But the "incentive" part of the Incentive Socialist Principle, viz, "To each according to his contribution," would be clearly applicable.

(d) What I said under (c) about the need canon in situations of relative abundance or abundance, applies, *a fortiori*, to situations of superabundance. There—though for the opposite reason from situations of extreme scarcity—caring, like love, upsets that canon's delicate balance, rendering both the canon and the Socialist Principle superfluous. Love and caring, which are often given to excess, are apt to be even more lavishly giving when no need whatever for material giving exists.

We saw that caring and the need canon can and do complement and reinforce each other in certain types of situations. We also saw that in certain other circumstances, the need canon and the need principle of distributive justice, such as the Socialist Principle of Justice, cease to apply. But the opposite may also be true. I mean in situations of moderate scarcity [(a)] and even relative abundance [(c)], where need exists but caring, or sufficient caring for the needy—including caring about those related to oneself by blood or by law—is well-nigh nonexistent.

Even if a society or community is blessed with a period of abundance or relative abundance, philanthropy by the well-off, however widespread and genuine, and reinforced by such incentives as tax breaks, is almost never enough to satisfy the material and other basic needs of all who still need help in that society or community: *a fortiori*, in other, much less fortunate parts of the world.

This is clearly seen in the United States, the world's most affluent nation, in relation to the country's poor, and, especially, in relation to the Third World. In these cases, a considerable share of the burden of helping the poor (to the extent that they are willing to do so) cannot but fall on the shoulders of the governments of the wealthy countries.

Oftentimes, caring is not matched by the ability to help, or the demands on the caring may become progressively greater and more difficult to satisfy if the need is too great or continues for a long time. Then caring may turn to resentment and even ill will. But genuine caring too has its limits, and it may come to a stop when it entails giving part of one's hard-won earnings to the needy, especially if they are total strangers.

Some of the familiar corrosive effects of private charity and public welfare systems on the recipients are psychological dependence, loss of self-respect, anger at one's situation and the society or government that may be held responsible for it, and resentment at the caregivers. Given the population explosion in the Third World, the coming depletion of nonrenewable global resources, the environmental cost of the utilization of existing, partially renewable resources, and the continued search for new natural resources, the numbers of the world's poor are bound to continue to rise. The elimination of existing welfare systems, and even private giving in an effort to do away with their negative effects on the recipients, would be both morally and practically unjustified. The recent welfare reforms implemented by the United States government, if properly applied, should help reduce the aforementioned self-destructive feelings and behavior patterns, provided the public and private sectors cooperate to train those who are on welfare, and help them put that training to practice in decent, meaningful employment.

Needless to say, such measures, however effectively applied, would not eliminate all material need and the negative effects it brings in its train. Nor, I fear, would help, even when flowing from love or caring, enable the recipient to escape the debilitating sense of inadequacy and dependence, however much he or she may be assured and reassured that the help is motivated by caring or love.

But love and caring can, I believe, prevent loss of self-respect and dignity if those who receive the help are continually made to feel that their self-respect as persons is independent of their material means. For that to be possible in a country such as the United States, the stigma unjustifiably attached to poverty by those who have "made it," must be eliminated. It is significant (and quite understandable) that in parts of the world, such as the Arab Middle East, where the majority of the people are poor, no such stigma attaches to poverty, and where charitable organizations and close-knit families and communities are largely responsible for helping the especially needy, the sense of dependence and inadequacy appear to be much less in evidence.

To sum up. The main purpose of this long chapter was to establish the role of justice in a comprehensive care-centered ethic. For, contrary to the view of feminist moral philosophers who reject impartial justice in relation to an ethic of caring, replacing it with "equity," it was argued that, in addition to fairness and equity, formal, no less than substantive, justice has or should have an important place in such an ethic. In agreement with Brian Barry's general thesis in *Justice as Impartiality*, that if justice (in the present author's view, formal justice) is understood as second order impartiality, as Barry maintains, no real conflict would exist between an ethic of caring and justice. For he convincingly argues that universal second-order impartiality does not entail universal first-order impartiality, but leaves room for individual discretion.

To make a convincing case for that thesis, and to ascertain the roles of formal and substantive (mainly distributive) justice in an ethic of caring, as well as to describe some of the main ways in which individual and judicial discretion, including equity in the term's legal meanings, the nature of justice "in all its aspects"had to be first ascertained. After a discussion of some alternative theories of justice, Barry's view of justice as second order impartiality was accepted, but with respect to formal justice alone. The primary defining characteristic of substantive, e.g., distributive, justice, it was argued, is desert, with (second order) impartiality as its lexically secondary defining characteristic. In other words, *justice in general* or generically speaking is a "quasi-essentialist," not an "essentialist"concept, contrary to Barry's theory and the other theories discussed.

Notes

1   Miller, *Social Justice* (Oxford, 1976), 20; Campbell, ibid., 4.

2   Miller, op. cit., 24; Campbell, ibid., 4.

3   "Radical Egalitarian Justice: Justice as Equality," in *Social Theory and Practice*: 5, 1974.

4   "Justice as Desert," in *Social Theory and Practice*: 3, 1974.

5   Campbell, ibid. The reference is to Walzer's *Spheres of Justice* (Oxford, 1983).

6   Walzer, op. cit.

7   Campbell, ibid., 9.

8   Ibid.

9   Ibid., 151.

10 Ibid., chapter 6, 150–178.

11 Ibid., 6.

12 Ibid., 6.

13 That is why I used the parenthetical remark "or not simply because . . ."

14 Fittingness is another member of the family of concepts related to merit and desert, justice, and fairness. A fitting reward or punishment is a merited or deserved honor or punishment. A fair/just reward or punishment is a fitting reward or punishment.

15 We can also say that it is the due of all human beings, but in a sense in which "what is due to them" does not mean, is not identical with, "what they deserve," since human beings do not deserve justice simply as human beings. This marks one difference between the uses of "A is due to Y," in the present sense, and "Y deserves A."

16 See ibid., 6, for Campbell's statement of what (or whom) he means by the "first level of analysis."

17 Ibid., 31.

18 In *Today's Moral Problems*, 2nd ed., ed. Richard A. Wasserstrom (New York, 1979), 471–491.

19 As well as in arguing invalidly against a system of therapy for lawbreakers.

20 Just treatment includes fair, equal treatment. Since I maintained in chapter 6 that the human right to be treated as a person entails the right to equal treat-

ment, it follows from that and the present discussion that the (equal) human right to be treated as a person entails a right to justice.

21 One may wonder whether a conflict between the right to justice and the right to life is possible. But that question must be left for the future.

22 Campbell distinguishes "material" from "formal" justice as follows: "Material justice may be said to relate to the formulation of rules which embody reference to the deserts which are to be punished or rewarded, or reflected in other distributions of benefits and burdens, while formal justice is a mix of the analytically necessary efficient application of these rules, the existence of second-order rules which allow for excuses and exculpations where the standard assumptions of responsibility do not apply, the treatment of individuals as publicly answerable through fair procedure in court, and the underlying assumption of a commitment to judicial impartiality." (Op. cit., 31.)

Note also Rawls' definition of formal justice: "If we think of justice as always expressing a kind of equality, then formal justice requires that in their administration, laws and institutions should apply equally (that is, in the same way) to those belonging to the classes defined by them. As Sidgwick emphasized, this sort of equality is implied in the very notion of a law or institution, once it is thought of as a scheme of general rules. Formal justice is adherence to principle, or as some have said, obedience to system (*A Theory of Justice*, 58).

23 Ibid., 232.

24 Ibid., 191.

25 Ibid., 194.

26 Cambridge, MA., 1970.

27 Fried, ibid., 227. Barry, ibid., 229.

28 Fried, ibid. Barry, ibid.

29 Fried, ibid., 227. Barry, ibid., 229.

30 *Moral Luck: Philosophical Papers, 1973–1980* (Cambridge, 1981), 18.

31 Op. cit., 232. Italics in original.

32 Ibid., 230.

33 I have elsewhere argued that human beings have a positive, not merely a negative human right to life. See my "Need and Distributive Justice: A Defence," in *Practical Reason and Theories of Justice*, eds. Werner Maihoff and Gerhard Sprenger (Stuttgart, Germany, 1992), 115–123.

34 Barry, op. cit., 230.

35 Ibid., 19.

36 Ibid., 194.

37   Ibid., 195.

38   Ibid., 192.

39   Ibid.

40   Set out in chapter 1, Section 2 of *Justice as Impartiality*.

41   Ibid., 194.

42   Ibid., 241.

43   Ibid.

44   Ibid., 235.

45   Ibid., 236.

46   Ibid., 242.

47   Ibid., 242–243.

48   Ibid., 244.

49   Ibid.

50   Ibid., 245–246.

51   Ibid., 231.

52   (Oxford, 1961), 42.

53   Ibid., 42–43.

54   "Institutions, Practices, and Moral Rules," *Mind*, LXXXVI, no. 344 (October 1977): 479–496; and "Language and Speech as Institution and Practice," *Teorema*, IX/1 (1979): 5–38. Reprinted in my *Philosophy of Language and Logical Theory: Collected Papers* (Lanham, MD, 1995).

55   Chapter 10 of *Justice as Impartiality*, entitled "Kohlberg and the feminist critique of impartiality."

56   Ibid., 232–233.

57   Ibid., 233.

58   Ibid., 195.

59   Ibid.

60   Ibid., 249. Barry mentions Susan Moller Okin, *Justice, Gender and the Family* (esp. p. 15) as taking that position. See also Marilyn Friedman, "Beyond Caring: The De-Moralization of Gender," in Marsha Hanen and Kai Nielsen (eds.), *Science, Morality and Feminist Theory* (Calgary, Alb., 1987), *Canadian Journal of Philosophy*, supp. vol. 13 (1987): 87–110. But the way I attempt to incorporate caring and justice in the ethical theory outlined in this book is different from Friedman's (see Barry's remarks in footnote "*e*," ibid.,

249.) Barry himself has "some reservations about the terms of reconciliation that both of them [Okin and Friedman] propose" (ibid).

61   Ibid., 247.

62   Held, op. cit., 3.

63   Op. cit., 34.

64   Ibid., 249.

65   Ibid., 5–6.

66   Barry, op. cit., 250.

67   Gilligan, "Moral Orientation and Moral Development," 28.

68   Nel Noddings, *Caring: a Feminist Approach to Ethics and Moral Education* (Berkeley and Los Angeles, 1984), 52–53. Barry, op. cit., 250.
        For Barry's and my critical discussion of Noddings' feminist view, see later in this chapter.

69   Barry, ibid.

70   Ibid., 251.

71   Ibid. The same is true of the desert aspect of justice, insofar as (a) the concept of desert as such is not, as far as I can see, an issue between feminist and other moral philosophers. Similarly with (b) the element of second-order impartiality included the concept of desert, since as we have seen, impartiality in that sense is compatible with first-order partiality.

72   Barry's reference here is to Noddings' rejection of second-order impartiality, since he says: "there are some partisans of an 'ethic of caring' who wish to reject not only Kohlbergian justice but justice as impartiality." (Ibid., 251–252.)

73   Ibid., 252.

74   Noddings, op. cit., 86.

75   Barry, op. cit., 252.

76   It would be interesting to inquire whether praying to God would qualify as a relationship with Him in Noddings' sense.

77   It might be thought that the narrowness and inadequacy of Noddings' conception of the domain of moral obligation (and duty) can be established by showing that special moral obligations presuppose the existence of at least one human right, a person's human right to be free, including the moral right to choose to enter into special transactions and relationships, which result in the creation of special obligations and correlative special rights. Such an attempt is made by H.L.A. Hart in "Are There Any Natural Rights?" (*Rights*, David Lyons, ed. [Belmont, CA, 1979], 14–25. Unfortunately, the attempt is unsuccessful, as I shall briefly show.

Hart's thesis is that "if there are any moral rights at all, it follows that there is at least one natural right, the right of all men to be free"(ibid., 14). His argument is essentially that (1) to have a right entails having a moral justification for limiting the freedom of another person and for determining how he should act; (2) "the assertion of a special right . . . invokes it immediately"; (3) "the types of justification for interference involved in special rights . . . [are] independent of the character of the action to the performance of which there . . . [is] a right but dependent on certain previous transactions and relations between individuals (such as promises, contracts, authorization, submission to mutual restrictions)"; and (4) just as "in . . . saying in the case of promises and consents or authorizations that this claim to interfere with another's freedom is justified because he [the promiser, etc.] has, in exercise of his equal right to be free, freely chosen to create this claim [,] . . . in the case of special rights [in general] . . . recognition of them implies the recognition of the equal right of all men to be free" (ibid., 24–25).

Premises (1)–(3) are perfectly true: the problem lies with premise (4), the crucial part of Hart's argument. What Hart says in premise (4) is only true in the trivial, weak sense of "a right." But a promiser's creating a special right in the promisee does not presuppose the former's having a natural (human) right to be free in the desired *strong* sense of "a right"; the sense in which a natural (human) right is a very strong moral right (chapter 6). Obviously, promising restricts the promiser's freedom and presupposes her actual freedom to make or not to make the promise. But that only entails that she had *a* right to that freedom in the weak sense; that she did nothing wrong in making the promise. In other words, we cannot validly equate (a), "human beings naturally have the actual capacity or freedom to choose or not to choose to act in various ways," with (b), "they have a *natural* (human) right (entitlement) to be free." All that the existence of moral and other kinds of special rights implies or presupposes is (a)'s truth. Again, Hart's argument does not imply or entail that one's putative right to freedom is (i) a moral freedom, or that it is (ii) an equal right; and Hart provides no additional or independent arguments in support of the latter two claims.

The basic question here is the way in which promising, or entering into contracts or other types of special transactions or relationships, creates certain special norms, special rights, and obligations in the parties involved. Hart's answer is essentially that these norms can only arise from, presuppose, another norm, a natural human right; or stated negatively, that "ought" cannot be derived from "is." With that I fully agree; but as I noted earlier in this chapter, a quite different line of argument from Hart's is necessary to show how special rights and obligations arise, which, again, I shall leave to the interested reader to explore.

Finally, Hart states that "there may be codes of conduct quite properly termed moral codes . . . which do not employ the notion of a [*moral*] right, and there is nothing contradictory or otherwise absurd in a code of morality consisting wholly of prescriptions or in a code which prescribed only what should be done for the realization of happiness or some ideal of personal perfection" (ibid., 15). That is true. But to show that at least one natural right does exist, Hart assumes, without evidence, that there are special moral rights and obligations.

78   Ibid., 253.

79   Ibid.

80   Ibid.

81   Ibid.

82   Ibid., 254–255. Note that Barry correctly distinguishes mutual advantage and reciprocity, and argues that justice as reciprocity involves a "sense of fair dealing" (ibid, Part I, 48ff). But he argues that the "lack of fit between the motive for behaving justly and the criteria of justice that is inherent in justice as reciprocity would propel . . . [people] into the acceptance of justice as impartiality" (Ibid, 255).

83   Barry, op. cit., 253.

84   The kind of legal rule relevant here is what H.L.A. Hart calls "primary rules," which include, for example, criminal laws.

85   *WMT*, 154–177.

86   Ibid., 164.

87   Ibid.

88   Ibid.

89   It is significant that "historically, 'equity' developed as a separate body of law in England in reaction to the inability of the *common law* courts, in their strict adherence to rigid *writs* and *forms of action*, to entertain or provide a *remedy* for every injury. The King therefore established the high *court of chancery*, the purpose of which was to do justice between *parties* in those cases where the common law would give no or inadequate redress. Equity law to a large extent was formulated in maxims, such as "equity suffers not a right without a remedy," or "equity follows the law," meaning that equity will derive a means to achieve a lawful result when legal procedure is inadequate. Equity and *law* are no longer bifurcated but are now merged in most jurisdictions, though equity jurisprudence and equitable doctrines are still independently viable." (Steven H. Gifis, *Law Dictionary*, Woodbury, NY, 1975, 71.)

90   By Steven H. Bifis (Woodbury, NY, 1975).

91   Ibid., 75, col. 1. Italics in original.

92   Ibid., 56, col. 2. Italics in original.

93   In "Care and Context in Moral Reasoning," Marilyn Friedman speaks of "contextual relativism" in emphasizing what she considers women's sensitivity to detail. But the word "relativism" is a clear misnomer in that connection. Attention to detail, to context, is not relativism. One can readily see that if, for

example, we recall Gilligan's example of the woman who killed her neglectful husband after he strangled her pet canary.

94   Some if not all members of the radical Critical Legal Studies Group of legal scholars claim that judges have total judicial discretion, which means, in effect, that there are no legal rules. Or as one Harvard law professor put it, a judge can always choose either rule "p" or rule "not p." This view greatly exaggerates the judge's (even the most liberal Supreme Court Justice's) freedom in interpreting and applying the law, and is contrary to actual judicial practice in the United States—or elsewhere. With regard to case law, even the most liberal judges tend to respect the doctrine of "stare decisis" in relation to past precedents.

On the other hand, in the European Civil Law system, judges have little discretion in interpreting the Code, raising in an acute form the kinds of feminist concerns about abstract rules we have been addressing.

Unfortunately, fear of creating a precedent by making individual exceptions sometimes becomes an obsession with those who run institutions of all kinds; just as the fear of abuse tends to make courts and legislators leary of legalizing certain proscribed drugs or medical procedures that may or would benefit certain groups of people; e.g., marijuana for those suffering from cancer, and assisted suicide in the case of terminal patients, respectively. In these and other kinds of moral issues, the spectre of the "slippery slope argument," is always present for many people, including some moral philosophers.

95   Harold J. Berman and William R. Greiner, *The Nature and Functions of Law* (Mineola, NY, 1980), 74. The authors point out that at present the term "has the general meaning of equality or justice" (ibid, 73). But I am concerned here with its historical meaning, which seems to be the way in which feminist moral philosophers use the term, in *contrasting* equity and justice and advocating replacing the concept of justice with the concept of equity in moral theory. (See Part II of this chapter.)

96   It is worth noting that some feminists, for example, Christina Sommers and Paulia Camilli, distinguish "equity feminism" and "gender feminism," and describe the former as championing women's equal opportunity and equal treatment with men. In that sense of "equity," women's demand for equity requires the assigning of an important place for fairness and for formal justice in the ways described in Section I of this chapter.

97   Ibid., 125.

98   Ibid., 125.

99   Ibid.,126.

100   Ibid., 127.

101   Legal Realism in American jurisprudence was pioneered by Oliver Wendell Holmes.

102 For an excellent discussion of developments in English law regarding the legal rights of the "house-mate" or common-law wife, see chapter 8 of Antony Allott's *The Limits of Law* (London, 1988), pp. 259–286, entitled "The 'house-mate' or common-law wife." The epigraph to the chapter states: "An example of the competing contributions of state, courts and people in the making and unmaking of law."

103 Jeffrie G. Murphy and Jules L. Coleman, *The Philosophy of Law, An Introduction to Jurisprudence* (Totowa, NJ, 1984), 41.

104 For a discussion of cases, see, for example, Sanford H. Kadish and Monrad G. Paulsen, *Criminal Law and Its Processes, Cases and Materials*, Third Edition (Boston, 1975), *passim*. For a provocative theory regarding mental disabilities and criminal responsibility, see Herbert Fingarette and Ann Fingarette Hasse, *Mental Disabilities and Criminal Responsibility* (Los Angeles and Berkeley, CA, 1979).

105 It is interesting that so far, women have not taken up as actively the struggle against the largely male domestic and international forms of violence, such as terrorism, revolution, civil war, and war, though feminist political thinkers have written about the putative (innate?) male proclivity to aggression, and love of war.

106 Paper read at the Fifteenth World Congress of Philosophy of Law and Social Philosophy, Göttingen, Germany, August 1991.

107 Ibid., p. 5 of typescript.

108 Ibid., p. 6 of typescript.

109 The recent attacks on and repeal of affirmative action laws in higher education in California and Texas show how legal battles once won can be later lost, illustrate the need for unending effort to prevent such legal losses, as well as to regain lost ground.

110 The latest biomedical breakthrough, the cloning of a sheep in Scotland announced in late February 1997, may turn out to be an exception to that trend: since some religious leaders have already spoken against the idea of cloning human beings. The same recommendation was made to President Clinton by the special committee the White House created for that purpose.

111 In "Need and Distributive Justice: A Defence," *Praktische Vernunft Und Theorien Der Gerechtigkeit*, eds. Werner Maihofer and Gerhard Sprenger (Stuttgart, 1992), 115–123.

112 The "need principle" states that "society has the moral obligation to help its needy or disadvantaged members to satisfy their basic (a) "survival" and (b) "social interests." (a) includes physical survival, security, education and leisure; while (b) includes the satisfaction of people's basic psychological-existential needs as essentially social beings, and the realization of their physical, mental and emotional potentials" (op. cit., 115).

113   Robert McNamara, former President of the World Bank, defines "absolute poverty" as "a condition of life so characterized by malnutrition, illiteracy, disease, squalid surrounds, high infant morality and low life expectancy as to be beneath any reasonable definition of human decency." (Quoted from Peter Singer, *Practical Ethics* [Cambridge, 1979], 159.

114   In "Justice Under Socialism," *Justice: Alternative Political Perspectives*, ed. James Sterba (Belmont, CA, 1980), 200.

115   "Distributive Justice," in *Justice: Alternative Political Perspectives*, James Sterba, ed. (Belmont, CA, 1980), 149ff. The selection is reprinted from Nozick's *State, Anarchy, and Utopia* (New York, 1974).

116   Nozick writes: "Let us call a principle of distribution "patterned" if it specifies that distribution is to vary along with some natural dimension, weighted sum of natural dimensions, or lexicographic ordering of natural dimensions. And let us say that a distribution is patterned if it accords with some patterned principles. . . . The principle of distribution in accordance with moral merit is a patterned historical principle" (Nozick, in Sterba, op. cit., 153).

117   In Sterba, op. cit., 149.

118   "Like the Socialist Principle of Justice, it pictures a society in which all are required to work in proportion to the talents that have been developed in them" (Nell and O'Neill, op. cit., 201).

119   Ibid.

120   Ibid.

121   Ibid., 208.

122   Nell and O'Neill, ibid., 201. The following passage summarizes well the fundamental reasons why Marx and Engels ultimately reject that principle: "One man is superior to another physically or mentally and so supplies more labour in the same time, or can labour for a longer time; and labour, to serve as a measure, must be defined by its duration or intensity, otherwise it ceases to be a standard of measurement. This equal right is an unequal right for unequal labour. *It is therefore a right of inequality in its content, like every right.* . . . Further, one worker is married, another not; one has more children than another and so on and so forth. Thus with an equal share in the social consumption fund, one will in fact receive more than another, one will be richer than another, and so on. To avoid all these defects, right, instead of being equal, would have to be unequal" (Karl Marx and Friedrich Engels, "The Socialist Ideal," in *Justice: Alternative Political Perspectives* (Belmont, CA, 1980), ed. James Sterba, 197–198. Italics in original. Reprinted from *The Communist Manifesto* and the *Critique of the Gotha Program*).

123   Ibid.

Chapter 9

Persons, Community, and the
Ethic of Caring

A fundamental tenet of the contemporary communitarian Michael Sandel is that "*moral subjects*" or selves are "encumbered," partially constituted by their "values and ends." He rejects the "unencumbered" concept(ion) of the individual self, which he thinks is presupposed by Kantian and contemporary liberalism, most notably in Rawls' "deontological liberalism." Thus, in his *Liberalism and the Limits of Justice*,[1] he proposes to challenge the 'deontological liberalism' of "Kant and of much contemporary moral and political philosophy,"[2] describing "the deontological view" of the self as "the notion of a self barren of essential aims and attachments."[3] But he cautions that the latter view "does not imply that we are beings wholly without purpose or incapable of moral ties, but rather that the values and relations we have are the products of choice, the possessions of a self given prior to its ends."[4] Again, "deontology insists that we view ourselves as independent selves, independent in the sense that our identity is never tied to our aims and attachments."[5] Again, for Rawls as a deontological liberal, "[e]ven those attributes, such as a person's character and values, that intuitively seem closest to defining an essential self, are relegated to contingent status."[6] For Sandel, on the contrary,

> We cannot regard ourselves as independent in this way without great cost to those loyalties and convictions whose moral force consists partly in the fact that living by them is inseparable from understanding ourselves as the particular persons we are—as members of this family or community or nation or people, as bearers of this history, as sons and daughters of that revolution, as citizens of this republic. [7]

Instead, "those more or less enduring attachments and commitments . . . taken together, partly define the [moral] person I am."[8]

Feminist moral philosophers too stress what appears to be a similar if not identical relational conception of individuals as moral subjects, and their interdependence, but frequently characterize that view with the graphic but rather misleading metaphor of "embeddedness in others."[9] That relational conception of "concrete" individual selves is contrasted by these philosophers with what they call the "disembodied" and "disembedded" conceptions of Hobbes and Kant. Some contrast the concept of the "relational," "concrete" self with the concept of the "generalized" other, which they also attribute to Kohlberg and Rawls. It may also be recalled that in examining the logical grounds for the feminist moral philosophers' rejection of "the rights and justice perspective" in earlier chapters of this book, we met Seyla Benhabib's claim (1) that that perspective rests on the untenable Enlightenment liberal conception of the self as a nonrelational self, a Hobbesian "mushroom." In contrast to that view, the feminist moral philosophers posit (2) a conception of the individual person as a self-in-relation, a self "enmeshed" in others.

I

A. Sandel's "Encumbered" Conception of the Self

In this section I shall examine Sandel's view, and will compare the feminist view to it. In the next section I shall consider the implications of Sandel's "encumbered" and the feminist relational conception, for the ethic of caring outlined in this book, with specific reference to the concepts of caring, individual freedom and autonomy, and human rights. Their possible implications for the concepts of fairness and justice will be left for chapter 12.

If as moral selves we are partially constituted by our values and ends, hence by the commitments, attachments, and relationships they involve, it follows, as Sandel notes, that our moral identity changes, especially if our "deepest convictions" undergo a radical or revolutionary change. For example, if we undergo a religous conversion, such as Saul's on the road to Damascus, or Ignatius Loyola's during his convalescence from battle-inflicted wounds.

It will be recalled from our discussion in chapter 1 that Sandel invariably employs the term "community" to refer to a T-community—a kind of community that would clearly be a "constitutive community" in his sense. For a community whose members are continually engaged in the common pursuit of common ends, the communal telos or teloses, would be, as selves, partially constituted or defined by their relationship to one another by virtue of these shared ends and the values they entail. Thus a T-community can be correctly described as a "constitutive community," as Sandel does.

Since I have argued the possible (and actual) existence of a second kind of community, namely an N-community, we need to determine whether (1) the members of an N-community would also be necessarily "encumbered" as moral persons or selves, and so, whether an N-community too necessarily is, or at least can be, a "constitutive community"; since by definition no communal ends exist in an N-community. (2) More generally, we need to determine whether the "encumbered" conception of the self is true of members of noncommunal kinds of societies or social organizations. Since a positive answer to (2) would entail a positive answer to (1), I shall concentrate on that question.

To be able properly to answer question (2) we need to distinguish first (a) a "descriptive," nonnormative, empirical concept of the individual person or self;[10] and (b) a normative, moral (in general, axiological) concept of the self.[11]

(a) The self as an empirical entity, the "empirical self," is complex and includes, as the basic aspect or dimension, (i) a particular "biological self" in the form of a particular living biological organism with a particular body and mind[12]; together with another dimension or aspect, consisting of (ii) an individual (indeed, unique) "social self," in a broad use of "self," which is all that the particular individual's experiences, values, and goals, attachments and relationships, contribute to his or her being or becoming, as a particular biological self, a unique "empirical self."

The "social self" is "constructed" from and upon the individual's biological self and consists in the partial, incomplete actualizations, over time, of the latter's natural physical and mental qualities and capacities under the influence of the physical and social environment. The empirical self as a whole is, therefore, a complex product of the biological and social self.

Of course, the concepts of the "biological" and "social self" are analytical constructs or logical abstractions, and do not refer to any entities, over and above or distinct from the complex concept of a person or individual self. Similarly with the normative concept of the self, e.g., the "moral person." The metaphors of aspect and dimension, facet, or component that I am using in speaking of the biological self and the social self, and so on, are awkward if not misleading, though difficult to avoid. It is also difficult to avoid mixing these metaphors in speaking of their interaction in the total self, the person as a whole.

(b) Besides the empirical self, a person is a moral—indeed, an axiological—self. The entity we call an individual person or self—which I shall henceforth call the "moral subject"—is an organic whole consisting of the empirical-*cum*-axiological self. A person's moral/axiological "dimension" ontologically presupposes the empirical self as a whole; just as the social self presupposes or rests upon the biological self. As in any organic whole, the individual self's components—its biological, social, and axiological/moral aspects—are essentially related to one another; and through their particular essential relations, they create the moral subject as a whole.

I said that the individual self's various components are essentially related to one another, and are partially defined by their relationships. In addition, each of them is partially defined by the particular kind or kinds of its external relations. That is, the total self or person is biologically, socially, and axiologically related to other persons and to other animate beings, and to inanimate nature.

On the biological level, as a biological self, the individual is genetically related to, and is partially defined by, a complex web of genetic relationships to parents, ancestors, and relatives, as so-and-so's father, mother, son, daughter, brother, sister, etc.

The same is true of the individual as a social self: he or she is also partially defined by a web of important personal and social attachments and relationships: as a particular member of a particular nuclear and extended family (in a social sense of "family"), clan, etc.; as part of a network of friendships; as a citizen of a certain country; and as a member of a certain ethnic, racial, or religious group, and, possibly, a particular N- or T-community.

Finally, as a moral self, the individual is also partially defined by his or her moral responsibilities, duties and obligations, commitments toward others, and deep convictions, ends and values.

If the preceding analysis is correct, Sandel's encumbered conception of the individual self as a moral subject, appears to be correct.

But some of Sandel's remarks in relation to constitutive community suggest a second, stronger claim than the one I have so far considered. For in speaking of one's being partially constituted or defined, among other things, by one's personal and other deep attachments and relationships, what is really meant is that one's personality or identity is partially shaped or determined by the psychological, moral, and various other influences of others, through their relationships, etc., to oneself. But in the passages I have in mind the language he uses suggests the belief that the participants in a constitutive (T-) community, in so far as they relate to one another in the common communal endeavors, somehow become part of one another as moral subjects, reminiscent of the feminists' notion of "embeddedness." That view seems at first sight to follow from the thesis that one's values and ends are partially constitutive of one's moral selfhood. Thus on pp. 147ff. of *Liberalism and the Limits of Justice*, Sandel writes as follows in criticizing two so-called nonconstitutive, hence inadequate, accounts of community, which he labels the instrumental and the sentimental conception:

> But neither the instrumental nor the sentimental account of community, presupposing as they do the antecedent individuation of the subject, can offer a way in which the bounds of the subject might be redrawn; neither seems capable of relaxing the bounds between the self and the other without producing a radically situated subject.
>
> For this, one would have to imagine a conception of community [the constitutive community] that could *penetrate the self* more profoundly than even the sentimental view permits.[13]

For this more profound "penetration of the self" to be possible, the good of the community must be "internal to the extent of engaging the aims and values of the self . . . so thoroughgoing as to reach beyond the motivations to the subject of motivations."[14] And, "what [*inter alia*] marks such a community . . . [is] a common vocabulary of discourse and a background of implicit practices and understandings within which the opacity of the participants is reduced if never finally dissolved."[15]

Earlier, in relation to affirmative action, Sandel states what appears to be his own view, viz:

> [W]hat at first glance appear as "my" assets ["for admission to any particular opportunity"] are more properly described as common assets in some sense; since others [my "parents, family, city, tribe, class, nation, culture, historical epoch, possibly God, Nature, and maybe chance"] made me, and in various ways continue to make me, the person I am, it seems appropriate to regard them, in so far as I can identify them, as participants in "my" achievements and common beneficiaries of the rewards they bring. Where the sense of participation in the *achievements and endeavors of (certain) others en-*

gages the reflective self-understandings of the *participants*, we may come to regard ourselves, over the range of our various activities, less as individuated subjects with certain things in common, and more as members of a wider (but still determinate) subjectivity, less as "others" and more as participants in a common identity,[16] be it a family or community or class of people or nation.[17]

In other words, rather than merely holding that (some or all of) the *other* participants, in the (T-) community "C," to which they and I belong, partially make me who I am, Sandel seems to be suggesting here a quite different view. That is, in becoming participants in "C," all the other numerically distinct moral subjects and I acquire a common qualitative identity, larger, more inclusive than our erstwhile separate identities. But its poetry aside, there lurks a familiar ambiguity in the use of the word "same" in speaking of "the same achievements and values," that infects Sandel's foregoing idea and reasoning. As a result of their common endeavors, etc., the participants in "C" come to *share* the same values and achievements in a qualitative sense of "same." They would all value (say) responsibleness, benevolence, caring, solidarity, cooperation, and interdependence. But the unity that results would be a unity of "deep convictions." They themselves remain numerically separate moral selves, though as moral subjects, they would be partially constituted by qualitatively identical characteristics.

B. The "Relational Self " in Feminist Moral Theory

I now turn to a brief examination of the "relational" or "enmeshed" conception of the "concrete," moral self of contemporary feminist moral theory.

Different contributors to *WMT* describe their conception of the "moral actor" in different terms. For instance, Gilligan speaks of the interdependence of moral agents while Addelson and Benhabib "stress that the moral agent is enmeshed in a network of social and institutional relations."[18] In describing the views of the volume's contributors in the Introduction to *WMT*, the editors, Kittay and Meyers, contrast "the self-in-relation" with "a separate self."[19] Gilligan herself writes:

As a framework for moral decision, care is grounded in the assumption that self and others are interdependent, an assumption reflected in a view of action as responsive and, therefore, as arising in relationship rather than the view of action as emanating from within the self and, therefore, "self-governed." Seen as responsive, the self is *by definition* connected to others, responding to perceptions, interpreting events, and governed by the organizing tendencies of human interaction and human language.[20]

The phrase "self-in-relation," and even more clearly the words I italicized in the preceding passage, as well as the contrast that Benhabib draws between the moral agent as "enmeshed in a network of social and institutional relations" and the view of "a separate self" in Hobbes' "mushroom" account of men—or, correspondingly, between what she calls "the perspective of the concrete other" versus "the perspective of the generalized other"[21]—strongly suggests that these thinkers conceive of moral selves as partially constituted by a network of certain kinds of relationships, in essential agreement with Sandel's "encumbered" concept of the moral subject. The difference between the two accounts is that the feminist thinkers do not speak of one's "deep convictions," values, and ends as the self-constituting factors; though in the care ethic the relevant network of social and institutional relations clearly involves interdependence and responsibility, avoidance of conflict and mutual concession, and other values. As a physician said, in effect, on a public television program entitled "When Doctors Get Cancer," we are valued when we are cared about. The values of caring about another are relational values by definition, and so, morally bind the caring subject and the cared-about other, thereby valuing the latter.

II

I shall now argue that individual freedom and autonomy and human rights are not only compatible with but fit in well with a relational conception of the moral subject. If that attempt is successful, it would follow that an ethic of caring, such as the one I outlined in Part II, can consistently adopt a relational conception of the moral self without jettisoning human rights, and individual freedom and autonomy in certain relevant senses. For as will be recalled, I argued in Part II for the necessity of including human rights (as well as justice) in that ethic, as well as for the compatibility of that ethic with autonomy in these senses.

The rejection of human rights (and justice) by some feminist moral philosophers is a result of their rejection of the "atomistic" conception of the moral subject, which they think underlies the "rights and justice perspective." From that they implicitly or explicitly infer that a care ethic—which they believe rests on the relational conception of the concrete person[22]—is incompatible with a theory of human rights and abstract justice. But that conclusion does not follow, even if we suppose that an ethic of caring presupposes the relational conception of the "concrete" person.

The answer to the question: "Does an ethic of caring presuppose the relational conception of the concrete person?" is, I think, a definite "No"; although, because of that conception's important theoretical and practical implications, it is not surprising that the champions of a care ethic go too far, or misunderstand, the putative relation between the two. Let me explain.

First and most important, the relational conception does not logically affect in one way or another, or significantly alter the central concept of, any care ethic; namely, the concept of care or caring itself. What does underlie a care ethic, such as the one outlined in this book, is the real possibility of unselfish other-regarding attitudes and actions, of unselfish caring by human beings. (A solely and wholly self-seeking caring is, of course, possible, both in a psychological and an ethical egoist theory; but that is not the kind of "ethic of caring" outlined in this book!) Such unselfish caring about others can and would exist so long as there are people from whose hearts flows the milk of human kindness and compassion, and empathy and sympathy, whether, as moral subjects, they are wholly isolated and solely self-interested Hobbesian "mushrooms" or "atoms," or are inescapably "enmeshed" in others.

But to realize clearly that we are, metaphysically, essentially relational beings, not an island, but part of the main, has important existential, including ethical implications. They include the fact that to be able to actualize ourselves, in any degree, as moral subjects, we must "grapple" others to our souls "with hoops of steel"; we must be compassionate, caring, empathetic and sympathetic, responsible, and so on. That in turn may impel those of us who aim to realize themselves as moral subjects to strive to become moral, virtuous human beings, to do what the film The Indian in the Cupboard suggests: that "[g]rowing up . . . [is] the discovery of compassion—recognizing that others have needs too."[23] (These considerations are also important in relation to good and moral N- and T-communities; where the web of caring, respectful, and just relationships would enmesh the whole or a large part of these communities. Compare and contrast, in this connection, Plato's and Aristotle's view that in the Greek community/

polis one can realize one's human good, i.e., realize onself and attain happiness, only as a good member of the community, as a good citizen. That is, by furthering the realization of the communal telos, the polis' collective good.

Let me expand a bit on the important link between the relational conception of the moral subject and self-actualization. Comradely, affectionate and loving, responsible and caring relationships are, by definition, bonds of shared endeavors, values, and ends. As a result, in (and by) working to realize these interests, values, and ends by cooperative and caring endeavors, such as in a good community, one simultaneously helps realize oneself and the other as a moral subject.

The relational character of the moral subject has also important implications for the age-long and much vexed opposition between egoism and altruism, alluded to above, as Kittay and Meyers themselves observe:

> The contrast between a separate self and self-in-relation throws new light on the egoism altruism controversy. If the boundaries of the self extend to others, the boundaries between self-interest and altruism blur. Virginia Held, in exploring the possibilities of a feminist morality, suggests that this debate is defused once the self is no longer conceived as an atomic entity. [24]

In her contribution to *WMT*, Virginia Held argues that the traditional attempt to reconcile the conflicting claims of egoism and altruism:

> has called for impartiality against the partiality of the egoistic self, or it has defended the claims of egoism against such demands for a universal perspective.
>
> In seeing the problems of ethics as problems of reconciling the interests of the self with what would be right or best for everyone, moral theory has neglected the intermediate region of family relations and relations of friendship, and has neglected the sympathy and concern people actually feel for particular others. [25]

She stresses the essential "entwining" of the self with others, claiming that "[t]o focus on either self-interested individuals or the totality of all persons is to miss the qualities of actual relations between actual human beings." [26] True, but she does not tell us how it follows that if "moral theories . . . pay attention to the neglected realm of particular others in actual contexts, . . . problems of egoism vs. the universal moral point of view appear very different, and may recede to the region of background insolubility or relative unimportance." [27] More precisely, she does not establish the supposed (logical) connection between the relational conception of the self and the "defusing" of the egoism vs. altruism controversy. She simply assumes that other-regarding "empathy" and "trust and consideration" do exist.

It remains that the relational character of moral subjects is compatible with both egoism and altruism. Of course, the ethic of caring and the entire communitarian theory propounded in this book, assumes that human beings are capable of selfless acts. If that assumption is false, a nonegoistic ethic, albeit coupled with psychological egoism, would still be possible. Although I believe that that assumption is true, its vindication must be left for the future.

Whether or not Held's supposition that the egoism/altruism problem may appropriately "recede to the region of background insolubility or relative unimportance," it is true that "[t]he important problems may be seen to be how we ought to guide or maintain or reshape the relationships, both close and more distant, that we have or might have with actual human beings."[28] That is certainly a central concern for any communitarian conception of society, such as the one sketched in this book.

The relational conception of moral identity is perfectly consistent with individual moral (including human) and legal rights, as well as with individual autonomy in any of the senses distinguished in chapter 7; viz, in Hill's sense (2) of "autonomy," and in Primoratz's three interpretations of it. We can readily see this with regard to Hill's sense (2), in which autonomy "as a right to make otherwise morally permissible decisions about matters deeply affecting one's own life without interference by controlling threats and bribes, manipulations, and willful distortions of relevant information." The reason is that interference in any of the ways described is clearly incompatible with the kinds of deep relationships that partially define moral subjects.

Similarly, the relational conception of the moral subject is perfectly compatible with Primoratz's three interpretations of autonomy, viz.: (a) "concern for seeing things from the point of view of the other person," (b) as including safeguarding "a certain area of personal freedom," and (c) as including one's being free to weigh and consider other people's actions without being constrained in one's deliberations by others; being free to decide for oneself whether or not to assent to the actions. In contrast to that, the "unencumbered" conception of moral identity, as a metaphysical account of the self, leads to the untenable Kantian deontological liberal concept of autonomy, as Sandel argues at length.[29]

Another totally inadequate concept of autonomy is the Hobbesian concept of autonomy, resulting from Hobbes' radically "unencumbered" "vision of men as mushrooms." That vision, as Benhabib says, "is [more correctly, leads to] the ultimate picture of autonomy." In that sense, "the autonomous self . . . is a narcissist who sees the world in his own image, who has no awareness of the limits of his own desires and passions; and who cannot see himself through the eyes of another. The narcissism of this sovereign self is destroyed by the presence of the other."[30]

This discussion naturally leads to two other questions: (a) whether the relational account of the moral subject is compatible with autonomy in the sense of positive moral freedom, or vice versa, and, if so, (b) whether a moral right to positive moral freedom presupposes the relational account of the self.

The answer to question (a) is "Yes." The freedom to strive, in some degree or other, to actualize one's potentialities and to seek to realize one's welfare and happiness is perfectly compatible with the relational account of the self, provided that the relationships that partially define one are "I" and "Thou" and not "I-It" relationships: relationships that nurture, nourish, and sustain one in the lifelong quest for fully actualized moral selfhood. I mean relationships of caring, compassion, concern, and responsibleness, and the like. On the other hand, destructive relationships that only nurture resentment, anger, or hate restrict if not destroy one's freedom or ability to actualize or even to seek to actualize oneself morally.

The absence or loss of certain self-defining relationships, no less than the presence of certain self-defining relationships, can affect one's ability, hence actual freedom, to strive to actualize oneself morally. The absence or the loss of a parent or of parents or other members of one's family, especially during one's formative years, and of close friends, are some telling examples. Their effects on one's moral selfhood often leave lasting scars on one's psyche, sometimes stunting or crippling the individual for life. Similarly, with the lack or loss of home or country. Sometimes, however, the absence or the loss can be liberating rather than ultimately destructive.

Unlike the answer to question (a), the answer to question (b) is "No": there appears to be no logical relation between positive freedom and the relational account of the moral self. Positive freedom is logically compatible with a nonrelational and a relational account. The freedom to seek to actualize oneself as a moral subject can equally coexist with an encumbered and an unencumbered self. Nor is its scope or the scope of its proper exercise materially different in the two cases. In either case, the moral agent is oneself. Although on the unencumbered account no relationships, even the closest and deepest, define the self in any degree, they are, nonetheless, quite likely to do so, albeit not in the same way and perhaps not to the same degree as on the encumbered account. In neither case can one actually be a dominion unto oneself, an island isolated and insulated from all others. Only on the encumbered account is one part of the mainland in a more intimate way than on the unencumbered account. Here the crucial difference is that the relational account gives direction and meaning to one's positive freedom or liberty: one's self-actualization cannot be separated from, independent of—indeed, often to the detriment of—another's self-actualization. Rather, if one is joined to another by strong, sometimes unbreakable bonds of mutual caring, commitment, and responsibility, one's self-actualization is only attained—to the extent that it is attainable in a mere lifetime—in and by the other's self-actualization.

To sum up. This chapter offered an analysis of the concept of a moral subject or self, and traced its relation to the concept of a community and to the ethic of caring. To that end it examined Michael Sandel's account of the moral subject or self as "encumbered," as partially defined by its essential attachments and aims, which Sandel contrasts with what he contends is an "unencumbered" (or "atomistic") account of it, presupposed by Kantian and contemporary—most notably, Rawls'—liberalism. Examination appeared to show that, as Sandel maintains, a T-community is indeed a "constitutive community," a community whose participants or members *are* partially constituted by their shared values and ends.

The discussion next turned to the question whether the "encumbered" account of the moral self is true of the participants in any kind of social organization whatever, including an N-community. To answer that question, (a) an empirical and (b) normative moral conception of the self (which rests on an empirical self) were distinguished and analyzed. As an empirical self, a person is partially defined by complex biological-genetic, and personal and social attachments and relationships, while as a moral self, a person is partially defined by his or her moral responsibilities, duties, and obligations toward (oneself and) others, and deep convictions, ends, and values. Consequently, Sandel's "encumbered" account of the moral self appeared to be correct.

However, certain passages in Sandel's *Liberalism and the Limits of Justice* seemed to suggest a stronger view regarding a "constitutive community" than the one considered earlier, namely, the suggestion that a constitutive community "could penetrate the self" so profoundly that the participants somehow become *part* of one another as moral subjects.

The relational self, the moral self "enmeshed in a network of social and institutional relations (Seyla Benhabib), in contemporary feminist moral thought"—which, according to Carol Gilligan, for example, underlies the care framework for moral decision—was next briefly examined and contrasted with the concept of a separate self or Thomas Hobbes' "mushroom" account of men, as Benhabib describes it. Since the feminist relational self is essentially the same as Sandel's encumbered account of the self, it too passes muster.

The rest of the chapter was devoted to some of the important implications of the relational account of the moral self for individual freedom and autonomy, human rights, self-actualization, and the distinction between egoism and altruism. It was argued that positive (but not untrammeled negative) freedom, autonomy in Hill's sense 2, and Primoratz's three interpretations of autonomy distinguished in chapter 7, are not only consistent with, but fit in well with, a relational account of the moral subject, so that an ethic of caring like the one outlined in Part 2 can utilize that account without jettisoning any of these crucial things. But it was noted that no logical relation existed between positive freedom and the relational account of the moral self.

Notes

1   Cambridge, 1982.

2   Ibid., p. 1.

3   Ibid., 176.

4   Ibid.

5   Ibid., 179. The following passage encapsulates Sandel's view of Kant's concept of a subject: "The concept of a subject given prior to and independent of its objects offers a foundation for the moral law [in Kant's philosophy] that, unlike merely empirical foundations, awaits neither teleology nor psychology. In this way, it powerfully completes the deontological vision. As the right is prior to the good, so the subject is prior to its ends." (Ibid., 7)

6   Ibid., 74.

7   Ibid., 179.

8   Ibid. Note relation between this and Bernard Williams' concept of personal integrity, whose validity and importance we have had occasion to discuss in this book.

9   "Embeddedness" can easily mislead one into thinking that what is being claimed is that *I* am somehow *part* of the being of others with whom I am bound by reciprocal affection or love: my wife and children, my brother, my friends, etc. And vice versa.

10   I shall use "individual," "person," and "self " interchangeably, though the latter two are often distinguished in philosophy.

11   I shall avoid speaking of "the metaphysical concept" of the self, of the self as a "metaphysical entity," whatever that vague expression may mean; though if I were to hazard a guess, the "metaphysical self" would be some kind of combination of the "empirical" and the "normative" self.

12   The putative subconscious "mind" or aspect of the self constitutes another aspect of the empirical self's ultimate "substratum." My use of the phrase "body and mind" is not intended to preclude materialist conceptions of the empirical self.

13   Ibid., 149. My italics.

14   Ibid.

15   Ibid., 172–73.

16   A common *qualitative* identity, we should add.

17   Ibid., 143. My italics. This, stronger thesis sounds very much like an organic conception of the self, and, to that extent similar to the organic conception in Objective Idealism. This raises a question concerning Sandel's consistency, since Sandel rejects the Hegelian organic conception of a community in *Liberalism and the Limits of Justice* (see chapter 13).

18   Ibid., Introduction, 10.

19   Ibid.

20   "Moral Orientation and Moral Development," op. cit., 24. My italics.

21   "The Generalized and the Concrete Other, . . ." op. cit., 161, 163.

22   For example, Gilligan writes: "From a justice perspective, the self as moral agent stands as the figure against a ground of social relationships, judging the conflicting claims of self and others against a standard of equality or equal respect. . . . From a care perspective, the relationship becomes the figure, defining the self and others" ("Moral Orientation and Moral Development," *WMT*, 3). Similarly, Benhabib speaks of [T]he antagonism-between autonomy and nurturance, independence and bonding, sovereignty of the self and relations to others. . . . ("The Generalized and the Concrete Other, . . ." *WMT*, 163. Cf. also her discussion of the standpoint of the "generalized" and the standpoint of the "concrete" other, and the moral (and political) implications of each (ibid., 163ff.).

23   David Ansen, "The Kid Finds His Inner Adult," *Newsweek* (July 17, 1995): 60.

24   *WAMT*, Introduction, 10–11.

25   "Feminism and Moral Theory," op. cit., 117.

26   Ibid., 118.

27   *Ibid.*

28   Ibid.

29   Sandel's critique is primarily directed at Rawls: at what, in *Liberalism and the Limits of Justice*, he takes to be a metaphysical "unencumbered" account of the subject, a theory of human nature. But Rawls has responded by stressing that, in *A Theory of Justice*, his "concepts of individual rights and individual liberty are not based on a theory of human nature . . . but rather . . . on the specific twentieth-century American experience of democratic individualism." That is, his "unencumbered" account is political, not metaphysical. (Harold Berman, "Individualistic and Communitarian Theories of Justice: An Historical Approach," *University of California, Davis Law Review*, 21, no. 3 (Spring 1988): 551).

30   Op. cit., 161. Compare Peter Singer who, in arguing in support of a positive human right to life against Locke's (and Nozick's) championing of untram-

meled negative freedom, describes Locke's (and Nozick's) view of human beings as the "unhistorical, abstract and ultimately inexplicable idea" of "isolated, independent individuals in the state of nature." He correctly observes that "our ancestors were and we ourselves are social beings" ("The Famine Relief Argument," in *Morality in Practice*, 3rd. ed., James Sterba, ed. (Belmont, CA, 1991), 92.

And "if we consider people living together in a community it is less easy to assume that rights must be restricted to rights against interference. We might instead adopt the view that taking rights to life seriously [i.e., as a positive right] is incompatible with standing by and watching people die when one could easily save them" (ibid). See also my "Need and Distributive Justice: A Defence," in *Practical Reason and Theories of Justice* (Stuttgart, 1992), 115–123.

PART 3

HUMAN RIGHTS, JUSTICE, AND MORAL COMMUNITY

Chapter 10

Human Rights and Moral Community

I

In Part 1, chapter 1, I analyzed the concept of a community in general, and in chapter 2, I sketched my conception of a good and moral community. In the first part of this chapter I shall explore the place of human rights in the creation, promotion, and maintenance of a moral community and chapter 12 will deal with their place in institutions and practices in general.

There are two distinct sets of claims I shall consider, a weaker and a stronger set of claims. The former, (A), consists of two related claims concerning the dispensability or indispensability of respect for people's personhood in the sense defined in earlier chapters. These claims are (1) that equal respect for everyone's personhood is indispensable for all actual, no less than ideal, moral communities; and that that respect is an integral part of what constitutes a moral community, or, indeed, any moral society. And (2) that equal respect for everyone's personhood is indispensable for a moral community's coming into existence, including a society's transition from a noncommunal to a communal social organization.

Claims (A) (1) and (2) must be distinguished from the stronger claim (B) that the protective norms of human rights themselves are indispensable in the sense that they must be explicitly acknowledged by a community or would-be community in addition to being widely respected in practice. In less than ideal moral communities, that allows for some members' occasional forceful standing on their rights and defending them in morally permissible ways, whenever these rights are threatened.

In the next section I shall defend claim (A)(1). Since claim (A)(2) would be true if claim (1) is true, establishing claim (1) would also establish claim (2). For if these norms are necessary for a moral community's continued existence and flourishing, they would also be necessary for the transition from a noncommunitarian to a (moral) communitarian form of social organization. As for (B), a restricted or qualified form of it will be defended in Section III.

II

Respect for people's personhood, including respect for their human rights, is a foundation for any morally good relationship, whether close or distant, social, economic, personal, or other. There are both negative and positive reasons for this. Negatively it is indispensable, because of the ever-present possibility of individual and group interest conflicts: conflicts that, as we shall presently see, lead Steven Lukes to maintain that the protective norms of justice and human rights are indispensable even in a community of angels. These conflicts may be of two sorts. The first results from opposed or divergent visions of the good (or of one's own good), the second, from differing conceptions of the most efficient, or the morally permissible means for the attainment of particular desired goods. Conflicts of either kind are probably unimaginable in a community of angels, though one might perhaps imagine an angelic host with competing ideas of how to please the Almighty. More plausibly, a "true" community of angels would be a community in which complete harmony of ends and means reigns supreme. But at their very best, human beings are a strange mixture of the angelic and the demonic (often vastly more demonic than angelic). In their case the possibilities for conflicting interests are very real—and numerous. If A and B, whose interests, "X" and "Y," conflict, show equal respect for each other's interests, overt conflict would be averted or minimized. Such respect presupposes a spirit of cooperation and compromise rather than an adversarial, confrontational stance, and would lead to compromises and mutual adjustments. Or if the differences run too deep, A may defer his or her pursuit of "X," to allow B to pursue "Y," with the understanding that later on B would reciprocate. In short, in the situations described, temporary sacrifices would be made willingly and voluntarily.

Two paradigms of relationships based on mutual respect for one another's personhood are families blessed with love and close friendships,[1] although other paradigms are to be found in other, albeit relatively rare attachments in which mutual adjustments, and the spirit of compromise and sacrifice, are common occurrences. The entire life of these noble and saintly individuals may be dedicated to the service of others. Their own interests are almost completely identified with the interests of those they serve. In such cases, sacrifice and self-sacrifice really cease to have meaning.

It should be emphasized that such adjustments, compromises, and other ways of harmonizing the self's and the other's interests, or one party's changing its interests or deferring its pursuit to allow the fruition of the other party's interests—provided it is freely undertaken—does not violate the human right of those who make them to seek their own actualization. In these circumstances, the agent temporarily refrains from exercising her right to satisfy the relevant needs and interests for the higher good of solidarity and caring, love or friendship.

Not uncommonly, conflicting interests or projects may be too important and central (commitments in Bernard Williams' sense) for the aforementioned ways of conflict resolution to succeed. To overcome the impasse, the protective norms of fairness or justice, which as we saw in Part 2, can be quite sensitive in various ways to differences in the strength, importance, and other relevant circumstances relating to the parties' strong preferences for their projects and ends, may have to come into play. In these cases, strictly equal weighing of the conflicting interests would obviously not help. Alternatively, in the manner of preference utilitarianism, the probable consequences of the pursuit of the competing interests would need to be carefully weighed. The weightier or weightiest would be allowed to be pursued. That way of resolving an interest conflict is most at home when love or friendship is absent; in the impersonal or less personal political and economic domains.

Apart from the above negative reason for the indispensability of equal respect for personhood in any actual, imperfectly moral attachment or relationship, there is at least one major positive reason that argues for the same conclusion. It is similar to the basic reason for the indispensability of Kant's categorical imperative, in its third formulation, if interpreted as MacIntyre does in *After Virtue*.

MacIntyre argues that Kant fails to provide a rational justification for his categorical imperative since ethical egoism is a perfectly self-consistent position. If he is correct, would it not be also true that respect for personhood in my sense is not indispensable in a moral community? The answer, I think, is "No." Assuming for the sake of argument that MacIntyre is right concerning the categorical imperative, it remains that treating all others equally as "ends," as MacIntyre interprets it, is a necessary demand of morality.[2] In fact he himself says that the egoist's making an exception for himself "may be immoral." For he says that what Kant "means by treating someone as an end rather than [merely] as a means seems to be the following

> I may propose a course of action to someone either by offering him reasons for so acting or by trying to influence him in non-rational ways. If I do the former I treat him as a rational will, worthy of the same respect as is due to myself, for in offering him reasons I offer him an impersonal consideration for him to evaluate. . . . By contrast an attempt at non-rational suasion embodies an attempt to make the agent a mere instrument of *my* will, without any regard for *his* rationality.[3]

For to treat someone as an "end" in the described sense is to treat her as a moral subject or person in my sense.

The positive reasons for equal respect for personhood in a moral community rest on the fact that human rights are moral entitlements, protections, and defenses. A loving relationship is fundamentally one of mutual respect for the other's autonomy. It is the paradigm of the "I-Thou" relationship, as Søren Kierkegaard, Martin Buber, and other religious existentialists have emphasized. The relationship embraces all varieties of human love and friendship. In the absence of equal consideration and treatment of the other as a free agent, love and friendship cannot take root or flourish. But if these qualities are essential for the existence and flourishing of loving and affectionate relationships, how much more so they are in less personal, and, above all, in impersonal relationships!

The operation of the individual's right to equal consideration or equal treatment is interestingly reflected in American common law in relation to the traditional "freedom of contract" principle. In certain notable cases the courts have attempted to limit or restrict that freedom in light of the need to give equal consideration to the contracting parties' interests. I have in mind situations in which one party had taken advantage of the other through fraud or misrepresentation of pertinent facts, and the like.

III

Human Rights and Moral Community

If my contention in Section II is correct, equal respect for the personhood of others is indispensable for a moral community: indeed, for any form of social organization. I now turn to thesis (B). Here we must distinguish two variants or subforms of that thesis. The first, strong claim is (a) that the *exercise* of a community member's human rights, including his or her standing on them, is at least sometimes indispensable. The weaker claim is (b) that only the *concept* of human rights is indispensable, or that the *concepts* of particular human rights are indispensable, not necessarily their exercise by anyone.

In what follows I shall concentrate on the strong thesis, (B)(a), which presupposes thesis (B)(b). I shall argue that the former is true with respect to economic and other impersonal or relatively impersonal relationships and transactions, and less frequently, in close relationships, in which love, friendship, or altruism in general is present. The occasional need for the exercise of their human rights and (perhaps only rarely) even to defend them, stems from the imperfection of human nature: an imperfection that may sully the noblest and most selfless friendship or love.

In "Protective Norms as a Basis for Cooperation between Non-Privileged Constituencies,"[4] Carl Hedman presents and criticizes two opposite views that concern claims (B) above; namely, whether the protective norms of human rights and justice are an indispensable feature of morality.[5] Hedman finds the two opposite alternatives wanting and suggests an intermediate or "mixed" position.[6] One of the opposite alternatives is maintained by Steven Lukes, who argues that these norms are indispensable for a community; while Michael Sandel takes the opposite position.[7] Hedman argues that we "shouldn't say that protective norms will always be needed, but neither should we rule out the possibility that they might play a progressive *transitional* role"[8] ; i.e., as "an indispensable means to a social order where protective norms could lose their importance."[9] Hedman, like Lukes and Sandel, fails to distinguish theses (B)(a) and (B)(b). But the following makes it clear that all three are concerned with the stronger thesis (B)(b). To illustrate what he considers a "misplaced standing on the demands of justice among friends," Sandel gives as an example a close friend's repeated insistence "on calculating and paying his precise share of every common expenditure" or refusing "to accept any favor or hospitality except at the greatest protest and embarrassment." This is also seen in Sandel's, Lukes', and Hedman's discussion of interest conflicts in a community and whether they render the "protective norms of rights and justice" indispensable. The "social order" referred to is a moral community. Lukes speaks of the protective dimension of morality as follows: "It is a fundamentally important part of morality as a whole, deeply rooted in every possible form of social life and inseparable therefore from any attainable social ideal."[10]

The "underlying intuition" of Lukes' position, Hedman observes, is that "there will always be interest conflicts that call forth protective norms. Such interest conflicts may be due to differing visions of the good, but they need not be. Nor need such conflicts reflect a lack of solidarity between individuals."[11] They arise out of the fact that the community members would enter into many different social relations. Since conflicts can occur, protective norms would be necessary to protect the interests of the conflicting parties.[12]

Interest conflicts may be either individual or group conflicts, including community-wide conflicts. The idea of interest conflicts between individuals or groups in a community is straightforward; but the idea of "community-wide" interest-conflict requires some explanation. In the case of N-communities, 'community-wide interest conflict' can only mean a conflict involving the divergent interests of large segments of the community, resulting in a split or division in the community. In the case of T-communities there may be a further sort of general division: divisions regarding the nature or desirability of the communal teloses themselves, and/or the means employed or proposed to realize them. Even those communities of which *all* members are committed to a common telos or vision of the good, are not immune to communal conflicts: either because of changes or revisions in some members' original conception of the good, or because some members feel that the community had abandoned or betrayed its original vision.

Even when the majority of the community's members share a common ethical position, e.g., if they are all (say) rule-utilitarians, or all Kantian deontologists, the familiar ethical problems they face, and attempts to harmonize them, can be sources of conflict. For example, such familiar abuses as "telishment" and scapegoating, to which utilitarianism, including rule-utilitarianism, is open in principle, would require the constraints of the protective norms of human rights.[13] More generally, the inevitable differences in the members' values or their ranking of them even if we imagine all the members to be utilitarians, or deontologists, are sometimes bound to result in interest conflicts. The treatment of offenders can be one such example. I mean disagreements about the fairness or justice of certain penal measures or their application to particular cases. Differences about other laws or certain of the community's social conventions or traditions may be other examples.

(A) The diversity of visions of the good can be particularly serious in relation to groups interested in creating a T-community, or in maintaining one already in existence. The problem can also arise in N-communities, in relation to the members' various relationships. In addition to possible divergent conceptions of the good, there would always be differences in the degree of people's individual physical or psychological-existential needs and interests, and the ways in which they seek, or would like to seek, to satisfy them.

(B) Again, complete solidarity between members of a community is all but impossible because of people's limited capacity for altruism and benevolence, affection, love and caring, and the general predominance of self-centeredness and possessiveness.

(C) Lukes gives additional reasons why "people, after all, get it wrong," and consequently why protective norms would be needed even if "divergent conceptions of the good, and of basic and vital interests, were to converge within a single moral and political conception."[14] These reasons are that "even under cooperative abundance, altruism, and the unification of interests within a common conception of the good, people . . . may fail to act as they should toward others, because they do not know how to or make mistakes, with resulting mis-allocation of burdens and benefits, and damage to individuals' interests."[15] But Hedman is, I think, correct in thinking that "such cognitive deficiencies are too weak a basis for showing the importance of protective norms."[16] The possibility of conflicts, particularly of the sorts I have enumerated, remains for me the main basis for Lukes' correct intuitions.

(D) Despite the weakness of the argument from "cognitive deficiencies," the argument nevertheless points to an important source of conflict. I mean specifically such things as honest mistakes, lack of foresight or understanding, or sufficient knowledge, even with regard to those close to oneself,[17] and human irrationality or deficient rationality.

We can only speculate, *pace* Lukes, whether rights would be indispensable in a community of angels, or whether as Sandel would maintain, the opposite would be true. What we can say with greater assurance is that a world in which no protective norms exist because they are not needed, would be a decidedly better world than one in which they are indispensable. One reason is that, as R. M. Hare observes, standing on one's rights frequently creates conflicts. Note how preoccupation with, and continual insistence on one's *legal* rights, has created incredible amounts of litigation in the United States, in sharp contrast to the paucity of litigation in countries where the concept of individual rights plays an insignificant role, for example, in the Arab Middle East. It is interesting that the situation there is significantly different with regard to the territorial and other international rights of these countries, but quite like the situation in most other countries.

Hedman notes that Sandel's view "sees a focus on protecting individual interests as one of the main obstacles to creating a social order where protective norms could lose their importance."[18] It can create the very circumstances that make it seem so important, for example, if "a close friend of long-standing repeatedly insists on calculating and paying his precise share of every common expenditure." Clearly, as Sandel says, such concern with justice leads to the diminution of the circumstances of benevolence, as the circumstances of justice grow.[19] Hedman thinks Sandel's primacy concern is with "finding ways to avoid a situation where protective norms become indispensable just because they have created a social order where people can't deal with interest conflicts in any other way."[20]

The thesis I shall endeavor to establish here, and in greater detail later in this chapter, is intermediate between Lukes' and Sandel's views, and hence is in partial agreement with Hedman's view. It maintains (C) (a) that in actual, imperfect moral communities the protective norms of human rights are neither indispensable in all societal relationships, nor dispensable in all. They are indispensable in certain kinds of relationships, but *normally* dispensable in others.[21] They are normally dispensable in close, loving, caring relationships such as in loving nuclear and extended families and in close friendships, but generally indispensable in the public domain, where only superficial or totally impersonal relationships exist. (b) It follows, in agreement with Hedman, that the protective norms of human rights are indispensable (in the types of cases I mentioned) in the transition from a noncommunitarian to a communitarian social order. But (a) differs from Hedman's view in so far as he believes that these norms would be dispensable once community (hence solidarity) is achieved.

(1) I have already discussed the possibility of interest conflicts in considering claims (A) in Section II. Here I merely wish to point out that the two opposing camps represented by Lukes and Sandel respectively concentrate on conflict to the exclusion of other important

reasons for the necessity of protective norms. Take justice for instance—to anticipate the discussion in chapter 12. Legal justice, in the form of procedural, substantive, and, perhaps, rectificatory justice, is concerned with settling disputes or anticipating the causes of conflict. But distributive justice in the narrow sense is concerned with fair distribution of benefits, while penal or so-called retributive justice is concerned with the fair distribution of burdens: in the latter, with, among other things, the fair assessment of penalties for violations of the law. More directly germane to our present purposes, human (and special moral) rights are extremely important not only for the extra-legal adjudication of actual conflicts but also for the prevention of possible conflicts, and arbitrary and unequal treatment of others. Another function of these rights is to provide to all the members of a community a sense of their physical and psychic security, anchored in the knowledge that they have fundamental moral protections, and that as moral persons, all community members are worthy of respect; that they are not objects to be exploited and even disposed of at will.[22] That is absolutely essential for self-esteem or self-respect, and consequently, for the existence of a secure sense that if one exercises, claims, stands on, or defends one's rights, one is doing what one is morally entitled to, not acting improperly or wrongly. In the absence of self-respect or self-esteem, one finds it extremely difficult to muster the inner resources necessary to strive and struggle to satisfy one's basic needs and realize one's goals and potentialities in the face of life's obstacles and pitfalls. The sense of psychic security one gains from self-esteem or self-respect makes for healthy, or healthier, loving and caring relationships, and helps satisfy one's basic need for acceptance and belonging.

(2) Solidarity is rightly emphasized by both Sandel and Hedman as an essential feature of a (moral) community. To see whether its existence in a community renders the protective norms of human rights dispensable, as both philosophers believe, we must see what its sources are; what makes it possible. Clearly these sources are various. In a T-community, one obvious source is the communal telos(es), the "shared vision of the good." That particular bond is absent from N-communities.[23] But in these as well as in T-communities, love and friendship, and the caring that blossoms from both, are the preeminent sources of community solidarity. In the absence of one or another of these powerful bonds, even the solidarity of like-minded people held together and moved by a shared vision of the good can easily fray and eventually break. In their absence, centrifugal forces would tend to dominate.

Personal ambitions, inflated egos, abrasiveness, competitiveness, professional jealousies and rivalries take over, even in professional communities with well-defined common goals, and solidarity goes by the board. Such divisive and destructive tendencies are not uncommon in artistic, educational, scientific, industrial-military, and business institutions and practices.

One might argue that such rivalries, and consequent secretiveness and reluctance to share vital information, show that the individuals purportedly pursuing common goals are not really interested in realizing them as quickly and as efficiently as possible—things which require honest sharing of information, ideas, and discoveries—but only in personal aggrandizement. There is some truth in this; but the "only" is too strong and, in a way, unfair. The desire for recognition, it will be remembered, is rooted in basic human needs, and, as far as it goes, is perfectly in order. What is undesirable in the kind of situation described is the way these needs are satisfied, or their satisfaction is pursued. They interfere with the communal goals of the medical, scientific, industrial, or other discoveries or inventions made, and so, fail to further the general welfare.

A consideration of the possible place of human rights in a moral community would be grossly incomplete unless it comes to terms with Karl Marx's claim that in all class societies "every right is a right of inequality,"[24] that equal rights perpetuate the inequalities of unequal, class society. If that contention is true, it would also be true, as Marx maintains, that a truly egalitarian society, consequently a moral community, would have no place for rights, human rights included.[25] In fact, as a ("pure") consequentialist (whether or not he can be called a utilitarian of sorts is another question), Marx has and can have no place for human rights in his ethical theory.[26]

My response to this argument is as follows. In the transition from the present, inegalitarian society to a moral community in which, among other things, the ideals of equal individual freedom, opportunity, and treatment would be increasingly approximated, the following steps would be essential.

(1) To lessen the inequality of treatment and opportunity, affirmative action legislation (as in the case of the laws enacted in the United States during the 1960s and 1970s) would be a necessary step. By the laws' utilizing the principles of rectificatory justice, past injustices against oppressed groups (certain ethnic minorities, women, children, etc.) would be compensated for, as much as circumstances permit: either by direct payment or by the provision of special educational,

employment, and other opportunities. The legislation would have to include provisions for the temporary preferential treatment of members of these groups by the provision of some degree of priority in education, the job market, promotions, and the like until the gap between them and the more advantaged sectors of society is appreciably narrowed.[27]

But reverse discrimination must be carefully avoided, by, for instance, banning hiring or promotion quotas. Hard cases, where the line between legitimate preferential treatment and reverse discrimination is hazy, would be decided in the courts.[28]

These and other measures, intended to help equalize treatment and opportunities, would also apply, mutatis mutandis, to the physically or mentally disabled or handicapped, though the limitations imposed on them by their disabilities or handicaps greatly reduce the areas in which they can compete with those who are not. Consequently, the occasions for putative "reverse discrimination" would be, in principle, more limited in their case.

(2) Although the Socialist Principle of Justice would be perfectly fair to those whose needs are great but whose ability to work and to contribute to society is limited or nonexistent, fairness requires that those who bear its burdens should be somehow "compensated," e.g., by tax breaks, in proportion to their contribution to society, as, to a limited extent, in the United States. Fairness also requires that those in need contribute to society to the extent of their ability, rather than have their needs satisfied by society without their working for it in any way.[29]

Affirmative action and an implemented "need principle," as I shall presently describe it, are intended to meet, among other things, Marx's criticism that equal rights are rights of inequality in an unequal society. They are intended to do so by progressively lessening the inequalities of a basically inegalitarian, e.g., capitalist or, even, welfare state, a state that enables the advantaged to use their (equal) rights to protect their unjust privileges at the expense of the less advantaged and disadvantaged.

The "need principle" (or N-principle) states that "society has the moral obligation to help its needy or disadvantaged members to satisfy their basic (a) "survival" and (b) "social interests." (a) includes physical survival, security, education, and leisure; while (b) includes the satisfaction of people's basic psychological-existential needs as essentially social beings, and the realization of their physical, mental, and emotional potentials.[30]

But can a society consistently implement affirmative policies, if not also the "need principle," without being forced to jettison equal human rights protections? For the fact is that affirmative action and especially the need principle appear to be needed not just in the transition to a progressively more egalitarian community but in an egalitarian community as well, for the simple reason that even the most exemplary actual community is bound to fall short of ideal equality.[31]

If the preceding is true, would not *human rights* become completely unnecessary, and have no place either in the transitional stage or in the resultant moral community? In the case of the latter, that would seem to be true for two reasons. First, because in a moral community as I have characterized it, the need principle, like Marx's Socialist Principle, would seem to be, if not the only principle of distributive justice, certainly the principle of distributive justice *par excellence*.[32] Second, given the imperfection of all human institutions, affirmative action policies too would be indispensable throughout a moral community's existence.

My own view is that the implementation of the need principle would not render human rights dispensable in actual, imperfect moral communities. First, the striving of the needy for the satisfaction of their basic psychological-existential needs, and the actualization of their potentialities, can only be *indirectly* protected by the implementation of the need principle, insofar as it would help them to pursue these interests and goals by directly ameliorating their physical condition. Second, it is *possible* for the need principle to be optimally implemented without the imposition of onerous burdens on those who provide the (re)distributed holdings. That would be true provided that a sufficient number of people enjoy the requisite material wealth. Clearly, the need principle can come into play only if a part of, not the entire community, is in great need. Then human rights would be needed to help morally protect the rest of the community: the well-off or relatively well-off, if not the disadvantaged as well.

Again, I see no logical conflict between affirmative action and the need principle, on the one hand, and the rights to individual freedom, equal treatment, and opportunity, on the other. I shall try to establish this first in relation to the need principle, then in relation to affirmative action.

It is obvious that the need principle conflicts with the freedom of the advantaged to do with their wealth whatever they please, as they please (cf. Robert Nozick, in *Anarchy, State, and Utopia*). But that putative negative freedom or liberty is not one to which, in my view,

individuals are morally entitled *qua human beings*. On my more restricted concept of a positive human right to freedom,[33] the ability of
the more advantaged individuals to exercise their right to satisfy their
basic needs and to actualize their potentialities is hardly curtailed or
compromised by the need principle's just implementation, assuming
that relative plenty exists. For just and fair redistribution requires that
after the community's just transfer of part of their holdings to the
needy, enough be left to those who contribute the holdings. What is
justly left over would be defined either by what Nozick calls the Lockean
proviso or by Nozick's own weaker form of it, in his account of the
"principle of justice in acquisition." Locke's proviso is that "there be
enough and as good left in common for others,"[34] and is meant, as
Nozick notes, "to ensure that the situation of others [here the well-to-
do or advantaged[35]] is not worsened."[36] Nozick's weaker proviso would
exclude someone's being made worse off "by no longer being able to
use freely (without appropriation) what he previously could."[37] Communities in which everyone is poor but where solidarity and caring are
such powerful forces that people willingly share the little they have
with the most needy at the cost of great sacrifice to themselves, would
constitute noteworthy exceptions to the normal conditions for the need
principle's implementation. Such generosity of spirit in the case of the
poor is far from inconceivable. It tends to exist most in time of general
stress or calamity, such as great scarcity brought about by war or a
very meager harvest.

Since the need principle was defended in general in chapter 8, I
shall not attempt to defend it here against either the libertarian, for
example, Nozick's, principles of distributive justice, or other principles
of distributive justice. What should be noted here is that that principle
fits in well with this book's overall thesis about the importance of our
satisfying our basic survival and social, including our psychological-
existential needs and actualizing our potentialities. As for the Socialist
Principle of Justice, the interested reader is referred to Marx' and
Engels' forceful presentation and defense of that principle in the *Communist Manifesto* and *Critique of the Gotha Program*,[38] as well as
Edward Nell's and Onora O'Neill's defense of it in "Justice Under
Socialism."[39]

What about affirmative action, it may be asked? On the face of it,
the enactment and implementation of civil rights legislation seem to
be inconsistent with the social ideal of equal rights for all: in fact, it is
inspired by it and endeavors to create the conditions under which
everyone's equal rights would be increasingly protected. Seen in light

of the conception of basic human rights in this book, it is an important mechanism designed to help provide various sorts of opportunities to the disadvantaged sectors of society, and to help them realize their political, economic, educational, and other interests, on as close to an equal footing with all others as imperfect human conditions permit. The progressive approximation to equal educational opportunities is a key to the success of affirmative action. As ideally envisioned, inequalities in them and in economic and political opportunities are progressively reduced with successive generations so that a return to blatant discrimination in the treatment of particular sectors of society would become more difficult. In actual fact, the struggle for equality in these areas cannot be realistically considered as a transitory phase that would eventually give way to a classless society, to communities of free and completely equal men and women. Consequently, I do not think that affirmative action (though perhaps not preferential treatment) will ever become completely dispensable in any actual moral community.

In the transition from present, grossly inegalitarian and unjust societies all over the world to more moral or less immoral societies, the goal of protecting everyone's ability to exercise unhindered his or her equal human rights must be kept fully alive as an ideal to which society should aspire. Correspondingly, the struggle of the disadvantaged to gain equality requires their utilizing their moral and legal entitlements to approach that ideal, ever careful not to lose the equalities they gain, or allow them to be taken away from them. For the struggle to succeed, it is also essential that the more fortunate recognize, even if only grudgingly, that affirmative action is not tantamount to reverse discrimination.

Alasdair MacIntyre, in defending a broadly Aristotelian virtue ethic in *After Virtue*, rejects out of hand the very idea of "natural rights." What specifically concerns us here in relation to that work is whether the communitarian character of Greek, Roman, Medieval, and Renaissance European societies provides historical support for the claim that the protective norms of human rights are dispensable in a moral community. The question is raised by MacIntyre's statement that "It would of course be a little odd that there should be such rights attaching to human beings simply *qua* human beings in light of the fact . . . that there is no expression in any ancient or [sic] medieval language correctly translated by our expression 'a right' until near the close of the middle ages: the concept lacks any means of expression in Hebrew, Greek, Latin or Arabic, classical or medieval,[40] before about 1400."[41] And so on.

The nonexistence of the concept of "natural rights" in the afore-mentioned societies—assuming that human rights exist in some sense—provides no rational support for the claim that they have no place in a moral community. It is possible to provide satisfactory historical explanations of why these societies lacked the concept, but that is unnecessary here. What is important for our above question is that, with the exception of, say, the Christian monastic communities (such as the community founded by St. Benedict in the Sixth Century.[42]) the Greek, Roman, Medieval, and Renaissance communities in Europe were anything but moral communities and cannot provide counter-examples to our thesis. It suffices to note that the Greek and Roman societies were based on slavery and were blatantly sexist to boot, and that serfdom formed the infrastructure of Medieval European society. Owing to the foregoing reasons, even Athens during the brief Periclean period—though less flawed than the tyrannies that preceded or succeed it—could not qualify as a moral community. One may also question whether ordinary Greek, Roman, and Medieval European men and women exhibited in any appreciable degree the moral virtues that MacIntyre considers as the cardinal virtues of the Greek T-communities during the Homeric period, or during the fifth and fourth centuries B.C., and later. Similarly with the Roman and the Medieval Christian virtues, including, in the latter case, hope, faith, and love—or these together with patience, forgiveness, and repentance. And so on.

Essentially the same considerations apply to present-day Middle Eastern Arab communities, where the so-called Mediterranean ethic and morality of honor, dishonor, and shame continue to be a powerful force, and where the concept of human rights still lacks a significant role in people's daily lives. Although these communities exemplify a considerable number of the virtues of a moral community, they too have serious moral flaws, due to the absence of sensitivity to or clear consciousness of the idea that women and men, young and old, rich and poor, the powerful and the powerless, all have—indeed, have equal—human rights. I particularly have in mind the society's grossly inegalitarian and discriminatory hierarchism and male sexism.

IV

Continuing the discussion of the place of human rights in the creation and sustenance of a moral community, I shall now focus on the possible role of human rights in the personal relations that exist within the institution of the family, between other relatives, and between friends, together with the more tenuous relations between acquaintances and the completely impersonal relations between total strangers. The next chapter will then explore the place of human rights in the institutions and practices in a moral community other than the family.

My general approach will be as follows. I shall begin with (A) the institution of the nuclear family, as the ultimate—at its best, the most organic—unit at the heart of a community, and will systematically broaden the scope of the inquiry to (B) the extended family and the cluster of blood-related families or clans, thence to a community as a whole, which, in addition to (A) and (B), includes (C) (1) friends, (2) next, acquaintances, and (3) finally, total strangers. Using that approach, I shall attempt to establish—what I believe is, however, quite obvious—that in light of their nature and function, human rights are least operative, hence the need to protect them least necessary, in a *good*, that is, loving nuclear family. They, together with their protection, normally become increasingly important as relationships radiate further from the nuclear family center. Within a given community, they normally become most important in people's dealings with casual acquaintances and, above all, strangers. That is, in what Søren Kierkegaard calls "I-It relationships." I said "within a given community" since the need to have their human rights protected and respected becomes theoretically even greater in intercommunity transactions and relationships. That is especially true if the communities have very different basic values and attitudes.

A. Human Rights and the Nuclear and Extended Families

The traditional, heterosexual family is a unique institution and a unique community unit, a microcosm of an N- or a T-community; and a good family is a special if not unique kind of moral community. It has features not found in socioeconomic, political, legal, or other types of public institutions. In certain ways, its basic structure and mode of operation are, among other things, importantly different in certain ways from those of the latter institutions.

Among the differences, a few may be mentioned here. To start with, the traditional family is created by a special religious or civil practice in the semi-technical sense of *practice*, defined by John Searle in *Speech Acts*. In that respect, it is exceptional, since, as far as I know, only language—if it is an institution—has been created by a practice, the practice of speech. In other instances, institutions create associated or ancillary institutions and/or practices, such as religious schools created by religious institutions. "Institutional activities," the activities of an institution's membership, are defined by the constitutive conventions or rules (C-conventions or rules) of the particular institution. In many cases these constitutive activities are simply the institutions' normal day to day operations. In the traditional family, at least some of its C-conventions are provided by the wedding's religious or secular practice. That practice also provides the regulative rules (R-rules) that regulate and assess the marital and parent-child and child-parent relationships, as well as evaluate the family's goodness or badness as a whole.

The traditional family has something distinctive in another important way. Justice and the principles of justice—at least of moral justice—do not arise in relation to it. In that respect John Rawls is correct. But it is otherwise with fairness as distinct from justice, as we shall see later. Again, unlike other institutions, where "good institution," in the narrow sense, is logically distinct from, although overlaps with, "moral institution," "good family" is identical with "moral family."

But the first question is whether the *concept* of human rights itself is applicable at all to the traditional family. My answer is (a) "yes," but (b) *standing on, asserting*, and, above all, (c) *fighting for* one's human rights, have no practical place in a *good*-moral, *i.e., loving* family. Let me explain., I shall attempt to establish—what I believe is, however, quite obvious—that in light of their nature and function, human rights are least operative, hence the need to protect them least necessary, in a *good*, that is, loving family. Let me explain.

(a) It is obvious that, as human beings, the members of a family have human rights. As *right-holders*, they stand in the same moral relation to one another as they do to all other individuals, with whom they also stand in a rights-relation. But only certain of these rights, such as the rights to security of person and personal privacy as understood in chapter 5, are pertinent to them as members of the family institution. In the case of children, another pertinent right is the right to have their special needs and interests satisfied, and by and by, to become emancipated as adults.

These and other pertinent rights have practical application to the members of a family, not only theoretical application, e.g., as concepts. Among these rights are various legal rights, such as the right of family members to "recognition everywhere as persons before the law."[43] Another, political human right is the right to "freedom of movement and residence within the borders of the state"[44] and "the right to leave any country, including . . . [one's] own, and to return to [one's] country."[45]

B. Good-Moral Family

Much of what I have to say in the rest of this chapter, including my remarks about love, friendship, and the like, is quite obvious and common knowledge. But for our purposes it is useful to remind ourselves of it.

A good family, ideally speaking, is essentially a loving family: a family founded firmly on mutual love, with all that love entails, including loyalty, selflessness, and a profound and lifelong commitment to sacrifice—in extreme cases, to sacrifice life itself—for one another's life or happiness. But love in general also involves the ability to identify oneself with the loved ones, so that the others' happiness and unhappiness, successes and failures, joys and sorrows, become one's own. It is, therefore, the very antithesis of that egoism and self-centeredness whose results are envy, resentment, and extreme competitiveness, and hence sorrow at the another's successes and achievements and delight in his or her frustrations and failures.

Ideally, these qualities are associated particularly with loving parents; though siblings too, of course, may exemplify them in a very high degree, both in relation to their parents and their siblings.

Again, ideal love entails respect for the loved persons' moral personhood, and their rights. The importance of this cannot be exaggerated, for love without respect and without equality—if it can be called love at all—is a deeply flawed love. Haughtiness and arrogance, a holier than thou attitude toward those one claims to love, is a sure way of killing love. For arrogance and a sense of superiority cannot coexist with respect for others as persons, and as equals.

Apart from the fact that I have been describing perhaps a humanly unattainable ideal of love, certain difficulties inhere in love itself. The desire not to cause the other the slightest unhappiness or pain tends to inhibit lovers from open and honest discussion of the deepest, most serious stresses and strains affecting their relationship. Indeed, being able truthfully to speak one's mind, so important for a healthy relationship, is often quite difficult in one's relations with members of one's immediate family and close relatives, as well as with one's closest friends. Ironically, such openness is least difficult where it matters least: in one's superficial contacts and passing relationships with acquaintances and strangers! Not surprisingly, *complete* honesty (assuming that it is humanly possible, even in relation to oneself) can jeopardize the best relationships, in any walk of life. In that area "the truth, the whole truth and nothing but the truth" can be utterly ruinous. The appreciation of that fact is, I think, one main reason why "make-believe" is so pronounced and so widespread in traditional societies with a strong communal lifestyle; societies in which people's need to belong and be accepted is particularly acute, where one's self-image depends so much on other people's good opinion. The Arab world is a prime example.[46]

Nevertheless, it must be stressed that a family can only have unshakable foundations if its members shun all forms of deception, pretense, lying, or make-believe in their interrelations. Only then can it approach, as much as human frailty will allow, the condition of an ideal family. But then the same is true of any other kind of human relationship.

Leaving aside the rather obvious differences in the case of the fledgling and still-evolving Western institution of "live-in" couples, much of what I have said about the qualities of a good family apply to these relationships.

If the ideal family—whether nuclear or extended, conventional or unconventional—is characterized by love, commitment and loyalty, helpfulness, kindness, identification and empathy, solidarity, understanding, a forgiving spirit—consequently, by a total absence of aggressiveness or a carping and critical attitude, and, last but not least, an almost godlike patience, it becomes clear why human rights would not be needed in such ideal circumstances. The situation is quite different with regard to the imperfect families of the real world. Their imperfections give the human right of respect for personhood and such other rights as equal freedom, treatment, and opportunity important roles in the family. The not uncommon tendency of parents to favor one child over another, violating the equal consideration rights of the less favored, can have profound and lasting ill effects on the less, or least, favored.

Again, human love is rarely if ever free of the taint of possessiveness and jealousy, seemingly increasing in strength with the love's strength. Aristotle's noble idea that to love a person is to desire the loved one's self-realization, unfortunately, is much truer of the angelic hosts than of mere mortals. The possessive lover's self-centeredness and jealousy constantly threaten the other's right to personal freedom and the fulfillment of her basic needs and potentialities.[47] They also violate the other's right to privacy, as defined earlier in this book. Sibling rivalry, particularly during their formative years too, mars brotherly and sisterly love; while the child-parent relationship may be sorely strained by an unresolved Oedipus or Electra complex.

It may seem outrageously paradoxical to speak of the possible ill-effects of "too much love," as I did earlier in this book, albeit it is not too *much* but too *little* love that many families and the world at large suffer from. One can starve from the absence of love, but one can be also straitjacketed, hemmed in, buffeted, and choked by too much solicitousness and love. "Too much love"—another name for possessive love—means continual interference in the others' lives, leaving them little room to live their life as they choose. To change slightly Oscar Wilde's famous hyperbole, we must always be vigilant lest we kill the thing we love.

For the reasons I have given, it is often necessary for those who suffer from unfair domestic treatment in the ways described to remind the perpetrators of their right to their own lives, and to ask, even demand, that it be respected. The family essentially ceases to exist whenever internal disputes and dissension reach the courts. It also ceases to exist if physical force is resorted to or contemplated, even if the parties involved continue to live under the same roof.[48]

It is true, as R.M. Hare observes, that insistence on rights *can* be a recipe for conflict. As he puts it, "The rhetoric of rights, which is engendered by . . . [the question,"What rights do I have?"], is a recipe for class war, and civil war."[49] But first, Hare is referring not to individual relationships but to entire segments (classes) of society or a society as a whole. Second, the statement is not true without qualification, even with respect to what it refers to, as a little reflection will show; although it is true that, in a litigious country such as the United States, a good deal of the litigation is initiated by individuals, not just entire segments of the society. Clearly, the means people resort to, and the persistence and vehemence with which they assert or try to defend their rights, the lengths to which they are prepared to go, and the price they are willing to pay to ensure success, determine the human cost to the parties involved. For instance, it is unfortunate that in their struggle for equality with men, some women tend to become their husbands', male lovers,' or business associates' competitors, perceiving them as threats. The same is true of men who feel threatened by their wives' successes and achievements, and are unable to identify with their wives and feel proud of them. This does not mean that all struggle for equal moral or legal rights in any shape or form must be avoided for the sake of harmony between spouses or other family members, oppressed minorities and oppressive majorities, women and dominating men, and vice versa. From a moral point of view, the essential thing is that moral and legal rights should be furthered by moral means. In extreme cases, when entire groups, peoples, or countries are denied their moral and legal rights, and where legal measures are unavailable or ineffectual and armed struggle appears to be the only recourse, the struggle must be furthered by just use of force, such as just uprising, civil war, rebellion, or "just war," in accordance with the rules of just war theory.[50]

Notwithstanding the human, all too human tendency to possessiveness and the numerous other infirmities that "flesh" is heir to, mutual respect for rights is far from impossible if a family is bound by mutual love, so long as everyone is continually mindful of and attentive to the others' rights and is willing and ready to rectify his or her lapses in that regard. The purer, less tainted the love (both within and outside the confines of the family), the more it engenders respect for the others' moral integrity and freedom. For it is not love as such that leads to possessiveness and irrational jealousies but the selfishness and self-centeredness of the "old Adam" in all of us. They tarnish not only love but all other-regarding human actions, sentiments, and relationships.

Again, it must be stressed that one can respect the human rights of others, can treat others as moral persons, and can act in accordance with their dictates, and be totally unaware that that is what one is doing: in fact, even if one lacks the concept of human rights itself.[51] For example, the lover may spontaneously treat those she loves with respect in our sense, without thinking, or stopping to think, that she is actually respecting their human rights.

C. The Extended Family

Although the extended family is almost a thing of the past in American society, it is very much alive in other cultures, and much of what I have already said in relation to "the family" applies to the extended family. Some of the differences between the nuclear and the extended family regarding the place of human rights in them are only a matter of degree. For instance, there is a special need for those at the top of the traditional authoritarian-hierarchical structure of the extended

Middle Eastern family, to be sensitive to the human rights of those poised precariously on the hierarchy's lower rungs: the grandchildren and, not far above them, their parents, particularly their mothers. But whatever the extended family's specific structure in different cultures, its greater hierarchical complexity makes the problem of unequal treatment of its members, from the oldest to the youngest, more acute than in the nuclear family. For instance, grandchildren have to answer to both parents and grandparents, and their own parents often have to answer to the latter (or vice versa; for example, if the grandparents depend on their children for financial support). In general the greater the number of one's relationships, the greater the difficulty of preserving one's personal freedom and one's treatment as a person who is equal to all others.

Children, the weakest members of society, are particularly vulnerable in this as in all other respects. The need to protect their human rights cannot be exaggerated, and not just within the family. The paucity of their legal rights even in such countries as the United States makes that all the more necessary. It is a sad irony that because of a common rationalist dogma concerning the necessary conditions for the possession of human rights, such philosophers as H. L. A. Hart claim that children lack human ("natural") rights: for Hart, the right to be free. But as I argued earlier in this book, his or her intellectual immaturity and inability to make rational choices is not a valid ground for not acknowledging a child's human right to be treated as a moral person, in the sense of a right to be treated with consideration in the second sense of 'consideration' I defined. Nevertheless, a child's and, to a lesser extent, an adolescent's inability to make any rational or fully rational choices, respectively, justifies measured and reasonable but gradually diminishing parental moral and legal control over the child's or adolescent's actions and activities, and physical and mental development; thoughtfully geared to his or her special, changing needs and abilities. In other words, the child's and the adolescent's entitlement to *exercise* his or her right to freedom is justifiably limited prior to adulthood.

D. Relatives, Friends, and Human Rights
In addition to grandparents, traditional extended families sometimes include adult uncles, aunts, cousins, and nieces; but the above observations about human rights essentially apply to that more complex form of the extended family, as well as to those family clans—clusters

of interrelated extended families—whose members feel, as is sometimes said, almost like brothers and sisters.

The foregoing observations also essentially apply to close friendships, except for a noteworthy difference between the best friendships and close blood relationships. I mean that the former can be more disinterested[52] and altruistic than is possible with close blood relationships. Part of the reason, I think, is that friendship is on the whole calmer, less emotional, and hence tends to be less subjective than parental love, and less likely to blow hot and cold like romantic love. In addition, the purest friendship, I believe, is less prone to possessiveness, jealousy, or envy than romantic or domestic love. As a result, Aristotle's characterization of love, mentioned earlier, is generally truer of friendship than of other forms of love.

What friendship shares with all forms of love as distinguished from liking is that (pace Nozick) it is not due to any characteristics of the friend, the person loved.[53] But as Nozick correctly observes, "It is the other person, and not the characteristics [or, I might add, any other of his or her characteristics] that is loved. The love is not transferable to someone else with the same characteristics, even to one who 'scores' higher for these characteristics."[54] Unfortunately, it is not always true that "the love endures through changes of the [sic] characteristics that gave rise to it," although I agree that "one loves the particular person one actually encountered."[55] It is commonplace that sometimes friendship sours, just as love between family members and relatives turns to indifference, dislike, or outright hatred, if one deeply disapproves of the friend's behavior, or due to significant changes in his or her characteristics. The uncontrolled urge or temptation to impose one's will on the other is a familiar cause of the withering of friendship and of love.[56] But the urge to control others finds less scope in friendship than in domestic and romantic love. Love is the lover's strength but also her Achilles' heel, makes her particularly vulnerable to manipulation by the one she loves. Her love makes it tempting and sometimes easy to do so: sometimes to such an extent that she may unconsciously cooperate with the other in her own manipulation, becoming a willing participant in her own exploitation and enslavement.

E. Acquaintances, Strangers, and Human Rights

By definition, mere acquaintances are not bound by affection or love, except sometimes, by *Caritas*—caring or concern. But sympathy and benevolence (and toleration of differences), arising either out of or apart from *Caritas* and enjoined by religion, can certainly extend much farther and embrace total strangers. As history amply shows, sacred love can reach beyond particular groups to all humanity and, even to nature as a whole.

I mentioned earlier that at its best, friendship can be more disinterested and selfless than other forms of love. But we must clearly except sacred love: the love that St. Paul spoke of in his *First Epistle to the Corinthians*. Ideally, that love is the *non plus ultra* of selflessness.[57] In that respect, it is like what Spinoza describes as the "intellectual love of God": a love that expects no reciprocation or return from God. As Spinoza describes that love in Prop. XIX of Part Five of his *Ethic*, "He who loves God cannot strive that God should love him in return."[58] I say "in that respect," since I am not claiming—what would be palpably false—that the selflessness of Christian love, whether in a human-human or human-divine "I-Thou" relationship, necessarily precludes any expectation of reciprocation.[59]

Whenever sacred love is found, distinctions between people and their limited human relationships are transcended: in its ideal form, all humanity is embraced in universal sisterhood and brotherhood. All human beings become subjects of deep equal concern, and all need for the assertion and defense of their human rights disappears. By contrast the "taint" that attaches to imperfect, profane love also attaches to sacred love in its actual, imperfect form, making the acknowledgment of everyone's human rights necessary in practice.

F. Human Rights and Community

So far I have considered the possible place of human rights in loving and other praiseworthy domestic and extra-domestic interpersonal relations, but without considering the societal matrix in which such relationships exist. The question that must now be raised is whether the very nature of a community, particularly a T-community, seriously restricts its members' ability to exercise the freedoms to which they are entitled in principle.

My answer will be brief, since it will mainly consist in bringing together the different parts of the answer already stated in earlier chapters. It lies essentially in seeing how three important concepts fit together into a whole: (a) the concept of the freedom to which all persons are equally entitled as human beings, consisting in a form of *positive liberty* together with the necessary negative freedom, (b) the relational concept of a *person* outlined in chapter 9, and (c) the concept of a *T-community*, in chapter 2.

As we saw in these chapters, the freedom to which I claimed we have a (an equal) human right is essentially the freedom *to satisfy our basic needs and interests and* realize our potentials. It is, therefore, as I said, a form of positive liberty.

In his review of Lawrence Crocker's book, *Positive Liberty: An Essay in Normative Political Philosophy,*[60] Carl Hedman summarizes Crocker's description of positive liberty as "liberty [which] is taken to be a matter of the presence of diverse opportunities rather than the absence of human interference [negative liberty]."[61] As for "negative liberty," Charles Taylor speaks of it (in "What's Wrong with Negative Liberty?") as the "independence of the individual from interference by others."[62] Ronald Dworkin similarly defines negative freedom as "the absence of constraints placed by a government upon what a man might do if he wants to."[63]

For our purposes the term "negative freedom" will be used to refer specifically to the absence of constraints by society as a whole, not just by the government or the law, on what a person may do if he wants to. *Positive liberty,* in Taylor's understanding, is quite similar to the concept of freedom delimited in this book, since he thinks of freedom as "including something like the freedom of self-fulfillment, or self-realization according to our own pattern."[64] But the idea "that each person's form of self-realization is original to him/her, and can therefore only be worked out independently"[65] (which, Taylor says, is "one of the most powerful motives behind the modern defence of freedom as individual independence"[66]—for example, in J. S. Mill's *On Liberty*—does not necessarily apply to the views I have been defending in this part of the book. In fact, in light of the relational concept of a person, self-realization is only possible in, and by virtue of, one's important commitments and relationships; in continual, lifelong cooperation with others.[67] That is specifically true of the actualization of our basic human needs and potentials, notwithstanding their variable individual manifestations or expressions, for the promotion of which, among other things, individual freedom is absolutely essential.[68]

Taylor finds the deeper doctrinal differences between the negative and the positive theories of liberty in Isaiah Berlin's observation that "negative theories are concerned with the area in which the subject should be left with who or what controls."[69] Doctrines of positive freedom are "concerned with a view of freedom which involves *essentially the exercise of control over one's life.* In this view, one is free only to the extent that one has effectively determined oneself and the shape of one's life. The concept of freedom here is an exercise-concept."[70] Negative theories "can [he adds that they do not necessarily] rely simply on an opportunity-concept, where being free is a matter of what we can do, of what it is open to us to do, whether or not we do anything to exercise these options."[71] Despite the similarities between the present author's and Taylor's conception of positive liberty, the ideas in the passages by Taylor I have italicized are different in some respects from the present author's views. In Taylor's view, one has a human right *to be free to* "effectively determine oneself and the shape of one's life," not that one is free *to the extent that* one has effectively determined oneself and the shape of one's life.[72] From that it does not follow that "we can't say that someone is free, on a self-realisation view, if he is totally unrealised, if for instance he is totally unaware of his potential, if fulfilling it has never even arisen as a question for him, or if he is paralysed by the fear of breaking with some norm which he has internalized but which does not authentically reflect him."[73] What *does* follow, I think, is that in the circumstances described, his right to positive liberty would remain completely unexercised or unrealized, and so, utterly useless in practice.

It should be stressed here that membership in a *good* and *moral* T-community does not abridge its members' positive liberty, since membership in any community and participation in its institutional activities, including its communal enterprises, would necessarily be optional and voluntary (see chapter 11). Again, the members would be free to work to change the community's goals if they do not like them, or to leave the community as a whole or any institution or practice in the community, or the community itself. A fundamental condition of a community's being a moral community is voluntary membership. The same is true of membership in any particular institution within a community. A corollary of the human right to positive liberty on my account is that if a T-community's goals interfere with a member's ability to exercise that right, he or she is morally entitled to try to change those goals or bid that community farewell.

Again, the members' right to positive liberty makes it imperative for a community to commit itself to furthering it in its institutions and practices and helps to make it a desirable matrix for individual growth. But the existence of that right only entails that the community as a whole is morally obligated not to interfere with the right's exercise. It does not obligate it to actually further the exercise of that right. The desirability of "collective self-government" in a community does not provide grounds, *pace* Taylor, for identifying positive liberty with it.

The equal right to positive liberty entails the desirability of collective self-government only if certain special propositions are true and can be added as premises. The human right to something "X" entails the desirability of realizing "X." Whatever anyone has a moral right to is, by definition, a positive value. If, therefore, it can be shown that political democracy is a necessary condition for the realization (or full realization) of *everyone's equal* human right to positive liberty, the desired conclusion would follow.

Finally, an individual's human *right* to freedom in pursuit of self-actualization in the sense described, morally obligates everyone else not to interfere with that freedom, and gives him or her the limited, correlative negative liberty.

As stated by Hedman, Crocker argues that "unlike a society committed to a negative notion of liberty—where diversity would be protected but not encouraged, a society committed to his positive account would undertake such things as 'support for affirmative (and probably expensive) programs aimed at the development of human capacities, the provision of free time, the supply of equipment, facilities, and other means to the enlargement of life's possibilities (p. 70).'"[74] That view clearly goes beyond the idea of collective self-government, and (as in the case of arguments in support of collective self-government) requires special arguments for its support, along such lines as the Platonic-Aristotelian idea that society's function is to provide the matrix or conditions essential for its members' self-realization, or else, by appeal to a special form of social contract theory. To provide a theory of that nature is beyond the scope of this book. Let me merely observe that the acknowledgment of an equal human right to equal treatment and opportunity would provide *some* support for the sort of view Crocker espouses. To make that "double equality"possible in practice, it would appear that, whenever necessary, a community must actually do considerably more than merely intervene to prevent some members from receiving less (if not also more) than equal treatment and fewer (if not also more) opportunities than others. A society would presumably also need to create and maintain institutions and practices that would effectively promote that equality in positive ways.

If all of the foregoing can be convincingly shown,[75] it would provide an additional answer to the central question of this section with respect to T-communities. For one of the goals of any *good* and *moral* T-community is the fulfillment of the moral obligation to treat everyone fairly and equally, and would be, *inter alia*, organized precisely with that end in view. From that it could be concluded that a good and moral T-community, far from being in fundamental conflict with its members' positive freedom, would in fact nurture and promote it. To state the matter differently, a T-community, by definition, cannot be an effective community, let alone a moral community, if any one of its goals interferes with its members' positive freedom.

The ordinary "existential" concept of a person (E-person) outlined in chapter 9, adds a further important element to the picture that I am sketching. As a "communal" concept, it fits naturally the idea of a good community in general, whether an N- or a T-community. In the act of fulfilling one's important commitments and maintaining one's important relationships, sketched in this chapter, and so, in the very act of actualizing oneself, one exercises one's positive freedom. These relationships and commitments in no way restrict that freedom: indeed, as we have seen, the preceding is the only way in which, by definition, positive freedom *can* be exercised. Correspondingly, a moral community is a community whose members, through the exercise of their positive freedom in loving and harmonious relationships, actualize themselves as moral E-persons. And vice versa.

To sum up. This chapter explored the place of human rights in the creation and maintenance of a moral community, concentrating on the personal relations within the institution of the family, between other relatives, friends, and the more tenuous relations between acquaintances, and, later on, the impersonal relations between strangers. It attempted to establish that human rights function least in a good, loving nuclear family, but that they and the need for the moral protection they afford normally increase in importance as relationships radiate from the nuclear family center and become most important in the members' dealings with casual acquaintances, and, above all, with strangers in the community, if any.

Starting with the nuclear and extended families, the love-and-respect-centered virtues of an ideally good, moral family, together with the latter's respect for its members' moral personhood, were described, followed by a discussion of the ways in which actual imperfect families fall short of the ideal—for example, in the not uncommon dissensions and lack of respect for their members' rights—which may lead to their demise.

The discussion of the extended family that followed particularly stressed the problem of the pervasive unequal treatment of the weakest members of the authoritarian family hierarchy, particularly children, in traditional societies, and took issue with H.L.A. Hart's view that children lack the "natural" right to be free.

After briefly considering human rights in relation to friendship, the discussion turned to their role in relation to acquaintances and strangers. Next it was maintained that a good, especially a moral, community, not excepting a T-community, does not restrict a member's positive freedom, or her ability to exercise it, since participation in any of its institutional activities would be perfectly optional and voluntary; in addition, it allows a member the freedom to work to change the community's goals (if it is a T-community), withdraw from any institution or practice in it she does not care about, or even leave the community altogether. Since an individual has a human right to positive freedom, it is morally incumbent on the community—indeed, on any form of social organization—to commit itself to protecting a member's positive freedom, including her right to seek to actualize herself. By definition, no community of either kind can be a good community, let alone a moral community, if any of its goals interferes with its members' positive freedom. By the same token, the members have the moral obligation not to interfere with one another's pursuit of their self-actualization.

Notes

1   Aristotle, as Alasdair MacIntyre tells us, distinguishes three types of friend-ship. The one I have in mind throughout this book, which is the only concep-tion of friendship we now have, is friendship based on affection and love, and usually includes admiration and respect for the friend's personal qualities, accomplishments, and abilities, as well as certain shared interests or goals. The latter is what Aristotle considers the best kind of friendship. See *After Virtue,* Second Edition (Notre Dame, IN, 1984), 154. MacIntyre's discussion of friendship and its importance in a community is excellent and important.

2   I have italicized the phrase, "as MacIntyre interprets it," since I took issue earlier in this book with a different, common understanding of Kant's impera-tive to treat all persons as "ends."

3   *After Virtue,* 46. Italics in original.

4   *Social Theory and Practice,* 17, no. 1 (Spring 1991): 69–84.

5   Ibid., 69.

6   Ibid.

7   In *Liberalism and the Limits of Justice* (Cambridge, 1982), especially 30ff.

8   Ibid. My italics.

9   Ibid. Hedman, like Lukes and Sandel, fails to distinguish theses (B)(a) and (B)(b). But the following makes it clear that all three are concerned with the stronger thesis (B)(b). To illustrate what he considers a "misplaced standing on the demands of justice among friends," Sandel gives as an example a close friend's repeated insistence "on calculating and paying his precise share of every common expenditure" or refusing "to accept any favor or hospitality except at the greatest protest and embarrassment" (op. cit., 35; quoted by Hedman, 71). This is also seen in Sandel's, Lukes', and Hedman's discussion of interest conflicts in a community and whether they render the "protective norms of rights and justice" indispensable.

10   Op. cit., 109; Hedman, op. cit., 69.

11   Hedman, op. cit., 70.

12   Hedman, ibid. Lukes, op. cit., 106-107.

13   John Rawls' defense of rule-utilitarianism in "Two Concepts of Rules," e.g., in relation to "telishment," does not, in my view, adequately answer H.J. McCloskey's criticism in "A Note on Utilitarian Punishment," *Mind,* 72 (1963): 599. J.J.C. Smart, in his defense of (act-) utilitarianism, in *Utilitarianism For & Against,* 68ff., essentially acknowledges the force of McCloskey's criti-cism.

14   Op. cit., 105. Hedman, op. cit., 70.

15   Ibid., 105.

16   Op. cit., 71.

17   See chapter 11.

18   Hedman, ibid., 71.

19   Sandel, op. cit., 35.

20   Hedman, op. cit., 71.

21   See also chapter 12 for a more detailed discussion of these issues.

22   Westerners, with their tradition of human and legal rights, would find it hard
to appreciate the corrosive sense of psychic insecurity that sensitive people in
the non-Western world tend to experience, wherever the idea of human rights
is absent or is not deeply rooted. In these circumstances, maintaining a healthy
sense of self-worth is a continually uphill fight. In colonial times, this was
most acutely felt by the so-called "natives" vis-à-vis their "masters," and is felt
(or continues to be felt) by present-day members of some racial, ethnic, or
religious minorities transplanted into the Western world.

23   Sandel would not countenance this eventuality, since as I have had occasion
to observe, he invariably uses "community," in *Liberalism and the Limits of
Justice*, to mean "T-community."

24   Richard W. Miller, *Analyzing Marx: Morality, Power and History* (Princeton,
NJ, [1984]), 24.

25   Let me illustrate this in relation to *legal* rights. Marx and Engels maintain that
in communist society the State (or at least its oppressive functions) will wither
away. It follows that law, as a coercive arm of the State, and consequently
legal rights, will also disappear. At the higher stage of its evolution the communist society will be able to drop "the narrow legal point of view" (*Critique
of the Gotha Program*, 90). "Law by its very nature can only consist in the
application of an equal standard" (ibid., 89). But every equal right in capitalism (as also in the lower or transitional stage of socialism) is a "right of inequality" (ibid).

26   One of Marx's important arguments against human rights is that interest conflicts set up conflicts between equally basic rights. "These conflicts are properly resolved by treating rights as means for enhancing people's lives, not as
ultimate standards" (Miller, op. cit., 22). In other words, rights-conflicts can
only be resolved by weighing the probable agathistic consequences of their
exercise.
   Note that whatever weight this argument may carry, it does not entail that
rights themselves are totally dispensable in *any* society, consequently, in a
communitarian society. At best, only their exercise is constrained in the way
described.

27   Preferential treatment should be distinguished from affirmative action proper, though as Burton Leiser states, the phrase "preferential treatment" is ambiguous. But "the general aim of all affirmative action programs is to raise the level of those groups that have suffered from discrimination in the past to a position of proportional equality in education, housing, employment, and other areas with those who have previously been relatively free from the disadvantages imposed by discriminatory policies" (*Liberty, Justice, and Morals*, 2nd ed. New York, 1979, 317). Affirmative action, defined as the elimination of discrimination or segregation, is distinguishable from "preferential treatment" as a special way of reducing discrimination.

As is common knowledge, affirmative action has recently been under strong attack by conservatives in the United States, especially California and Texas, and is incorrectly equated with the quota system, and with the "preferential treatment" of minority members by use of lower standards than those applied to whites. At the same time, "preferential treatment"—the very idea of which is anathema to the critics—is incorrectly equated with reverse discrimination.

28   In the famous United States case of Bakke v. Regents of the University of California, the Court struck down quotas in admission to medical school essentially on the ground that "the guarantee of equal protection cannot mean one thing when applied to one individual and something else when applied to a person of another color. If both are not accorded the same protection, then it is not equal." (Quoted from Burton M. Leiser, *Liberty, Justice, and Morals*, 2nd ed. New York, 1979, 327). Thus as Leiser adds, the Court ruled that "racial and ethnic distinctions of any sort are inherently suspect" (ibid). Justice Powell, who spoke for the Court, "rejected the suggestion that discrimination against members of the white "majority" is not suspect if its purpose is characterized as benign" (ibid). This statement dramatizes the difficulty of distinguishing reverse discrimination, at least in certain cases, from legitimate affirmative action.

However, the Court—correctly in my view—also concluded, in Leiser's words, that "the consideration of race as one factor in an admission program may serve a legitimate state interest," and is permissible, provided it did not exclude "*any* applicant from competing for a place merely because of his race. . . ." (ibid., 329. Italics in original). That means, as I understand it, that "one" special factor *can* legitimately serve as a *secondary* criterion. For instance, if two *equally qualified* applicants, one white and the other black, apply for a single available position, hiring the black rather than the white applicant would not constitute reverse discrimination (cf. also Leiser, ibid).

29   With the recent welfare reform bill recently signed into law by President Clinton—which is, however, still a "work in progress"—those receiving welfare benefits have to find a job and get off welfare within two years. One major problem—acknowledged by the White House—is adequate job training for the welfare recipients and their finding a job if and when the training has been done.

30   "Need and Distributive Justice: A Defence," in *Practical Reason and Theories of Justice* Werner Maihofer and Gerhard Sprenger, eds. (Stuttgart, 1992),

115. In that article, I attempted to ground the N-principle in the theory of human rights outlined in chapters 5 and 6 of this book.

31   Not all psychologists agree that economic and social equality are desirable in a society. Those who think that inequality is desirable believe that it provides an incentive to those on the lower rungs to strive to climb the ladder of success. This is certainly sometimes true, but it remains that vast numbers of economically and socially disadvantaged people all over the world simply cannot—because of the lack of the necessary education, skills, and connections—escape their lot, no matter how hard and long they may honestly try to do so. In fact, the hopelessness of their condition and their consequent bitterness and frustration are a major familiar cause of violence and crime in society.

32   I do not say that it will necessarily be the only principle of distributive justice. As I mentioned in chapter 8, I believe that no single canon of distributive justice is properly applicable in all relevant circumstances. Although the need principle occupies a special place in a moral community, the same is true of desert and merit. In addition, the putative canons of effort, productivity, or social utility may also play a significant role there.

33   For a fuller discussion of positive freedom, see later in this chapter.

34   "Distributive Justice," in James Sterba, ed. *Justice: Alternative Political Perspectives* (Belmont, CA [1980], 166). Reprinted from *Anarchy, State, and Utopia* (New York, 1974).

35   It is interesting that Locke's proviso turns Nozick's proviso upsidedown, so to speak. The latter, like Locke's proviso, is intended to apply to those, e.g., the needy, to whom the well-to-do property owners choose not to transfer any of their legitimately acquired holdings.

36   "Distributive Justice," 166.

37   Ibid.

38   Reprinted in "The Socialist Principle," in *Justice: Alternative Political Perspectives*, 188–199.

39   Op. cit., 200–210. See also O'Neill's critique of Nozick's entitlement theory of justice in *Reading Nozick*, ed. Jeffrey Paul (Totowa, NJ [1981]), 305–322.

40   MacIntyre strangely forgets Thomas Aquinas, who is a notable exception. But it is interesting that some contemporary legal philosophers take Aquinas to task for failing to make much use of the concept of "natural rights" in his ethics and legal philosophy.

41   *After Virtue*, 69. MacIntyre admits that "from this it does not of course follow that there are no natural or human rights; it only follows that no one could have known that there were. And this at least raises certain questions. But . . . the truth is plain: there are no such rights, and belief in them is one with belief in witches and in unicorns" (ibid; my italics).

The preceding strongly suggests that in talking about human rights MacIntyre is thinking of the traditional idea that human rights are natural properties of human beings, hence may (or may not) be somehow discovered at some particular time or other. It will be recalled from chapter 6 that, in agreement with Ronald Dworkin, I rejected that conception of human rights.

The reader may also recall from the discussion in chapter 6 that MacIntyre's fundamental reason for rejecting human rights is that "every attempt to give good reasons for believing that there are such rights has failed" (ibid., p. 69; italics in original).

42   Cited by MacIntyre in *After Virtue*, 263.

43   United Nations Universal Declaration of Human Rights, Article 6.

44   Ibid., Article 13. (1).

45   Ibid., Article 13. (2).

46   See, for example, my "The Mask and the Face: A Study of 'Make-Believe' in Middle East Society," *Ararat* (Summer 1963): 52ff., and "Moral Make-Believe in Arab Society,"*Ararat* (Autumn 1963): 47ff.

47   But Jean Paul Sartre's claim that all relationships turn the Other into an "object," an "être en soi," goes too far, although one should be always vigilant lest that happen in one's love relationship.

48   An adversarial relationship between members of a family is tantamount to the death of part of or the whole family, even when the litigants are siblings and not spouses seeking separation or divorce.

49   "Justice and Equality," in Sterba, op. cit., 119.

50   For a discussion of the conditions of a just war, see my "Self-Defense and the Just War," *World Futures*, 20, no. 3/4 (1985): 151–178. See also, "Just Revolution," *Shaping Revolution*, Elsbeth Attwooll ed. (Aberdeen, 1991), 182-189, for another morally justified form of "freedom fighting."

51   In that respect, among others, acting in accordance with the dictates of another's human or other moral rights differs from acting in accordance with the latter's legal rights.

52   In the English, not the common American usage of this word.

53   He says: "An adult may come to love another because of the other's characteristics." (*Anarchy, State, and Utopia*, New York, [1974], 168.)

54   Ibid.

55   Ibid.

56   In the same passage, Nozick states that love is historical, "In that . . . it depends upon what actually occurred. An adult may come to love another because of the other's characteristics," and finds the fact that love is historical

puzzling. But in talking about adult love Nozick is clearly limiting himself to (some) friendships and to romantic love. If I am right that love is utterly spontaneous, happens for no apparent reason at all and, sometimes, even against one's will, not because of any of another's characteristics, Nozick's explanation of love's "historicity" fails. The explanation, I think, is that love is a sentiment and a relationship that may develop and grow in time, with repeated encounters with the other. In any given stage of the love, the other is loved as he or she is at that time, and, sometimes if not always, as he or she was during the relationship's earlier stages.

57   It is true that Christian love ("charity" or *Caritas*) does not enjoin us to love others more than ourselves, but only as ourselves. Consequently it does not consist in *absolute selflessness*. But as James Rachels points out in *The Elements of Moral Philosophy* (New York, 1986), 60–61, self-interest or self-regard is distinct from selfishness and should not be confused with it. Moreover, self-interest and unselfishness are perfectly compatible. Another confusion he points out is "the common but false assumption that a concern for one's own welfare is incompatible with any genuine concern for others" (Ibid., 61). Absolute selflessness, unlike unselfishness as it is commonly understood, entails the sacrifice of one's interests whenever they appear to conflict with the welfare of others; but that does not mean *absolute* lack of concern for one's own interests and welfare.

Although not enjoined by Jesus, absolute selflessness, the Gospels tell us, was ideally exemplified in his life and death. But then, the Nazarene believed that he was the Son of God. For us, mere mortals, absolute selflessness is supremely difficult, hence supererogatory. More often than not, one's striving to attain absolute selflessness would sharply conflict with one's natural, often unreflective or unconscious human striving to realize one's own needs, interests, and potentials. On the theory of human rights propounded in Part II of this book, that is a main reason *why we need* to acknowledge everyone's equal human rights.

58   *Spinoza Selections*, edited by John Wild (New York, [1930], 380. It will be remembered that Spinoza's God is not a Person but Natura Naturans, consequently, man's intellectual love of God cannot be reciprocated.

59   A proviso even more obvious with respect to the altruism and disinterestedness of true friendship.

60   *Melbourne International Philosophy Series, 7* (The Hague, 1980).

61   *Ethics*, 93, no. 3 (April 1983), 598–600.

62   *The Idea of Freedom*, Alan Ryan, ed. (Oxford, 1979), 175.

63   *Taking Rights Seriously*, chapter 12, 267. There Dworkin, like Crocker, rejects negative liberty.

64   Taylor, op. cit., 176.

65   Ibid., 176.

66   Ibid.

67   An excellent account of the evils and ills of competitiveness in American society and in defense of cooperation, is found in *No Contest: The Case Against Competition*, Alfie Kohn, revised ed. (Boston, New York, 1992.

68   Taylor responds to the defense of negative liberty by arguing that the striving for self-realization "can fail through inner fears, or false consciousness, as well as because of external coercion," and that Hobbes'/Bentham's moral psychology "is too simple or too crude for its purposes." (Op. cit., 176.)

69   Ibid., 177.

70   Ibid. My italics.

71   Ibid.

72   Ibid. This too is incomplete, since, as I have pointed out before, the *right* to positive liberty entails everyone else's obligation not to hinder or prevent a right-holder from seeking to realize herself.

73   Ibid.

74   Hedman, op. cit., 598.

75   But see Crocker's arguments for his claim, including his conclusion that "his account would require an extension of 'democracy into the economy, from the shop floor and local union to the 'commanding heights' of the financial system' (p. 78)" (Hedman, ibid).

Chapter 11

The "Institutional" Role of Human Rights in a Moral Community

I

In chapter 2, I sketched the essentials of what I consider to be a good and moral community; while in chapter 10 I discussed the possible roles of human rights in interpersonal relations in such a community. There I argued, *contra* Sandel and in agreement with Lukes, that the protective norms of human rights are indispensable, in interpersonal relations, in actual, imperfect human moral communities; leaving open the highly speculative question of whether these norms would be dispensable in morally ideal communities, communities of angels so to speak. But except for the role of human rights in the institution/practice of the family, considered, among other things in chapter 10, I have not so far considered the role human rights ought to play in the institutions and practices of a modern moral community. That was left to the present chapter.

Basic Structure of Institutions

For a proper understanding of the place human rights ought to have in the institutions and practices of a moral community, it is useful to recapitulate what was said about the basic structure of institutions and practices in part 2, in relation to human rights and the ethic of caring.

The term "institution"[1] is a "functional" word. Its normal uses involve the idea of one or more related functions, purposes, or goals, or one or more teloses. An institution's goal-directed, teleological character is a defining feature of an institution, not a contingent feature that all actual institutions happen to share.[2] By virtue of that conceptual fact, we ordinarily speak of a scientific, religious, cultural, or other institution as a scientific, religious, cultural, etc., community. As teleological organizations by definition, these institutions are important examples of T-communities designed to further common scientific, religious, cultural, or other teloses.

All institutions share a *basic* logical structure or organization; but different kinds of institutions, and individual institutions of a particular kind, differ in size and complexity, and with respect to their goals or teloses, and so on. These differences do not affect the way in which institutions are logically set up or defined, or the way in which various normative principles, such as human rights and other moral principles, evaluate and regulate the basic structure and operations of institutions *qua* institutions.

An institution's basic structure and mode of operation or administration are defined by its constitutive rules (C-rules); viz, its various offices, roles, or positions, and the specific functions and responsibilities of each office, role, or position. Finally, the C-rules define the special practical (nonmoral) obligations and correlative rights and prerogatives of each office, role, or position. But the C-rules themselves, hence all that they themselves define, are ultimately determined, in a general way, by the institution's particular (or particular kind of) telos or teloses.

In addition to its C-rules, moral and other regulative rules (R-rules), including the protective norms of human rights and of fairness and justice, regulate and evaluate the institution: by regulating and evaluating (a) its telos or teloses and (b) prescribing the moral and other norms to which the institution ought to conform. The latter include prescribing the special moral obligations and correlative special moral rights of the institution's various participants or office holders. Thus, Rawls is right in maintaining that the R-rules determine (or can determine) "the rights and liberties referred to by them" [the institutions], but is mistaken in supposing (following John Searle) that these rules do so by defining "the public [constitutive] rules of the basic structure" of institutions.[3] For as I argued in *IPMR*, regulative rules/principles cannot determine or define an institution's C-rules. Nevertheless, through their positive or negative evaluation of an institution's organization and administration, the R-rules can help bring about reforms or other desirable changes in the institution. Indeed, that is precisely the *raison d'être* of the R-rules and of their evaluation of an institution's efficiency or inefficiency, practical or moral goodness or badness, and so on.

Stating the foregoing more precisely, R-rules, including various types of moral principles and rules,[4] regulate and evaluate an institution "I" by (a) evaluating/regulating its immediate and especially long-range aims or goals G (its telos(es)). Logically, this is the primary way in which R-rules can help determine, *inter alia*, "I's" efficiency and morality. For (b) G theoretically determines a certain large but finite set of subsets of possible C-rules, S1, S2, S3, etc., each of which can theoretically provide a blueprint for some institution I1 or I2, I3, etc. Which subset happens to define a particular institution I1 or I2, etc., depends on various contingent factors, such as the choices of I1's or I2's, creators or designers. If the institution *realizes* its intended goals or telos(es), and functions properly as its creators intended, it would be a successful, efficient, and perhaps morally good institution: depending on the kinds of its intended (and realized) goals or telos(es).

For various contingent reasons relating to their organization and the extent to which those who operate them fulfill or fail to fulfill their special responsibilities and obligations, and use or misuse their corresponding rights, no actual institutions realize perfectly their intended goals or *telos*(es). Institutions are never static, and even with the best design and will in the world, they never completely measure up to the ends for which they are designed.

Conditions of Moral Institutions

The general function of R-rules is to guide the activities of individuals and groups, institutions, communities, etc., and to judge, among other things, their goodness or badness as individuals or groups, institutions or communities, etc. This is true of the principles of fairness and of justice as well as of the fundamental human rights principle (what I shall call Principle P) that we ought to treat others impartially and equally as persons, with consideration and respect. Similarly with those moral rights that can be grounded in Principle P. In the case of institutions, this means that theoretically speaking, an institution "I" would be perfectly moral if its immediate, intermediate, and long range goals, its basic organization and administration, all perfectly exemplify the equal human right to freedom and the right to equal treatment and opportunity. An organization of that description would also encourage its members or office-holders to respect these rights in their day-to-day official activities and relations with one another and with outside persons and groups with whom they have official dealings, and would reward them for doing so.

Conditions of Moral Institutions with Respect to Principle P

A. To begin with, the goals G of an institution "I" may conform to Principle P in either of two ways. (1) G may consist in the defense and promotion of human rights in a particular community or country, or in the world at large. A goal G of that nature would be moral in a strong sense of the word. For instance, the goals of the institutions (and practices) comprising the United Nations, as promulgated in the Universal Declaration of Human Rights, include the defense and promotion of human rights. The same is true of Amnesty International, which, among other things, is dedicated to the promotion of respect for the rights and personhood of prisoners in general and prisoners of conscience in particular. But (2) G may conform to Principle P in the weaker sense of being consistent with it without consisting in its defense or promotion. It may be, say, a particular social, political, or economic goal whose realization is consistent with the Principle. By contrast, G, and to that extent "I" itself, would be immoral if "I" arrogates to itself the alleged right to set aside Principle P or any other moral right grounded on it. The Ku Klux Klan and neo-Nazi organizations are excellent examples of such immoral organizations.

The preceding is particularly important whenever, as in monastic communities, the goals of a T-community's important institutions coincide with, or are part of, the community's teloses. The overall religious and societal ends of the faith to which a monastic order is dedicated define the order's religious telos(es) and raison d'être. As a consequence, monastic life is instrumental to the realization of the order's immediate goals and, through them, the faith's larger ends. Religious schools and hospitals too help to realize the overall religious goals of the particular faith that runs them.

Some institutions have subsidiary or ancillary goals clustered around or radiating from a central, dominant telos. This is again illustrated by parochial schools and hospitals that are run by religious groups.

B. An institution "I's" C-rules conform to Principle P whenever they are (a) a subset of the set of the C-rules determined by "I's" goals G; and (b) G satisfies Principle P as described under (A)(1) or (2) above. That is, if the C-rules faithfully reflect "I's" intended moral goals. If (a) and (b) are satisfied, and if (c) these C-rules do in fact determine "I's" organization and administration, "I" as a whole would conform to Principle P. To that extent it would be a moral institution.

C. If "I" satisfies the preceding two conditions—if its goals and its C-rules are moral—its basic organization and administration would also conform to Principle P. For as we saw, in speaking of "I's" basic organization, we specifically refer to the various offices, positions, or roles attached to "I"as defined by its C-rules; and the basic operations of these positions, constitute the institution's administration. In such an institution (to speak in related Kantian terms) the office-holders would treat one another as beings possessing dignity. They would not exploit or discriminate against one another.[5]

In hierarchical institutions, which have historically been the norm everywhere, the preceding is particularly difficult to realize in practice. The differences in power, authority, and prestige that go with the different offices and positions and are directly connected with the special rights attached to them, are serious obstacles to equality of treatment.[6] But the satisfaction of Principle P is not impossible in hierarchical institutions, if the privileges and rights of those higher up do not exceed what their rank or office—the proper fulfillment of their special obligations and responsibilities—requires; and if the higher ranks can be attained fairly and squarely, in accordance with our fourth condition below.

D. As far as Principle P is concerned, a fourth condition of a moral institution "I" is that all positions and ranks in it must be public and open to all qualified persons, irrespective of color, race, ethnic background, sex, age, creed, or ideology. The satisfaction of this condition means the satisfaction of the human right to equal opportunity and treatment.[7]

Respect for the right to equal opportunity and treatment also means giving office-holders an equal opportunity for continued advancement in the institution. No rank or position should be closed to particular individuals or groups, particularly for reasons unrelated to the qualifications requisite for that rank or position. Additionally, wages, raises, promotions, and the granting of additional rights and privileges to an office-holder or position should be based on merit: on know-how, dedication, effort, skill, and achievement.[8] The management must not use any positions as tools to manipulate office-holders or as a weapon to coerce them.

An institution's granting special favors to particular office-holders in the form of greater rights or perks than the position justifies is an abuse of power. Similarly with the unjustified withholding of rights or powers necessary for a particular office's proper functioning. The injustice is compounded if as a result the office-holders are denied deserved promotions, or are terminated.

Consider what the abuse of a position P in an institution "I" logically involves. Every special right R or obligation O has proper limits, imposed by two sorts of factors. The first is the nature of the particular position P and its function, which define O and consequently R. R's abuse consists in the officer's overstepping R's limits as defined by O, etc. As an essentially legal—procedural or administrative—abuse it may carry a legal penalty. The second, moral limit is imposed by, among other things, the regulative principles of justice, fairness, and human rights; which means that a special right can be used in morally wrong ways. This is true of nonmoral special rights as well as special moral rights.

Cheating in examinations is a simple example of a special right's abuse in both of the preceding ways. A student who cheats violates his or her special nonmoral obligation to himself or herself as a learner, if not also toward his or her teacher and the educational institution in which he or she is enrolled. I mean the obligation he or she undertook to fulfill when enrolling in the particular school or college. But cheating is also a morally wrong act: a moral abuse of the student's special rights as a student.

E. A fifth condition of a moral institution is that office-holders should be at liberty to leave an institution at will, except when a binding contract stipulates otherwise. In the latter case, negotiations should be the first recourse. Only if they fail would legal means be a just recourse. In no case should physical or mental coercion be used against an office-holder to stay on against her will. The significance of this condition in the economic sphere is obvious. Equally, if not *more* significant, is its relevance to other spheres of life; e.g., in relation to certain highly authoritarian or fundamentalist religious groups and institutions, and in relation to political institutions in a dictatorship.

The preceding conditions of moral institutions coincide almost perfectly with the conditions of moral institutions entailed by Rawls' First Principle of Justice. All except our fourth condition follow from that principle. More significantly still, as Ronald Dworkin convincingly shows, Rawls' "deep theory" in *A Theory of Justice* rests on a natural right, "the abstract [natural] right to equal concern and respect, . . which [Dworkin argues] must be understood to be the fundamental concept of Rawls' deep theory."[9]

Some of the implications of conditions (A)–(D) can be justified in terms of the equal human right to positive freedom. In addition to providing a justification for the special rights and obligations attached to institutions that satisfy these conditions in an appreciable degree, that right can provide justification for the setting-up of good and moral institutions if we look upon the creation of an institution as the result of a hypothetical social contract, involving equal mutual constraints. It is true that an institution's C-rules restrict in certain ways the behavior of those who voluntarily join it by officially channeling their activities in certain specified ways and by stipulating certain required role- or position-linked institutional activities. But the creation of institutional modes of behavior also makes possible and gives rise to new kinds of relationships and collective forms of behavior not possible in the absence of that or a similar institution. The creation of an institution, therefore, also means a considerable enlargement of freedom. If the mutual constraints and the possible new forms of behavior work for the benefit of all office-holders or members and anyone else associated with the institution, it would be morally justified to that extent.

Since those discriminated against and excluded from a particular institution will be theoretically exempt from the duties and obligations associated with it, it might be thought that, on balance, they would not be unjustly treated. But that is false, especially if the excluded individuals are willing to bear, and to bear equally, the legitimate costs or burdens of participation. Moreover, other unfair burdens may be, and often are, imposed upon them even as they are prevented from enjoying the institution's legitimate fruits. As taxpayers, they may be burdened with financial obligations to help support that very same discriminatory institution. Discrimination against blacks and other minorities in public schools and in the job market in the United States illustrates this.

At this point it may be asked whether society has a duty to create, nurture, protect, and strengthen moral institutions, in the strict sense of "moral institution"; i.e., those expressly concerned to instill, protect, and promote the human right to freedom and other moral rights. For example, to support such institutions as the United Nations and Amnesty International. My view is that the acknowledgment of human rights imposes a *general* obligation on us, individually and collectively, to create legitimate means for the realization of these noble goals, but not an obligation to adopt or create any *particular* means to them. It does not obligate us to create any particular moral institutions but only moral institutions in general. It obligates us in the way any value does by virtue of being a value; namely, to promote, disseminate, defend, and multiply it.

The five conditions of moral institutions I distinguished can be stated more abstractly but more precisely in terms of the relation between the rights and *corresponding* obligations of a position R, and, directly or indirectly, the *correlative* obligations and rights, respectively, of the institution's other positions. For these conditions are relatively specific regulative rules that directly or indirectly serve to assess the extent to which the various office-holders in an institution, hence the institution as it is actually structured and operated, is moral or immoral. To the extent that the obligations O and corresponding rights R attached to a position P are justifiable by reference to the conformity of the institution's goals G to Principle P, O's fulfillment (by R's proper exercise) is a partial gauge of the institution's morality. The other determinant of its morality or immorality, as far as human rights are concerned, is the extent to which R and so the powers it bestows are used to further the institution's (moral) interests and goals, or are abused by being misdirected to irrelevant or opposite ends.

II

The Rationality and Goodness of Institutions

In considering the possible roles of human rights in determining the morality of institutions in Section I, I left out the question of the relation of an institution's morality to its rationality or irrationality. I now turn to that question.

Earlier I stressed the crucial role an institution, ("I's") goals G play with respect to "I's" basic organization and administration. It should now be added that an institution "I," whose organization O and administration A are perfectly geared to G's realization, and gives evidence of exceptional capacity for realizing G under optimum conditions, would be a perfectly *rational* institution in the relevant sense of "rational." It would be perfectly efficient. In other words, O and A would be (1) wholly, though not uniquely, determined by G, and "I" would be (2) a model of efficiency. As a consequence, (3) all positions in "I" would exemplify features (1) and (2). Finally, the special obligations and right attached to these positions, being perfectly attuned to the perfect fulfillment of "I" functions, would be (4) wholly though indirectly determined by G. In short, a perfectly rational institution in the present sense would be an institution in which all office-holders fulfill their prescribed functions in accordance with its goals, in perfect concert with all others.

The degree in which an institution is rational in the present sense, relative to its special goals, is determined by the degree in which it advances them. But what about these goals themselves? What would make *them* rational or irrational goals? The answer is their conformity or lack of conformity to the society's or community's social, economic, political, or other relevant ideals, hence to the regulative principles that reflect or are inspired by the latter. If these ideals themselves are moral ideals, ideals of equal universal human rights and of fairness and justice, together with ideals of an adequate moral code or system (e.g., an adequate form of ideal rule-utilitarianism), the institution would be perfectly rational. Similarly if these ideals consist of other positive values.[10]

An institution may be moral though inefficient; but it cannot be perfectly moral if it is completely irrational, assuming that complete irrationality is actually possible. If I am right that the rationality or irrationality of ends is ultimately determined by their moral and/or nonmoral goodness or badness, an institution can only be perfectly rational if it is perfectly moral. It cannot be perfectly rational and immoral, or serve other kinds of evils.

One mark of an eminently moral institution is its capacity for constant if not indefinite improvement, its responsiveness to internal and external criticism, and its inclusion of institutional mechanisms for the fair and objective evaluation of criticism and the expeditious implementation of reforms. For that free discussion and exchange of ideas on all levels, together with periodic evaluation of the institution's various functions and positions, and those who fill the latter, is requisite. In the prudentially and morally best institutions, critics would be positively commended and honored, rather than resented or penalized (Compare Socrates' defense in Plato's *Apology*, and contrast his actual fate).

In short, an essential part of the machinery needed to improve institutions and to prevent the decline of moral institutions is the existence and implementation of accepted institutional procedures for the rectification of moral abuses and other misuses of the positions in them, without jeopardizing the rights of innocent office-holders or anyone else, and disrupting normal operations as little as possible.

III

A discussion of the conditions of moral institutions needs to be supplemented by an analysis of the main conditions for the successful creation of an institution or practice. For simplicity's sake I shall concentrate on promising: a practice as simple in its basic structure as it is morally important. The analysis should throw light, *mutatis mutandis*, on the corresponding conditions in relation to institutions.

(1) A promise's being freely and voluntarily made is an obvious condition for a promise's obligating the promiser to keep her promise. A coerced promise is morally null and void, morally not binding—but a bona fide promise nonetheless![11] Despite its moral nullity the promiser *may* be obligated to keep the promise on other moral grounds, e.g., based on the fact or likelihood that the promisee is likely to suffer if the promiser fails to keep the promise.

(2) A related condition is this. Suppose I wish to promise you something: would your accepting my would-be promise constitute a condition for my successfully making a bona fide promise? The answer I think is "No." That, rather, is a condition of my being obligated to keep the promise; assuming that I satisfy the conditions for successful promising and have succeeded in making a *bona fide* promise to begin with. But if you do not accept my promise, you would not be *obligated* to accept what I promise, even if I try to keep my promise out of friendship or benevolence, and the like.

The implications of condition (1)—which may seem quite surprising when explicitly stated—is that voluntariness is not a condition of a would-be promise's being a successful act of promising and its result's being a bona fide promise. Therefore, an act X's being (or not being) a successful act of promising on the one hand and its not being morally binding *qua* coerced, are logically distinct matters. Ordinary usage clearly shows this. It is not odd to say: "I was forced to promise such-and-such to so-and-so," or "The promise was extracted from me by force." That voluntariness is not a condition of successful promising is also seen from the fact that in attempting to ascertain whether a speech act constitutes a bona fide act of promising, we do not inquire whether it was or was not made under duress.

The next question is whether (a) coercion in the creation of an institution or a practice necessarily makes it an immoral institution or practice; and similarly, if (b) an institution or practice coerces people to join it or participate in its activities. The answer to both questions depends on whether coerciveness is a structural-administrative feature of it, as in the case of the institutions and practices of slavery and white slavery. Consequently, a sixth condition of a moral institution or practice needs to be added to our earlier conditions. That is, (F) that the way an institution or a practice is created or is staffed and operated must be completely noncoercive. However desirable a would-be institution or practice may be, people should be free to decide whether to participate in its creation. People should also be free to join or not to join a desirable institution or practice.

On the other hand, if an institution or a practice is not coercive in nature, its morality would be determined by conditions (A)–(E) alone, but with the proviso that even occasional violations of a single individual's freedom in relation to either (a) or (b) above, if due to some defect in an otherwise moral institution's or practice's organization or administration, would diminish its moral goodness.

Finally, the basic issues discussed under condition (1) above can be put more precisely in terms of the distinction between two sorts of conditions. The first relates to an institution's or practice's legitimacy in general, which depends on the institution's or practice's moral and/ or nonmoral goodness or badness. The second consists in the conditions that determine in principle *who* should be subject to the institution's or practice's moral authority (if any). These individuals or groups would then be bound by the special legal and moral responsibilities and obligations attached to the institution or practice and would be entitled to the special moral and legal rights corresponding to their obligations. Consent is a condition of the latter sort: a condition of a legitimate (e.g., moral) institution's authority over consenting individuals. That authority includes legitimate expectations of loyalty and service, and the right to impose penalties on those subject to its authority if they fail to fulfil their duties and responsibilities.

IV

In speaking of "the morality of an institution"[12] in general and in distinguishing six conditions of "moral institutions," I have assumed without evidence that (a) institutions as a whole are in some sense moral agents; that an institution's so-called morality is logically distinct from (b) the morality of the individual office-holders, in relation to their ex-officio actions and activities. Since institutions are not literally individuals or collections of individuals but are categorially different from them, it is not clear whether they can be meaningfully said to be moral agents, hence moral or immoral. If they could, they would have moral duties and obligations and would be bearers of (special) moral rights.

The following considerations should provide fairly strong evidence in support of a positive answer to question (a).

Regarding the obligations of professions as a whole, Michael D. Bayles correctly states: "It is important to recognize obligations of professions as a whole and not to confuse them with the obligations of individual professionals. For example, some professions are said to have an obligation to provide services to all who need them. However, individual professionals do not have an obligation to serve all those who are in need."[13] Again, "obligations of a profession as a whole cannot be directly reduced to similar obligations of each member. . . . An obligation of the medical profession to provide services equally to everyone is not so reducible to a similar obligation of each physician. . . . Nevertheless, obligations of a profession as a whole can support some obligations of individual professionals—for example, to work for some disadvantaged client who would otherwise not receive services."[14]

A profession consists of a complex of institutions and practices; consequently its external obligations essentially boil down to the latter's obligations toward one another in the complex and toward the community or society as a whole. Its duties include moral obligations that are correlative to the community members' human rights. Therefore, a further condition of a moral community over and above those detailed in chapter 2 is its member institutions'/practices' respect for these rights. Similarly with the putative special rights of institutions/practices in their external relationships.

Some writers maintain that businesses, and presumably other institutions and practices, are not moral agents. One such writer is Nani Ranken. In "Morality in Business: Disharmony and Its Consequences,"[15] she argues against the so-called "harmony thesis," which "suggests that what is 'really' good for business will be in harmony with a course of action which is also correct from a moral point of view."[16] As Kevin Gibson states her position in his reply to her article, Ranken claims that "in order to make sense of 'the good' for a business . . . we need to make an analogy to the 'true good' of man."[17] Such an analogy, she thinks, is nonexistent.

> The "true good" of man . . . is something which goes beyond self-interest. Traditional philosophical models of morality apply uniquely to persons, and hence we cannot treat businesses as moral agents. Businesses are characterized as being necessarily subject to considerations of survival, growth and profit, and are thus incapable of altruism(behavior from a disinterested motive).[18]

The question then is whether institutions and practices are sufficiently analogous to persons to qualify as a bona fide, albeit a special kind of, moral agent, and so, constitute potential members of a moral community. In attempting to establish that they are moral agents in some sense, Gibson appeals to an ethic based on the "obligations and immunities of rights-holders":[19] precisely the kind of moral theory that animates the present work. He writes: "Given that we can recover some sense in which a business can be said to be a moral entity, then not only is the harmony thesis meaningful but also the morality of business will not be just a matter of the acts of autonomous individuals."[20]

Gibson concedes—what is obvious—that businesses are not literally persons, though they are regarded as *persona ficta* in the law. But as he adds, they are imperfectly analogous to persons; since they have characteristics analogous to those of persons; e.g., dynamism, coming into and going out of existence, and often a mission statement "which does not reflect the direct best interest of any individual in the company, but is instead geared to long term survival and benefit of the company itself. . . . A business has enough individuating characteristics [i.e., has a character, though not as Ranken demands of moral agents, "an inner nature"] to be described as a member of the moral community."[21] Moreover, a business can be "an intentional moral agent."[22] Gibson, therefore, posits company responsibilities resulting from a company's acts and decisions, over and above the personal responsibilities of the individual members. He concludes that companies, like individuals, are rights-bearing entities.

Gibson's reasoning and conclusions appear to me to be perfectly sound; and the characteristics of a business or company he stresses tie in nicely with the analysis of an institution's basic organization and administration that were discussed earlier in this chapter. I should add that a T-institution's overall teleological character (which is often explicitly formulated in a mission statement, as Gibson says) concern its external, societal relationships, as well as those internal to it. Its goal-directedness is clearly analogous to the normal goal-directedness of human beings, a characteristic essential for the latter's being "rational animals" in the sense in which the Greek philosophers understood that phrase.

I am also in agreement with both Bayles and Gibson in rejecting "the full reducibility of descriptions about organizations to descriptions about the individuals of whom...[they are] composed."[23] Rights and obligations are good examples. But the rights and obligations of institutions and practices, consequently of businesses and professions, are limited to special legal and (sometimes, also) moral rights and obligations. They obviously cannot include human rights.

The state provides a clear example of special institutional moral obligations and rights. In any system of government, but especially in a democratic government, the complex of institutions and practices that comprise the state, and the individual institutions and practices in that complex, unquestionably have moral obligations toward the citizens. That is perhaps most obvious given a two-step social contract theory of a democratic state, à la Locke, for instance. That is one reason why the contract remains in force (if it is a binding contract to begin with) from one generation to the next, despite the transitoriness of those who govern the country.

As Gibson, following J.L. Mackie, says, the special internal and external legal rights and obligations of institutions and professions are "granted within the context of a political and legal system."[24] In contrast to that, moral rights—special rights no less than human rights—are independent of any social organization or any legal or political system. This is clearly true of the special moral rights and obligations of persons, institutions, and professions; though the special relationships and transactions that give rise to these rights and obligations cannot exist except within some social or political framework, in a way that is not necessarily true of individuals. Once they arise, the special moral obligations and rights acquire an independent existence of their own. Further, although all individuals live in some society or other, some of their moral relationships do not logically presuppose the existence of any society. To take a simple example, we can imagine Friday promising Robinson Crusoe to help him with some chore. Or we can imagine the two forming a mutually satisfying compact, resulting in the creation of two special moral rights and two correlative/corresponding obligations; but the two-men-in-relation do not constitute a society or even a tiny community.

To return to Bayles. Bayles distinguishes three main facets of the external responsibilities of the professions. "First are activities of social leadership, such as service with charitable organizations, government commissions, and so on. . . . A second facet of responsibility for public good is the improvement of professional knowledge, tools, and skills. . . . A third facet of this responsibility is to preserve and enhance the role of the profession itself."[25] All three facets have important dimensions of moral responsibility, of special interest to a community.

To Bayles' three facets a fourth needs to be added: the obligation of institutions to cooperate in order to create or help sustain a good and moral community: an obligation absolutely essential to T-communities, particularly those whose communal teloses consist of the inter-related goals of their member institutions.

An institution's internal and external responsibilities and obligations are not unrelated. For one thing, the institution's respect for or violation of the equal human rights of its members or office-holders may have a bearing on its satisfying or not satisfying its external responsibilities; and vice versa. For example, a company's discriminatory treatment of some, especially a sizable number of its employees, may give rise to a general dissatisfaction with its management and hurt its ability to fulfil its responsibilities toward other institutions on which its and the community's welfare may depend. Again, the human rights of the employees tend to become a casualty of cut-throat economic competition between institutions in the same or different professions. The danger then would be that the management may look on the employees as mere means for the maximization of the institution's profits, power, and prestige, ignoring the need to provide for their physical and emotional welfare by giving them a decent standard of living and a healthy working environment.

To sum up. The discussion of the role of human rights in a moral community in the previous chapter focused on the private sphere, principally on the institution/practice of the family, and on friendship. This chapter, continuing the exploration of the role of human rights in a moral community, considered their institutional role in general, in a modern moral community. It therefore drew upon the conceptual framework or basic structure or organization and mode of operation of an institution/practice in general, sketched in Part II of the book, which exhibited the logical relations between an institution's/practice's constitutive conventions or rules, its goals, and the relevant moral regulative rules. Respecting human rights, five conditions of a moral institution/practice were distinguished (a sixth was later added). On that conceptual framework, an institution/practice is perfectly moral if it exemplifies, in its basic structure and administration, and in its goals, the equal human rights to freedom, treatment, and opportunity (Principle P).

The following are the five conditions distinguished. One, the goals of an institution/practice must conform to Principle P, by themselves consisting in the defense and promotion of human rights, or two, by being consistent with their promotion and defense. Three, the institution's/practice's constitutive rules must conform to Principle P, whenever they are (a) a subset of the constitutive rules determined by the institution's/practice's goals, and (b) the institutional goals themselves satisfy Principle P. Four, all positions and ranks in the institution/practice must be public and open to all qualified persons, irrespective of color, race, ethnic background, sex, age, creed, or ideology; and five, office-holders should be free to leave the institution/practice at will. If their employment agreement or contract requires them to stay with the institution/practice, they should be able to negotiate the termination of that agreement or contract. These conditions coincide almost perfectly with the conditions of a moral institution/practice entailed by John Rawls' First Principle of Justice, while some of their implications are justifiable in terms of the equal human right to positive freedom or liberty.

The aforementioned five conditions are regulative rules that, directly or indirectly, serve to assess the degree to which the office-holders, and so, the institution/practice as actually organized and operated, is moral or immoral.

The discussion turned next to the conditions of a rational institution/practice. It was maintained that an institution/practice is rational if (1) its organization and administration are geared to the institutional goals G and show evidence of exceptional ability to realize G under optimum conditions, and (2) the goals themselves conform to ethical social, economic, political, educational, or other relevant ideals—for example, to the ideals of an adequate rule-utilitarian or some other adequate normative ethic.

The earlier discussion of the conditions of a moral institution/practice further led to a consideration of the conditions for the moral creation of an institution/practice, taking as a paradigm the simple but normally important practice of promising. It was found that a promise—indeed, any practice or institution in general—should be freely and voluntarily created or established. If any coerciveness is built into any aspect of an institution's or practice's organization or administration, the institution or practice as a whole would, to that extent, be immoral. That means that a sixth condition of a moral institution/practice was also needed, viz; that the way an institution/practice is created, or is staffed and operated, must be completely non coercive.

In speaking of "a moral institution/practice," and of "the conditions of a moral institution/practice in this chapter and elsewhere in the book, it was assumed that an institution/practice, as a whole, is a moral agent in some sense. To justify that claim, it was necessary to show that a sufficient analogy existed between institutions/practices and actual persons, qualifying the former to be considered as bona fide—albeit a special—kind of moral agent, and making them potential members of a moral community. The author concurred with Kevin Gibson in arguing that a business has "sufficient individuating characteristics [i.e., has a character], to be described as a member of the moral community," and that it can be "an intentional moral agent." It was also pointed out that the rights and obligations of institutions/practices as a whole are not reducible to the rights and obligations of their members—in general, of those who participate in their institutional activities or perform their institutional functions—albeit the rights and obligations of institutions/practices—as, for example, in the case of the state—are limited to special legal rights and, sometimes, also to special moral rights and obligations.

Finally, following Michael Bayles, some main facets of the external responsibilities of the profession—activities of social leadership, improvement of professional knowledge, tools, and skills, and preservation and enhancement of the role of the profession—were briefly distinguished.

Notes

1   What I say here applies, *mutatis mutandis*, to practices.

2   For a general discussion of "functional" words, see my "Common Names and Family Resemblances," *Wittgenstein: The Philosophical Investigations*, George Pitcher, ed. (Garden City, N.Y., 1966), 205–220. For an analysis of the concept of an institution, see also "Institutions, Practices and Moral Rules," *Mind*, LXXXVI, no. 344 (October 1977): 479–496 (hereafter referred to as *IPMR*), as well as "Language and Speech as Institution and Practice," *Teorema*, IX/1 (1979): 5–38. For a partial analysis of legal institutions, see H.L.A. Hart's "'Primary' and 'Secondary' Legal Rules and the Institutional Character of Law," *Proceedings of the 12th World Congress of Philosophy of Law and Social Philosophy* (Athens, 1986); *Theory and Systems of Legal Philosophy*, Supplementa, III, S. Panou et al., eds., 204–213.

3   Quoted from "Justice as Rational Choice Behind a Veil of Ignorance," from *A Theory of Justice*; in *Justice: Alternative Political Perspectives*, James Sterba, ed. (Belmont, CA, 1980).

4   For simplicity, I shall ignore the differences between moral principles, standards, and rules.

5   This would be more likely to occur in institutions whose express aim is to further human rights, and whose basic structure and administration are attuned to that goal.

6   This is not true of all *practices*, since practices may be nonhierarchical, as in the case of games. In games, the idea of a hierarchy does not make much sense. Whether it is also true of language is an interesting question that I shall leave to the reader to decide.

   By contrast, practices that form part of an institution's rule-governed activities or are otherwise associated with an institution reflect the latter's hierarchical nature. Good examples are religious practices. Church services are an excellent example.

7   As we noted in Part II, affirmative action and preferential treatment of particular individuals or special groups in order to help rectify past inequities and injustices, and to enable the individuals or groups to compete on a roughly equal footing with the more advantaged, require for their justification special moral principles, such as Rawls' Second Principle of Justice. For a good discussion of discrimination in the United States in relation to admission to the professions and related moral issues, see Michael D. Bayles, *Professional Ethics* (Belmont, CA [1989]), chapter 8.

8   I leave out need, since it cannot be justly tied to people's positions or occupations, hence their position in institutions as such. It becomes relevant in rela-

tion to people as human beings; generally if not universally by virtue of the circumstances in which they find themselves. Need properly arises, e.g., in relation to the economic obligations their special obligations impose on them. (See chapter 8.)

9   *Taking Rights Seriously*, 181.

10   For a discussion of various classical concepts of rationality, including my view that ultimate ends, not just means or proximate ends, can be rational or irrational, see my "What is Rationality?" *Theoria*, XXIV, no. 3 (1958): 172–187.

11   I leave aside the legal conditions of valid promising in some particular legal system.

12   This entire discussion also applies, *mutatis mutandis*, to practices.

13   *Professional Ethics* (Belmont, CA [1989]), 28.

14   Ibid., See also chapter 5, "Obligations to Third Parties," Chapter 7, "Obligations To The Profession," and *passim*.

15   *Journal of Applied Philosophy*, 4, no. 1, 1987.

16   Ibid. Quoted from Kevin Gibson, "Ranken on Disharmony and Business Ethics," *Journal of Applied Philosophy*, 6, no. 3 (1989): 209.

17   Gibson, ibid.

18   Ibid.

19   Ibid.

20   Ibid., 209–210.

21   Ibid., 211.

22   Ibid.

23   bid.

24   Ibid., 212.

25   Op. cit., 166–167.

Chapter 12

Justice and Moral Community

I

Chapter 11 explored the place of human rights in the creation and maintenance of a moral community. There I distinguished a stronger and a weaker claim regarding the dispensibility or indispensability of the protective norms of human rights in such a community. This chapter parallels that exploration by investigating the place of principles of fairness and of moral and, to a lesser extent, legal justice: including their dispensability or indispensability in such a community. And as in the case of human rights, we must consider both a weaker and a stronger claim or sets of claims. The weaker claim I shall consider consists of two related theses. They are: (A1) that respect for fairness and justice, fair and just treatment of others, are indispensable in a moral, including an ideal, community; and (A2) that that respect is an integral part of what constitutes a moral community or, indeed, any moral society.

The stronger claim (B) is that fairness and justice are indispensible in a moral community, in the sense that a community's (1) explicit adoption and promulgation of some set of existing principles of fairness and justice, and (2) the members' general acknowledgment of and conformity to them are indispensable for the community's being a moral community. In actual, nonideal moral communities (2) allows for some members' occasional forceful standing on their entitlement to fair and just treatment and their defense of them, in morally justified ways whenever they reasonably believe that they are unfairly or unjustly treated. That may also include their challenging in the courts or in the forum of public opinion, laws they believe are unfair or unjust to them or to certain others, such as members of their ethnic, religious, or other groups.

Michael Sandel on the Dispensability
of Justice in a (Moral) Community

Paralleling his claim that the protective norms of human rights are dispensable in a (moral) community, and, *mutatis mutandis*, for essentially the same reasons he gives for them, Sandel envisages, in *Liberalism and the Limits of Justice*,[1] such a high degree of coincidence of people's interests and ends in a (moral) community that it would result in the "relative absence of the circumstances of justice." He agrees with Rawls[2] that principles of justice are needed to "sort out" conflicting claims in society. He characterizes society as a "cooperative venture for mutual advantage." Conflict as well as an identity of interests mark it. The identity lies in the benefits all receive from mutual cooperation, while, because of their "divergent interests and ends," they differ about the distribution of the benefits they derive from their cooperation. Since it is the role of justice to provide "arrangements by which such claims can be sorted out," principles of justice are needed to that end.[3]

But he argues that, while the modern nation-state, for example, might empirically satisfy the requirements of justice conceived of as primary, the participants' values and ends in smaller-scale and "more intimate or solidaristic associations" may coincide so closely that the circumstances of justice "prevail to a relatively small degree." As Hume observes, such conditions can be real enough, discoverable by "common experience and observation" (1739: 495).[4] Sandel agrees with Hume that such "enlarged affections" are approached by families, and that the greater the benevolence between individuals, the closer it approaches complete instances of enlarged affections. In such instances, "all distinction of property [may] be, in a great measure, lost and confounded among them" (1777: 17–18). He thinks that a range of human associations may be imagined, "characterized in varying degrees by the circumstances of justice." Among them are "tribes, neighborhoods, cities, towns, universities, trade unions, national liberation elements and established nationalities." But there are also a "a wide variety of ethnic, religious, cultural, and linguistic communities with more or less clearly-defined common identities and shared purposes," and these attributes would mean the *"relative absence of the circumstances of justice."*[5]

The arguments I have urged in chapter 11 in response to Sandel's claim regarding the alleged dispensability, in a (moral) community, of the protective norms of human rights also apply, *mutatis mutandis*, to his claim regarding the relative dispensability of the circumstances of justice, and so, of justice itself, in a (moral) community.[6] Consequently, I shall leave it to the interested reader to apply that discussion to justice. Let me only remind the reader that the distinction I drew there between a strong and a weaker sense of "dispensibility" of human rights also applies here. Hume and Sandel are right that e.g., nonideal communities can be imagined in which the coincidence of interests and ends is so great that no actual occasions arise for anyone's brandishing, so to speak, any justifying principles of justice; for the reasons Sandel gives. In that strong sense of the word, justice may be relatively, or even totally, dispensible. But that still leaves the possibility of circumstances of justice, hence the indispensability of justice in the weaker sense of the word. That is, most members of a (moral) community at least would *implicitly* treat one another justly and fairly; just as they may naturally respect their human rights; in circumstances in which scarcely any occasions arise for anyone's insisting on or defending her entitlement to be justly or fairly treated. This may be true even if such communities may have the language of fairness and justice, and even explicitly formulate principles of justice.

The relative or even total dispensability of justice in the strong sense is more likely in the case of (moral) T-communities than N-communities, in which no communal teloses exist; where more divergences of interests and ends, hence conflicts, are more likely to occur than in T-communities.

A community in which justice is indispensable in the weaker sense of that word would clearly be morally better, more desirable than a community in which justice is indispensable in the *strong* sense. That is because, in addition to not presupposing people's frequent standing on their rights, justice in the weaker sense would characterize an ideal community, setting a standard for actual communities. In an angelic community, justice in the weaker sense would not be, as Sandel thinks of justice, a negative or remedial virtue. That is, a second-order virtue presupposing certain first-order evils. In the weaker sense its indispensability in an actual moral community and even in an ideal community would be a positive virtue or value. Just as a state of affairs in which people respect the moral rights of others spontaneously and unreflectively, as naturally as the air they breathe, so also in the case of fairness and justice. In both cases such a state of affairs is without doubt much to be desired. Contrast that with, say, a family in which, in Sandel's words, we find continual "demands for fairness." In that kind of situation justice would be indisputably remedial. The virtue of benevolence (or rather, caring), which "must be a virtue of at least correlative status,"[7] is a positive virtue which, I claim, coexists with, indeed includes rather than replaces, fairness and justice in a harmonious, affectionate, "more or less ideal family situation," to quote Sandel again. Likewise with friendship and other caring relationships.

In sum, Sandel's thinking of the remedial aspect of justice ties in with his and Hume's understanding of the (relative) dispensability of justice in the kinds of circumstances they envisage, but only in the stronger sense of dispensable. In contrast to that, justice (and fairness) in the weak sense, which I believe is indispensable to *all* moral communities, is a positive virtue, not a remedial virtue presupposing disharmony or conflicts of interest.

Sandel's exclusive understanding of justice as a remedial virtue, leads him to claim that one of its consequences is our inability to predict whether, in any given instance, an "increase in justice is associated with an overall moral improvement." The reason is that an increase in justice can come about in either of two ways: (1) where before injustice prevailed, or (2) where before there was neither justice nor injustice, but a "sufficient measure of benevolence or fraternity such that the virtue of justice had not been extensively engaged." In (1), other things being equal, we clearly have overall moral improvement. But in (2), where an increase of justice reflects a change in the "quality of preexisting motivations and dispositions," the "overall moral balance might well be diminished."[8]

It is significant that Sandel's very definition of the "circumstances of justice"[9] automatically rules out the kinds of "circumstances of justice" that render justice indispensable in a community or society in which conflict is largely or totally absent; i.e., the very circumstances of justice that render justice indispensable in the weaker sense, even in a moral community! The narrowness of Sandel's conception of the circumstances of justice is particularly evident, and serious, in the case of legal justice; which Sandel is strangely silent about. For as I hope will become clear, the resolution of disputes and conflicts between individuals and groups is only *one* important kind of circumstance of legal justice.

In *The Nature and Functions of Law*,[10] Harold B. Berman and William R. Greiner argue for a comprehensive, balanced functional approach to law. They distinguish four main functions of law, three of which concern us; viz, (a) to resolve disputes, (b) to facilitate and protect voluntary arrangements, and (c) to mold and remold the moral and legal conceptions of a society, . . ."[11] They illustrate law as a process of resolving disputes [(a)] from civil and criminal procedure, and from labor law and the law pertaining to racial discrimination and law as a process of resolving acute social conflict (which they, unlike Sandel, correctly distinguish from disputes and so is additional to it). They also distinguish law as a process of protecting and facilitating voluntary arrangements [(b)] from the law of contract.

In as much as fairness and justice are involved in all the foregoing functions of the law their scope is measurably greater than Sandel envisages for justice, and affects the nature and scope of the circumstances of fairness and justice, going well beyond conditions of conflicts resulting from differences in individual and group interests and ends. Indeed, the circumstances of the civil law of contract, which facilitates voluntary arrangements, are quite different from the circumstances of tort law, which involves the resolution of disputes, as well as from the circumstances of labor law and law concerning racial and gender discrimination; e.g. laws defining affirmative action in the United States. Although Berman and Greiner subsume criminal law under "Law as a Process of Resolution of Disputes," that is not strictly correct. Crime and violence against persons and property may often result from various kinds of disputes or conflicts between individuals or groups: they are not themselves disputes or conflicts. Criminal law as such is, therefore, not a process of resolving disputes or conflicts. Crime and violence are threats to social order, and Berman and Greiner themselves stress the social function of law as ". . . a tendency of law to contribute to the maintenance of social order,"[12] "primarily as one of the order-creating, or ordering, processes, . . . [of society]."[13] And "law . . . is something that is done when things go wrong."[14]

Thus, although resolving disputes and conflicts over how the fruits of cooperation are to be distributed, i.e., distributive justice,[15] is one of the important functions of moral principles of justice as well as of positive law, Sandel's specification of the circumstances of justice is too narrow and circumscribed. A moral theory of justice is also concerned to resolve other kinds of conflicts among individuals and groups. Further, a moral theory of justice no less than a legal system must include principles of criminal justice. For example, criminal justice falls under the rubric of individual and collective security and cannot be subsumed under "conflict resolution." For example, it must provide a moral justification for punishment, restitution, and rehabilitation, as well as therapy for psychopaths and sociopaths.

Even in a community of largely caring individuals the old Adam of self-interest and self-seeking tendencies remain so long as human nature continues to be what it has been at least since the evolution of Homo sapiens from his prehuman ancestors: tendencies which color, sometimes dilute, distort, or stain the noblest sentiments of love and affection, fraternity or sisterhood, comradeship and friendship. The recognition of these tendencies in oneself and others, even in a community of caring individuals and institutions, requires constant vigilance to avoid or prevent unfair or unjust treatment of others, even members of one's own family and closest friends, let alone others.

But such awareness and vigilance presuppose the existence of the guiding principles of fairness and justice, and the community's awareness of them. But as with human rights in a moral community, that does not mean the members' continual or, perhaps, occasional standing on their moral and legal right to fair and just treatment; even defending them against attack either by appeal to the law or informally by appeal to the others' sense of justice within some generally accepted morality.

II

If fairness and justice are indispensable for a community's being a moral community, in the ways described in Section I, what sort of theory of justice is requisite for a moral community, in which caring and respect for human rights are the norm?

In a seminal article,[16] Harold Berman endorses a central thesis propounded by Edgar Bodenheimer,[17] and provides a historical perspective in its support. Berman describes Bodenheimer's thesis thus: "Edgar Bodenheimer has shown that human nature contains both individual and social characteristics and that injustice results unless a symbiosis of these two conflicting sets of characteristics is achieved."[18] Again, ". . . Professor Bodenheimer is surely right in stressing that the fundamental moral problem is to maintain the proper balance between the two . . . ["justice and rights, individual and community"]."[19] But Berman stresses that it has a historical, in addition to a political, dimension (Rorty[20]).

In a footnote (footnote 5) Berman elaborates.

> Bodenheimer lists in some detail affirmative aspects of both the individual and social interpretation of human nature. He states: "The concept of justice prevailing in a symbiotic society would require that individual rights (especially the rights of liberty, equality, and security) be recognized to the greatest

extent compatible with the common good." He defines the common good not in Benthamite terms of the sum total of private goods but in terms of "the highest material and cultural development of society."[21]

I wholeheartedly agree that a moral and legal theory of justice should balance individualistic and communitarian concerns or contain both kinds of elements. But, going further than Berman and Bodenheimer, it needs to be reiterated that an adequate moral theory as a whole, not just a moral theory of justice, would balance the moral demands of the individual, the moral subject, and the moral demands of society as a whole, including the special demands of any N- and T-communities it may consist of or contain.

There are two main ways in which a theory of justice may be *individualistic*: (1) by *defining* the principles of justice in terms of the human right to liberty, (like Rawls' definition of the first principle of justice), understanding these principles in terms of individual equality and liberty (as Rawls also does in his hypothetical original situation), or (2) *grounding* the principles of justice on a human right or a set of human rights (as Rawls' "deep theory" does, in basing the First Principle of justice on the human right to equal concern and respect[22]). Berman is, therefore, correct in pointing out these two ways in which Rawls' principles of justice are individualistic. But in stipulating the *equality* of individual rights and liberties, Rawls' First Principle is also universally impartial in relation to all human beings.

The individualism of Rawls' two principles of justice is a consequence of the deontologism of his theory of justice as a whole. Individuals may give up to society ". . . only so much of their liberty and equality as is necessary to prevent arbitrary interference in the liberty and equality of others"[23]; whereas I believe that the exercise of individual human rights (as well as special moral rights) may be restricted not only for the preceding reason but also in extreme circumstances that deeply affect the welfare, happiness, or survival of the human race as a whole or a sizable part of it, as well as to ensure a moral society's/community's survival in the face of internal crime and violence or external aggression. (Cf. Etzioni's views concerning the equilibrium of autonomy and order, discussed in chapter 3 of this book.) That to be achieved by enforceable and properly enforced humane and enlightened penal law and defensive measures conforming to the traditional rules of just war.

A theory of justice is universalistic or collectivistic (or "communitarian," to use Berman's term[24]), if (a) the principles of justice are defined in terms of the general welfare (or exclusively in terms of a T-community's telos(es), or (b) furthering the general welfare is taken as the criterion for bona fide principles of justice. Utilitarian theories of justice are universalistic-collectivistic in sense (a) or sense (b). The ethic of caring sketched in Part II fulfills a considerable part of the balance envisioned by Bodenheimer and Berman by striving to place a balanced self-caring and other-caring squarely at the center of a moral theory: a balance which in an ideal moral community would embrace an entire community.[25] In other words, that ethic of caring is by definition fundamentally universalistic; particularly in the way a good and moral community in Part I and the ethic of caring in Part II were portrayed; as we saw, by complementing other-caring and constraining self-caring by the acknowledgment of universal human rights.

To complete the fundamentals of the moral theory sketched in Part II, and to make the relation between individualism and communitarianism more closely balanced, a similarly balanced theory of moral (and legal) justice is required. As noted earlier, impartiality means treating relevantly like cases alike, and relevantly unlike cases unlike. I shall now argue that justice, conceived of as impartiality-*cum*-desert, provides the desired balance.

As we saw in chapter 8, impartiality and desert are two essential elements in (fairness and in) justice in general: neither impartiality nor desert by itself exhausts justice (or fairness). To begin with impartiality, I noted that impartiality is a common element in both fairness and justice; yet fairness and justice, albeit closely related, are distinct. Though both include impartiality and desert, justice in general is not the alter ego of fairness, or fairness simply the alter ego of justice. What justice in general and fairness include over and above impartiality is desert: treating everyone (impartially) according to her desert, including her merit or demerit, what she deserves and, in that sense, what is her due (Plato). That is, treating all who deserve one kind of treatment alike, impartially, differently from all others who deserve something else (Aristotle).

Thus, both those who define justice as impartiality and those who define it as desert pick out one defining element and explicitly or implicitly exclude the other. Together with impartiality, desert combines the meritocratic classical Greek conception with modern egalitarian and meritocratic conceptions of justice. Justice as impartiality-*cum*-desert provides the necessary balance between individualism and universalism in ethics, politics, and law, as follows:

(1) Again, as we saw in chapter 8, justice in general consists in second-order impartiality. That is, as purely formal justice, it applies

to rules, and—but not necessarily universally—to the particular cases to which these rules are applied. Likewise, desert is a second-order canon and criterion of social justice.

Impartiality, as the formal element in all species of justice, constitutes—and morally *guarantees*—*formal* moral and legal justice, but not moral and legal social justice. "Treat all slaves equally" is only formal justice; while "treat all human beings equally" is not only formally but also "socially" just; though it does, of course, have content and is not a purely formal moral rule in the sense in which, for example, Kant's first two formulations of his categorical imperative are purely formal. It morally enjoins the nonexistence or abolition of a slave class and a "free" class. One can treat all human beings equally if, by transcending conventional distinctions, one recognizes in practice the sameness of all human beings in their humanity (humanness).

Insofar as distributive justice is a species of justice in general, distributive justice includes (second-order) equality or impartiality; but insofar as it is a special species of justice, generally speaking, it also involves partiality with respect to those members of society that differ from others in desert. In short, it combines equality-with-difference, or difference-with-equality.

For a harmonious relationship between impartiality/equality and desert to exist in practice, the following must be borne in mind: that whenever reflection is possible (unlike, e.g., in Fried's example), a judge or agent must give equal, i.e., impartial, consideration to the particular cases or situations before her[26] in order to assess justly the merits or demerits—in general, the possible deserts—involved in each case. She must weigh the deserts involved, if any, impartially; or stating the matter in terms of caring, if one cares equally about (say) two friends and is able to put aside all irrational, subjective factors that would favor one friend over the other, one ought to be able to give their cases or situations equal consideration, weighing their deserts impartially. In that way the just weighing of desert itself is conditioned by impartiality, as the foundation on which just moral and legal practical reasoning and decision-making are built.

We can see why one might think of desert as constituting the whole of justice, and incorporating impartiality into it as one basic element. On that view (a), whenever the deserts of two persons "A" and "B" differ, justice would consist in rewarding (treating) "A" and "B" according to their different deserts; and (b) whenever the deserts of two other persons "C" and "D" are the same, justice requires that they be treated similarly. In fact, even when "A's" and "B's" deserts are different, whereas "A's" and "C's" deserts are the same, and likewise, "D's" and "B's" deserts are the same, justice requires that "C be treated impartially like "A," and "D" be treated impartially like "B."

(2) As we saw in chapter 9, a person is essentially relational, essentially involves others in a web of attachments and relationships. Consequently, attending to a person's concerns also necessitates, requires, or presupposes attending, in some degree, to the concerns of all those who form part of that web of attachments and relationships. In a good and moral community that would ideally mean helping to realize their moral personhood, their values and ends.

(3) Again, a balance between the impartiality and desert elements of an adequate theory of justice would be struck if a theory of justice attends to both (a) what distinguishes different persons and (b) what they have in common as human beings, what is essentially the same in all human beings. The "general welfare" of utilitarian ethics is nothing more or other than the sum total of the welfare of the individual members of the group.

(4) To be fair and just does not mean ignoring differences: impartiality is not tantamount to blindness as to what is individual, provided what is individual is not utterly *unique, completely* unlike anything else. But uniqueness in that very strong sense does not exist in the case of human actions and situations, for very simple and obvious reasons. First, because of the universals found in all human beings, our common human nature.[27] Thus, our intentions and motives, desires, needs, interests, and goals are not and cannot be altogether different but have (must have) certain commonalities. Second, the actual situations in which human beings find themselves or put themselves—in short, the conditions of human existence on earth or "the human condition"—are also fundamentally the same, have certain common, indeed universal components.

(5) Ideally, procedural legal justice consists of the impartial protections and defenses of the legal (and underlying moral) rights that everyone has before the law, limiting to a considerable extent the state's power to use the law to discriminate against or oppress "undesirable" individuals and groups. That is, to prevent their unfair treatment vis-à-vis those whom the law would otherwise unjustifiably favor.

Impartiality is also a fundamental element in statutory law and, in common law systems, such as in Britain and the United States, in case law as well (without, however, forgetting the important element of judicial discretion in common law systems, discussed in chapter 8).

But it should be noted that the champions of the Critical Legal Studies movement greatly exaggerate the scope of actual judicial discretion in supposing that the judge can always set aside an existing rule (e.g., a statute or a case law precedent) "p," and apply its very opposite, "not p."

(6) A majoritarian, democratically elected legislative body is essential for the enactment of positive laws that serve the community's practical needs and moral ends while protecting individual rights. The existence of such a body constitutes still another way in which a system of moral and legal justice can strive to harmonize the general welfare and individual rights and liberties. In theory or principle, that is precisely what, e.g., the U.S. Supreme Court is supposed to be doing in its deliberations and the decisions it hands down; viz, endeavoring to somehow balance justice and individual rights with what they believe are the demands of "public policy"; what they believe is in the interests of the country as a whole, whenever these demands or concerns are, or seem to be, in conflict.

To sum up. Following the discussion of the place of human rights in a moral community in the preceding two chapters, this chapter focused on the place of fairness and justice in a moral community. In relation to that question too, a weaker and a stronger claim or set of claims was considered. The weaker claim (A) consisted of two related theses: that (1) respect for fairness and justice are indispensable for a moral community, including an ideal community, and (2) respect for them is an integral part of a moral community, or, indeed, any moral society. The stronger claim (B) was that fairness and justice are indispensable for a moral community, in the sense that, to qualify as such, a community must (1) explicitly adopt and promulgate some set of principles of fairness and justice, and (2) its members must explicitly acknowledge them in addition to conforming to these principles.

Paralleling his claim that human rights are dispensable in a constitutive (moral) community, Michael Sandel argues, for essentially the same reasons as with regard to human rights, that "the circumstances of justice" would be relatively absent in a (moral) community. Analysis showed the correctness of Sandel's view (following David Hume's) that one can imagine (nonideal) communities where the coincidence of interests and ends is so great that no actual occasions arise for anyone's standing on any justifying principles of justice. Consequently, that justice (and similarly fairness) may be dispensable in a nonideal (moral) community in the stronger, second sense. However, the situation is significantly different with the weaker claim. Although the participants in a moral community would generally not have occasion explicitly to acknowledge these principles, most of them would implicitly acknowledge them by treating one another fairly and justly.

Sandel's claim that justice is relatively dispensable in a nonideal community, essentially stemmed from his exclusive concentration on the remedial aspect of justice, on its role in resolving disputes and conflicts, and his neglect of the other important functions of moral and legal justice; that is, the facilitation and protection of voluntary arrangements, the molding and remolding of the moral and legal conceptions of society (Berman and Greiner), and fair and equitable distribution of benefits and burdens. These too are ways in which justice would be indispensable in a moral community.

But if fairness and justice are indispensable in a moral community, in the weaker sense, one is led to ask what sort of theory of justice is requisite for a community in which caring and human rights are the norm. The answer was that, as Berman and Bodenheimer maintain, the requisite moral and legal theory would contain, and would balance, individualistic and "communitarian"—universalistic or collectivist—concerns. The two ways in which a theory of justice may be individualistic, and the ways in which it may be collectivist, were spelled out. A theory is individualistic if (1) the principles of justice are defined in terms of the human right to liberty or if (2) they are grounded on a human right or a set of human rights. It is collectivist or "communitarian" if, for example, (a) the principles of justice are defined in terms of the general welfare or if (b) furthering the general welfare is considered as the criterion for any acceptable principles of justice. The ethic of caring sketched in Part II fulfills a considerable part of the balance envisaged by Berman and Bodenheimer since it strives to place a balanced self-caring and other-caring squarely at the center of a moral theory. Moreover, the balance provided by that ethic is also reflected in the conception of justice as impartiality-*cum*-desert put forth in Part II. Evidence in support of the claim that justice, conceived of in that way, balances individualism and collectivism in ethics, politics and law, completed the discussion.

Notes

1   Ibid., 28–29.

2   Sandel writes: "The circumstances of justice are the [empirical] circumstances that give rise to the virtue of justice. In their absence, the virtue of justice would be nugatory; it would not be required nor for that matter even possible. 'But a human society *is* characterized by the circumstances of justice' [emphasis added] ([Rawls] 129–130). Therefore, the virtue of justice *is* required" (ibid., 291; italics in original).

3   Ibid., 28–29.

4   Ibid., 30–31.

5   Ibid., 31. My italics.

6   Although I focus on community, what I say applies, *mutatis mutandis*, to families, clans, tribes, etc., which Sandel mentions.

7   Sandel, ibid.

8   Ibid., 32.

9   The same idea is also implicit in Hume's view of the circumstances of justice that Sandel is interested in in his discussion; namely, that justice arises whenever conflicts of interests and ends arise or are present.

10   Fourth Edition (Mineola, NY, 1980).

11   Ibid., 36. Italics in original.

12   Ibid., p. 28.

13   Ibid., 26.

14   Ibid., 27.

15   This includes remedial or rectificatory justice in relation to past inequities regarding the distribution of the fruits of cooperation.

16   "Individualistic and Communitarian Theories of Justice: An Historical Approach," *University of California, Davis Law Review*, 211, no. 3 (Spring 1988): 549–575.

17   "Individuals and Organized Society from the Perspective of a Philosophical Anthropology," 9 *Journal of Social and Biological Structures*, 207 (1986).

18   Berman, op. cit., 550.

19   Ibid., 554.

20   Ibid., 554–555. Berman adds in footnote 14: "This is implicit in the title of Rorty's essay, . . . ["The Priority of Democratic Politics to Philosophy,"] 12 (1988), *The Virginia Statute of Religious Freedom*, M. Peterson and R. Vaughan, eds., 1988.

21   Berman, ibid., 550; Bodenheimer, op. cit., 224.

22   "The original position is well designed to enforce the abstract right to equal concern and respect, which must be understood to be the fundamental concept of Rawls' deep theory." Ronald Dworkin, *Taking Rights Seriously*, 181.

23   Berman, op. cit., 549.

24   A universalistic/collectivist conception of the good should be distinguished from a conception of the good where society is organically conceived, as, for example, in Hegel's philosophy, such that the good of society as a whole is supposed to transcend its members' collective good.

25   It would be interesting to compare the idea of a balance between individualistic and collectivistic theories of *justice*, with, or relate it to, Etzioni's conception of the "golden rule" of a balance or equilibrium between autonomy and order in a good society, which was discussed in chapter 3.

26   Note also the role that equal consideration plays—or rather, ought to play—in consequentialist deliberations. For example, in utilitarianism, including contemporary preference utilitarianism.

27   Empirical evidence that all human beings, members of the species *Homo sapiens*, have a common nature has been mounting in recent years and is now generally recognized by scientists.

Chapter 13

Feminist and Postmodern Challenges to Communitarianism

The debate between liberals and their communitarian critics, called "the central debate in Anglo-American political theory during the 1980s,"[1] continued in the 1990s, has been joined by some feminist and postmodern challenges to communitarianism. The literature on the communitarian critique of liberalism is now quite extensive. Rather than rehashing (an impossible and unrewarding task) the extensive communitarian criticisms of liberalism in articles and books, this chapter will mainly focus on the less well-covered feminist and postmodern challenges to communitarianism, without totally ignoring some main liberal responses to communitarian criticisms.

I

A. The Feminist and Postmodern Challenge(s) to the Ideal of (Moral) Community

For what follows it is essential to remember that the ideal of (moral) community has taken different historical forms and takes different contemporary forms; and many, perhaps all, may or may not correspond to the ideal of (moral) community sketched in this book. Consequently, some possibly valid criticisms of a particular ideal of community may or may not be also valid against that ideal of (moral) community.

(1) In the words of Drucilla Cornell in *The Philosophy of the Limit*,[2] a fundamental argument urged by postmodern critics, and shared by some feminist thinkers, concerns the opposition of the individual and community, or the public role of the citizen. For the critic, a main form this opposition takes is the community's denying "the difference between subjects."[3] For example, "Iris Young has argued that the very

idea of community as a unit of ethical being in Hegel's sense must be rejected as philosophically wrong and normatively suspect."[4] Her reason is that it denies "the difference between subjects. The desire for community relies on the same desire for social wholeness [and] identification that underlies racism and ethnic chauvinism, on the one hand, and political sectarianism on the other."[5] But in claiming that "the ideal of community presumes subjects who are present to themselves and presumes subjects can understand [one] another as they understand themselves, . . .denies the difference between subjects,"[6] Young goes beyond the Hegelian conception of community to "the ideal of community"[7] in general.

Cornell comments that Young replaces the ideal of the community with a vision of a "nonrepressive city," which stresses difference. Her skepticism regarding the ideal of community rests on her "deep suspicion" that, lying behind that ideal, is a nostalgia for an "organic wholeness" that inescapably excludes those who are perceived not to fit into the community.[8]

(2) Since the conception of a (good and moral) community, including the conception of a T-community sketched in this book, is far from the Hegelian metaphysical-"organic" (Idealist) conception of community, it is not affected by Young's *specific* strictures against that particular type of conception. In the course of examining her criticism of "the ideal of community," some of the main differences between the conception of a good and moral community presented in this book and the Hegelian conception of a community should emerge.

(3) It is true that, *in a sense*, the desire for community—at least the desire for a T-community as I characterized that type of community— is a desire for "social wholeness." But that desire is not (a) a desire for the kind of wholeness—i.e., a desire for an "organic whole"—that the Hegelian conception of a community, for example, involves. Nor, consequently, does it (b) rely "on the same desire for social wholeness [and] identification that underlies racism and ethnic chauvinism, on the one hand, and political sectarianism on the other."[9] It does not deny individual differences and certainly does not raise the community to the level of a metaphysical entity, or conceive of it as an aspect of some all-embracing metaphysical Reality, such as Hegel's Absolute Reason. Indeed, several decades earlier I argued in detail against F.H. Bradley's organic conception of the world of Appearance and Brand Blanshard's organic conception of Reality—and by implication, Hegel's organic conception of reality—by rejecting, *inter alia*, the doctrine of

"internal relations" in the requisite sense(s) of "internal relations" logically presupposed by *any* organic conception of reality.[10]

The "wholeness" that constitutes a community in the Hegelian sense consists in (a) a unity in which the individual members are *wholly* defined by their internal, essential relations to all the other members of the community, hence to the community as a whole.[11] In fact it is (b) a community in which the value of the "whole" is putatively[12] greater than the sum total of the values of its parts and is an aspect of Ultimate Being, the Absolute.[13] Whereas on the relational conception of the moral agent defended in chapter 9, the moral subject is only partially defined by her personal relationships and attachments, and important projects and ends. Consequently, the communal telos(es) in a good and moral T-community can at best only partially define the members as moral subjects; and no special (indeed, any) metaphysical status is assigned to the community as a whole, either as such or as a supposed part of an all-encompassing monistic, monolithic reality. Since by definition N-communities lack communal teloses, not even such partial communal definition of the members can exist in their case.)[14]

Yet neither (a) nor (b), nor (a) and (b) together, entail a denial of difference. An organic whole characterized by (a) and (b) is logically compatible with the acceptance and valuing of individual difference. *A fortiori*, the conception of community broadly presented in chapter 1, is logically compatible with difference. That includes the concept of a T-community and specifically the idea of a communal telos or teloses.[15] To discover what aspect of the Hegelian conception of community is logically responsible for the denial of difference we need to consider the crucial concept of a communal telos. The issue of the denial of difference is particularly relevant to T-communities, of which the Hegelian community is one special kind.

B. "The Ideal of Community"

Whether or not any feature or combination of features of a Hegelian organic community logically entails a denial of difference, it is patent that, unfortunately, Young's strictures about "the ideal of community" in general are supposed to be empirical, not logical ones. I refer to her claim that "the desire for wholeness . . . is the same as the desire that leads to racism and chauvinism. . . ." She unfortunately mixes logical-metaphysical and empirical claims, or jumps from the one to the other without distinguishing them.

Basic to Young's argument is the claim that the desire for wholeness is the same desire that leads to chauvinism, racism, etc. But that is an error. The desire for wholeness and the unthinking, frequently irrational impulse or desire to deny difference, are two quite different, and, indeed, opposed, psychological forces. That impulse or desire has little or nothing to do with the ideal of community, and with the desire to approximate it or to attain it. It is true that a minimal condition for the *existence* of any societal form of human existence at all, communities included, is the existence of like-minded individuals who share a strong desire to cooperatively live and work and play in relative proximity. And no community, or any other form of societal organization, can *survive* without the continual cooperation of its members. But only in a T-community does the cooperation necessarily include *general* agreement, like-mindedness on the community's goals and how to achieve them. Thus *attraction* or a centripetal force is the essence of the impulse or desire, natural to human beings as social animals, to band together in common pursuits. But general agreement does not mean (a) absence of all discussion, debate, or disagreement about means and ends, as the community is faced with changing conditions over its lifespan. More than that: a T-community needs to periodically rethink and even redefine its telos(es), through open, democratic discussion and debate, and correspondingly, on the best ways to realize it (them).

The impulse or desire to deny difference is the psychological counterpart of the impulse or desire to unite. But Young's error of identifying the two impulses or desires stems from the conceptual fact that exclusion presupposes inclusion. That logical fact leaves undecided the factual question of (a) what in a given period of time happens to be the "in" group and what the "out" group of a given tribe, city, community, or country. Similarly, (b) what groups happen to be excluded altogether from that tribe, city, community, country, etc.

Another reason Young gives for her claim that the ideal of community "denies the difference between subjects" is the astonishing claim that "it presumes subjects can understand [one] another as they understand themselves."[16] There we have two basic errors. First, Young's claim is a palpable *non sequitur*: the presumption Young describes simply does not follow from "the Hegelian ideal of community" that Young criticizes—and certainly not from the conception of an ideal moral community sketched in this book. On Hegel's coherentist conception of (human) knowledge, the knowledge or understanding of any entity in the universe is always necessarily incomplete. A complete knowledge or understanding would require knowledge or understanding of its internal relation to every other entity in the universe—an impossible task indeed! (Cf. Tennyson's lines from "Little Flower in the Crannied Wall": "If I know you,/ root and all,/ and all in all,/ I would know/ what man and God is.")

Even complete human knowledge is impossible on the preceding grounds; and, more importantly for us, no plausible "ideal of community," including the one sketched in this book, does or can plausibly require it, even as an ideal.

To focus on the conception of community in this book, such a requirement is neither requisite nor possible for a good and moral community; and there is understanding and there is understanding. The kernel of truth in Young's claim is that, as emphasized in earlier chapters, an appreciable degree of sympathetic understanding of other people's needs, concerns, interests, and goals, and their view of themselves and others, is necessary for empathy with them and for a stable and sustained harmonious relationship between them. But that is true not only of a community but of any other possible form of social organization. Requisite for this understanding in this "existential" sense is that people care enough about others to make them want to understand them and to make a sustained effort to do so. As the American philosopher Brand Blanshard observes, wrong action is often not a result of deliberate evil but of lack of imagination; the inability to put oneself in another's shoes.

Some of the ingredients of the complex and powerful atavistic impulse or desire to deny difference (going back no doubt to our evolutionary past and intimately connected with our prehuman and early human struggle for survival) are suspicion, dislike, and fear, even paranoia: emotions and attitudes that have infected human society throughout history, encompassing every conceivable sort of difference the feverish human imagination could conjure up. The ideal of community has nothing to do with it, and certainly not in any degree responsible for it.

Some examples of long-festering suspicions, distrust, and fear of difference are, e.g., the recent and ongoing religious and ethnic conflicts in the former Yugoslavia; the century-old territorial conflict between Arabs and Jews for the land of Palestine; and, in the United States, historical white racism in relation to blacks and more recently, in relation to Latinos and other minority groups.

The brief sketch of the Armenian community in Jerusalem in chapter 1 serves as a telling contrast to this dark picture.

Although Young's strictures against community are intended to be factual criticisms, she gives no empirical evidence that people who desire or cherish mutual closeness and caring, cooperation and solidarity, tend to deny difference; that the two desires are even generally present together, are intertwined. It is natural and indeed desirable for people to want to be with those who share the same language, history, and culture: the same customs and traditions, values and ideals. It makes them feel at home and makes life simpler for them. Self-expression and communication, consequently mutual understanding, cooperation and teamwork, and close relationships become easier to come by. As a result group activities generally run more smoothly and efficiently than otherwise.

The tendency to deny difference, to the degree that it exists, is clearly greater in a T- than in an N-community, by virtue of the fact that the former involves certain common goals that all the adult participants have to agree to and work together to realize. But if these goals are broadly defined, and if the means of pursuing their realization allows for flexibility, innovation, and constant experimentation (as they are, for example, in good scientific research centers and artistic communities) the tendency to exclusion of any of the community's participants would be greatly minimized. The tendency would be further minimized if the communal goals themselves are open to revision or modification through periodic democratic discussion and decision. The denial of difference would be also minimized if the community is open to innovative new members who can bring new vitality to it, even if that would mean the community's revising or modifying its goals or the means it has hitherto employed to realize them.

Even in the case of T- and N-communities based on ethnic, racial, or historical-cultural heritage, an open-door policy would be possible if a community's members are willing to admit individuals who lack that heritage but whose membership would enrich the community and would in turn enrich them.

Again, though communal existence may sometimes give rise to, or may itself be based upon the tendency to deny difference, that tendency is unfortunately not confined to it but is a general failing we find throughout human history, in all forms of social organization.

As mentioned earlier, the particular element in the Hegelian conception of community responsible for its denial of difference we have been looking for has to do with Hegel's understanding of the community's teloses and how they are to be pursued. Whether or not a T-community denies difference is determined by these two factors: the nature of the teloses, and, the way or ways in which they are to be realized. A T-community necessarily denies individual difference if (i) its members are forced to put aside or sacrifice their needs, interests, aspirations, and attachments for the sake of pursuing the communal telos(es) conceived as of greater value than their own individual concerns and good. That is, if it violates their integrity in Bernard Williams' sense. Or if (ii) they are forced to do so on the supposition that their self-realization itself either consists in or crucially depends upon their doing so. Ancient Sparta, as well as Hitler's Germany, Stalin's U.S.S.R., and Mao's China are classic examples of (i); though only Sparta was a T-community. Characteristic of such societies were the Iron or Bamboo curtains that prevented citizens from leaving or fleeing to less coercive environments. The Hegelian conception of community exemplifies both (i) and (ii). Isaiah Berlin's following description of that conception of community makes this clear.

> The real self [as the Hegelian conception does] may be conceived as something wider than the individual (as the term is normally understood), as a social "whole" of which the individual is an element or aspect: a tribe, a race, a church, a state, the great society of the living and the dead and the yet unborn. *This entity is then identified as being the "true" self which, by imposing its collective, or "organic," single will upon its recalcitrant "members," achieves its own, and therefore their, "higher" freedom.* The perils of using organic metaphors to justify the coercion of some men by others in order to raise them to a "higher" level of freedom have often been pointed out.[17]

In other words, in both (i) and (ii) we would have a community that denies its members a modicum of liberty. I include (i) since the realization of no communal telos, however noble or desirable—such as a selfless philanthropic or humanitarian communal goal—can completely realize the members' selfhood as individuals. No human being—whether a Socrates, the Old Testament prophets, a Jesus, a Gandhi, an Albert Schweitzer, a Martin Luther King or a Mother Teresa—is totally self-fulfilled by his or her service to the truth, or to others. The same is true of much lesser men and women.

(iii) A virulently exclusive, discriminatory communal telos can be singlehandedly responsible for the denial of difference; as with Nazism, whose nationalistic goals had no place for non-Aryans, particularly gypsies and Jews.

The moral of the preceding analysis is that a truly democratic T-community (and, similarly, an N-community) is the *sine qua non* of a nonoppressive community. More specifically, a community that requires diverse talents and skills, visions and ideas for the realization of its communal telos or teloses, and prizes that diversity. That would be the case if:

(a) the ideal goal of a T-community is securing the welfare and happiness of *all* its members without exception; or if,

(b) as in good scientific communities, such as laboratories, scientific centers, etc., where cooperative research on interrelated scientific questions is the set-up's overall purpose, the special knowledge and skill, imagination and creativity each scientist brings to the task is requisite for its success. Likewise with good artist communities, where an important goal is to permit each artist or student of art "to do his or her own thing," in his or her individual, distinctive way. Similarly with orchestras and other musical ensembles blessed with open-minded, nonauthoritarian, and flexible leaders, teachers, or conductors.

Like the tendency of other forms of social organization, the tendency of real, nonideal T-communities to deny differences would be obviated to the extent to which a community's goals are freely, democratically chosen. Similarly with the means chosen to pursue these goals. And third, if those who are unhappy with the generally chosen means are given opportunities to find and to employ their own different (but nonviolent) means to help realize the communal goals. All this, provided the various means employed complement rather than interfere with one another.

A further necessary condition is (c) that communal goals must not be carved in granite, but must be open to periodic debate and democratic change if not complete abandonment; allowing other, more desirable or more practicable goals to replace them. Finally, (d) individuals and groups should be free, without any detriment to them, to their belongings or property, or to any relatives or friends that stay behind, to leave a particular community any time they wish to do so.

However, the question whether, under any circumstances, it is morally right to *exclude* certain individuals or groups who may wish to do so, from participation in a particular T-community, has no straightforward answer. There is absolutely no question in my mind that it is utterly wrong and evil for a country's, society's, or community's dominant majority or minority to deny difference by (1) excluding from that country, society, or community (and so, deny difference in that sense) those "outsiders" they consider as "undesirables," in addition to "cleansing themselves" from the "undesirables" living in their midst, by deportation, banishment, massacre, or genocide, because of their race, color, age, gender, or religion, language or history, customs and traditions, economic or social status, or physical or mental handicaps.

(2) This situation should be carefully distinguished from the case of highly specialized professional or other T-communities, such as special religious or educational institutions, scientific research labs, special artists' colonies, special religious (e.g., monastic) communities, or gay or lesbian communities, etc.; viz, T-communities designed for individuals with special knowledge, know-how, or skills, who band together to realize a special (or specialized) common goal or set of goals. My view is that in this type of T-community, it would not be wrong or undesirable to limit participation to those who are or would be able (or would be able with some help) to (a) benefit from the institution *and* (b) contribute to its life and goals. For instance, requiring (or continuing to require, as is the practice) that admission to a particular college or kind of college be limited to those students who satisfy certain entrance requirements. In short, the condition for admission should be merit and merit alone.

The *practical* problem of difference in a (an N- or a T-) community as I have sketched it, indeed, in any form of social organization, boils down to the problem of finding and implementing the proper means for the inculcation and encouragement, indeed, the nourishing and rewarding of caring and respect for the rights and freedoms of others and for fairness and justice, and spreading these ideals across the entire community; and in that way indefinitely approaching the ideal of a good and moral community. As Iris Marion Young states it in relation to the United States, "Social justice, . . . requires not the melting away of differences, but institutions that promote reproduction of and respect for group difference without oppression."[18] To that end the emphasis of thinkers like J.S. Mill on proper education and legislation, in relation to the inculcation of utilitarianism in society, are also essential here. Yet however closely it may approximate in its principles and rules the ideal of fairness and equal justice for all, the law would be little more than ink on paper unless the community's members are willing and ready to abide by it.[19] This means that a democratic economic, social, and political system is an integral part of a moral community, and an educational system geared to the inculcation of democratic attitudes and practices in the young; since respect for individual rights and freedoms, hence for individual difference, is an integral part of a democratic system. We can agree that the educational system should be "cooperation-promoting" education, "designed to give young people opportunities to discover the value of participating in constitutive communities. Once they have experienced this, . . . [the] hope [is] they will choose to maintain their ties to their communities."[20]

One important way women can be instrumental in realizing a moral community is by continuing to exercise their traditional role, where, as Jean Baker Miller observes, "they have used their powers to foster the growth of others—certainly children, but also many other people. This might be called using one's power to empower another—increasing the other's resources, capacities, effectiveness, and ability to act. For example, in "care-taking" or "nurturing," one major component is acting and interacting to foster the growth of another on many levels—emotionally, psychologically, and intellectually."[21] "This is a very powerful thing to do." Indeed! For one thing, historically, a very valuable quality of a woman is her "being attuned to and responding to her context and to the needs of everybody in it. . . . "[22] But as Miller notes earlier, "enhancing other people's power [what feminists call "power to" as against the traditional male domination or "power over"[23]] is difficult for the world to comprehend."[24]

For just laws to be enacted in a community there need to be individuals and groups who not only cherish the ideals of a moral community but are also willing and able to implement them; accepting all the risks involved in attempting to "cut the cake of custom." For instance, concerned participants like the feminist activists in the West and the developing world who have been struggling to achieve equality with men.

Let us return to Derrida and Cornell. We saw earlier that according to Cornell, Derrida rejects not only the Hegelian but also Rousseau's conception of a democratic community, claiming that violence inheres there too.[25] Nevertheless, Cornell contends that Adorno and Derrida do not "reject the *ideal* of a community as the hope for a nonviolent ethical relationship to the other."[26] She writes: "Both Adorno and Derrida clearly guard against the violence of self-enclosed community. But is their message, then, that we must remain ever vigilant against the violence of the *ideal* of community? I suggest that the answer to this question is complex indeed."[27] In fact, in chapter 3 she goes on to suggest that "the entire project of the philosophy of the limit [as she calls Derrida's deconstructionism] is driven by an ethical desire to enact the ethical relation."[28] By the "ethical relation" she "means to indicate the aspiration to a nonviolent relationship to the Other, and to otherness more generally, that assumes responsibility to guard the Other against the appropriation that would deny her difference and singularity."[29] For instance, she states (pp. 81ff.) that Derrida's practice of deconstruction, "conceived as a practice of reading, can be interpreted as an exercise of responsibility to otherness,"[30] and thinks that, being concerned to examine political institutions as well as texts, he is also ethically committed to taking responsibility for the Other and for himself as he relates to and "signs for" her. His recognition of the Other's precedence also means the Other's dependence on him. Derrida takes responsibility "for who he makes the Other become when he reads her."[31]

Unfortunately, her account provides little more than hints about what Derrida means or might mean by "community," and why she thinks the philosophy of the limit only "*aspires* to enact the ethical relationship," why she takes it for granted that "the ethical relation cannot be enacted in the sense of actualized but only adhered to as an aspiration."[32] Indeed, what it is for Derrida to *aspire* to enact, rather than actualizing the ethical relation; especially as she admits that "[b]y making the claim that the philosophy of the limit does aspire to enact the ethical relation, I am going beyond Derrida, who, in spite of his brilliant salvaging of Levinas' project, remains wary of the very word "ethical."[33] For example, whether Derrida is in any degree influenced by Jean Paul Sartre, who completely rules out the possibility of nonobjectifying relationships; in significant contrast to Albert Camus' humanism in *The Plague*. Perhaps it is our aspiration—but also our failure—to have "communion through a love that as a love becomes divine"; since Cornell says that "Derrida is not as optimistic as Irigaray. . . ." [concerning the latter's "dream of love," in his "The Divinity of Love"[34]] about communion through a love that as a love *becomes divine*."[35] Perhaps we can understand Derrida's "ethical relation" better by understanding what he understands by "unethical"—which is clearer. For one thing, Cornell states that Derrida considers gender hierarchy as unethical, and that for him "there can be no aspiration of the ethical relation within the gender hierarchy."[36] That, of course, is true. But one may then ask why, if Derrida rejects the "inevitability of gender hierarchy . . ."[37] by deconstructing it, he does not or would not consider the possibility of overcoming gender hierarchy as a partial actualization of the aspiration to community, to communion? Are Derrida and Levinas too pessimistic about the admittedly always hesitant, always partial, and never complete (or completed) move of caring and loving individuals toward the ideal of community? As far as Levinas, at least, is concerned, the answer appears to be "No." Although Cornell states that "in Levinas we must constantly remind ourselves of our inevitable failure to fulfil our responsibility," that statement appears to be only a hyperbole, since she also says that according to Levinas "we must constantly seek to do more for the Other. We can never do enough"[38]—which, of course, implies that we can partially fulfill our responsibility. We can increasingly move toward the ideal of the ethical relation. From this it does not follow, however, as, according to Cornell, Irigaray thinks, that "Levinas' emphasis on the inevitable lack of fulfillment of the individual [specifically, his view that "we do not have much fun in "the ethical relation"] allows the source of dissatisfaction of women to be ignored."[39] But we can grant that "no woman finds enjoyment in her *reduction* to either the good wife or the bad mistress."[40] And though it may tend to do so, it is not inevitable, psychologically or otherwise, that "concentration on the failure to the stranger diverts attention from the failure that is closer to 'home.'" Still, as Cornell comments: "In Irigaray, . . . nonsatisfaction [of our responsibility] may well not be "sublime." In Iragaray, it may be explicitly 'sexist'."[41]

III

In the discussion of community in general and of good and moral community in particular in this book, I have not dealt with the important practical challenges and obstacles facing attempts to create moral communities, or how to reduce indefinitely the denial of difference, in one form or another, in existing societies and communities. The challenge to provide a practical answer to these questions is not a challenge to the ideal of community itself, to the claim that good and moral communities are highly desirable to create and maintain. The following is a modest beginning or prolegomenon to providing such an account, confined to a few brief observations about male domination of women. A full, far more adequate account must be left for the future.

Although some matriarchal societies have existed in certain parts of the world, they are the rare exception to the long-standing patriarchal societies of which European and American societies are but a few examples. Domination of one group by another has historically been a main thread running through the numerous forms of denial of difference in human history; a relationship of profound unfairness and injustice and (and consequent upon) inequality in power. And like other forms of inequality and discrimination, women have been socialized ("brainwashed") by the male-dominant societies to accept an inferior, subordinate position. The same brainwashing is evident with respect to e.g. the blacks and some other ethnic and religious minorities in the United States and elsewhere, and in the brainwashing of the "natives" in Asia, Africa, and the Middle East by their former masters in the former European colonies. In considering the struggle of women throughout the world to escape their invidious socialization, their "femininity" as feminists call it, I shall turn to the issues Will Kymlicka raises in Appendix I of Daniel Bell's *Communitarianism and Its Critics*,[42] (entitled "Some Questions about Justice and Community") which evaluate Bell's central views from a liberal point of view; and Bell's response in Appendix II. Both the Appendix and the book are in dialogue form, in which "Anne" represents Bell and "Louise" represents Kymlicka.

The dialogue between "Anne" and "Louise" in Appendix I stresses the difficulties feminists face in their attempt to 'escape the grip' of their socialization and their constitutive identities; namely, their becoming a "disturbed" or "damaged" person as a result (p. 100), but also the greater damage caused by not escaping from their socialization. That brings up the question whether it is impossible to escape completely the grip of their socialization. As Louise says, "Femininity had become constitutive of our identity, and it is profoundly damaging to have to fight against it."[43] "Domination and subordination were built into the social construction of masculinity and femininity."[44] Therefore, though feminists "will insist that [they] . . . be free to question [their] . . . constitutive attachments, not just when they break down, but even when they are working as expected, . . . the subordination of women is built into [their] . . . everyday expectations about men's and women's behavior."[45] Morever, feminists believe that "subordination occurs even where there is no external coercion. Subordination, feminists believe, is built into the very construction of femininity and masculinity (and hence "husband" and "wife"), and many women accept their subordinate role in the family as natural or appropriate."[46]

Granting all this, I want to concentrate on the question of the extent to which we can "stand back from our constitutive attachments and evaluate or reject them," since I agree that it is probably impossible to do so completely. As Louise says, "vast areas of our life are governed by learned dispositions that have not been consciously chosen"; and if liberals deny that, "then clearly they are wrong"[47] (thus disagreeing with the liberal conception of self determination).[48] Second, that feminists must be able to (as they insist they can) question and "evaluate [their] constitutive attachments,"[49] if they are to be able to "escape the grip" of their socialization, give up those constitutive attachments that are "damaging to give up, but . . . [which] can themselves be damaging."[50]

The view of moral personhood elaborated in chapter 9 enables us to see how we can change our moral identity in fact and not just in principle; hence how those who wish to escape their socialization, including their "constitutive attachments," can do so. Theoretically, that is possible because, as moral subjects, we are only partially defined by our constitutive attachments and important goals at any given period in our life. We have an inborn, genetic biological-psychological/mental "core" of personhood prior to any constitutive attachments, which enables us to relate to things around us and to forge relationships with and form constitutive attachments to others.

Second, though inborn, that "core" of selfhood is malleable and dynamic, since it is a bundle of genetic dispositions, and so is capable of continual change, especially during childhood and youth, through "self-creation." We are, in varying degrees, self-determined. As Anne and Louise in Appendix I of Bell's book agree, not all our attachments and relationships are unconsciously formed: at least the conscious ones can be changed by sustained effort. What is more, the advances made by feminists in the United States, in Europe, and, to a much lesser extent, in other parts of the world, constitute clear empirical evidence that individuals and groups can escape their socialization at least partially, and move toward greater equality; though some ethnic or racial groups have moved further than others in their struggle for emancipation.

The claim that partial self-creation is possible is convincingly defended by Jonathan Glover in *I: The Philosophy and Psychology of Personal Identity*.[51] It is only partial because there are environmental influences on us which we do not create, as well as "genetic differences [which] contribute to the different ways . . . [we] behave."[52] Since hard determinism (which Glover calls "fatalism") denies the possibility of even partial self-determination, Glover argues in support of soft determinism and against hard determinism; and attempts to establish that "our decisions play a role in the causal process. This is part of the defence of the possibility of self-creation."[53]

More detailed and substantial support for the possibility of self-determination, consequently, of partial self-creation, is found in Daniel Dennett's similar view in *Elbow Room*.[54]

I shall now turn to Glover's criticism of two variants of the view that "our identity is constructed by society,"[55] and his defense of the possibility of self-creation. "The first [argument is] a variant of what is known as role theory, says that the idea of an inner core of a person is an illusion. The inner core can be analysed without remainder into the playing of various social roles. . . . The second, more sophisticated variant accepts that people have an inner core which transcends the roles they play, but says the inner core is itself a social construct."[56] On the first view, "we want relationships that are personal, where we respond to each other's particular characteristics, and where it is not just as good if someone else is here instead. Relationships require society. But, . . . social life obliterates anything distinctively ours to be recognized."[57]

Glover raises doubts about the putative evidence for role theory, with regard to (1) "the way people seem to behave inconsistently in different contexts"[58] and (2) cases of regimentation and extreme pressure, which are supposed to support role theory. Glover thinks that one problem with (1) is that "apparently inconsistent actions may reflect a character that is consistent [hence stable] but complex."[59]

The assumption underlying the behavioral inconsistency argument in support of role theory is that any (real) behavioral inconsistency is wholly ascribable to the influence of society and not partially due to the influence of one's heredity, one's genetic equipment. For if one's heredity does influence one's behavior, the argument would only succeed in showing that the individual's character or personality is in part socially determined. The idea of a core of personality that is not socially determined would remain a "hidden side" of one's character, and so, may be only apparent as Glover thinks. Glover does not offer evidence that that is always so—but then he does not need to, since only partial self-creation is at issue. Rather, our experience with ourselves and others appears to show that many if not all of us sometimes do actually act out of character. In fact, if such writers as Dostoyevsky are to be believed, human beings are a mass of deep inconsistencies and contradictions.

On the other hand, it is quite possible that some of our inconsistent actions are due to tensions between some of our genetic dispositions and our basic biological or psychological needs and drives; or more likely, that they are due to the different ways in which these dispositions, needs, or drives are socially channeled or actualized; that in varying degrees nature and nurture conspire. Now behavioral inconsistency, what we call acting out of character, does sometimes "reveal or bring about inconsistent or conflicting behavior."

Again, on Glover's side, it may be noted that acting "out of character" is sometimes caused not by society's influence but by natural causes. For example, the effects of certain medications, hard drugs, or heavy alcohol consumption—let alone certain psychiatric conditions—responsible for people's acting out of character, are quite familiar.

Glover's second doubt is "whether the role pressures on us are really too great to allow any distinctively personal characteristics."[60] He imagines a community in which regimentation "squeezes" self-creation through the prohibition of activities "except the standard role-bearing ones, such as serving the food and sweeping the floor. . . . Everyone has to answer to a number, not a name. There are no customs where particular people or particular kinds of people perform certain tasks: everyone takes a turn at all of them."[61] And so on in the same vein. In such circumstances, Glover says, "some sense of individuality might be preserved by 'internal emigration': the inner life of thought might be the last refuge of the self. But even this might be largely obliterated by some mental version of a treadmill, such as constant pressure to call out answers to problems in mental arithmetic."[62] Alternatively, "those who have been tortured, terrified or starved know how consciousness can be pared down to a single desperate concern,"[63] such as hunger as the "essential governor of survival."[64]

Glover's point is that there are degrees of pressure and that instances of extreme, irresistible pressure are extremely uncommon. Thus "it is an illusion to think that we are utterly malleable, submitting entirely to social moulding."[65]

This point and the notion of "internal migration" are well taken. For example, in *Man's Search for Meaning*, Viktor Frankl describes "internal migration" as man's last bastion of freedom in relation to his experience as a prisoner in Auschwitz.

Glover correctly concludes that "we have an inner core that enables us to bring something distinctive to the roles we play,"[66] a view accepted by role theory's more subtle and sophisticated version (2). But on that version "the inner core is itself a social product."[67] Glover comments: "This is less threatening, as it attempts to explain, rather than undermine, our uniqueness. And this version would only be a threat to the possibility of self-creation if the way society constructs our inner core has to bypass any decisions and choices of ours."[68] This is true. But the bypassing of the individual's decisions and choices is precisely a sore point with African-Americans, and with feminists, homosexuals, people living in dictatorships or under an oppressive foreign rule, together with many other disenfranchised groups! This brings us back to the basic question with which we started, whether it is possible for these groups to "escape the grip" of their socialization.

A fundamental problem with both the role theory and the "more sophisticated" version (2), which I shall call "social environmentalism," is their exaggeration of the role of the social environment at the expense of heredity in determining us as human beings and as individuals; biologically, psychologically, and mentally.[69] For example, their denial of psychological universals,[70] such as our universal basic needs as human beings, which, on the contrary, is finding increasing support among personality psychologists, including those referred to in Part II, chapter 6.

Glover points out that the "more sophisticated" version recognizes a "central core" of personality but claims that it is also socially determined. But if the latter is true, it is difficult to see how such a core can be conceptually distinguished or demarcated by the "part" of the personality "outside" that "core"; since that part too is supposed to be socially determined. That is, it is difficult to make sense of that notion unless that putative core is conceived to be the product of both heredity and environment. Further, in order that it may be a core of personality, properly speaking, distinguishable from the "rest" of the personality, the part that changes with changing social and other environmental forces, it must be relatively stable or unchanging, and consequently not a product of the variable social environment alone. That also means (and this harks back to the inconsistency argument of the role theory) that behavioral inconsistency cannot apply to the "central core." On the other hand, if the central core is changeable, it cannot be a core distinguishable from the admittedly changing part of the personality. Thus what Glover thinks is the more plausible version turns out to be at least as implausible as the role theory.

Finally, social environmentalism does not logically entail a hard determinist position, though social environmentalists are likely to be hard determinists. (A good example is B.F. Skinner, with respect to his behaviorist brand of environmentalism.) It is quite possible to maintain (along Dennett's lines of argument) that, assuming that we are causally wholly determined, we nonetheless have the ability to help determine the course of physical and societal events, to influence others, and to help determine ourselves, by utilizing the information, the feedback we continually receive from the environment. This is well illustrated by Dennett's example of the little boy who, by continually observing the flight of his toy electric plane, is able to control it by pressing the right buttons of his remote control, keeping it from flying too high or too low, or crashing.

IV

Liberals Vis-à-Vis (Some) Communitarians

A central issue between contemporary liberals and some communitarians concerns morality, and is of very considerable importance in relation to the central ethical claims put forth in this book. These communitarians contend that "morality cannot be conceived in universal terms. Universal and absolute justice, for example, is . . . [an] illusion of individualism. Since the values that people hold in general, and the concept of justice in particular, derives from their communities, there is no way for this concept to be universal or absolute. This is Walzer's argument."[71] In terms of Hegel's distinction between *Moralität*, "the abstract or universal rules of morality," and *Sittlichkeit*, "the ethical principles that are specific to a certain community,"[72] liberals consider *Moralität* to be "a higher level of morality,"[73] while Hegel and the contemporary communitarians who follow him in this particular respect argue that "*Sittlichkeit* is the higher level of morality, for it is the only way that genuine moral autonomy and freedom can be achieved."[74] In "Solidarity or Objectivity,"[75] Richard Rorty draws a similar distinction between communitarian "solidarity" and liberal "objectivity." He notes that "we are the heirs of this objective tradition [going back to Socrates and Plato], which centers round the assumption that we must step outside our community long enough to examine it in the light of something which transcends it, namely, that which it has in common with every other actual and possible human community."[76]

From his particular pragmatist perspective Rorty defends "solidarity" against "objectivity,"[77] arguing that it is only "ethnocentric," not relativist as liberals have accused communitarians of being.[78] "To be ethnocentric is to divide the human race into the people to whom one must justify one's beliefs and the others. The first group—one's ethnos— comprises those who share enough of one's beliefs to make fruitful conversation possible. In this sense, everybody is ethnocentric when engaged in actual debate, no matter how much realist rhetoric about objectivity he produces in his study."[79]

(1) Rorty thinks of "objectivity" and "solidarity" as (a) mutually exclusive and (b) jointly exhaustive of the logical possibilities. A crucial passage regarding both (a) and (b) is Rorty's characterization of "solidarity" and "objectivity." I quote:

> Insofar as a person is seeking solidarity, he or she does not ask about the relation between the practices of the chosen community and something outside that community. Insofar as he seeks objectivity, he distances himself from the actual persons around him not by thinking of himself as a member of some other or imaginary group, but rather by attaching himself to something which can be described without reference to any particular human being.[80]

Now ethical objectivity and nonobjectivity or ethical relativism are mutually exclusive: the latter is the former's negation; and Rorty is correct that if one embraces the universalistic, "internationalist" position, one cannot be "ethnocentric" with regard to values, justice and injustice, etc. But he fails to see that it is perfectly possible, perfectly consistent for someone both to belong to a community and to "attach himself to," to be, a "citizen of the world," to care about the welfare of humankind as a whole. This is precisely the present writer's existential position.

Thus, *pace* Rorty, I contend that it is not logically contradictory for someone to seek objective universal moral principles and rules and then, if she finds them, proceed to apply them to existing and to potential communities; including communities to which she desires to contribute and with which she identifies. That is precisely the way I have approached the ideal of moral community in this book: characterizing a moral community in terms of caring, "objective," universal human rights, fairness, and second-order universal principles/rules of formal justice. Although the caring relationships and the special obligations they create vary with the individuals involved, the *kinds* of caring relationships and the corresponding kinds of special moral obligations they may involve apply to all human beings in all societies and all communities.

In the last analysis, Rorty avoids ethical (and epistemological) relativism by understanding solidarity not as the antithesis of objectivity
but as a *third* thing. That is, he interprets "ethnocentrism," hence
"solidarity," in terms of a pragmatist conception of morality, knowledge, and truth. In other words, by espousing an anti-realist position,
and urging us to drop the traditional realist distinction between knowledge and opinion, "construed as the distinction between truth as correspondence to reality and truth as a commendatory term for well-
justified beliefs."[81] He claims that "as a partisan of solidarity, his [the
pragmatist's] account of the value of cooperative human inquiry has
only an ethical base, not an epistemological or metaphysical one."[82]

But suppose one rejects, as I do, Rorty's pragmatist antirealism
with regard to truth[83] and knowledge in general? One consequence
would be that the "realistically" understood distinction between objectivity and solidarity would not be mutually exclusive. From the general
characterization of the desire for solidarity itself, quoted earlier (Rorty,
ibid., 3), it does not follow that an individual or group, including a
community, cannot adopt certain axiologically (e.g., ethically) objective, second-order universal principles or rules together with certain
other, axiologically (e.g., ethically) "provincial"[84] principles or rules.
Second, it would not be logically contradictory to ground solidarity,
"realistically" understood, on objectivity—as, Rorty says, "realists" wish
to do in contrast to pragmatists, who wish "to reduce objectivity
to solidarity."[85] The latter is a correct "antirealist" pragmatic
move.[86]

To return to a point I made earlier, I should again stress that for
different but complementary reasons, we need both morally objective,
in the sense of general or universal, intercommunal or societal principles or rules, and axiologically "provincial" moral guidelines. In effect, the solidarity moral position in Rorty, Walzer, or other solidarity
advocates, essentially sees all moral duties/obligations as special moral
obligations, and rejects the possibility of any general, non-special moral
duties.[87] That view, it may be recalled, was criticized in an earlier
chapter. In fact, the present book as a whole attempts to overcome
the supposed exclusive moral either/or of objectivity (or "universalism") versus parochialism (and ethnocentrism), by attempting to show
the compatibility, nay complementarity of objective, universal, and
parochial ethical elements. I attempted to do so by defending the necessity of complementing a provincial care ethic with the universal
norms of human rights[88] and principles of fairness and justice. But as

I also reiterated, in its noblest albeit rare instances, caring can embrace all humankind and even nature as a whole, and hence is non-relativistic.

True, some people may, like the present writer, experience a strong psychological tension between a need or desire to be part of a good and moral community, and a desire to be morally, politically, and humanly "citizens of the world." Moreover, various moral circumstances and situations may arise that create a tug of war between a strong need or desire to appeal to general or universal impartial norms and a tendency or need to appeal to provincial guidelines; or else, to follow one's "heart," such as an ethic of caring, where moral responsibility is usually predicated on the presence of certain attachments or relationships.

In *Contingencies of Value*,[89] Barbara Herrnstein Smith finds Rorty's "complex of ideals involving 'community' and 'solidarity'" to be unsatisfactory, and "not only . . . 'provincial' (p. 12) but, it appears, determinedly naive."[90] I shall discuss some of her criticisms here. Other criticisms are considered in the Introduction to this book.

One of Smith's criticisms concerns Rorty's distinction between objectivity and solidarity. She thinks that what Rorty offers as an alternative to objectivity is another monolithic principle, rather than what is needed, viz, "the development of an altogether different *type* of conceptualization."[91] She criticizes, as I did, Rorty's oversimplification in supposing that objectivity and solidarity are mutually exclusive, asserting that "there are more than two kinds of stories that people tell about themselves."[92] She also correctly asks "whether—and at the cost of what else—any of us ever does or could 'give sense to our lives' in some single, particular way,"[93] given "the multiple, heterogeneous, shifting, and more or less mutually inconsistent and conflictual . . . nature both of our desires, beliefs and actions and also of the relations among them."[94]

Other telling criticisms are directed against Rorty's ethical and political "ethnocentrism" (Rorty, p. 13), which divides the human race "into those to whom one must justify one's beliefs and the others,"[95] together with Rorty's making much of the idea of "local cultural norms."[96]

As Smith observes, Rorty's conception of a community ignores "the mobility, multiple forms of contact, and numerous levels and modes of interconnectedness of contemporary [Western] life and forgets, accordingly, that contemporary communities are not only internally complex and highly differentiated but continuously and rapidly reconfigured."[97]

And

> To the extent that the concept of communal solidarity denies or obscures both differences and dynamism, including internal differences and dynamism, it can only encourage the illusion, undesirable for political practice, that there is some mode of thought or set of principles that would ultimately eliminate all difficult and disagreeable encounters with other people.[98]

Another fundamental criticism of Rorty's conception of community occurs in these lines:

> What Rorty's (and other current invocations of community miss and obscure, is that at any given time as well as over the course of anyone's life history, *each of us* is a member of many, shifting communities, each of which establishes, for *each* of its members, multiple social identities, multiple principles of identification with other people, and, accordingly, a collage or grab-bag of allegiances, beliefs, and sets of motives. . . . Recognition of this situation requires a conception of "community" and an image of individual social life and mental life that is considerably richer, more subtly differentiated, and more dynamic than that articulated by contemporary communitarians. Indeed, the current invocation of "community" as a replacement for "objective reality" is not only a problematic gesture but an empty one. Where it is not (as it seems to be in Rorty's case) a conceptual retreat and apparent move toward socio-political isolationism, it is usually a form of neo-objectivism.[99]

Although these criticisms are damaging to communitarians who, in the words of Daniel Bell, think "that only one community constitutes the identity of the members of a society,"[100] it is especially telling against Rorty and other anti-realist communitarians who, by thinking of community "as a replacement for 'objective reality,'" embrace ethnocentrism. The idea of an individual's "solidarity" with only *one* community runs like a thread through all of Rorty's claims regarding community, solidarity, and ethnocentrism.

Fortunately, Smith's foregoing criticisms do not apply to the conception of community—and of a good and moral community—put forth in this book. Although I invariably spoke of an individual's being a member of *a* (constitutive) community, etc., for simplicity's sake, there is nothing in the concept(ion) of a community described in chapter 1, or of a good and moral community in chapter 2, that negates what Smith says about the multiplicity of shifting communities, etc. to which we may belong in the course of a lifetime, and the complexity, dynamism, and mobility of actual communities. Nor does that concept(ion) preclude one's membership, at the same time, in more than one community, or the possibility of one's moving from one community to another or to others. The Armenian community in the Old City of Jerusalem, of which I was a part during my formative years, briefly described in the Introduction and chapter 1, illustrates some of the features Smith stresses.

Nevertheless, not all actual constitutive communities exemplify all the foregoing characteristics. Not surprisingly, Smith's description applies most to the complex, highly dynamic, mobile, and rapidly changing Western society, and much less to the essentially static, stable, and structurally simple tribal, or rural and urban communities, in traditional non-Western societies in Asia, Eastern and Southern Europe, Africa, and Latin America. The Armenian community in Jerusalem was (and I believe still is) a good example. Until recently, many communities in the world consisted of long lines of extended families and clans: communities into which generations of men and women were born, grew up, worked, grew old, and died. In such communities, especially in the rural areas, things changed very little, except when some members, particularly the young, moved to the towns and cities, or migrated to other parts of the world, in search of a better life. Those who were uprooted from their native soil by discrimination, persecution, or other forms of oppression, or by civil war, revolution, war, or genocide, were sometimes fortunate enough to put out new roots in their new communities, while others remained rootless in an alien new environment. In our sad century of displaced persons, refugees, and *Heimatlos*, millions have been cruelly forced to abandon their communities because of the ravages of assorted forms of mass violence, and vast numbers have been huddled together in refugee camps for years or decades, under almost inhuman conditions, condemned to languish there the rest of their miserable lives. On the other hand, even the refugees who end up in ethnic ghettos do sometimes find some measure of community existence in their new environment.

As Daniel Bell ("Anne") stresses, when individuals or groups leave their ancestral constitutive communities that had helped shape their being and identity, it is often more because they are running away from something rather than *running toward something*, as a colleague whose ancestors emigrated to the United States from Eastern Europe once told me. In the case of traditional societies, those who voluntarily leave their ancestral communities—where their roots are strong and have spread deep and wide—in quest of freedom, greater economic rewards, and so on, are normally the exception to the rule.

As Bell also correctly observes, many of those who leave continue to look back, dreaming about and yearning to return; often not knowing, or deceiving themselves into believing, that they can "go home again."[101]

In American and other highly complex and mobile societies, the situation is markedly different. For example, in the United States, in addition to their simultaneously participating in a variable number of different, continually shifting communities in the ordinary meaning of the word, individuals and families frequently relocate in different parts of that vast country in search of "the American dream," successively participating in different communities with different compositions, concerns, preoccupations, and so on. And everywhere in the world except in the simplest communities, people normally participate in a number of different, sometimes overlapping—educational, professional, or other—institutions: little T-communities that are part of the particular societal communities as a whole, or exist *outside* them. In these respects Smith's remarks are perfectly *à propos*.

To sum up. The chapter focused on feminist and postmodern challenges to communitarianism, without totally neglecting some liberal responses to communitarian criticism.

A main argument urged by postmodern critics and shared by some feminist thinkers, concerns the opposition of the individual and the community, or the citizen's public role. In one form of that opposition, Iris Young charges that community denies "the difference between subjects." In place of the ideal of community, Young offers a vision of a nonrepressive city, one that emphasizes differences. Since Young's strictures are specifically addressed to the Hegelian, "organic" conception of community, they leave unaffected the significantly different ideal of moral community sketched in the present book. To make clear the differences between the two types of conception, a brief sketch of the Hegelian conception of community is included.

Examination of Young's reasons for her view that community denies the differences between subjects revealed that they involved certain empirical or logical errors, such as *non sequiturs*. Again, although her criticisms are intended to be factual, she provides no empirical evidence that the desire for closeness and caring, cooperation and solidarity, tends to lead to the denial of difference.

To Young's negative view of community, the present author opposes, as the sine qua non of nonoppressive community, the vision of a truly democratic T- (and N-) community: in particular, T-community that requires diverse talents and skills, visions, and ideas for the realization of its communal teloses. Several necessary conditions for such a socially just community, which include proper education and legislation, are then described. With Will Kymlicka, it is maintained that the educational system should aim at "cooperation-promoting," while with Jean Baker Miller, the importance of "enhancing other people's power" is stressed, although, as Miller says, that is "difficult for the world to comprehend."

Lucinda Cornell's discussion of Derrida's and Adorno's views on community followed. Cornell maintained that the two thinkers do not reject the ideal of community, but guard against the violence of self-enclosed community. In fact, she argues that "the entire project" of Derrida's deconstructionism is "driven by an ethical desire to enact the ethical relation" to the Other. Unfortunately, her account leaves unclear what Derrida actually means, or might mean, by community, and why, for example, she thinks that, according to him, "the ethical relation"can only be "adhered to as an inspiration."

The discussion next turned to the issues raised by Will Kymlicka in Daniel Bell's *Communitarianism and Its Critics*, and to Bell's response to them. Kymlicka's imaginary dialogue between Anne and Louise stressed the difficulties feminists face in attempting to "escape the grip" of their socialization, that is, their becoming disturbed or damaged persons as a result, but also the greater damage caused by *not* escaping from their socialization. That led to the general question of how one may change one's moral identity, and to an evaluation of Jonathan Glover's claim, in opposition to the "role theory" and "social environmentalism," that *partial* self-creation is indeed possible.

The last section, on liberalism vis-à-vis some communitarians, was largely devoted to Barbara Herrnstein Smith's and this author's criticism of Richard Rorty's antirealist, pragmatist defense of an "ethnocentric" but putatively nonrelativist conception of community. It was concluded that Smith's criticisms do not affect the account of community developed in this book.

Notes

1   Susan Moller Okin, "Humanist Liberalism," *Liberalism and the Moral Life*, Nancy Rosenblum, ed. (Cambridge, MA), 46. Quoted from Daniel Bell, *Communitarianism and Its Critics* (Oxford, 1993), 2.

2   (New York and London, 1992).

3   Iris Young, "The Ideal of Community and the Politics of Difference," *Social Theory & Practice*, 12, no. 12 (1986). Quoted by Cornell, ibid., 39.

4   Ibid., 39.

5   Young, op. cit., 1–2. Quoted from Cornell, op. cit., 39.

6   Young, ibid. Cornell, ibid., 39.

7   Young, ibid.

8   Cornell, ibid., 39.

9   Young, op. cit., 39.

10 *The Coherence Theory of Truth: A Critical Evaluation* (Beirut, 1961), Chapters II and III. A possible exception to what I say there is Spinoza's organic conception of reality.

11 Thus F.H. Bradley's statement that "the 'individual' man, the man into whose essence his community with others does not enter, who does not include relation to others in his very being, is, we say, a fiction, and in the light of facts we have to examine him" ("My Station and Its Duties," *Ethical Studies*, 447), does not fully express the Absolute Idealist view that the web of internal relations between everything and everything else in the universe wholly exhaust their essence. But then Bradley held that relations are limited to the world of Appearance and so, are ultimately unreal, do not qualify Reality, the Absolute.

12 I say "putatively" since, as it is well-known, G.E. Moore's "principle of organic unities" in *Principia Ethica* maintains (with what effectiveness I am not here concerned to decide) that "*The value of a whole must not be assumed to be the same as the sum of the values of its parts.*" (*Principia Ethica*: chapter I. Reprinted in *Readings in Ethical Theory*, Wilfrid Sellars and John Hospers, eds. (New York, 1952), 85. Italics in original.

13 Cf. Isaiah Berlin on the organic conception of society: "the real may be conceived as something wider than the individual (as the term is normally understood), as a social 'whole' of which the individual is an element or aspect: a tribe, a race, a church, a state, the great society of the living and the dead and the yet unborn. This entity is then identified as being the 'true' self which, by imposing its collective, or 'organic,' single will upon its recalcitrant 'mem-

bers', achieves its own, and therefore their, 'higher' freedom." ("Two Concepts of Liberty," *Four Essays on Liberty* (Oxford, 1969). Quoted from *Liberalism and Its Critics*, Michael Sandel, ed. (Oxford, 1984), 24.

14   Whether a nonmetaphysical organic conception of a community—a conception compatible with realist, idealist, or other conceptions of reality—is logically possible is an interesting question. But whatever its answer, a T-community entails the denial of individual differences if its communal telos(es) and their realization or conservation is(are) the *end*(s) to which the individual members' own needs, interests, desires, and projects are subordinated; are regarded as only means, hence have inferior, derivative value.

15   Perhaps the Hegelian "logic of identity," as Adorno calls it, is responsible for the putative denial of difference. But I shall not go into it here.

16   Young, op. cit., 1–2. Quoted from Cornell, op. cit., 39.

17   Isaiah Berlin, op. cit., 24. My italics.The rest of the section, pp. 24–25, is also directly relevant to our discussion of Young's criticism of the Hegelian conception of community.

18   "Five Faces of Oppression," *Rethinking Power*, Thomas E. Wartenberg, ed. (Albany, NY, 1992), 180.

19   Until the *pax syriana* of the past few years, Lebanon was a classic example of the dire consequences of general lack of respect for the law. That fact was one of the main factors that made the tragic civil war possible.

20   Will Kymlicka, "Some Questions about Justice and Community," in Daniel Bell, *Communitarianism and Its Critics*, Appendix I (Oxford, 1993), 215–6. Like Bell, Kymlicka uses the dialogue form, with Anne (representing Bell) and Louise (presumably representing Kymlicka). The quoted passage is part of Louise's statement of Anne's proposal regarding education for community in the book—a proposal with which Louise agrees.

21   Miller, "Women and Power," *Rethinking Power*, 242.

22   Ibid., 245.

23   For the problem of the oppression of women and other groups, see e.g., Iris Marion Young, op. cit., 174–195. The "five faces" of oppression she distinguishes are exploitation, marginalization, powerlessness, cultural imperialism, and violence. But some authors in that volume express outrageously intemperate views, supported by little or no empirical, e.g., scientific evidence and full of unsupported and very dubious sweeping generalizations. I have specifically in mind Nancy C.M. Hartsock's "Gender and Sexuality: Masculinity, Violence, and Domination," in relation to male (or masculine) sexuality and alleged violence (ibid., 249–276), and Roger S. Gottlieb's. "Masculine Identity and the Desire for War: A Study in the Sickness of Power." Ibid., 277–288.)

24   Ibid.

25   See Cornell, op. cit., 49–53.

26   Ibid., 56.

27   Op. cit., 40.

28   Ibid., 62.

29   Ibid. She defines the "ethical relation" "more broadly than the thinker Emmanuel Levinas, with whom the phrase is usually associated." (Ibid., 62.)

30   Ibid., 82.

31   Ibid.

32   Ibid., 84. At the end of chapter 3 (p. 90) she speaks of "the recognition that we can never fully meet the promise of fidelity to otherness inherent in the ethical relation to which we aspire."

33   Ibid.

34   Luce Iragaray, "Questions to Emmanuel Levinas: On the Divinity of Love," *The Iragaray Reader*, Margaret Whitford, ed. (London and Cambridge, MA, 1991).

35   Cornell, ibid. Italics in original.

36   Ibid., 86.

37   Ibid.

38   Ibid., 88.

39   Ibid.

40   Ibid.

41   Ibid.

42   (Oxford, 1993).

43   Ibid., 210.

44   Ibid.

45   Ibid.

46   Ibid., 211.

47   Ibid.

48   Ibid., 212.

49   Ibid., 213.

50   Ibid., 210.

51   Ibid., 179.

52   Ibid.

53   Ibid., 183.

54   There Dennett argues in support of compatibilism with detailed empirical evidence drawn from evolutionary science and from analysis of our folk-psychological conceptual framework.

55   Glover, ibid., 170.

56   Ibid.

57   Ibid., 171.

58   Ibid., 172.

59   Ibid.

60   Ibid., 173.

61   Ibid.

62   Ibid.

63   Ibid.

64   Ibid., 174. This occurs in a passage in which David Piper "described this effect of hunger he and others experienced in Japanese camps in the Second World War" (ibid.,173). Almost identical effects were described by Viktor Frankl in *Man's Search for Meaning* concerning the effects, on him and other victims, in Auschwitz.

65   Ibid.

66   Ibid.

67   Ibid., 175.

68   Ibid.

69   In that respect, compare also B.F. Skinner's environmentalist behaviorism.

70   Which an increasing number of contemporary psychologists and linguistics experts now recognize.

71   *Communitarianism and Individualism*, Shlomo Avineri and Avner De-Shalit, eds. (Oxford, 1992), Introduction, 4.

72   Ibid., 2.

73   Ibid.

74   Ibid.

75   *Post-Analytic Philosophy*, John Rajchman and Cornell West, eds. (New York, 1985), 3–19.

76   Ibid., 4.

77   He says that "realists" "are those who wish to ground solidarity on objectivity" while "pragmatists" "are those who wish to reduce objectivity to solidarity." (Ibid., 5.)

78   The liberal's criticism of the putative relativism of the particular communitarian moral-political position we are considering goes along the traditional lines familiar to students of the History of Ethics; e.g. that "once a standpoint of moral relativism is taken, it makes no sense for a Westerner to raise an argument against the caste system in India, or for an American to complain about the abuse of human rights in Iran. The debate becomes fruitless and meaningless" (Avineri and De-Shalit, op. cit., 5).

79   Rorty, ibid., 13.

80   Ibid., 3.

81   Ibid., 6. Although Rorty is right that "true" is "an expression of commendation," it is not only that. See "About," in my *Philosophy of Language and Logical Theory: Collected Papers* (Lanham, MD, 1995).

82   Ibid.

83   Although I cannot defend here my "realist" conception of knowledge and truth, let me just note that the pragmatist conception of empirical truth is a revisionary, stipulative conception and does not correspond with what we ordinarily mean by "true" and "truth" in relation to putative matters of fact. Further, I believe (though I cannot show here) that no good reasons exist for abandoning the ordinary use/conception and adopting the pragmatist's recommended use/conception.

        I should add that Rorty's pragmatist conception of truth differs in an interesting way from John Dewey's and, perhaps, William James' pragmatist conception of empirical truth.

84   The term "ethnocentric" can be misleading in this discussion since in present-day parlance it refers to an ethnically homogenous group in the contemporary sense of "ethnic" and "ethnicity," and there is a suggestion in Rorty's article that he necessarily has that in mind in relation to "community." In fact, in *Contigencies of Value* (Cambridge, MA, 1988), 170, Barbara Herrnstein Smith correctly criticizes him for thinking of *ethnos* as constituted, at least in the first instance, by those who share beliefs; e.g., "the community of the liberal intellectuals of the secular modern West" (Rorty, op. cit., 12), who he considers to be "the pragmatist's own *ethnos*." (Note how Rorty's use of "community," though a perfectly ordinary one, is significantly different from our use of the term in this book.) For instance, she writes: "Shared beliefs and the possibility of fruitful conversations neither establish nor sustain tribes but are, rather, the emergent by-products of those other, more significant and determinative aspects of cohesive social relations" (ibid., 169). She is also correct that "[w]hat will matter with regard to *justifying* our beliefs are not those

people whose views we already share but, rather, those whose attitudes and actions in relation to our beliefs (which perhaps they do not share) have *consequences* for us." (Ibid. Italics in original.)

85   Op. cit., 5.

86   However, this characterization of "pragmatism" does not describe William James. Whether it applies to John Dewey is an interesting question into which I cannot go here.

87   There is, of course, a lot of difference between holding that there are no "objective," universal or even inter-societal/cultural moral principles, hence corresponding moral duties and, and holding that such principles and duties cannot possibly exist. In so far as Rorty is an "anti-realist" pragmatist in morals, as well as in relation to truth and knowledge, the stronger view must be attributed to him.

88   For Rorty's account of the traditional view of human rights, see op. cit., 13.

89   Cambridge, MA, 1988.

90   Ibid., 167.

91   Ibid. Italics in original.

92   Ibid.

93   Ibid.

94   Ibid.

95   Ibid., 169.

96   Smith is skeptical, as I am, about Rorty's description of "the habits of modern democracies," the "local norms" which he wishes to praise as a pragmatist; viz, "toleration, free inquiry, and the quest for undistorted communication." (Rorty, op. cit., 11). She asks: "is the identity of the societies that exemplify the virtues of contemporary civilization [viz. "toleration, free inquiry, and the quest for undistorted communication"] altogether self evident?" (op. cit., 171). Cf. also her criticism that, "in defining his [the pragmatist's, i.e., Rorty's own] *ethnos* in terms that do not engage with, and effectively obscure, the issues of contemporary political life, the pragmatist virtually bows out of both political analysis and political action." (Op. cit.,170. Italics in original.)

97   Op. cit., 168.

98   Ibid., 167–8.

99   Ibid., 168–9. Italics in original.

100   Op. cit., 114, footnote 8. Bell says: "One communitarian, Michael Sandel, can be interpreted in a way that suggests he thinks that only one community constitutes the identity of the members of a society."

101   Cf. for example, my "Going Back," *Ararat*, XXIX, no. 3 (Summer 1988): 36–
       38. The essay's epigraph is Walker Percy's statement: "Every man has to
       stand in front of the house of his childhood in order to recover himself" (*Con-
       versations*, 67).

Chapter 14

Conclusion

I

As the reader will recall, Part 1 of this book sketched an ideal of a good and moral community, together with three alternative conceptions of "the good society," two of which identified the good society with community conceived of in a particular way. Part 3 continued, and put the finishing touches on the sketch begun in Part 1, by locating important roles for human rights and justice in—this time—not ideal but (to borrow an epithet from John Kenneth Galbraith) an actually achievable moral community. In this chapter I shall conclude the discussion of good and moral community in this book with some remarks concerning the need for our continual striving to create or recreate, and maintain good and moral communities, and to strengthen and improve community living wherever it exists in the contemporary world.

II

If "community"[1] is understood in its everyday dictionary meanings, as in this book, i.e., not as a place but, in Amitai Etzioni's words, as "a set of characteristics" that define a certain form of social living, "community" can not only characterize the small ancient Greek polis or medieval European town, a contemporary Arab village, an Israeli Kibbutz, or an ethnic American neighborhood, but also, in principle,[2] an entire country or society, or even perhaps a group of countries: in the latter two cases, not merely as constellations of individual communities but as complex communities themselves: in Etzioni's phrase, as "communities of communities."

Although this book argued at length that good and moral community living is an eminently desirable form of human association, it was not claimed that an ideally good and moral community constitutes *the* ideal form of social organization: assuming that it makes sense to describe in that way any actual or possible kind or form of social organization, particularly in the abstract. But if this book provided convincing reasons that the ideal of good and moral community sketched in it constitutes a desirable state of affairs, it follows that, as with all other desirable things, we ought to strive continually to approximate that ideal; although, given our deeply flawed nature as human beings, and the always imperfect natural and societal conditions and circumstances under which we live, that ideal can never be perfectly realized. Where good and moral communities do exist, we ought to strive to preserve, sustain, strengthen, and morally improve them, guarding them against the forces of alienation in the contemporary world that, if left unchecked, would destroy them. Our awareness that kindness, compassion, love and caring, solidarity, loyalty and commitment, fairness and justice, and respect for human rights are fundamental to the ideally good and moral community, should not weaken our resolve. For in Spinoza's famous words in the *Ethic*—"all noble things are as difficult as they are rare."

Except in the case of professional institutions and practices that quality as teleological communities, the creation and the maintenance of nonteleological communities are generally less difficult to effect than the teleological communities. The latter tend to be less stable, because, with time, the participants' interest in the community's goals (or teloses) tends to wane, or because disagreements or conflicts concerning them may grow or remain unresolved. In such cases the community may either modify its original or current goals, or replace them with others. Or it may cease to pursue any common goals and turn into a nonteleological community.

It is worth remembering at this point the close, centuries-long historical association of the so-called morality of honor and shame (also known as Mediterranean morality of honor and shame[3]) with communal societies in Europe and the Middle East, as well as other parts of the world. Whether that morality, which formed an important part of their collective memory, predated the rise of community living, for example, in the Mediterranean basin, or whether it developed along with it, there is no doubt that it served well (if it was not expressly designed for) the nonindividualistic, highly collectivist character and aims of traditional communities, by maintaining or strengthening the strong personal bonds between their members.

That being so, it is highly probable that contemporary communities characterized by a morality of honor and shame, would stand a good chance of surviving if they are able to coexist peacefully with other moralities: as they do with Muslim and Christian morality and values, for example, in the Arab world.

In striking contrast to Middle Eastern Arab and other communal societies, the concept of honor, as Peter Berger writes, is obsolescent in contemporary Western society.[4] As Berger states, "Honour occupies about the same place in contemporary [Western] usage as chastity."[5] And "the social location of honour lies in a world of relatively intact, stable institutions, a world in which individuals can with subjective certainty attach their identifies to the institutional roles that society assigns to them. The disintegration of this world [in the Western world] as a result of the forces of modernity has . . . made honour an increasingly meaningless notion."[6]

The following passages should give the reader an idea of the nature of honor and shame in a small scale community or society: "Honour and shame are the constant preoccupations of individuals in small scale, exclusive societies where face to face personal, as opposed to anonymous, relations are of paramount importance and where the social personality of the actor is as significant as his office."[7] And,

> Even when honour is inherited with the family name it has to be asserted and vindicated. To accept this is to accept the all-powerfulness of public opinion rather than that of a hierarchical superior. When the individual is encapsulated in a social group an aspersion on his honour is an aspersion on the honour of his group. In this type of situation the behaviour of the individual reflects that of his group to such an extent that, in his relations with other groups, the individual is forcibly cast in the role of his group's protagonist.[8]

Honor and dishonor are both individual and group attributes. With regard to the latter, Julian Pitt-Rivers observes that "social groups possess a collective honour in which their members participate; the dishonourable conduct of one reflects upon the honour of all, while a member shares in the honour of his group." Further, he points out that honor "pertains to social groups of any size, from the nuclear family whose head is responsible for the honour of all its members to the nation whose members' honour is bound up with their fidelity to their sovereign."[9]

In traditional Middle Eastern society, female honor essentially consists in chastity, and shame is the consequence of the dishonor of loss of chastity. Male honor, on the other hand, includes strong loyalty to, and solidarity with, the family, clan, the community, and genuine concern for their welfare. Thus, it importantly includes defending the family, clan, and community honor: for example, avenging the dishonor suffered by a female member of one's family by rape, abandonment, etc.

Given the close historical tie between traditional communities and the morality of honor and shame, one would expect that the obsolescence or disappearance of that morality from contemporary communities would weaken the bonds between the community members, and may lead to the community's demise; although the possibility that that morality is a result rather than a cause of the existence of at least some traditional communities, would mean that a community may survive the disappearance of that morality. Be that as it may, one may wonder whether the *recovery* of the obsolescent concept of honor would help revive community living in the contemporary Western world, by, among other things, helping to redefine individual identity in the desired way. If the answer is "Yes," as Berger speculates, it would provide an important way in which community may be recovered. After rightly applauding the "specifically modern discoveries of human dignity and human rights"[10] (the former, he points out, replaced honor in modern Western society), Berger correctly writes:

> A rediscovery of honour in the future development of modern society is both empirically plausible and morally desirable. Needless to say, this will hardly take the form of a regressive restoration of traditional codes. . . .[11] Man's fundamental constitution is such that, just about inevitably, he will once more construct institutions to provide an ordered reality for himself.[12] A return to institutions will *ipso facto* be a return to honour. It will then be possible again for individuals to identify themselves with the escutcheons of their institutional roles, experienced now not as self-estranging tyrannies but as freely chosen vehicles of self-realization. The ethical question, of course, is what these institutions will be like. Specifically, the ethical test of any future institutions, and of the codes of honour they will entail, will be whether they succeed in embodying and in stabilizing the discoveries of human dignity that are the principal achievements of modern man.[13]

Notes

1   As opposed to "*a* community."

2   A familiar factual reason for the difficulty of establishing a large-scale community is the difficulty of creating any but impersonal relationships between the inhabitants of the particular region or area; and where personal relationships do exist, both space and time often conspire to make them languish or die.

3   See *Honour And Shame*, J.G. Peristiany, ed. (London, 1965).

4   "On the Obsolescence of the Concept of Honour," *Liberalism and Its Critics*, Michael Sandel, ed. (Oxford, 1984), 149–158.

5   Ibid., 156.

6   Ibid.

7   *Peristiany*, Introduction, 11.

8   Ibid.

9   Julian Pitt-Rivers, "Honour And Social Status, in *Peristiany*, op. cit., 35-36.

10   Ibid., 157.

11   This should be strongly emphasized, since certain aspects of the traditional concepts of honor, dishonor, and shame, are quite bad or morally wrong and should be abandoned. Fortunately, improvement in these respects in the more Westernized parts of the Arab world, a society in which we still find that morality, has occurred. Whether the same process is occurring in other honor-and-shame societies I do not know.

12   Cf. Bellah et al., *The Good Society, passim*.

13   Op. cit., 158.

Index